The Guitar Greats

Also available from BBC Publications

The GUITAR GREATS

John Tobler & Stuart Grundy

BRITISH BROADCASTING CORPORATION

Picture credits

ASYLUM RECORDS pages 159 (photo Jim Shea), 169, 171 & 172 (photo Henry Diltz); BLACK STAR page 25; ADRIAN BOOT page 107; DECCA RECORDS page 60; IAN DICKSON page 130 below; ROBERT ELLIS pages 87 top left, 90 & 140; EMI pages 57 & 186; H. GOODWIN page 86; JOHN GREENWALD page 19; FRANK GRIFFIN page 143; STUART GRUNDY pages 31, 41, 43, 79, 155, 174 & 175; GISBERT HANEKROOT page 16 top; ISLAND RECORDS pages 63 right & 78; LONDON FEATURES INTERNATIONAL pages 46, 61 top & centre left, 70, 76, 82, 84, 102, 104 both, 106, 122, 124 below, 137, 138, 141, 148, 161, 166, 178, 179 & 182; 153 (photo J. Bellissimo), 177 (George Bodnar), 127 (Fin Costello), 92 (Paul Cox), 128 (Richard Creamer), 113 below (David Hill), 53 (courtesy BBC), 63 left, 87 below right, 88, 91, 151, 163 & 165 (Mike Putland), 162 (Janet Macoska/Kaleyediscope), 156 (Retna Ltd/Andy Freeberg), 77 (Retna Ltd/Garry Gershoff), 118 (Tom Sheehan), 59, 61 below, 72, 85, 103, 105 & 124 top (SKR), 62, 89, 116 & 125 (Chris Walter); MCA RECORDS page 18; MELODY MAKER pages 48, 110, 135 & 154; PHONOGRAM pages 132 & 144; PHOTO-FEATURES pages 113 top left & 130 top right (photos David Wainwright); BARRY PLUMMER pages 64, 108, 149 & 183; W. E. G. PRIOR page 39; RAREPIC pages 10, 12, 13, 47, 56, 66, 109 & 134; KEITH RENTON page 94; REX FEATURES pages 99 (Dezo Hoffmann) & 123; MIKE STOLLER COLLECTION page 26; JOHN TOBLER COLLECTION page 74; VIRGIN RECORDS page 22; ELIZABETH WALKIDEN pages 45, 61 centre right, 68 & 181; WEA page 40; VALERIE WILMER pages 16 below & 113 top right. The publisher would like to thank *Melody Maker* for making their photographic files available.

Cover illustration by Jim Kane

Published by the British Broadcasting Corporation
35 Marylebone High Street
London W1M 4AA

ISBN 0 563 17957 0

First published 1983
© John Tobler and Stuart Grundy 1983

Typeset by Phoenix Photosetting, Chatham
Printed and bound in Great Britain by
Mackays of Chatham Ltd

CONTENTS

INTRODUCTION

To say that the electric guitar holds a unique place amongst modern instruments is to understate the case. Although it has never quite achieved the 'one in every boy's front room' ratio threatened a couple of decades ago, it is undoubtedly the most popular musical instrument of the twentieth century, a prospect that would have evoked only laughter until the runaway success of rock music turned it into one of the most desirable of man's inventions.

It is only too easy in retrospect to see the reasons for the electric guitar's dramatic success. It is firstly very portable and capable, not only of producing a wide range of sounds and effects, but at its most powerful can vibrate seats or, as the 'have guitar, will travel' brigade would claim, 'can kill pigeons in mid-flight'. It has also not gone unnoticed that it is a very sexual instrument, both in terms of shape and power, and this constitutes an immensely powerful psychological reason for picking it up in the first place. It is quite simply as macho a prop as man has ever devised. Add to these features the fact that it can be played to some effect with only limited experience, and you find that you are talking about something so damnably clever that not even armies would have halted its inexorable progress.

You will perhaps be relieved to discover that it is impossible to trace the person first responsible for adding electric amplification to the guitar, but it is generally agreed that a number of people were experimenting with electrostatic pick-ups in the early 1920s, notable amongst them an American called Lloyd Loar, who worked initially with the Gibson Guitar company before leaving in 1924 to manufacture his own electric instruments. Loar was one of many striving to produce something reliable and acceptable with the limited technology available. It was ten years before such experimentation and development began to pay off.

1931 was the year that the first commercially produced electric guitars became available. They were the Rickenbacker A-22 and A-25 'frying pan guitars'. Made in all-aluminium or solid bakelite, these oddly-shaped instruments demonstrated from the beginning that, once electrified, the guitar's shape could be altered dramatically. The 'resonator box' was far less critical and, as would be demonstrated, could be dispensed with altogether.

Development continued for another twenty years before the invention in 1954 of what is probably the most popular electric guitar, the Fender Stratocaster.

In those intervening years, jazz musicians carried much of the responsibility for promoting the electric instrument with Eddie Condon, Freddie Green and, in particular, Charlie Christian helping to create a space for the guitar as a solo instrument.

In the world of country music, Chet Atkins pioneered work on pick-ups, and Merle Travis helped to develop the first 'solid body' electric guitar to be used conventionally. Another great musician/innovator is Les Paul, credited not only with discovering the solid body guitar (he was having them made for himself in the 1930s) but with pioneering multiple recording techniques and development of eight-track recording equipment.

So, 1954 brought the Fender Stratocaster, 1955 brought Rock'n'Roll, and large scale manufacture brought the price of an electric guitar within the reach of almost everyone's pocket. End of equation, or almost. As with any area of human endeavour, there have to be heroes. There have to be those people whose playing inspires, provides a standard for others to at least aim for. The fourteen guitarists profiled in this book are simply amongst the greatest rock/blues players alive today. It is sheer coincidence that there are an equal number of American and British players featured, but a happy one which reflects the overall picture.

More than one of the subjects in this book believes that the age of the rock guitar hero is over, and that could well be the case. Certainly, synthesisers have grown increasingly popular of late, but it will be a sad day when a lead guitarist no longer struts the stage, threatening, coaxing, brandishing the lethal weapon that makes him at once part poet, part Samurai Warrior.

Thanks to all the guitarists who co-operated with us and Victoria Huxley, Judy Moore, Ralph Baker, Ernest Chapman, Bruce Payne, Elliott Abbott, Sidney Seidenberg, Tina, Brian Goode, Linda Komorsky, Greg Fishbach, Gail, Paul Prenter, Sara Juszkiewicz, Rex King, Mick Brigden, Ray Etzler, Larry Salters, Martyn Smith, Eddie Tickner, Bill Fowler, Judy Totton, Susanne Olsen, Ava Reich, 'BeBop' Willis Edwards, the staff at 'Close Quarters' in Nashville, Mrs James Burton, Carole Marvin, Clive Banks, Maurice Schneider, Allan James, Barbara Baker, Mike O'Mahoney, Peter Jay Philbin, Glo Williams, Harold Bronson, Ray McCarthy, Martin Satterthwaite, Margaret Wells, Alison Hunt, Glyn Davies.

B.B. KING

In considering the dozens of potential candidates for this book, one essential ingredient was a representative of the blues/R&B heritage, for without the inspiration of this essentially black tradition, very few, if any, of our subjects would have ever bothered to badger their parents or friends into acquiring that first cheap guitar. Regrettably, the substantial majority of these pioneers are now either dead or fading into senility, or their whereabouts are a matter for conjecture. While this is not necessarily true of every country blues player, the final selection could only be Riley B. King, better known to guitar lovers throughout the Western world (and some parts of the East) as B. B. King, the Mississippi Blues Boy.

Having made what we thought were concrete arrangements to interview B.B. via his manager, Sidney Seidenberg, we arrived at Howard Johnson's hotel in Miami on the correct day and inquired of the desk clerk the scheduled arrival time of the King entourage. A feeling of impending doom descended as the clerk seemed impervious to our enquiries concerning B.B., and seemed totally intent on booking us a room for the night, something which was only avoided after a desperate request to see the manager. While less intent upon forcing on us the legendary Howard Johnson's hospitality, he was little better informed, and our last hope seemed to be a visit to the auditorium where B.B. was due to play that evening. Fortunately, after further panics relating to our inability to enter the hall, we finally discovered a charming lady named Ava Reich, one of the organisers of a series of concerts of which this would be the climax. Ava was involved with an organisation known as PACE, whose aim is to provide a series of both free and normally subscribed concerts in Southern Florida. B.B. and his band, we learned, were travelling overnight from a previous engagement several hundred miles away by coach – the party usually travels in this manner unless extreme distances make it impractical – and would undoubtedly be at the 'prophylactic palace' (so called because it was erected with money provided by the rich owner of the contraceptive franchise to American servicemen during World War II) in time to perform that evening. This provided some small relief – although the ideal situation for an interview is not the small hours, the opportunity to point a tape recorder at a legend must be taken at whatever time or place it is offered.

After watching B.B. entrance a packed hall with his lyrical playing, we were invited to his dressing room. It was already crowded with admirers, predominantly young and attractive black ladies for, despite being fifty-five, B.B. can still stir the hearts of those less than half his age. We were watched during the interview by a small but most attentive audience, whose initial vociferous reactions were soon quietened by B.B.'s faithful and long-serving tour manager, BeBop Edwards. It was now midnight and the time and place meant that our interview was somewhat less than a complete look at the man. However, if this dip into his history whets the appetite for greater detail, *The Arrival Of B.B. King* by Charles Sawyer, published in 1980 by Doubleday (USA) is a sympathetic and substantial history of the great man and also authorised by him.

Riley B. King was born on 16 September 1925, in Itta Bena, a small cotton plantation town in the Mississippi Delta, the closest conurbation being Indianola. His childhood, while not dissimilar to that of many of his contemporaries, seems outwardly to have been at least unfortunate and at worst tragic. By the time Riley was four-years-old, his parents had separated, and his mother, Nora Ella King, had little alternative but to base her infant son with his grandmother, seeing him when she could – at times the infant even accompanied his mother into the cottonfields. Despite this less than ideal parental situation, Riley was close to his mother as a child, so that when she died shortly before Riley became ten-years-old, he was heartbroken. Reflecting on his childhood nearly fifty years later, B.B. displayed no trace of permanent scars . . .

'When you say I was deprived, I don't think I can really agree. I don't feel I was deprived any more than most of the kids in my area, with the exception of losing my mother when I was nine – I was deprived of that. But we didn't know a lot of the things that are happening today, or were happening in cities around us – we didn't know about it anyway, so we didn't feel like we were being deprived, other than with the buses. They had buses for the white kids in the area and they didn't have any for us, so we felt deprived of that, but other than that, we didn't really feel like we were being deprived of anything.'

Riley King's education was sparse by present-day standards, although his teacher, Luther Henson in Elkhorn school, was, according to Charles Sawyer's biography, highly influential in providing the young man with good advice on the way to proceed through life. However, further potential disasters were to occur – in 1939, Riley's grandmother died, although by this time, his father, Albert King, had made himself known, and was able to offer the fifteen-year-old shelter in Lexington. It was a Godsend, but soon the boy was desperately missing his schoolteacher and also the company of the other members of the gospel group which he had formed in Itta Bena.

By the start of the Second World War, music had made an initial impact on Riley King, although he did not become deeply involved with the guitar until later. 'I used to fool around with playing guitar, but I didn't take it seriously until I was about eighteen, because I never thought of making a living with it. It was just like something around the house and everyone would fool with it, and I guess nobody ever took it seriously. I didn't know anybody personally that was popular, that used an instrument to make a living, for instance, except my cousin Bukka White. He was the only person I ever knew, so I guess I didn't have enough to motivate me to want to play.'

It seems to have purely been a lack of imagination which prevented Riley from connecting his love of

Portrait of the artist as a young man

music with a potential career – his memory of first being captivated by the instrument obviously remains crystal clear in his mind. 'My uncle, my mother's brother, his brother-in-law was the preacher in the church, and he played guitar. His name was Archie Fair – when I heard him play electric guitar, I felt that if there was any such thing as heaven, I was there when I heard this guitar.

Nothing else I had ever heard sounded so good to me. I'd heard acoustic guitars around the house, but he came with this guitar with a DeArmond pick-up on it, and an amplifier, and man, I went bananas. I just couldn't believe it, and that's what really made me want to play.'

From the age of ten, Riley had also been involved in a gospel singing group known as the Elkhorn

Jubilee Singers (named after his beloved school), and it was in this direction that his first moves towards a musical career were made. But before that, 1942 saw several significant events take place. First, Riley moved back to Indianola from the town of Kilmichael, where he had been living under the patronage of one Flake Cartledge, a white sharecropper who had earlier acted as patron for Riley's parents. He also bought a guitar for $2.50 from a friend, intending to form a new group as soon as he had become settled domestically. 'Yes, I sang with another group when I was a teenager, and that group got to be very popular in fact. We were kind of like the warm-up group on stage for groups like the Soul Stirrers, which the late, great Sam Cooke was in, and the Spirit of Memphis.'

The group in which Riley sang was known as the Famous St John Gospel Singers, and as well as singing, he would also provide guitar accompaniment. To supplement his low income, he earned extra money by 'busking' the blues on street corners, and after seeing such contemporary black stars as Sonny Boy Williamson and Louis Jordan, Riley developed a yen to become a full-time performer himself, although many obstacles still remained. The war was still continuing and during 1944, Riley married his first wife. After registering for the draft, Riley was set to serve his country, but his sharecropper employer, Johnson Barrett, found himself short of labour and suggested that Riley apply for a deferment because of his occupation/ and recent marriage. The choice between risking his life in the war and making money for his employer amounted to little advantage either way, and while he obviously survived the war, working for 'The Man' was unrewarding and fuelled Riley's desire for a change in his circumstances. It was then that his unique guitar style began to take shape, under the influence of several master players whom he either saw playing live or more frequently heard on record.

'There was a guy called Lemon Jefferson, who we called Blind Lemon, because he was born blind, I was told. Another was Lonnie Johnson – I like to think of myself as Lonnie Johnson, because he was associated with the great jazz musicians as well as the great blues people, so he seemed to me to be that link between jazz and blues. And then, of course, I liked jazz at the time, and I was crazy about a guy called Charlie Christian, and another was Django Reinhardt, who only had three fingers. His little finger and his ring finger had been burned, and I heard that he was in a trailer that caught on fire, and he burned his left hand, so he had two free fingers, and his ring finger and his little finger were kind of webbed together from the burn. We called him three-fingered lightning.'

During May 1946, increasingly discontented with his lot and catalysed after a tractor accident which nearly resulted in the loss of all his earnings, Riley took his courage in both hands, and set out for Memphis with his guitar and very little money. He hoped to find his mother's cousin, Bukka White, there, and having made enquiries, he located White after a few days, and stayed with him. In 1981, B.B. does not acknowledge that Bukka was an influence on his playing, as has been suggested elsewhere. 'No, but

he was a very good friend to me. As well as being my mother's cousin, he had that something that I hope I'll have maybe someday – he could make everybody smile, he could make you laugh. He was a jolly fellow, he always had something that used to turn me on, and I was so glad when he would come around. I lived with him for about a year then, when I was about twenty, and he got me a job at the place he worked, the Newbury Equipment Company.'

However, Riley was troubled about what he had left behind in Indianola, specifically his wife and an unpaid debt to his sharecropper landlord, so he returned in 1947 to settle his affairs, which took the best part of a year, after which he returned to Memphis determined to make a career in music.

'When I got to Memphis, I had heard of a guy called Sonny Boy Williamson, who we used to listen to before I left Mississippi. I had heard that he was in West Memphis on the radio there, instead of in Helena, Arkansas, where he used to be – I'd been listening to him for so long it was almost like I knew him. So I went over that day to the radio station where he worked and begged him to let me go on the radio, so he made me audition for him. I thought I could sing pretty good, so I sang for him, and he said ''OK'' and let me do one number.' Sonny Boy's programme was a daily fifteen-minute live blues broadcast, and Riley King could see its obvious potential for exposure.

'On that first day, it happened that Sonny Boy had two jobs, one that he didn't want too much where he had been working quite a bit, and another one where he was going to get paid more money. So the lady that he had been working for, that he was trying to get rid of, you know, not wanting to work for her that particular night, he asked her if she'd heard me on the radio. She said she had, so he said, ''Well, I'm going to let him play for you tonight, and I'll be back next week. Is that OK?'' and she said it was fine. So I went there, and my job was to play for the young ladies while the men would go in the back. A few of them didn't gamble, but the ones that did, would go in the back to do it, and it was my job to make all the young ladies happy and keep them dancing. And that just knocked me out – I loved that, plus she paid me twelve dollars too, and I'd never made that much money in my life. I'd been working most of my life, and during the war everything was supposed to be very good moneywise, and I was making twenty-two dollars a week then, which was supposed to be a good salary, and here I was making twelve dollars in one night – unbelievable!

'So then the lady that I worked for told me that if I could get on the radio like Sonny Boy, where I could advertise her place, she would pay me for six days a week, and of course, I'd get paid twelve dollars a day plus room and board, and one day off. I couldn't believe that, man – there couldn't be anything like that, playing for these beautiful ladies and getting paid for it. Oh man! So at that time, a new radio station had just been bought by a couple of friends. It had been a Country & Western station, and they had just changed it and made it an all-black operation. I went there that same day, and they put me on the air that day, singing and playing, ten minutes a day by myself. I got to be very popular, and they gave me

several of the guys that had worked with me started to work with Johnny Ace as the Beale Streeters.'

The significance of Johnny Ace in the popular music pantheon is that on Christmas Eve, 1954, at the age of twenty-five, Ace, accidentally killed himself while playing Russian Roulette, thus becoming the first notable casualty of the rock'n'roll era. His record 'Pledging my Love', inevitably became one of the biggest hits of 1955 . . .

It was around this time that B.B. met Elvis Presley, although he could not confirm that his first manager turned down the chance to manage Presley on the grounds that he thought the latter lacked any talent. 'I don't know if that's true or not, but I do know that where I used to record, the gentleman who owned the studio, Sam Phillips, did have Elvis, and Elvis used to come to that studio. I knew Elvis – not that well, but I knew him – he was just like another dude then, because none of us was very popular at that time.'

If anything, B.B. was better known than Elvis before the latter's meteoric rise to fame in the mid-1950s – after 'Three O'Clock Blues' had topped the R&B chart in 1950, further R&B hits followed, including 'Woke Up This Morning' in 1953, apparently written in the wake of his almost inevitable divorce. Inevitable, because the man seemed never to stop working, although the intention was simply survival as opposed to the amassing of a vast fortune. B.B.'s records never sounded the same because all his work only served to synthesise new influences and fads, of which 'Woke Up This Morning' was just one example. 'Yes, that one was kind of a calypso beat, because during that time, music was changing quite a bit, and calypso was very popular. Through the years, I've been influenced by the music around me, so from time to time, I've always tried not to go all the way out and do exactly what the musical fad of the time is, but play something that I felt I could colour with that fad.'

During the 1950s, B.B.'s main arena for live performances was the 'chitlin circuit', an almost unending series of black night clubs fanning out from America's heartland, and life was a constant routine of performing, travelling and occasionally recording. 'I think the most one-nighters I ever did in a year was in 1956, when I did 342. I expect we'd have done the complete year except that we were busy trying to get to the next job – I didn't think about it though, because I was very young. When I'm on stage now, I enjoy it, especially when the group's sounding good and everybody's energetic – it seems to motivate me, and I really have a good time. Normally, a concert runs from an hour on, and many times I'll turn to my conductor and say, "Hey, what time is it? How much time have we played?", and he'll say an hour or whatever, and I'd think, "Already? I don't believe it!"'

Despite his obvious popularity, as evidenced by nearly twenty hit singles during the 1950s, the vast majority of these hits were confined to the R&B charts, and seemingly insufficient sales were logged to allow a crossover into the pop chart. 'Well, we didn't have as large an audience as we have today. At that time, most of my audience was blacks, usually my age and older, hardly ever the young

fifteen minutes, and then they made a disc jockey out of me. I think working as a disc jockey helped me as far as the way I am on stage today.'

A little clarification – Sonny Boy Williamson II, whose real name was Rice Miller, once hosted a radio show which is still enjoyed throughout America today, the King Biscuit Hour, on station KWEM. The station on which B. B. King began to broadcast (his epithet B.B. was applied to him by a fellow disc jockey, Don Kearn, who called him the 'Blues Boy') was WDIA, on which he became famous, among other things, for a commercial for Pepticon Health Tonic. B.B. became a familiar name in Memphis blues circles, and before long, offers to play live began to occur, resulting in the formation of the Beale Streeters.

'The guy that started that group used to be my piano player, and his name was Johnny Ace, although in fact his real name was John Alexander Junior. He had been working with me, and we had made a record called "Three O'Clock Blues", which had gotten to be very popular – I don't know what it was about that record that made it become so popular, but if I did know, I'd have a hit every time I made a record – so I decided to sign with a booking agency out of New York called Universal. Universal said, "We want a single performer, we don't want a group, we don't need a band". I had decided by then that I was going to travel, but nobody except me wanted to travel, so I said to Johnny Ace, "I'll tell you what I'll do – I'll give you the band, you take the band, and I'll take off". Which was the same way I'd got to Memphis in the first place – I took off, left the gospel group I'd sung with in Indianola, and went to Memphis, so now I'm leaving the group we started in Memphis to go on the road as a single. So when I left,

B.B. during the early 1960s

blacks – a lot of the groups like the Dominoes, the Clovers, maybe Jackie Wilson, James Brown, people like that, had a young audience, so when you've got a young audience and an old audience all combined, you'll sell more records, but I was never really appealing to the young blacks. Then, in the middle '60s, we started to gain more white fans, and after I did "The Thrill Is Gone" in the late '60s, our audience then became young whites and old blacks. I guess in the latter part of the '70s we started to get a few more young blacks and a few more older whites, so now, if I could get a few more of both, I'd think I was a true artist.'

Little startlingly different occurred for B.B. during the '50s, other than a second marriage, which was unfortunately destined to be no more successful than the first. Musical experimentation continued, especially with regard to the size of his backing band. By the time he recorded one of his more famous songs, 'Sweet Sixteen', in 1960, B.B. was using what for him was a big orchestra. 'Yes, I think I had about a thirteen-piece group at that time, which was about the largest group I've ever had. But then, back in the '50s I used studio orchestras where we had strings, voices, the whole works – that was when we made "Do I Love You", "My Heart Belongs To Only You" and quite a few other things. With a full orchestra – I'm daring, I'm a real rebel!'

Talking of rebelliousness, one item which, on the face of it, appears bizarre in considering B.B.'s unique guitar playing is that he rarely, if ever, employs the bottleneck style which has characterised so many of his imitators. The suggestion has been made that this is not deliberate but rather because B.B.'s fingers are too large to be easily encased in a conventional bottleneck, be it made of glass or metal.

'I won't go along with that, because Bukka's fingers were larger than mine, and he used one. I've just got stupid fingers that just don't work. I could never get my fingers to work like most of the guys who use a bottleneck. I used to trill my hand after listening to Bukka and to Robert Nighthawk, and a few of the other guys like Earl Hooker – I felt that when I trilled my hand, I got this sound that my ears say was similar to using a bottleneck, because I never could do it the usual way. Like I say, I've got stupid fingers that just don't work, so I could never do it, and the more I trilled my hand, the more my ears would say I was sounding like I was using a bottleneck, therefore I keep doing it, and I'm still trying, and it still tells me, even now, because I like that sound. I'm crazy about the steel guitar.'

Certainly, the sound B.B. produces is sometimes not far removed from bottleneck, however he achieves it, although a much more archetypal part of his style is his remarkable and much copied (although never completely successfully) ability to sustain a note. 'That's technique, which comes from practising, and it also comes from having a pretty good ear that's able to work with the volume and feedback of the amp in such a way that it eventually becomes professional. What I'm trying to say is that anybody can just turn the guitar up and scream, but to be able to control it without going to your volume controls, but using your ear to tell you when it's getting too loud or not loud enough, takes technique, because you've got to work with the frets there . . . that part of it is rather hard to describe, but when I feel that it's not sustaining enough, I press harder, but at the same time, move the finger. When it's getting too loud, I let up off it a bit, but still keep it moving, because if you don't . . . it's like flying an aeroplane and your engine cuts out, you've got no way to start it again, you dig? So you have to keep working with it, and yes, that takes practice, but this is going on thirty-one years that I've been trying.'

Prior to the early 1960s, B.B.'s recording career was limited commercially by the labels to which he was signed – labels like Bullet, RPM and Kent/Modern were rarely able to appeal to other than the 'race' market and a few devoted blues scholars. His signing, around 1962, with the Bluesway subsidiary of ABC Records, a multi-national conglomerate, should by rights have broadened his market substantially. Although ABC reportedly paid $25,000 for the privilege of adding B.B. to their roster, early attempts at gaining ground were hindered by his previous record companies releasing or re-releasing his old recordings which inevitably competed with his new work. Together with an impending second divorce, the first half of the decade was not the pleasantest period of B. B. King's career, although several masterpieces did emerge, and conceivably caught the ears of several British teenagers who were still learning their craft as guitarists. One such record, released in Britain on the somewhat obscure Ember label, was 'Rock Me Baby', which later became a staple of the act of numerous R&B bands. In the '80s, B.B. is polite but hardly bubbling over about the song: 'I think it's a good song, and I was motivated to do it after I heard a guy called Little Son Jackson do it, and I rewrote the lyrics and played it my way. I like the feeling, that down home feeling, and I think that's one of the things that really made me want to do it.'

The same kind of reaction results from an enquiry about what many critics suggest is the ultimate B. B. King live album, *Live At The Regal*, released in 1965 on ABC. 'Yes, many critics have said that was *the* album, and as I've said before, I don't argue with my critics, especially when they're in my favour. That was produced by a guy called Johnny Pate, who at the time worked for ABC Records, and is also a bass player, a great musician and a great arranger. I think that the set up he had to record this was a once in a lifetime thing, and the audience seemed to be just right – it seemed that every ingredient was just so, because I don't think I played any better than I've played before, but the feedback from the audience was good, there was a rapport. I don't think it was nothing extraordinary, other than just the way it was set up and everything was just right. I think that's the best I can tell you about it.'

One of the stand-out tracks on the record is another B.B. classic, 'Everyday I Have The Blues', a title which seemed somewhat incongruous in the face of the obvious success which B.B. was experiencing. How difficult is it, then, to sustain a feeling for the blues when much of the reason for being afflicted has been removed? 'Well, first I think of it this way. It's kind of like a saying I heard from someone – I believe Dr (Martin Luther) King was one I heard say it – that no man's free until all men are free. I might make a good salary, but a lot of my friends and a lot of people I know don't – how can I ever forget what I had? You can't possibly forget it, and even today, being successful, there are a lot of things still denied to me. Even if I had money enough to buy them or do them, I still couldn't, so how can I forget? Not only that – and this happens to all people, I think – we all have problems, especially like it is now, and boy! do we have problems! So, yes, to make a long story short, I know people who make a much better salary than I do, but then I know so many that make much, much less than I do, so I don't ever feel comfortable, as if I've really made it, because I don't think I have. You've made it when all your buddies and everybody else are in good shape too, so you don't forget – you can't.'

In the second half of the 1960s, the pieces of the jigsaw finally began to fall into place for B.B., although once again not without some false starts along the way. Perhaps the biggest advantage came when young white guitarists from both sides of the Atlantic, who were playing the blues, acknowledged B.B. as one of their major influences. 'I felt happy about that, because even though a lot of doors were open to a lot of white kids that were playing the same thing I was, those doors weren't open to me, but when they spoke out and said they listened to B. B. King, they listened to Jimmy Reed, many doors opened then that had never been open for us before, so I started to think "Oh well, better late than never". I felt good, obviously.'

In 1968, this newfound white following provided another breakthrough – prior to that year, B.B. had rarely, if ever, played in front of a predominantly white audience. 'I was scared, frightened – the first big white audience I remember playing for was at the Fillmore West in San Francisco, and we used to play there when it used to be ninety-five per cent black. When I got there that day, there were all of these white kids there with long hair, and everybody sitting all over the place, so I thought I was in the wrong place, that's what I thought. Because I'd heard about the hippies and all that, but I'd never actually been involved with them, so when I got out there, our promoter was Bill Graham, and he said, "B., we're glad to have you", and then I felt a little comfortable, knowing that I was in the right place, even if it seemed to be the wrong audience. So I went into the same old place where we used to sit, up there in the dressing room, and I said I was nervous and that I needed something to drink – I've never used any hard drugs – and he said they didn't sell any alcohol, but he'd send somebody out to get me a bottle, which he did. And the kids didn't know me – they knew about me, but they didn't even know what I looked like. There were quite a few blacks there, but I'd say it was about ninety-eight per cent white. And I'll never forget that after I'd done had me two or three slugs of whatever it was that I was drinking – Courvoisier, I believe – I was kind of OK then, feeling good. And I remember Bill Graham himself introduced me, and I'll never forget it, it's ringing in my ears now – he said "Ladies and gentleman, I bring you the Chairman of the Board, B. B. King". And everybody stood up. I cried, I couldn't believe it, and from that time on, my fear kind of left.'

The following year saw a further breakthrough with a series of albums produced by Bill Szymczyk, a young white staff producer for ABC. Szymczyk recalls: 'B.B. was on the roster at ABC, and I kept bugging people to let me produce him, but they said, "Hey, what are you doing? You're a white guy, you can't cut that stuff". I finally convinced them that I could do it, and they said that if B.B. agreed, it was all right with them. He did agree, and he was due for a live album, so I suggested that we did it half live with his band at the Village Gate in New York, and for the other half, I'd put some different musicians together, maybe a little more modern people. B.B. got off on it, and we all liked it, and one of the tunes we did was "Why I Sing The Blues", and that was the first chart record I ever had in my life as a producer – it went to about 40 in the pop charts even. It did quite well on the R&B charts, but to get into the pop charts then was considered quite a big success.'

Despite what the ABC executives had intimated, B.B. had actually worked with white producers before, in the shape of Jules, Joe and Sol Bihari, the owners of Kent/Modern, and the reason for the serendipity between artist and producer was in no way connected with colour or race.

'He was a great producer, and he didn't try to tell me how to play the blues. He didn't do what a lot of other producers do and tell me what was selling and what wasn't selling – I sing and play what I feel, so what Bill would do was make sure that the engineer and my surroundings provided me with exactly what I needed to do what I do. That's what made him so unique, and in fact, I'm grateful to him today, because some of the best work I did was with Bill Szymczyk, and I think of him as an actor or an actress would a director. A lot of times, a director sees things in you that maybe you don't see, but usually, he'll tell you what it is that he'd like to get, but he'll let you do it. And that's another thing to add to Bill Szymczyk – think of it like this: I'm fifty-five now, and Bill is maybe two-thirds of my age, something like that, so how could he possibly feel the blues as I do, who've been playing them since before he was born? What I'm trying to say is that he could tell me how certain things should be put on tape or something, but I don't think anybody could tell me to sing, except how I feel.'

Live And Well was the title of the album, and to follow it, Szymczyk decided to make a second LP completely in the studio, understandably supplying a title of *Completely Well*. This was an even greater success than the half-live *Live And Well*, to a large extent because of the inclusion of a track which still stands as B.B.'s biggest chart item, 'The Thrill Is Gone'. The memories of producer and artist are somewhat dissimilar on this song, which was allegedly written by B.B. as an answer to his second wife's pleas for a reconciliation, although this seems somewhat unlikely in view of what B.B. recalls.

'Bill didn't like it when we first cut it. I had kept that song for about eight years, and every once in a while, I would bring it out at a session, but it never sounded right, so I'd put it back – you always have "x" amount of tunes, so you just lay them over if they don't sound right.'

Szymczyk: 'B.B. would bring the tunes in, and then everybody would work out kind of head arrangements in the studio.'

B.B.: 'That particular night, we had Hugh McCracken on guitar, Gerald Jemmott on bass, Herbie Lovelle on drums and Paul Harris on piano, and it seemed like the whole ingredients, everything, was right, and so I went into it. Nobody picked songs for me – somebody might suggest something, but if I don't like it, I won't do it. But this particular tune, I got into it, and it seemed to me like it was just right. I've always thought, and I still do, that when you

*The focal point on the stage
and even on the bus!*

make a good record, you make a good record – I don't try to make pop records, just good records – I don't try to make it commercial this way or that way, I just think in terms of making a good record. That night, I knew we had made a good record, and I told Bill that, and he said "OK".'

Szymczyk: 'The only quote brilliant unquote thing I did on that track was about the third time I heard it, I said, "Well, we've got to put strings on this", and everybody looked at me like "What? Strings? On a blues record? You're kidding me", but I said, "No, it'll be great".'

B.B.: 'About three-thirty or four o'clock, he called me at my apartment and I was half asleep and mad too – talk about a terrible sounding voice, you want to hear me first thing in the morning! – and he didn't say who he was or anything, he just said, "What do you think about putting strings on 'The Thrill Is Gone'?" I said that would be OK, and he said, "Well, I think it'll crossover to the pop charts, what do you think?" I said, "Bill, all I know is that it's a good record. You put strings on it if you want", and he said, "Man, I think we've got something", and I said, "I told you that when we got through".'

Szymczyk: 'I got my man Bert De Coteaux, who did all my charts, and we put these hypnotic strings on it, and B.B. came to check it out and said, "This is real nice, I like it", and the rest, as they say, is history.'

B.B.: 'I went down and listened to it, but as I said, although I never thought it would do what it did do, I knew it was a good record, and a good record's a good record. But every time I heard the radio, all across the country, everywhere was playing "The Thrill Is Gone", even some of the jazz stations. I started to think then "What was it that we did? Can I do it again? Ever?" I don't think so . . .'

The collaboration between Szymczyk and B. B. King continued for two further albums, *Indianola Mississippi Seeds* and *Live at Cook County Jail*. For the first of these, Szymczyk introduced a new discovery of his, a young guitarist from Ohio who was the leader of a trio whom Szymczyk had signed to ABC, the James Gang. The guitarist was Joe Walsh, and among the other notable white musicians who played on the record were Carole King and Leon Russell. On the face of it, there seems little point in using Joe Walsh on a B. B. King record . . .

'He's a great musician – I don't know him that well, but I've enjoyed working with him every time we've played together. It may not actually be necessary to have him on my records, but it always enhances a performer to have good musicians with them, and in my case as a blues singer, which is usually the bottom of the totem pole as far as music's concerned, to have a rock player on there, or a name in jazz, enhances the sales of a record without a doubt. Because Joe has a lot of fans himself – I don't know, but my name might be good on his record too, if he ever asked me.'

The *Cook County Jail* LP documents the first of a number of prison concerts which B.B. has performed since the early 1970s. 'It started in Chicago, where we were about to be the first blues group that had ever played a jazz club called Mr Kelly's. There was a newly-appointed black director of the Cook County Correctional Institution, and he called over to Mr Kelly's while I was working there, and told me that he'd invited many people over (to the prison), but nobody ever came. And he said that this was a first for me and Mr Kelly's and it was a first for him, and if I'd help him, we could both provide a first for the inmates, because he'd promised them that if they were orderly and what have you, he was sure that I would do everything I could to help them. So I spoke to my management, and told them I'd like to do it, and being managers, they think in terms of publicity and all that you can get out of it, so they invited the press, and at the same time, they got the record company to record this event.

'The press interviewed many of the inmates, and found that most of them were black or from minority races, and we also found that a lot of these people had been locked up for like seven or eight months or more, and hadn't come to trial, simply because they were poor. And then usually when they'd come to trial, if found innocent they weren't compensated for anything, and if they were found guilty, the time they had already spent locked up didn't go against the time that they got. Well, the press played it up real big the next day – all the Chicago papers had stories about it, and about four or five months later, one of the TV networks did an in-depth story kind of thing, and they interviewed some of the people that we had talked with and played to, and one of the results was that if a person had been locked up for a long time, they would set a calendar date for trial, instead of keeping them there for months and months. That made me very happy, because I felt that we really did something good, and that was one of the reasons I started doing it. In fact, I'm going to do another one pretty soon in my home state, which I've never done before.' The Mississippi prison which B.B. was going to play was in fact the celebrated Parchman Farm, which gave its name to one of the more notable modern blues songs.

The four albums which B.B. made with Szymczyk provided him with a new plateau which was substantially higher than those he had previously occupied, and on which he will doubtless remain for the rest of his career. However, it would be appropriate at this point to devote some space to B.B.'s love affair with the guitar – one notable facet of B. B. King's instruments is that all his guitars are known to him as 'Lucille'.

'That came about in 1949. I used to play a place called Twist, Arkansas, on Friday and Saturday nights, and Sundays too if it rained, because that meant that people didn't have to go to work the next day. It got kind of cold in Twist in the winter, so they would set something that looked like a big garbage pail in the middle of the floor, half-fill it with kerosene, light the fuel and use that for heat, and usually everybody would dance around without disturbing it. But one particular night, two dudes started fighting, and one of them knocked down the container and it spilled on the floor – it was already burning, so when they spilled it, it was like a river fire. Everybody started making it for the door, including me, but when I got outside, I remembered I'd run off and left my guitar, so I went back for it. Now the building was a log building, and it started to fall in

Cradling a recent Lucille

around me, so I almost lost my life trying to save that guitar. The next morning, we found two men had got trapped in one of the rooms above the dance hall and burned to death. We also found out that these two guys that were fighting were fighting about a lady, and although I never got to meet her, I did learn that her name was Lucille, so I named my guitar Lucille, to remind me never to do a silly thing like that again, because I think you can get another guitar, but not another B. B. King.'

Somewhat surprisingly, despite B.B.'s obvious command of the guitar, he regards himself as strictly a soloist rather than a chord player, and additionally finds it difficult to play while singing, although this latter item is partly explained by his self-confessed lack of expertise as a rhythm player – playing chords while singing is substantially simpler than simul-taneously singing and picking single note solos.

'My rhythm playing's worse than awful – I'm really strictly single strings. I've never played in a rhythm section – I wish I could, but ever since I've been play-ing, usually if I want to sit in a rhythm section, my fans and friends start saying they want to hear ''Three O'Clock Blues'' or ''The Thrill Is Gone'' or something, so I can never play rhythm just to enjoy myself. There have been times when I've gone to jam sessions where people wouldn't ask me to sing, but that's rare. So yes, I'm worse than awful chordwise. And I can't think that well to be able to sing and play at the same time. Really, I'm not putting myself down – I sing, though, in my mind with the guitar while I'm playing it, so I do play while I'm singing, but the singing's in my mind, and when I'm just singing, I'm singing to the guitar. I could never do it, and I never have been able to – in my home town, people used to say "Frail along", and I could do that, but I could never chord properly while I'm singing.'

The significantly enlarged audience for B.B. during the 1970s resulting from the recording activity which included 'The Thrill Is Gone' (the song won a Grammy Award, the musical equivalent of the cinematic Oscar) led to some remarkable achievements – during 1970, a year in which he toured with the Rolling Stones, B.B. played to more than three million people in concert, and his appearance the following year on the *Ed Sullivan Show* attracted a reported TV audience exceeding seventy million. 1971 also saw him embarking on a series of successful foreign tours, taking in Australia, the prelude to a 1972 world tour which took in Africa and Israel as well as most of Europe. Such travels seem somehow trivial compared with a 1978 trip to Russia, although B.B. still has ambitions to play in a still more remote part of the world, politically speaking.

'Yes, I want to go to China, mainland China, I mean Red China – I'd like to go there. And also I'd like to do a blues show. Every time I've been on television, usually it's a rock show, or a jazz show or something like that, and I'd like to do a special, a blues special, and I want it to be spelt out real big – B L U E S. And then I could invite some of the other people from jazz or rock or gospel or whatever on the blues show, like they've invited me on various shows. That's what I'd like to do. And a movie where I can at least say, "I'm B. B. King".'

In recent years, B.B.'s recording activities have been straightforward – while occasionally using predominantly white sidemen, as on 1971's *B. B. King In London*, where he was supported by such British notables as Ringo Starr, Peter Green and even Rick Wright of the Pink Floyd, or 1972's *LA Midnight* and *Guess Who* LPs, where he worked with, among others, Randy California and Jesse Davis as well as being reunited with Joe Walsh, B.B.'s major projects included a pair of albums with the renowned vocalist Bobby 'Blue' Bland, and several collaborations with the Crusaders, the largely black and highly acclaimed soul/jazz group.

'Bobby and I have been friends for a very long time, but we were never on the same record label until the end of the '70s, when the company I'm with, ABC, bought the company that he was with, Duke/ Peacock Records. We had worked for the same agencies before but never the same record company, and somebody decided that it would be good if we recorded together, although we had wanted to do it all the time. When we got the green light on it, Bobby doesn't like flying, but he flew out to Los Angeles to meet me, and that's how that came about.'

In fact, Bland had been a member of the Beale Streeters, but not, apparently, when B.B. was running that group. 'No, but we'd been around, been friends, and in fact, believe it or not, he used to work with me as a valet from time to time, helping me drive and do things like that, but that's the early years I'm talking about, a long time ago.' Working with the Crusaders was a somewhat different proposition, of course . . . 'It's like I told you a while ago, I like to feel that I'm the link between jazz and blues. I've known about the Crusaders for years, and in fact

The greatest living bluesman

the drummer that worked with me for a long time went to school with Stix Hooper (drummer with the Crusaders), so I'm familiar with the group and their progress and everything. And they had started to produce – in fact, they still produce records on many people – and when they wanted to produce one on me, it made me very happy. The only thing I asked them was "Don't change me, let me be myself". That was my only request, and I think they did that very well.'

Turning to B.B.'s preferred guitars, it comes as no surprise to learn that he currently plays a Gibson ES355. 'The company have just released a line of guitars like the model I play, and they call it the B. B. King Lucille model, and that's obviously been my favourite, ever since it's been available. I like it – it's slim, I like its name, it's a lady, and I can hold it very close to me and it doesn't argue and it doesn't talk back. I have played other guitars, of course, but I started playing this type of Gibson in the early '50s, and it's been my guitar since then. Prior to that time, I played various types, but this has been my favourite since the early '50s. There are others, of course, but it's kind of like automobiles – there's Fords and Chevrolets, but then there's Rolls Royces, Cadillacs and Mercedes.'

B.B.'s interest in the American penal system, or at least in its reformation, has already been noted, but this is by no means his only public-spirited activity, another being a company which he has recently formed through his management which aims to assist other blues artists. 'What I would like to do is share with them and counsel them on the things that have helped me to go as far as I've gone. That means, for instance, the various types of material, various types of people to work with, things to look for in negotiations with people like managers and record companies. There's a whole world of things that we could share with them – to try to see that the records get out, good distributors, many things, even little things like from the right guitar to what have you . . .'

At the age of fifty-five, B. B. King is without doubt one of the most famous and respected guitar players of all time. At such an age, many would be considering winding down to a quiet retirement, but it is a measure of the man's enjoyment of life and his commitment to his music that no such thoughts have entered his head. 'I won't retire until the people retire me. When the people stop supporting me recordwise and supporting my concerts, that'll be it. Other than that, until the great Creator says, "You've stayed down there long enough", this is it – other than that, I'll be here.'

B. B. King Discography

Early years
As more than thirty years have elapsed since B.B. started recording, his earliest works have been released on a bewildering variety of record labels. Charles Sawyer's biography, *The Arrival Of B. B. King*, lists eleven LPs on the Crown label, few, if any, of which appear to be available in Britain, and many of which may no longer be available in the United States. This may also apply to his work for Kent/Modern, although it seems that for much of the time, the Crown albums are simply repackages of Kent/Modern material. Sawyer lists eight Kent/Modern LPs, the most representative of which is *From The Beginning*, a double LP. In Britain, much of the Kent material was available during the early 1970s on three LPs released by Blue Horizon Records, although that company's closure in the mid-'70s has probably resulted in their deletion. Thus there is little definite information available concerning the acquisition of B.B.'s early recordings, although there are doubtless numerous albums available through specialist blues labels on both sides of the Atlantic.

Since he joined ABC/Bluesway in the early 1960s, B. B. King's albums have been much easier to find, particularly in Europe, although since ABC Records went out of business in 1979, after which their catalogue was taken over by MCA Records, the availability of many of the records listed below is in doubt.

Release date

1962	*Mr Blues*	1974	*Lucille Talks Back*
1965	*Live At The Regal*	1976	*Together For The First Time* (with Bobby Bland)
1966	*Confessin' The Blues*		
1967	*Blues Is King*	1976	*Together Again . . . Live* (with Bobby Bland)
1968	*Blues On Top Of Blues*	1977	*King Size*
1968	*Lucille*	1978	*Midnight Believer* (with the Crusaders)
1968	*His Best – The Electric B. B. King*	1979	*Take It Home* (with the Crusaders)
1969	*Live And Well*	1979	*Live B. B. King On Stage*
1969	*Completely Well*	1980	*Great Moments with B. B. King* (compilation – US only)
1970	*Indianola Mississippi Seeds*		
1970	*Live At Cook County Jail*	1980	*'Now Appearing' at Ole Miss*
1971	*B. B. King In London*	1981	*There Must Be A Better World Somewhere*
1972	*L. A. Midnight*	1982	*Royal Jam* (with the Crusaders and the Royal Philarmonic Orchestra)
1972	*Guess Who*		
1972	*To Know You Is To Love You*	1982	*Love Me Tender*
1973	*The Best Of B. B. King* (reissued 1982)		

SCOTTY MOORE

There can be few more graphic illustrations of the fact that rock'n'roll music is no longer some here today gone tomorrow speck of lint in the wind than the fact that Winfield Scott Moore, better known as 'Scotty', celebrated his fiftieth birthday on 27 December 1981. The last remaining member of the trio which recorded a string of timeless classics in the rocking '50s – the other two were bass player Bill Black and a certain Elvis Presley – Scotty Moore today lives and works in the Country Music Capital of the world, Nashville, Tennessee, where he operates his own tape duplicating plant. Against one wall stands a small amplifier from which emerged some remarkable sounds more than twenty years ago, while the instrument which made the sounds can be found in a nearby office, although the man who played it then rarely removes it from its case these days, more's the pity . . .

The influence exerted by the early Presley recordings released by Sun and later by RCA is quite incalculable – Scotty Moore, in essence, wrote the rock guitar primer which has been at least studied, if not openly copied, by every major rock guitarist, bar none. However, Scotty's early years, from his birth in Gadsden, Tennessee, until the end of the Second World War, gave no indication of what was to follow, aside from an early interest in the guitar largely fostered by his family.

'I started playing the guitar when I was about eight years old. My whole family – my dad and three brothers who were much older than I was – played guitar, and my dad played banjo and a little fiddle, and one of my brothers also played fiddle and mandolin. So when I got old enough to begin to see what they were doing and enjoying it, about that time they all left home. I guess I'm just hard-headed, and I said, "Well, I'm left out – I'm going to do it myself!" The best I remember, I think the first guitar I had was a Kalamazoo, which my brother had gotten for me, and which later, when I was really old enough to know, I discovered was a real good little guitar. This was during World War II, and my brother was in the Navy, and he had this real shiny guitar, as far as looks went – it wasn't a Gene Autry guitar, probably a Sears. So he conned me. He said, "I don't want to take this guitar and ruin the finish out on the ship",

In the Sun Studio, 1954 – the first publicity shot.
Left to right: Bill Black, Elvis Presley and Scotty Moore

A 1980s reissue album with Scotty Moore on the left in the picture

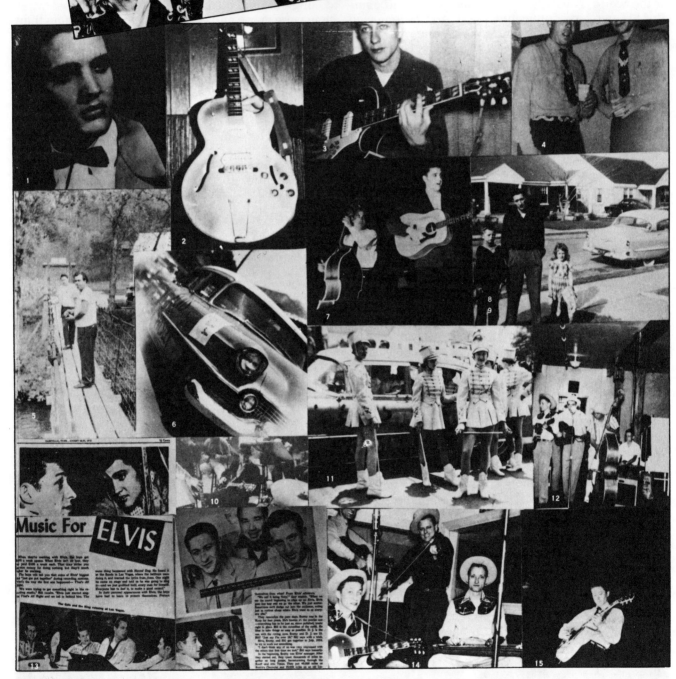

Scotty Moore memorabilia:

1 Elvis
2 Scotty's guitar from first recording
3 Scotty
4 With Bill Black
5 On Tour

6 Handpainted by Elvis
7 Bill and Elvis
8 Scotty and Kids
9 1953 Chevy
10 At Paramount Studios

11 Elvis' first fan club
12 VA Hospital
13 Newspaper cuttings
14 Starlite Wranglers
15 Scotty on stage

and so on, ''Let me trade with you''. You know who got the raw end of the deal on that?'

Scotty feels that even at the age of fifteen, at the end of the War, he was interested in the possibilities presented by making music for a living. 'I think I knew, even before I went in the Service in January 1948 – I had a little band in the Service, and then, as I went from ship to ship, kept forming bands, or going out and searching for people I could get together with to form a little group. It was always in the back of my mind that that was what I wanted to do.' However, despite his origins, his interest was not strictly concerned with country music.

'No, no, it really wasn't at that time, because I was learning, so I was listening. Anybody who played guitar was fine with me, and what sort of music it was didn't matter. I heard Muddy Waters, of course, and a lot of the jazz players, but I really wasn't into who they were – I'd just hear a record, or hear something on the radio, and that was fine. In fact, in later years that's probably one of the things I really regret – at the time that Elvis came along and his thing happened, I was at a point where I was really grasping and learning. No schooling, strictly by ear, and of course, as many musicians can tell you, when you're on the road you're in a rut doing practically the same thing day in and day out, and after a while, you lose the thing you had, and looking back, that's one thing I do regret.'

For Scotty, music was never a full-time occupation in the early days, primarily for financial reasons. 'Oh no, Lord no. When I came out of the Service, I went to work for my oldest brother in Memphis who owned a (clothes) cleaning plant. He had a hat department run by an elderly gentleman that was about to retire. To back up for a minute, I first had a job as a diesel mechanic, and one day my brother asked me if I'd be interested in learning about the hat business, so I said, ''I don't know – what happens in the hat business?'' So I went with the guy who was due to retire and learned the business in two weeks and took it over and ran it for a year and a half, maybe two years. And doing that, it was like going to work early in the morning and being through by two o'clock in the afternoon, and then I'd swing and get into the rest of it.'

His stint in the Navy had also provided Scotty with his first exposure, when one of his ad hoc groups had a regular Saturday morning slot on a radio station in Marsden, near Washington, D.C., for a few months when their ship was in dry dock – although nothing resulted in the form of records. Having returned to Memphis and begun to run his hat department, Scotty soon became aware of the legendary Memphis musical entrepreneur, Sam Phillips, who founded the Sun record label at the start of the 1950s.

'Sun was fairly new, although Sam had been producing a lot of black acts for other companies, like Chess Records in Chicago, and Don Robey's Peacock Records in Houston. Sam was working as a disc jockey at WREC, and while he was there, he set up his Memphis Recording Service, which was strictly a walk in and cut your demo tape type of thing, and that was when he was producing these other acts. From that, he decided, I'm sure, that there was no reason why he should record for other companies

when he could easily start his own thing, and that's when he started Sun. I met Sam after I had joined a group in Memphis – it was strictly a country group, called Doug Poindexter and his Starlite Wranglers, and we made a record for Sun called ''My Kind of Carryin' On'', which I wrote.'

This was not the only record made by Sam Phillips on which Scotty appeared (other than the numerous Presley sides he decorated), another being 'I'll Change My Ways' by Danny Stewart which was recorded in 1958. It was not long after the release of 'My Kind Of Carryin' On' that the Presley phenomenon began to occur and Scotty was readily available. Poindexter and his Starlite Wranglers had a singular lack of success with their single (330 copies sold in a year) so they were very much a temporary band. It has been suggested that Presley performed with Poindexter and the band on one or two occasions, although how he fared in view of what Scotty recalls of the Starlite Wranglers' music is difficult to imagine: 'It was just straight Hank Williams type country as far as the record went, but when we went out to play a club, we had to try, with whatever instrumentation we had, to play a little bit of everything for dancing.'

Legend has it that during 1953, a young truck-driver entered the Memphis Recording Service building at 706 Union Avenue, Memphis, and paid to make a record of himself singing the sentimental 'My Happiness', which he intended for his mother's birthday present. Some time later, when Sam Phillips found himself with what he thought was a potential hit song, he tried to think of an artist who might do the song justice, and was reminded by his secretary of 'that kid with sideburns'. The kid, of course, was Elvis Presley, nineteen-years-old at the time, and after some hesitation, Phillips rewrote history by putting him together with Scotty Moore and Bill Black to form perhaps the most potent rock'n'roll trio of all time.

'Of course, I didn't know anything about that making birthday records stuff, because that happened practically a year before I met Elvis. After we'd done that ''My Kind Of Carryin' On'' record, which none of us really expected to have any great success – we were hoping for a little local stuff that might get us a few more jobs, and then we could go back and cut another record. You know, the usual ''build as you go'' type of thing – Sam mentioned this kid to me one day after I'd got through with the Hat Department trick and had gone down to Sun Records and Sam and I had gone next door to drink coffee at Miss Taylor's restaurant. We'd talk about ''Well, we need to do something'' and ''What are we going to do?'', just general day-dreaming, and one day Sam said, ''Remember this kid that was in about a year ago? Best I remember, he had a real good voice''. And his secretary, Miriam (Keisker), was there with us, and Sam asked her if she'd look up his name and everything – which she did, after two weeks of me bugging them, because once they'd given me the name, I decided I'd call this kid up. Which I finally did – Sam said, ''Get him to come over to your house'', because in other words, he didn't want to be bugged if the kid wasn't any good, ''Do some things with him and see what you think?''

'So I did that, and then called Sam and told him I thought the boy could sing fine, and if he had the right song, the right backing, who knows? Then he called Elvis, told him who he was, and asked if he'd come in for an audition in the studio, and that was when he suggested that Bill (Black) and I should go into the studio and play just enough to provide a little musical background so that he could hear what it sounded like on tape.' The results were, of course, stupendous – Elvis' untutored but dynamic vocals counterpointed by Scotty's quite unique guitar licks, and the whole thing underpinned by the Black bass throb. Even Scotty isn't able to pinpoint the style in which he played, which quite obviously was something more than straightforward Country & Western.

'I cannot tell you, even though I've been asked quite a few times. It wasn't even really the lack of a drummer.' (Not long afterwards, the trio became a quartet with the addition of D. J. Fontana on drums, while Elvis played acoustic guitar, as well as singing, at the start of his career.) 'I guess it was just a combination of several different styles rolled into one. I was a big fan of Merle Travis, of Chet Atkins with his thumb and finger styles, and a lot of the blues players – it was just trying to roll different sounds together, and that's what came out. Like we used to say then, and probably people still do today when you ask them how they do something,'' I just did everything I could'', you know? That's what happened – I played everything I knew. I wasn't even looking for an individual style, and probably, I'd never have known that I had one if I'd stayed in a five or six piece group, but by pulling it down to a trio like that, you naturally had to do more. So that was how I developed the combination rhythm and a few notes type thing – we were forced into it really, I guess you could say.'

While freely admitting that his playing contained elements of black music, Scotty modestly adds that he didn't consider himself in any way unique at the time: 'I'm sure there were bunches of people around doing that same sort of thing – I can't remember hearing any specific players around Memphis at that time, but I'm sure they were there, and I'm sure I heard some playing clubs and so on. It was a funny thing – and I've said this a lot of times – but I think what happened came about because it was time for it to happen.'

Whether or not there were other young pickers working to the same equation is something which is a matter for conjecture – what is more definite is that Scotty's sound, at least to those who heard it in Britain, was unique, one particularly noticeable feature being his use of echo. 'It wasn't an echo chamber, it was tape slap. And I didn't have the first tape slap unit – Chet Atkins had one before me, and Les Paul did that with his multiple recording, and I'm sure he probably was the first, because he was doing it with overdubbing and multiple parts and so on. There was a guy who's retired and lives here in Nashville now, who lived up in Carroll, Illinois, a guy named Ray Budds, who was a good friend of Chet's. He was an accordion player, but he was also really an electronic genius, and he developed this amplifier, and in the bottom of it he stuck in a set of tape recorder heads – erase, record, playback, not like the later echoplexes and stuff where you actually move the

playback head to get the delay, because he did it electronically. And you could get this type of sound out of it – it just gave a fuller type of sound. A friend of Ray's had the first one – Ray built it for him, and more or less had him go out and debug it, then he built one for Chet, and I got the third one that he made. After that, Roy Orbison bought one, and a couple of other guys, and then Ray sold the right of sale to Rickenbacker. They brought it out on the market – how many they made I don't know – but I saw a couple and they'd cheapened it parts wise so that it became very noisy and it wasn't as good.'

At this early point in his career, Scotty was searching for innovation of some kind, and like many players of the time looked initially to Chet Atkins, the acknowledged king of the country guitar, for inspiration. 'I was a great fan of Chet's, and when I heard him use that tape echo, I wondered how in the world he was achieving it. Sam (Phillips) was the first one to capitalise on the tape slap sound on record for the overall thing, but what he did was put a tape slap on the whole record, but even Sam didn't recognise the sound that Chet was getting off his guitar. Boy, I can tell you that when I first plugged in and turned that thing on, I said "That's it!" The movies had had echo for years – any size or shape you wanted – but they used it for sound effects – and tape slap was the same thing, but nobody had thought about using it to enhance music or recordings. The first session we did for RCA, which is about a block away from here, on McGavock Street, they had a big RCA speaker set up at one end of a long hallway, and a microphone set up at the other end, and that's "Heartbreak Hotel" sound. It just sits in a well. Somebody had to stand guard on the door, in case somebody came in and slammed it. Gradually from that, somebody wondered how that sound was being produced, and started investigating, and found that you could do it in bathrooms, or get in a stairwell, so then they said, "We'll build our own room, and then we won't have to drag all these microphones and things out to the stairwell!"'

There can be no doubt that Scotty Moore was involved in the formative years of rock'n'roll although he maintains that he had no idea of the eventual significance of what he was doing. 'No, not at all – after we got started, we were just doing what we could and what we liked to do. I guess Alan Freed was the one who actually put the label on it, but the first label that was put on our music was Hillbilly Cat, the cat part referring to the R&B side and the Hillbilly coming from the fact that basically I was still playing country, although it didn't really come out that way. Then later they called it Rockabilly, and the only thing I can attribute that to is that we could do "Rock Around The Clock" and a few things like that. I don't know if this was actually before or maybe at the same time that Freed was starting his *Moondog* radio show, but it all kind of melded together.

'I don't really remember much specific about those early records we made, except that when Sam turned me on to all the Junior Parker stuff, the guy who did "Mystery Train", it was like finding a pot of gold. I'd

Opposite: An early show – left to right: Elvis Presley, Scotty Moore, D. J. Fontana, Bill Black's bass

heard a couple of things that Little Junior had done on the radio, but I didn't know where they'd come from or anything like that, and I was listening to these records a little before I'd even met Elvis, because knowing Sam, I'd got the records from him. But supposedly, Junior Parker had a sixteen-year-old guitar player that was playing all these licks – I can't recall what his name was, although I'm sure somebody once told me – and I almost broke my hands trying to figure out how he was doing them, because they just seemed so unorthodox. Once we'd got locked in rhythm-wise, we played all night usually, didn't want to quit.'

The first Presley release on Sun, which was credited to 'Elvis Presley – Scotty and Bill', coupled blues singer Arthur Crudup's 'That's All Right, Mama' with a 'rocked-up' version of the country standard made famous by Bill Monroe, 'Blue Moon Of Kentucky'.

'As a rule, we usually only played country standards on personals (live appearances), and didn't record them, but ''Blue Moon Of Kentucky'' was an accident really, after we did ''That's All Right'' which was also an accident. The way it came about was that we had gone through several songs and put them on tape, and during a break, Elvis started singing that, clowning and more or less jumping all over the studio and playing the guitar, then Bill picked up his bass and started slapping it and got the rhythm, and not to be left out, I grabbed my guitar and started trying to find something to play along with it too, just more or less jamming. Then Sam came to the studio door and said, ''What are you all doing?'' and we said we didn't know. He said, ''Hey, it sounded pretty good through the door'', and told us to go back to the microphones and see if we could do it again. We kind of looked at each other and said, ''Huh? You must be kidding'', but we struggled around for a minute there and figured out a halfway kind of format of something, and then I think we ran through it a couple of times and recorded it. And that was it – we just kind of blocked in on the feel. ''Blue Moon Of Kentucky'' was identical, the same way – Bill Black started during a break, and in fact I think he was sitting straddle of his bass, and for some reason or another, started singing ''Blue Moon Of Kentucky'' and clowning, and Elvis started playing rhythm with him. It was the same thing – we just jived it up, you know?'

Scotty's favourite track from the Sun days is probably 'Mystery Train'. 'Yeah, as far as really enjoying doing it, and ''Milk Cow Blues'' was another one that we enjoyed, although I can't remember quite how we fixed on that start, where Elvis stops it, and then we carry on a lot faster. It was probably Sam's idea, just like a tension getter, and it also gave a few spoken words of Elvis, which he hadn't done before. But it worked.' And how – by the end of 1955, after releasing five singles, Elvis was signed to the monolithic RCA Records for what was then the unbelievable figure of $35,000. However, this sum was of little account to Scotty Moore and Bill Black. 'We weren't actually involved in the contract, and it only included us to the point that we were working for Elvis. It didn't mean any more money for me personally – as far as recordings went, we just got paid recording scale and no royalties – but we knew that RCA was a

On the set of Jailhouse Rock. *Left to right: D. J. Fontana, Elvis, Scotty, Mike Stoller (partially obscured)*

definite advancement from the record side of things. We'd been out in the backwoods, so to speak, long enough to begin to see what was going on. We were a little apprehensive about whether they might try to clean our act up – no, not clean it up, I mean, try to regiment us as to how we played and ''You've got to hit this note on the head'' and ''No, no – B minor goes there. You're playing that wrong'', things of that nature.'

Moore is noticeably not bitter about the fact that he did not become substantially better off as a result of his work with Elvis, particularly in view of the fact that for some time he acted as Presley's unofficial and doubtless unpaid manager, and provided the trio's transport in the shape of his wife's car. 'Well, the first six months or better that we worked was in her car – she was the only one that had a job, working at Sears, and making enough for a car. It was a brand new BelAir with gold and white trim and I think it collapsed after about 40,000 miles, the best I remember. We did anything we could get – clubs, school houses, shopping centre openings – and a lot of them were good, and a lot were bad. It really wasn't such an overnight thing as it seems now, looking back – when you put it in real time, it really wasn't. I think the ''Louisiana Hayride'' was probably the first time I thought it was really going to happen – he had a large audience, and it was quite obvious that they were very receptive to what he was doing. And he loved it – he could work an audience, just absolutely work them to death.'

After RCA took over Presley's contract, the minor hits of the Sun days became international chart toppers, and life became much more hurried, to the point where casting his mind back twenty-five years is difficult for Scotty, especially about an individual track. 'Probably the first ones, like ''Heartbreak Hotel'' and ''I Was The One'', stand out most, because after that, what with the TV shows and all the rest, we started cutting them so fast, you couldn't really remember them, although we'd pull one out occasionally and put it into the stage act. RCA didn't try to change us at all, but they would have cut twice or three times as many tracks if the Colonel (Parker, Presley's manager) had let them – but he was smart enough to know that the minute we cut one, they'd put it on the market as fast as possible, so he was all for stretching it as far as it would go, and, of course, proved himself right.' Whether or not Parker's attitude ever did Presley any favours has been discussed at length in numerous other volumes, most of which seem to disagree with Scotty, who anyway worked with Elvis on more than twenty tracks that were released in 1956 alone, and possibly a number that remain 'in the can'. 'To my knowledge, there wasn't much else that we cut, at least nothing I can remember, because if it wasn't on a single, a track usually ended up on an album.'

While it is generally understood that RCA A&R man Steve Sholes 'produced' the early Presley records, according to Scotty the task was very much undertaken by Elvis himself. 'It was just strictly Elvis, if you had to give anybody credit. It was up to him to weed through the pile of material and the demos that were brought in for the songs, and once he found one he wanted to try, then it was just a group effort to work it out. Everybody made suggestions – sometimes a song would get thrown out even after we'd run through it two or three times, and he'd say, ''No, that's just not right'', you know, and we'd go on to another song.' Jerry Leiber and Mike Stoller were also involved with Elvis during the early RCA years, both as songwriters, and in order to protect their material, often as producers with other artists, although not with Presley, according to Scotty, 'I think they were just happy to get their songs cut with the way his record sales were going, and I don't think there was too much pressure from them to change anything.'

Another aspect of Elvis Presley's early career in which Moore was involved was films. 'We failed the audition for Love Me Tender – we didn't get a screen test for the movie, but the Jordanaires (the vocal backing group on early Presley discs), D.J. (Fontana), Bill and myself went out there. Nobody told us it was a period movie with a bunch of hillbilly music in it, so they took us out to this bungalow and had us set up, and then told us to play something. Great – we did what we did on stage every day, but it didn't fit Love Me Tender (laughs). We were in the next film, Loving You, and for all of us, that was a learning experience, because we hadn't been around the movie scene at all. We worked with Charlie O'Kern who became a great friend of all of us, and he was a dancer, choreographer, things of that nature, but he was quick to see that he wasn't going to be able to choreograph this bunch, so they changed it and just called it staging – ''We're going to stage this – we're not going to make a routine out of it''. We had a lot of

great times doing Loving You and a couple of other things that he also worked with us on, King Creole and G.I. Blues.

Shortly after Loving You, a ripple occurred which briefly disturbed the smooth workings of the Presley cash accumulation system. 'We were probably getting $200 a week by then. I suppose everyone gets greedy, and at that time we were making a good living wage, but maybe the movie thing was what made it a little more apparent to us, because we were making less than the minimum scale for actors on Loving You and we had to threaten to walk off the lot to get that. I think we were making $325 a week . . . But it wasn't a gauge technique, it was just a matter of the cost of living – as he grew, naturally our cost of living went up. Today, we could have run around in dirty blue jeans and an old slouch hat, and we could have a ball, but back then, you couldn't do that, and you didn't want to do anything to scar your image in any way. We were all very careful, and we never drank before a show or anything like that, even though Bill, D.J. and I got accused of being the rakiest trio in Lord knows what. When Elvis was being criticised for what people saw as his obscene stage act, we weren't under the same microscope, but we were definitely under one that was right next to it, I can guarantee you. I'm proud to say that Elvis, D.J., Bill and myself were all from very religious families, and we'd been taught matters, we knew how to act, and we acted accordingly, although that's not to say that we weren't all human, either. (Laughs.) There was no pressure from our families – my mother was so proud of Elvis as if he'd been her own son, and in fact, the one time that she met him, she said ''What a nice boy! Just like I figured he was going to be with his 'Yes, ma'am' and 'No, ma'am'.'''

As a result of feeling underpaid, Black and Moore to some extent disenfranchised themselves from Presley, although in the end, little changed. 'The first thing we did was go to Dallas, where we played the Dallas State Fair with a bunch of different acts, rock and country/rock oriented types of act, for sixteen days, four and five shows a day type of thing, and we got paid very well because we were being billed as ''Scotty and Bill, Elvis's original backing group'' and what have you. Shortly after that, when we got back to Memphis, Elvis was fixing to do a tour in Seattle and Vancouver, then swing down the West Coast, and they called and wanted to know if we'd work it, and I gave them a price – so much per day – and they said that was fine. It was never a thing where anybody was mad about anything, it was just strictly a financial thing, which Elvis could have straightened out himself at any time, but he chose to leave it in his manager's hands. But that was the last time, with Loving You, that we were actually on salary – from then on, we always worked on a per show type of thing.'

By then Presley was doing less live work as his time was taken up with films and recording, in which the group was also involved. This left Scotty, in particular, with spare time, but somehow he resisted the obvious temptation to become a session musician, for which he would have been much in demand. 'No, I was never a session man as such, although I've played a few sessions. I've never been in that daily grind, although I almost did when Elvis went into the Army – I almost came here to Nashville, just a breath away, but I didn't.'

Instead, Scotty began to work with a small Memphis label, Fernwood Records. 'The label was started by two friends of mine, Jack Clement and Slim Wallace, and the first thing we did together was "Tragedy" by Thomas Wayne. I've always said that was the cheapest session ever done, even cheaper than when we did "That's All Right, Mama" for Sun, because I think Sam at least used tape! No, I'm kidding, but it was only two instruments, Bill and myself, and three little girls who were friends of Thomas' in high school with him, who did the background singing, and that was it. Everybody was doing it for a lark, and nobody expected to get paid, and it sold a million. And what's also funny about that – I don't know if you've ever heard the other side of the record, which was a little up-tempo thing called "Saturday Date", but that's what we were pushing. When I say pushing, keep in mind that we're doing this out of a garage, and with no budget – Slim (Wallace) was a truck driver, so what bucks he could turn loose at the end of a week, and what bucks I could turn loose, we'd pool and that way we got a few records pressed and sent them out to so many radio stations and so on. Like I say, we were pushing the up-tempo side, because that's the kind of thing that was happening right then, but a disc jockey on a station which I think was called WACKY – wacky – turned it over late one night. At that time, we couldn't hear it, because the station boomed way up North East, but Steve Brodie from Buffalo heard it. He was a record promoter and so forth, and he called down and said, "Hey, I think you've got a winner there" and said he'd like to do a national promotion on it. We didn't know anything about national promotion, so we said, "How much?" and he said so much a record, and we said "Go". And I'll never forget it – keep in mind that this was with no budget, nothing – because we had three pressing plants, one in Memphis, one in Philadelphia and one on the West Coast, and the record started going great guns, with distributors ordering and we're shipping more and more records, and then all of a sudden, we said "Oh wait!" We stopped and called up all the pressing plants and told them we didn't have any money if the records weren't sold, but all three of them said they thought it was going to be big, and that they'd go with us. That was OK, but as record distributors, you've got at least sixty days before you're going to get a penny back, depending on how the record's selling, and I'll never forget sitting down and writing cheques for $40,000 for pressing bills at the end of sixty days – that's how fast the thing was moving. I don't know whether they could read my signature or not – and they didn't care!'

Unfortunately, 'Tragedy' was the biggest record ever made for the Fernwood label. 'It was the only one, apart from a few little regional hits, but I left Fernwood, sold out, and it was at that point that I started to come to Nashville. Then a friend of mine, Bill Fitzgerald, who ironically was the first one to sell any of the early Elvis records, when he was manager for Music Sales Distributors, left that distributorship and went to work for Sam Phillips, and then, Bill and

I having known each other for all these years, he got me to go back to work for Sun. And I did it – at that point, I thought it was really going to happen in Memphis, and things would bust wide open, because by that time, I was looking at the production side, and I wasn't really playing very much during all of this. So I decided not to go to Nashville, even though all the friends that I'd worked with were urging me to, and I stayed with Sam for about four years as production manager with his new studios. In the meantime, he had opened a studio here in Nashville, and when I came to the parting of the ways with Sam, I did come to Nashville, went into partnership with a couple of guys here and built a studio. I took over one that had become defunct, and we remodelled it and put it back in business, and lo and behold, six months later Memphis just blew wide open – I mean, Stax Records, you name it, The Mar-Keys, were coming out of there like great guns.'

During the early 1960s, Scotty played on several rather obscure records, such as one released under his own name titled 'Have Guitar – Will Travel'. 'That was for Fernwood, done in the garage, and it was just made up – we had to give it a title, and it just happened at the time that "Have Gun – Will Travel" was a big popular TV show.' He also played sessions for Dale Hawkins, who recorded for the Chess/Checker labels in Chicago. 'D.J. and I made those tracks with Dale and with the Mathis Brothers, who were an old act on the "Louisiana Hayride", and later on they joined up with Larry Henley, who had a real high voice, and became the Newbeats, who had a big hit with "Bread And Butter". I don't think we cut more than a couple of tracks with Dale – one was "Class Cutter", I think – but while we were there, Chess said that they had another group there, and would we mind cutting some stuff with them, and that was Harvey and the Moonglows. It was a great thrill working with them, but it's so long ago that I can't remember any of the titles – D.J., Bill and myself said many times that if we'd had someone like you guys around, with a tape recorder and a camera . . . If nothing else, just to remind us of what we did.'

Among the other artists upon whose records Scotty played at this time were Eddie Hill and Texas Bill Strength, although a good deal of his later work for Sun was as a producer, working with one Tony Rossini, but also with Jerry Lee Lewis, about whom he tells an interesting story.

'Jerry Lee was wild as a buck, always was – he was born that way. I worked with him at one time when Elvis was off the road for about a month, and Jerry's guitar player had quit or something and he called me and asked if I'd go on the road with him for a two week tour, and I said I would, because basically I knew the stuff he was playing. So we got to be friends, and after the tour – I can't tell you the date, I'm afraid – Jerry's contract was up, or at least Sam Phillips and Jerry were in crossways on their agreements and so forth, and it was that time that I went in the studio with him instead of Sam, and worked with Jerry cutting some things, a couple of which I thought were real good. Yeah, now I remember – it was something to do with the Musicians' Union, and Jerry wasn't allowed to play, or something, and on the sessions that I did, Jerry didn't play, but Larry

Muhoberac played instead. And as far as I know, that was the only time that Jerry made records that he didn't play on – one of them was an à la Ray Charles thing called "When I Get Paid". I did play on some of Jerry's tracks, but not on guitar – I usually played six string bass, which is known around here as "tick tack". I probably played guitar on some, but normally, he had a guy who worked with him all the time, Roland Janes, who did most of the guitar work on Jerry's early stuff.'

Of possibly greater interest in a book about guitarists is the celebrated Scotty Moore solo LP, *The Guitar That Changed The World*, which was produced by Billy Sherrill, more recently noted for having produced an album of country music for the other Elvis – Costello. 'I did that just prior to moving up here to Nashville, in the mid-sixties – Billy Sherrill suggested that title, and I fought him tooth and nail, but he won. I think the album's great, although I do say it myself, but more because of the guys working on it. We were so close – it was like a five day party, and it was just a fun thing to do. The only person that wasn't on the album from the people who were still around that had worked on so many sessions with Elvis was Floyd Cramer, and he was out of town so we couldn't get him, but we used Bill Purcell, who's an excellent piano player, and the Jordanaires, of course, and D.J., and Jerry Kennedy, Bob Moore, Buddy Harman, Boots (Randolph) – it was really a fun thing to do.' (Bill Black, the original Presley bass player, died during 1965, which was probably the year when this album was recorded.) 'I don't think I can choose a favourite track from that album – we did what we set out to do, and that was to do twelve of the hits Elvis had instrumentally, but when we actually got into the studio and got into it, we all seemed to have forgotten how much space his singing took up, and suddenly, you had to fill that space up, when most of us had been working as background. I'm the world's worst at carrying a melody – I've got to sit down and go "Doing, doing, doing" to get it, and it's much easier when somebody's singing, because you can stick a little lick here and a little lick there. You respect instrumentalists, people like Chet (Atkins) and Barney Kessel, when you've tried to do something like that, because it's just a different bag.'

On Presley's return from the Army, the backing group reformed, although, as already noted, on a different financial basis. 'Everything was sort of back to normal, being as he was out of the Army, and we immediately went into the RCA studio here in Nashville, and cut a full album, *Elvis Is Back*, and then we got on a train to go to Miami to do the Frank Sinatra TV show. And that was really an amazing trip for me, and for everyone – with the Colonel doing the press and promotion all down the tracks, even with that, at every little crossroads and in every small town, seeing people line the tracks like they did was real hard to believe. This was all the way, and even into the night you could hear people. It wasn't so strange during the day, because the train would slow down a little bit ...' Another Presley-related item was his comeback film, *G.I. Blues*, which was Scotty's fourth and last Elvis film, the others being *Loving You*, *Jailhouse Rock* and *King Creole*.

'There were musicians in some of the later films, but the storyline then got to be that the guys playing with him, or whatever it was, were actually actors, and had to be woven into the film, so then it wasn't like a "Here's my band" type thing. We were still working on the soundtracks on a lot of the movies, although I couldn't tell you where we stopped – it might have been *Kissin' Cousins* or *Flaming Star* or *Viva Las Vegas*, but I don't know which, because there were so many of them coming from right and left.' It takes a brave man to admit that he had anything to do with far too many Presley films ... The last thing on which Presley was backed by Scotty Moore was the 1968 TV Special, for which Scotty was specially invited back, having largely severed his connections during the previous years (and having eventually been replaced by James Burton).

'I'd got so involved with the studio here in Nashville, and I was hardly playing guitar anyway, so I just really didn't have the time. And then just taking up space wasn't my kind of thing to do, although the Jordanaires were still working with him, and so was D.J. It was really never a question of leaving, we just more or less drifted apart. After we did that '68 Special, his management called when he opened up in Las Vegas, and they wanted the Jordanaires, D.J. and myself to go out there and work with him. There again, it's the communication – we're dealing with management, and if you understand the life of a session player in a town like this, or if you're in business as a studio engineer, owning a studio, you're like a barber. You've got your clients, and if you're not there and they can't get you, they'll go some place else. So when they called us to go out and work on this thing, nobody said it was going to be an ongoing situation, that he was going back on the road – at that point, as far as we knew, it was a one shot deal for two weeks, although he did get extended to four or six or something. But originally, it was like a two week job, and the only way any of us could figure out a price, what we would charge, was to base it on what we'd lose by going. There were no personalities involved, nothing like that – it was strictly a matter of dollars and cents, or pences and pounds! But you know, you figure four sessions a day for the Jordanaires over a two week period, and you can get a general idea about what they'd have to ask, and obviously it seemed like a fortune. Of course, if somebody had known what was going to happen after that, it might have been a different story, although that's hindsight, of course, and there again, we're dealing with just one end of the story, and none of us knew what was being told to Elvis. But nothing ever came back to us that he was mad, or we were mad or anything like that – it was just a business thing really.

'Elvis really worked so hard on that TV Special. D.J. and I were in this segment – I don't know what you'd call it, because I don't know what they had in mind when we went out there – but Steve Binder, who was the director, got us all in Elvis' dressing room, and we sat around there for two nights and talked, just talked, while he and his assistant sat over in the corner. It was more or less like a homecoming or something – we just sat around and kibitzed, played this and that and the other, and he finally said, "That's it, that's what I want you to do. You've got this much time, and I want you to go out there and do whatever you want to do", and that's about basically what we did. I saw the thing the last time it was rerun, and they included some stuff they'd cut out to shorten it the first time round, and there's D.J. hollering in the background, and it's just bedlam! That was the last time I saw Elvis, and he was much like he was in the early days – he was glad to do something besides just those dumb movies, and that was it, in no uncertain terms. He talked about wanting to do a European tour, and he invited D.J. and myself for dinner at his house, and he wanted to know how the studio was doing. I said it was OK, and he asked what would be the chances of us going in there, and block it off for a week or two weeks, get in and do things like we used to, so I said, "No problem – all it takes is money" – you know, back to the same old thing – and he said, "Boy, it sure would be fun", and that's the thing, you see, that he was thinking, trying, wanting to go to Europe. He's wanting to get in and look for new sounds or get back to the old sounds, or whatever – what might have come out of it I don't know, but nothing ever happened after that.'

At some later point during the 1960s, Scotty and D.J. made an album which they titled *What's Left*. 'That was my group again, another of my little "put 'em together" type things. I just had this idea of trying to show where we got some of the sounds we used. I dug out a bunch of old 78 r.p.m. records by Jay McShann and Lowell Fulsom, and there's a little piano player/singer here in town who's just absolutely fantastic, named Willie Rainsford, and he did all the vocal work on it. Again, it was a fun thing to do, trying to show people – I'd play these old 78 records and they'd say, "You've got to be kidding!" And most of the tracks we did first take. The record's been out a couple of times.' One place where it seems never to have been released is Britain, but one hopes this will be remedied.

By the end of the 1960s, Scotty had moved from the part of the studio used by musicians into the control room, although he generally functioned as engineer rather than producer. 'Yeah. There again, I just got trapped, it was that simple. I came to Nashville and went into business with these two guys, one of whom was a lawyer, and the other had been doing studio mastering, disc mastering work with another place. Our main purpose for going in together was to have a workshop, and we were going to do our own production company and everything. So you've got to buy this, and you've got to buy that, and then you start taking in some sessions from outside, and then you get more sessions, and pretty soon, you don't have time to do what you started out to do. And then, when you finally do have an open slot that you can use, you're so darn tired and beat out that it's "Produce what? I want to go home and lay down".'

Perhaps the most celebrated album engineered by Scotty was Ringo Starr's *Beaucoups Of Blues*, a record on which the Beatle drummer was backed by a fine Nashville band led by steel guitarist Pete Drake, while Scotty thinks that perhaps the biggest successes he engineered were a series of hits by black singer Joe Simon, the best known of which was 'The Chokin' Kind'. However, in 1976, Scotty was persuaded out of retirement by Billy Swan, an ex-

studio janitor who idolised Elvis Presley, and who scored a major hit in 1974 with the classic 'I Can Help'. Swan's third, eponymous, LP includes Scotty playing on one track, 'I Got It For You', while a subsequent Swan LP, *You're O.K. I'm O.K.*, features the reluctant guitarist on three tracks.

'Yeah, that rat! (affectionately) That happened because he was a friend of mine. Chip Young, who produced his real biggie, "I Can Help", had a studio at that time at his house, about thirty miles out of town here, and Billy wanted me to put a piece of playing on something, on a couple of cuts – he said "I don't care what you put on it, but I want you on the record". So I went out there, spent about a week in one day (laughs) overdubbing a couple of songs, and then I did it again later when Booker T (Jones) was producing Billy. In fact, for that one, Chip had sold that original studio after he bought the one that's right here, next door, and Chip was in the process of remodelling – I sat in the drum booth with just a little amplifier, while Chip was running round doing things, in and out. Booker T was producing Billy out on the West Coast, and I overdubbed three tracks on the album here.'

Another recently released album on which Scotty appears as guitarist is a rather curious double LP tribute to Elvis Presley put together by Presley's finest imitator, Ral Donner, himself a significant rock'n'roll vocalist with several hit records to his name. 'Ral's manager or whatever called me, and wanted me to help with this thing, which I didn't want to do. From the time of Elvis' death, I only did a couple of interviews and nothing else really. But he explained the thing. He said he wanted me to engineer it, because I knew the sound, and maybe to play on a couple of the early songs.' (The album attempted to recreate Presley's career, both musically, and with Donner speaking as Elvis, narrating the singer's life story in the first person.)

'Over a conversation of several weeks, I finally said I'd do it, but I didn't have any idea what a monstrous project this could be when we got into it, and I didn't realise how little they knew what they were doing. It just got to be a big project – and we're talking about thousands and thousands of dollars – but I think overall it's a very good album. Ral did a great job on the vocals, and I think he did an excellent job on the narration, if you listen to it for what it's meant to be. It's not meant to be a direct copy, it's supposed to be a story, and it takes me back when I listen to it. It's hard to be objective when you're working so close to something like that, especially when it's in bits and pieces, four bars of this, eight bars of that, you know? But after we'd completely finished editing the whole thing, six weeks or two months later, I sat down here one night and played the thing and it really took me back. You're not having to look at something, it's just sound, and I think it came off real well, and I'm proud to have been part of it. I don't know if the word's reached Britain, but Ral has cancer now, and it's terminal . . . but he just got back not long ago from California, where he did some narration stuff for the quote unquote Estate sanctioned movie on Elvis' life. I'm glad he got to do that, because he was a very big fan of Elvis, yet he looks nothing like him whatever. Absolutely nothing, yet from the vocal standpoint, I think he was one of the best Elvis impersonators or soundalikes.'

Today, Scotty rarely plays his guitar. 'Really, I haven't played for years, but I'll be honest and say that if I had the time, and could contain my train of thought – I'd probably have to go to Mount Everest or somewhere to do that, because I seem to get interested in a lot of little things – and could get off somewhere and there was a purpose, spend about a month getting the old corns back and everything, I'd like to do some things again, I really would. But they'd have to be old things, because I'm not going to try to learn any new ones' (laughs).

As far as his choice of guitars goes, Scotty spent some early years experimenting. 'When I came out of the service, I bought one of those Fenders, a Telecaster or a Stratocaster or something, but I couldn't hold on to the thing with its little slim body. It might have something to do with it being a feminine shape, but I couldn't get on with the Fender. So I got a Gib-

son, a gold ES335, and that was the one I used on the first things we cut, and then I went on to the L5, and I had a blonde one of those, and from there, I went to a blonde Gibson Super 400, which is here in town, by the way. We had a big instrument trading thing in Memphis one time, trading vibes and guitars and all sorts of things. Chips Moman ended up with the Super 400, and I'd always wanted a Sunburst 400, and that's the one I've still got. I've always been partial to the sound of the big body guitars, although people today still say they get problems with feedback and so on. There were problems until they made feedback work for them, I should say. I never used a solid guitar, and I've never used small gauge strings – I just bled a lot!'

Our evening in Nashville with Scotty Moore, his exceptionally charming secretary Gail, and a bottle of Johnny Walker Black Label, was one of the pleasantest we spent while collecting material for *Guitar Greats*. The man's self-effacing personality

Scotty Moore in 1981, (above) with the guitar that changed the world, and right still proud of the first single by Elvis, Scotty and Bill, 'That's All right'. Lurking in the background is Scotty's secretary, Gail

31

was totally genuine, despite the fact that his guitar really did change the world – even at the age of fifty, Scotty must not be written off as some antique from a past age, because if he finds a new musical project which interests him, be sure he can still outplay many of those guitarists who are less than half his age.

Scotty Moore Discography

The major item in this discography almost inevitably concerns the recordings made with Elvis Presley. The albums listed are, to the best of our knowledge, the latest repackages of the Presley heritage, and while the list is not complete, everything included is at worst a desirable part of any serious rock record collection, and at best, totally indispensable.

Recording date

With Elvis Presley
1955	*The Sun Collection*
1956	*The '56 Sessions Volumes 1 & 2*
1957	*Loving You* (Film soundtrack)
Various	*A Legendary Performer Volumes 1, 2 & 3*
1957	*A Date With Elvis*
1958	*King Creole* (Film soundtrack)
1957	*Jailhouse Rock* (EP) (Film soundtrack)
1960	*Elvis Is Back*
1960	*G.I. Blues* (Film soundtrack)
1968	*TV Special*
Various	*Elvis Presley Sings Leiber And Stoller*
1957	*Elvis' Christmas Album*
Various	*Elvis' Golden Records Volumes 1, 2 & 3*
Various	*Worldwide 50 Gold Award Hits Volume 1*

A certain amount of duplication in the above list is unfortunately unavoidable.

Solo albums
1960s	*The Guitar That Changed The World* (also released as *Elvis Presley's Original Guitarist Scotty Moore Plays The Big Elvis Presley Hits*)
1970	*What's Left*

With Billy Swan
1976	*Billy Swan*
1978	*You're O.K. I'm O.K.*

With Ral Donner
1979	*1935–1977 'I've Been Away For Awhile Now . . .'*

With Phil Sweet
1981	*Memphis Blue Streak*

Various Artists
1982	*Rockabilly Stars Volume I* (one track)

JAMES BURTON

One of the great rock'n'roll guitarists of the 1950s, but a man who remained virtually unknown to all but the cognoscenti until comparatively recently, is James Burton. His series of scintillating solos on Ricky Nelson's late '50s and early '60s hits must have resulted in many potential guitarists throwing in the towel when they heard the speed and the flow achieved by Burton, whose solos were never long, but perfectly concise and in complete serendipity with the requirements of each record. Nowadays, James is one of the most in-demand session musicians in the world, frequently playing with several different artists each day. With most of his work centred on Los Angeles, James and his family live in a highly commodious house in Burbank, a suburb of LA. He also works on occasion in Nashville, perhaps a measure of just how highly his superb playing is rated, even among the most prolific hitmakers in America.

A most fascinating piece of information about James is that he keeps very few guitars at home – his array of instruments are left with a Safety Deposit Company, who deliver the instruments he requires to the studio where he's working, and collect them again afterwards.

James Burton was born in Shreveport, Louisiana, on 21 August, 1939, although not apparently to a particularly musical family. 'When I was about ten years old, some friends that I went to school with got into music, and as I'd always liked the idea of the guitar, I just started playing with them a little bit, but I didn't really get into it until my mother and dad bought me my first guitar when I was thirteen.' His early influences came from players who would later find themselves in the mainstream of rock, but at that point, were operating in different fields, including Chet Atkins from country music, B. B. King from the blues area, and such R&B masters as Bo Diddley, John Lee Hooker and (although presumably a year or two after the others), Chuck Berry.

However, it seems that what brought James his initial fame was not necessarily his ability to play the guitar, but rather his ability to perform with it behind his head, a difficult feat, for those who have yet to try it!

'I don't know how I learned to do that – I suppose I just enjoyed doing tricks with guitars, rather than just playing chords or something. I really got into the effects, and I think the guitar can do a lot more than what it's basically made for. I guess that's how I got into that – and showing off a little bit too, of course, because for some reason, I found it easy to do. It just looks complicated.'

His first professional work was with what he called the 'staff' band on the celebrated 'Louisiana Hayride', a weekly radio programme, which was extremely influential in the 1950s in introducing new sounds to an audience still recovering from the Second World War and looking for something new in musical terms that they could call their own. The artists whom James recalls playing behind were by no means all rockers.

'There was George Jones, the late, great Johnny Horton, Slim Whitman, who used to be our postmaster in Shreveport, an awful lot of people who were regulars on the show. I preferred the stuff that was country music slanted towards rhythm & blues, as opposed to the straight country that Slim Whitman, for example, played, but there's so many types of music that contain country backgrounds, and that country influence is what I always hear in whatever I play.'

Around the end of 1955, James recorded what must be presumed to be his first hit, after joining the band which backed another notable Louisiana rocker, Dale Hawkins. 'I worked with Dale playing clubs around town for about a year, and we recorded ''Suzie Q'' when I was still fifteen, I think. I actually wrote that song – it was originally an instrumental, and Dale added some lyrics and called it ''Suzie Q'', but very shortly after we recorded it, I left Dale and went to work with Bob Luman.'

Both Dale Hawkins and Texan Bob Luman recorded only one significant track which would mark them for posterity, 'Suzie Q' being Hawkins' best known record by far, while for Luman, the same could be said of 'Let's Think About Living', a semi-humorous item concerning the glut of 'death discs' which were becoming popular in the late 1950s. James Burton played no part in Luman's big hit.

'I joined him before that, and I played on almost all his earlier records, like ''Red Hot'' and ''Red Cadillac And A Black Moustache'', and ''Let's Think About Living'' was after I left. It was while I was working with Bob that I met Ricky Nelson. We were rehearsing one day in the studio for a new single for Imperial Records, the label that both Bob and Ricky were signed to. Ricky stopped by the studio and Jimmie Haskell and Lew Chudd brought him in and introduced him to us, and he stayed for about three hours, listening to us play. The next day, we had a telegram from his office to appear to meet his dad, Ozzie, and basically that's how I and James Kirkland, the bass player, got involved with Ricky, and we played as his backing group on the family TV show.' Later Ozzie offered him a contract.

'It was a pretty good deal for me at that time, because I was still only seventeen. You see, before I met Ricky that first time, I really wasn't familiar with what he was doing. I'd probably heard his early records, like ''I'm Walkin' '', but I didn't know much about him at all.'

From this point at the start of 1958 (which must incidentally mean that he was eighteen, not seventeen), James and Ricky Nelson became inseparable musically until 1966 or thereabouts. It would have been a golden opportunity for plugging their wares on a weekly TV show, let alone *The Adventures Of Ozzie and Harriet*, a family soap opera similar to *Happy Days*, with Ricky's parents in the star parts and Ricky and his brother also featured, and a failure to capitalise on it would be unthinkable. It became difficult to avoid getting a big hit when a huge audience saw Ricky, backed by his band led by the faithful James, play their new single at the end of the show, although this can hardly have resulted in realistic continuity . . . Not that anyone cared that much – Ricky was, after all, the nearest thing to Elvis Presley, whose induction into the US Army coincided with Nelson's rise to fame, and Ricky it was who filled the gap, making hit after hit with classics like 'Stood Up', 'Believe What You Say', 'Poor Little Fool' and 'I Got A Feeling', all before the end of 1958. It was a time when the careers of both Nelson and Burton were accelerating.

'I think that basically, our music at that particular time was quite well advanced, the sort of thing you might hear in a studio today, and even more advanced than some of today's stuff. I gather that a lot of people today are trying to recreate the kind of feeling we got in those days, playing the old sounds, and playing the way you feel, rather than sitting down in a studio and reading a bunch of charts (sheet music). We had nothing like that – we just walked in and did what was comfortable.'

And quite reasonably, because although the Nelson records are usually compared unfavourably with contemporary Presley product, the bone of contention usually centres around the vocal, as opposed to the instrumental side. We asked James to recall how he had approached the recording of an early up-tempo Nelson track, 'I Got A Feeling'. 'The basic style I played was a finger-picking style, using a straight pick and a finger pick – that was something I had gotten into, which was really strange, I even play slide dobro like that – rather than using a thumb pick and two finger picks, I just use a straight pick and one finger pick. A lot of people seem to think that my style, even on things like "Suzie Q", was going back to the way John Lee Hooker and Lightnin' Hopkins played, but I think the style I play is a combination of rhythm & blues with a country feel as well – it seems like they're so close anyway, but when you take the two and pull them into one, it creates a different feel for me, and I like that.'

A word or two of explanation – 'finger picking' can be described as plucking individual strings of the guitar, which is normally achieved by the use of thimble-like picks on two fingers and the thumb, while a straight pick is the more familiar triangular piece of plastic held between thumb and index finger. Turning to 'I Got A Feeling', it is powered throughout by James' finger picking rhythm playing, and also contains a typically concise guitar solo which forms the perfect bridge between verses – just one of many examples of the peerless Burton guitar style, which was ideally suited to the two and a half minute single format.

Combining country music and R&B was something which James feels occurred organically – 'I didn't have outside influences which made me do that, it was just basically what I felt, what felt good to me. I don't believe I was copying anybody – if there was something I liked, I would never actually copy it, because I never had that feeling for music. For example, I play sometimes in the same kind of style as Chuck Berry, but the way I do it is a completely different way of playing it, because I take what he played and play it my way.'

Working with Ricky Nelson was almost a full-time

occupation at this point, taking in recording, live shows, television and the rest, but this was apparently no problem as far as James was concerned. 'It didn't seem to affect me in any way, because I love playing live, and I'd rather do that than just sit around and cut records all the time, although we did do an awful lot of travelling, because I believe that Ricky was the next most popular artist to Elvis for three years in a row, so I went through all that excitement when I was very young. But I just enjoyed being there and being able to play and hear the crowds cheering us on.'

Ricky Nelson continued to score hit after hit – 1959 provided 'It's Late', 'Never Be Anyone Else But You', 'Just A Little Too Much', 1960 'Young Emotions', 'Yes Sir That's My Baby' and 'Milk Cow Blues', and 1961 'Travelin' Man', 'Hello Mary Lou', 'A Wonder Like You' and 'Everlovin'', each decorated to a greater or lesser extent by James. 'I like to go back and listen to all those things we did then, because apart from the hits, there are several album tracks that I felt should have been singles. Probably my favourite solos from that time are on "Hello Mary Lou" and on "Fools Rush In", which was also Ozzie's favourite solo, because he said it reminded him of a saxophone player he worked with at one time.'

Somewhat surprisingly, considering his enormous amount of session work today, Burton did little in that line during his time with Ricky Nelson. 'No, because I was under contract to Ricky, and there was a sort of agreement that they didn't want me to work with anyone else, although eventually, I wasn't too happy about that, and I did a few things with Joe Osborn, who became our bass player after James Kirkland left. Joe joined the group not knowing how people would feel if he worked with other artists, and he talked me into doing a couple of things with Dorsey Burnette – he said, "Nobody's going to know it's you anyway so why don't you just come and play with me?", and I enjoyed it, it was great, because it was at a point where Ricky wasn't working that much. Towards the end, before I actually left the group, Ricky was working less than one month in the entire year, so I did those couple of things with Joe, but of course, Ricky recognised me right away, so that didn't sit too good with him.'

By 1965, the initial impetus had all but left Ricky Nelson, who had already slightly changed his name to the rather less adolescent sounding Rick. Burton continued to do his best through these less successful years, and was influential in Nelson's two most artistically successful albums of the mid-sixties, *Country Fever* and *Bright Lights And Country Music*, which can be seen in retrospect as two of the earliest examples of the burgeoning country/rock hybrid which was so popular in the early 1970s.

'At that time, I was trying to get Ricky to do more country type things – his dad had a big influence on his career, and of course, Jimmie Haskell was doing all the arrangements, and I think they tried to push Ricky too far into the pop field. It's obvious that when you stop selling records, it's for a reason, because people aren't buying that particular thing – when the music changes, you have to change with it in order to keep the trend going. There were several things on those two albums that I thought I played well – I played a lot of slide dobro, although I can't remember too many titles, because I haven't played those albums in a long time. Then, when I left Ricky not long after that, he did exactly what we'd talked about doing, because he and I were going to produce his next album together. That didn't happen, of course, and then he came out with that Bob Dylan song, "She Belongs To Me", and after that, the song he wrote about Madison Square Garden, "Garden Party", was basically country music, and exactly what we'd talked about doing before I left.'

Shortly before he and Nelson parted company (and they may yet perform together again), Burton became involved in a seminal American rock TV show, *Shindig*, conceived and produced by the Englishman who had earlier revolutionised British television, Jack Good.

'Yeah, I had a group called the Shindogs, and the way that happened was that Leon Russell was putting a band, an orchestra, together for that show, and Jack also wanted to have a smaller group to do all the rock'n'roll tunes on the show, so he called me up and asked if Glen D. Hardin and I could put together a band, which he called the Shindogs. We actually ended up doing 75 per cent of the music in the show, while the orchestra did the other 25 per cent. The show was rated top for the year it ran, but then ABC wanted to change the way it was produced, and Jack didn't feel he'd be comfortable with a new format, so that was it. But it was an incredible show – Glen Campbell got his start, the Righteous Brothers, and Bobby Sherman, of course, and it was really popular.'

This same vague mid-sixties period also saw the release of what appears to be the first James Burton solo record, a single credited to Jimmy and Joe, and titled 'Jimmy's Blues', which was released on a small label called Miramar Records in 1964. '"Jimmy's Blues" and "Love Lost", yeah. Joe Osborn and I were doing a lot of work with this guy that came into town who had this label – we were working with just about everybody, had a sort of clique type band together, and this guy had some people he wanted us to work with, and then one day he suggested that we record an instrumental, and call it "Jimmy's Blues". And I wrote a thing called "Love Lost", which I think is a great tune. I think it should have lyrics to it, because it could be a big smash as the melody line's so great.'

Unfortunately, very few copies of this disc ever made it to Europe, so that evidence of the first Burton solo efforts are difficult to come by, although it is odd that James had never previously made records on his own account. 'I was really busy, doing like five or six sessions a day, and that seemed to take up so much of my time that I didn't sit down and think about it. I did do a couple of singles with one of the first guys I worked with, Faber Campbell, who was also with Bob Luman. I met Faber in 1956, and worked on "Having A Guitar" records – he was also involved with a group called the Browns who you've probably heard of, and I also did some records with the DeCastro Sisters, and tons of others. It's really hard to try and remember what I've played on, and I really should have written them down – I think it was probably a mistake not to keep a daily log of everything I did, because now people call me up and tell me

about records I played on that I've completely forgotten.'

This would turn out, in terms of this project, to be an insurmountable problem – despite having laboriously compiled a list of around sixty LPs on which James is credited, apart from a few obvious artists who will be discussed, James apparently has no memory for titles, and although he can recall working with numerous acts, pinning him down to precise tracks, or even to entire LPs, proved an impossible task. Fortunately, as the case of Hoyt Axton, James is known to have appeared on at least seven of his albums, so his memory is a little more enlightening.

'I met Hoyt some time before I played on his records, because we used to do demo sessions together, right after I left Ricky. We did tons of demos for publishing companies around town, and that's how I met Hoyt, because he was singing on a lot of them. We'd go in and do twelve songs in three hours, just incredible records with three or four instruments – Hal Blaine playing drums, and sometimes Glen Campbell playing rhythm guitar – and we cut a lot of those, sometimes three or four albums worth each week.'

In fact, much of Burton's credited work with Hoyt Axton did not occur until the 1970s, although one particular LP, *My Griffin Is Gone*, originated in the previous decade. Another more famous act from the mid-'60s was surfing duo Jan and Dean, on whose final album, *Save For A Rainy Day*, James played, although he may well have been on several more. 'Yeah, Joe Osborn and I lived real close together in North Hollywood at that time, four or five blocks apart, and Joe had a little studio in his garage where Jan and Dean used to come to record. And I even cut with them in somebody else's garage way before that – they were incredible records, and that's where they made their big hits.'

Nothing more specific, unfortunately – but does James recognise records he's forgotten if he hears them on the radio? 'Oh yeah, I can always remember my licks. They come straight back to me. Back in the '60s, a lot of record companies didn't give credits on albums covers – I don't even think Elvis gave credits back then – and I've never really known why.'

One act with whom James played during the 1960s for whom the time obviously wasn't right was an obscure folk-oriented vocal group known as the Shacklefords. 'That was with Lee Hazelwood and Marty Cooper – I did a lot of work with Lee, but that was the first time I'd met Marty. The guitar I played on that was a Stella that cost seven dollars – that was the one I played on the Glen Campbell album, and the sound was so unique that I started using it on a lot of dates, and I couldn't do a date after that with Marty Cooper unless I used that guitar. It was an incredible thing with a big body, which I bought from Red Rhodes, and I moved the nut, raised the strings up and used it as a slide dobro on that album for the Shacklefords. I never did find out who the group was – I think Marty and Lee formed the group and used studio singers for the backgrounds, so it was just something they put together.' The Shacklefords' only substantial item was a single titled 'Stranger In Your Town', and a glance at the sleeve note of the group's (presumably) sole album confirms James' impression that the group didn't really exist, but were purely a figment of the fertile imaginations of Hazelwood and Cooper.

Much better known are the Everly Brothers, for whom James apparently played on several albums along with Glen Campbell, although in many cases uncredited. Two that he felt able to identify positively are *Roots*, on which the Everlys retraced their musical steps back to the early 1950s, and *Beat And Soul*, a 1965 LP which includes a series of notable songs which were staples of the British R&B revival, although recorded in a somewhat different manner from their familiar format. 'That was interesting, because we took a song like Mickey & Sylvia's "Love Is Strange" and did some completely new arrangements which sounded incredible. That's another of my favourite albums.' One of the more famous fans of both James and the Everlys is British guitarist Dave Edmunds, who insists that James also plays on a 1965 Everly Brothers single, 'Ain't That Lovin' You Baby', while mention of *Roots* provoked some information from Burton that may not have been generally known. 'That *Roots* album has a couple of Merle Haggard tunes on it, and I played on most of Merle's early stuff, including "Mama Tried", which is on the Everly's record, "The Bottle Let Me Down" and "The Fugitive", although I've never played live with him.'

During the mid-1960s, James was heavily involved in studio work to the exclusion of virtually everything else. 'After I left Ricky, I did nothing but studio work until I joined Elvis in '69. I got so busy, working for just about everybody in the business, that there just wasn't time for anything else, and I turned down a lot of road travelling with quite a number of artists because I couldn't leave town — they keep you booked up here two months in advance, although I also did a lot of work in Nashville. It was all studio work, TV and movies, and that was when I worked with the Monkees. I was on a lot of the shows, and also cutting albums with Michael (Nesmith).' Arguably the finest Monkees record was the group's first single, 'Last Train To Clarksville', although once again James cannot be certain that the excellent solo on the record was his work.

Another now well known artist with whom Burton worked in the sixties was Randy Newman, more recently famous as a highly distinctive singer/songwriter. 'I did an awful lot of studio work with Randy, and with Lenny Waronker, who was producing him. With the things I did for Lenny, sometimes the artist wouldn't be there, so you never knew whose record you were playing on. Randy played piano on a lot of studio sessions we were doing at that time (late '60s), and all of a sudden, I went in one day to do a session that Lenny was producing, and found out that it was Randy's record we were working on. And it was the same thing with Ry Cooder — we did a lot of studio work together, and then Ry was doing his own album, again with Lenny producing.'

One less likely musician with whom James collaborated was Stephen Stills, on a pair of exceptional albums released in 1968, although his contribution was limited to a single track, Richie Furay's 'A Child's Claim To Fame', on the seminal *Buffalo*

Springfield Again album, and to four tracks out of nine on the best album made by Judy Collins, *Who Knows Where The Time Goes*.

'I remember doing several instruments on that Springfield track — two dobros, slide dobro and acoustic dobro, and that got played a lot on the radio, although I don't think I've ever even owned a copy of that album. The Judy Collins record was actually one of the first times I got to play with Stephen, because he was playing a lot of the guitar on that. When I went in to do the first session for the album, the producer said he needed a steel guitar player on some of the songs, and I told him I couldn't think of anyone better than Buddy Emmons. We really got into a trip working on that album for Judy, sort of cueing off each other — we converted the basic folk type of music we were doing into more of a real nice, laid-back country feel, and that's another of my favourite albums.'

The 'supersession' concept was coming into favour at the time the LP in question was recorded, and it is of interest to note that on a couple of tracks a basic instrumental unit of Burton and Stills on guitar, Emmons on pedal steel, Van Dyke Parks on piano, Chris Ethridge on bass and Jim Gordon on drums, is used, which must surely qualify as extraordinary . . . Among the pantheon of stars of the sixties who used James were the Mamas and Papas, although once again, precision is lacking. One definite connection with that group came when their erstwhile leader, John Phillips, used James on his celebrated solo album, *The Wolfking Of LA* — at the start of a track titled 'Mississippi', Phillips calls out 'Do it to me, James!'

'"Mississippi", right. John was a dobro freak, and he had to have dobro on that album. Working with people like that can be really amazing, because they like to give you something to do. They like to turn you loose, rather than just being another session player, and they like to present what you do, which is great, and I really appreciate it.'

Towards the end of the 1960s, Burton was given another chance to record on his own account, this time the result being an album titled *Corn Pickin' and Slick Slidin'*, on which he shared the credit with steel guitarist Ralph Mooney.

'Ralph and I were both doing lots of session for Capital Records, which Ken Nelson was producing – Merle (Haggard), Wynn Stewart, Kay Adams, just everybody on the label – and Ken told me one day that they had received a lot of requests for Ralph and I to do an album, and that they would let us make an album each, or we could do one together if we liked, and that was what we decided to do eventually. There was one track on that that I remember quite well, ''The Texas Waltz'', because several radio stations used it for play-ins and play-outs. I used a wah wah, a sort of talking wah wah pedal for that track. Overall, I think we did quite well on that album for a real quick country LP, which was done and finished in three sessions (nine hours). We did it live – it wasn't overdubbing this and that, and we just played it, mixed it down and released it.'

A suitable place, perhaps, to enquire how easy James found it to adapt to the enormous variety of music he was invited to play, from rock'n'roll to country to rhythm & blues to folk/rock to straight pop. 'I never took lessons in music, but I guess my background, all the different types of music I loved, just gave me the feel and the change for all those things. Naturally, if you go in to do a session-type thing, you get into the song and you have to play what complements the singer, and I don't know how or why, but I just have an art for making that happen for me, making what I feel fit right in with the basic music we're doing.'

When asked how many guitars he owns, James is once again predictably vague. 'I must have 150 to 200 guitars at least. I've lost count – I keep most of my instruments in cartage, and when I'm going to a session, my cartage company sends over a box in which I keep twelve or fifteen guitars, so that I have a gut string, and choices of 12-string, electric and acoustic guitars, and basically whatever I need is all in one box. Some of them are differently tuned, of course – if I'm using a high 3rd guitar, it's a different tuning, and sometimes there are open tunings, of course, depending on the type of music you're doing and what you're into.'

Talking of tunings, one innovation introduced by James was the use of a banjo string on his guitar to facilitate a Burton trademark, note bending. 'That was years ago, and if you listen to my old tracks, my basic style of playing involved a lot of string bending, and that was my feeling, the type of playing I think I created, which goes back to my country/bluesy playing, and for that, you bend a lot of strings, and the banjo string was more flexible.'

Then there's the question about a guitarist's inability to develop musically during periods of touring – unlike most of the others who were asked this question, James felt that touring was no particular hindrance to his development. Perhaps this is because his eminence is such that those who employ him to work live, tend to leave plenty of room for what is probably their most expensive acquisition! It hardly needs to be added that whatever he may cost in comparison to his rivals, James is worth his weight in gold, something which Elvis Presley would have confirmed were he still with us.

'I think that playing live shows creates a feeling for what you're doing, and sometimes that's really important when it comes to cutting records, because records that have a live feeling are nearly always better because of that. A lot of people do live albums, and after the basic live recording, they'll go in the studio and overdub everything and put the vocals back on, and to me that takes all the personal feeling and communication out of a record.'

A musician in James' position is invited to play, as we have discovered, on a great many records – how important is it that he likes the records he plays on? 'You don't have to like all the records. That's the other part of the business, because we play on an awful lot of records we don't like, although I'd say that being in my position and working with the people I do, I'd have to say that I enjoy doing 75 per cent of the things I do, and the other 25 per cent is stuff you do because you don't want to feel that you're letting somebody down just because they don't have a certain status in the business, like they don't have to be a big star. You have to be very careful with that – it's not fair to let those people down, because they're out there trying just as hard as all the people that are already on top and have made it, and I think it's good to work with semi-unknowns, because they need your help. Of course, some people seem to call me because of my reputation of having played with all these stars, but I don't like to feel that I'm terribly responsible for that situation – I prefer to feel that they're calling me because they really need me on their project.'

There can be little doubt that the three artists with whom James Burton has made the biggest impression are Ricky Nelson, Elvis Presley and Emmylou Harris. The time with Presley began in 1969, when it was decided that 'The King' should return to live work after a lengthy period when he was only visible to his public in the infamous series of films which almost destroyed a once great artist, and certainly contributed to his obvious artistic decline. Did James feel as delighted as one should when invited to become Elvis' guitar player?

'Oh, certainly. At that particular time, Elvis called me personally and we spoke on the phone for two hours. I assured him that I would get a band together for him, and that I would very much like to work with him on this project, which was working live in (Las) Vegas. As a matter of fact, I believe Scotty (Moore), D.J. (Fontana) and those guys had already been approached to do the Vegas thing, and I don't know what the problem was there, but I guess it was basically a lack of communication between them and the Colonel (Colonel Tom Parker, Presley's manager). So when Elvis called, we talked about putting a band together, which I did very fast as a matter of fact, because he was due to open a week later. I got on the phone and put together a band of musicians who I felt I would want to work with if I was doing a live show, and because Elvis didn't know these people, we had auditions and he came out for them. He and I hit it off really well – it was like we went to school together, and we had a great communication.

'Naturally, we got the band we wanted, but during all this time while I was putting it together and talking with Elvis, I was still convincing myself that that was what I wanted to do, because I was very busy doing studio work, six sessions a day – that's working round the clock – seven days a week. I once had to turn down a Bob Dylan tour – he wanted to go on a three months solid tour, and I talked to his manager, Albert Grossman, in New York, but we just couldn't get it together. I couldn't go out of town for three months – the price I'd want to go would have been astronomical, and it would have been foolish for me to turn down what I had going, plus the fact that I'd be leaving my family, which has to be considered, and I felt the same way about the Elvis thing when I first had the call. But it worked really well – we worked Vegas five weeks at a time, actually ten weeks in a year, because we had to work it twice a year. And we were really working – two shows a night, seven days a week, for four weeks solid, and that gets awful boring, doing the same thing every night with no nights off. It's tiring – it's work, it's fun sometimes, but it's work.'

While backing Elvis must have been an exciting and inspiring job for Scotty Moore, by the time Burton joined some fifteen years after Presley had first broken through, live shows were a different game – with a cabaret audience, communication is arguably more important than performance, which cannot

have often resulted in the build-up of tension so necessary for a star of Presley's magnitude.

'Well, live shows are like that, but the Vegas crowd is also different – you're dealing with people who come to see a show, a public which has seen almost every type of show you could imagine. Vegas is a part of the entertainment scene, and people go there to see good shows and good talent, and it's basically critics you're dealing with in a Vegas-type audience. I think Elvis didn't necessarily want to change his basic format, but what we did was a little more of an updated thing with an orchestra as well. I think it's probably one of the greatest feelings an artist can have to be able to walk out on stage to sing with a 30-piece orchestra behind him, although Elvis didn't really need a 30-piece orchestra, he could walk out there by himself and do what he was there to do. It was like he felt that the six guys behind him represented the real Elvis. Sometimes, of course, it was a bit frustrating playing with that big orchestra, but I felt that a lot of his songs required that, and on the other hand, he often keyed off the guitar, which was one of the main instruments in his band. It was drums, bass, guitar and a little piano, of course, but

Second solo album, 1971. The autograph is genuine . . .

those were his main instruments for the stage. He really did key off the guitar – we worked together so closely, it was like his right arm, but doing big band songs, the orchestra didn't give the guitar much room, although I managed to put a lick in here and there, like on things like "Johnny B. Goode" and a thing we would do which was a basic medley of his old tunes with "That's All Right Mama", "Mystery Train", and things where I could stretch out a bit.'

But wasn't there, we wondered, a temptation to copy Scotty Moore's original classic solos? 'No, I don't think I ever did that at any time, even when I was playing the songs that he had originally made with Elvis. Scotty's a fine guitar player, and he had the perfect style for the type of music that Elvis started out doing – it was so close to Elvis that the two went together perfectly. Elvis was great with the orchestra on the big band things, and he had a range in his voice, but the things with Scotty were classics, real classics. That basic style that Scotty plays goes back to the Chet (Atkins) style, and there's a lot of resemblance between their styles, although Chet plays more melody when he does that finger-picking style. Scotty has three things going, his rhythm, his bass, and his lead work but all in one, and anybody that can play three songs all in one is great.'

During 1971, James had another opportunity to make a solo album, although he seems less than totally enthusiastic about it in retrospect. Titled *The Guitar Sounds Of James Burton*, it was somewhat inaccurately sub-titled 'The solo debut album of the friend and player to Elvis, Haggard and (Waylon) Jennings'.

'I felt that album was a bit rushed, and I'll tell you how it came about. Felton Jarvis, who recently passed away – I lost a good friend there – produced Elvis' records, and he and I were real close, so we talked about doing a record which he said he'd like to produce. Now when I say it was a fast album, we were in Nashville doing an album with Elvis, and Elvis got sick – that was the time he had the glaucoma problem with his eyes. He had a whole week booked in the studio, and it was cancelled, so Felton suggested that we should take advantage of the fact that the studio time was booked, and make a start on the album. I said I hadn't picked out any tunes, because there hadn't been a chance to sit down and write anything. No preparation whatso- ever, but I knew I had two days before the session, so we decided to go ahead, and Felton got all the musi- cians from Nashville, but it was still a very rushed thing. We sat down and talked one night, put some songs together, and I wrote a couple of things just like that, and then we went in and did it. Three ses- sions plus an overdub session to put some more guitar on, and it was all done in about five sessions. There are several good things on there, I think – a Leon Russell tune called "Delta Lady", which was nice, "Fire And Rain", that I felt came off real good, and of course I did tunes like "Johnny B. Goode", that type of thing. I think I've probably recorded that with more artists than any other tune – I can prob- ably name ten or twelve people I've cut it with, plus I did it on my own album. There was another good one, an old Barbara George tune called "I Know", that was great, and we had this fantastic girl singer

James with his trademark Telecaster in the 1970s

on that, Jeannie Greene, who sang on Elvis' "Sus- picious Minds". But overall, I felt that album should have been a little more me and a little less rushed, and there should have been time to pick the tunes out – I went to Nashville to work with Elvis, and ended up doing my own album, and afterwards I felt that the timing had been bad.'

It seems to be a fact that however pre-eminent a session musician may be, the conversion from hired hand to principal is rarely achieved successfully, which is less a reflection on the abilities of studio players than a comment on the different mental approaches required for the two positions – while a star is available or not, depending on the machina- tions of his management and the needs of his public, a session musician must be always on call – an absence for as little as three months can result in the best sessions being allocated to rivals.

'I think it's very important for a studio player to work with certain people that rely on you and require you to be there, and a lot of studio players lose out, I think, by going out of town. Being a studio musician, you're booked up two months in advance, which I didn't much like, although I did it for several years, but now I've become able to do both types of work,

An open air gig with Emmylou Harris and the Hot Band

sessions and playing live. With Ricky, it was working the road and cutting records in town, with the *Shindig* thing, I was working every week, recording with other artists and also travelling, because the Shindogs went to South America and worked some live shows, and with Elvis, I worked with him and also did some studio work – an in and out of town type thing. I like the feeling of doing that, because it gives me the chance to get away from the studio scene and keeps me fresh, so that when I've been out working on the road, I'm ready to get back into studio work.'

During the first years of the 1970s, James became involved in the first line up of the band with whom he arguably achieved most, both musically and in terms of popular fame, during that decade. Gram Parsons, a rock star with leanings towards country music, had become noted for his attempts to merge the two musical forms, although not in exactly the same way as James himself had merged his differing guitar styles – the Parsons dream was to create a fresh musical hybrid, which he referred to as 'white soul music' or 'cosmic American country music', which he partially achieved in the Byrds, whose music he transformed almost overnight, and later in the Flying Burrito Brothers, a group he helped to form, and through which many of the most significant country/

rock musicians of the 1970s passed. After leaving the Burritos, Parsons embarked on a solo career, and it was decided that no ordinary bunch of session musicians would be appropriate to play with him.

'The first thing that was different about that was that Gram's manager, Ed Tickner, persuaded Warner Brothers, the company Gram was recording for, to supply enough money for a special band. Gram intended to hire this band that played on his albums to go on the road with him, but then he passed away, and Ed Tickner took over Emmylou Harris, who'd been working with Gram, and did with Emmylou what had been his intention of doing with Gram.'

This was to be the skeleton of what would become, when they backed Emmylou Harris, the Hot Band, which included, apart from James, notable players like pianist Glen D. Hardin, and recorded two classic LPs with Parsons before the latter's unfortunate death. At that point, Emmylou Harris, a featured singer in Parsons' band, assumed the role of front person, which she has retained to date, recording nine original albums up to the end of 1981, on all of which James has featured. Although Emmylou was almost unknown at the time she 'inherited' the band, all the musicians seemed eager to help her live out Gram Parsons' vision.

'I didn't think there was any real difference – I felt a great loss there with Gram dying, but since Ed Tickner was managing Emmylou, and I knew that he wanted to do with her what he had in mind for Gram, I felt good about it, because I knew that if Gram couldn't do it himself, he'd want it to happen for Emmylou.'

It was as a member of the Hot Band backing Emmylou Harris on her first British tour that James Burton also first performed in England, where he was treated like royalty. 'That made me a little nervous, to walk on stage and see fifty other guitar players watching from the front row, but I just got into my act – there was nothing else I could do. And the competition in that band was quite tight – the guys really respected each other, which was a very good thing, and we had to try hard to accomplish what we wanted to do.'

The Burton speciality which will never be forgotten by those who saw it came on a mid-'70s tour during an encore of 'Shop Around'. After pedal steel player Hank DeVito had played a sizzling solo, he would turn to James as if to say 'Your turn next', whereupon the Burton Telecaster would be hoisted behind its owner's head, and a five minute solo would result which left the entire audience speech-

less. The only regret is that no one had the foresight to record this magical moment legally – although bootlegs exist, as James noted, they are of poor quality in technical terms.

While working with Ms. Harris was obviously enjoyable and fulfilling, this period was proving difficult for James, who was also still contracted to Elvis Presley, although he was allowed to work with Emmylou when Elvis did not require his services, which in fact meant that the Hot Band could not tour when Elvis was working.

The work with Parsons and then with Emmylou Harris also led to a series of other fine albums featuring a variety of artists backed by the Hot Band, among them Rodney Crowell, Jesse Winchester, Jonathan Edwards and Mary Kay Place, although James did not return to tour with the Hot Band, even after Elvis Presley died in 1977.

'I loved working with Emmy, but I really didn't think I wanted to travel as much as I thought Emmy would be doing. I think I enjoyed just about everything I did with her, and there are so many tracks that stick out, like ''Till I Gain Control Again'' and ''Too Far Gone'' – I did the solo on that live.'

More recently, the two most interesting projects in which James has been involved, aside from hun-

James in his office, 1981 – no prizes for guessing what's missing!

dreds of sessions, are his work with John Denver, the latest superstar to add J.B. to an already star-studded backing band, and a more personal project, the TCB Band. 'I did a TV show with John in 1977, just about a month before Elvis passed away, which was the first time I'd worked with him, and he invited me to go with him on tour, and I told him I'd like to as long as I wasn't going to be out of town with Elvis. Then Elvis passed away about a month later, and right after I got back from the funeral I had a call from John's company to say that he wanted me to play on his new album, and then we talked about putting together a new band, because some of his old players had left. We had a great communication going, so I did it, and it's worked out really well, and I'm still with John.

'The TCB Band project is a bit different – that's the band I had with Elvis, and we made an album that was a tribute to Elvis, but we haven't yet released it, and I'm not sure that we will, because everybody in the band is so involved in different projects that there's a big problem about getting together to work. It's a real good album, and it's been pressed and everything, but it's two years old now, so we're thinking of not releasing it normally, although I'd like to see it released perhaps through my fan club.'

It has been said before, and perhaps this interview will confirm it, that James Burton communicates best through his Telecaster, a guitar which has been his favourite instrument for more than twenty years, although he claims to be in the process of building a new James Burton model guitar, which will undoubtedly become a popular item should it come to fruition. 'It'll probably compare closely with the Fender Telecaster, and also with the Les Paul model Gibson – basically, we're talking about one guitar that does everything. All those records I've played on during my years of music, I've mostly used a Telecaster, but being a studio musician, you're required to play different instruments – someone might prefer the sound of a Gibson or whatever, but my basic sound is the Telecaster.'

It would be fruitless to deny that we had hoped to learn substantially more about James, about the records on which he has played, the people with whom he works, and his unique ability as a guitarist. However, it is true that to hear him play the guitar – and the attached discography, although substantial, may be merely scratching the surface – tells you more about the man than words are able to convey.

James Burton Discography

The utter futility of trying to compile any kind of meaningful discography of James Burton's work is something which has to be attempted to be believed. As a result, what follows is far from comprehensive, and it should be noted that apart from those albums listed for his major employers (Nelson, Presley, Harris/Parsons, etc), James' participation is no guarantee of quality, due to the varying circumstances in which he was employed.

Solo Albums
196? *Corn Pickin' & Slick Slidin'* (with Ralph Mooney)
1971 *The Guitar Sound Of James Burton*

With Rick(y) Nelson
1957 *Ricky*
1958 *Ricky Nelson*
1959 *Ricky Sings Again*
1959 *Songs by Ricky*
1960 *More Songs by Ricky*
1961 *Rick Is 21*
1962 *Album Seven*
1963 *For Your Sweet Love*
1964 *For You*
1964 *The Very Thought Of You*
1964 *Spotlight On Rick*
1965 *Best Always*
1965 *Love And Kisses*
1966 *Country Fever*
1967 *Bright Lights & Country Music*
1968 *Another Side Of Rick*
1973 *Legendary Masters* (compilation)

With Elvis Presley
1970 *On Stage*
1972 *Live At Madison Square Garden*
1972 *Elvis Now*
1973 *Aloha From Hawaii*

1974 *Live On Stage in Memphis*
As has already been mentioned, Presley records do not usually list personnel (except, evidently, live LPs). There are obviously many more which include Burton, although uncredited)

With Gram Parsons
1973 *G.P.*
1974 *Grievous Angel*
1976 *Sleepless Nights*

With Emmylou Harris
1975 *Pieces Of The Sky*
1976 *Elite Hotel*
1977 *Luxury Liner*
1978 *Quarter Moon In A Ten Cent Town*
1978 *Profile – Best Of Emmylou Harris*
1979 *Blue Kentucky Girl*
1979 *Light Of The Stable*
1980 *Roses In The Snow*
1980 *Evangeline*
1980 *Cimarron*

With John Denver
1977 *I Want To Live*
1978 *J.D.*
1979 *A Christmas Together* (with The Muppets)
1980 *Autograph*

Various Sessions
James Burton has played on innumerable albums by a wide variety of artists, among them the following: Herb Alpert, Hoyt Axton, Buffalo Springfield, J. J. Cale, Glen Campbell, Johnny Cash, David Cassidy, Judy Collins, Ry Cooder, Rodney Crowell, Mac Davis, Delaney & Bonnie, Jonathan Edwards, Everly Brothers, Phil Everly, Mickey Gilley, Arlo Guthrie, The Hagers, Merle Haggard, John Hartford, Dale Hawkins, Ronnie Hawkins, Lee Hazelwood, James Hendricks, John Hurley, Jan & Dean, Waylon Jennings, Jack Jones, Nicolette Larson, Johnny Lee, Jerry Lee Lewis, Longbranch/Pennywhistle, Dan McCorison, Michael Nesmith, Joni Mitchell, The Monkees, Randy Newman, Phil Ochs, Buck Owens, John Phillips, Mary Kay Place, Gary Puckett, Billy Lee Riley, Johnny Rivers, Kenny Rogers, The Shacklefords, Silverado, Frank Sinatra, Nancy Sinatra, P. F. Sloan, Mark Spoelstra, John Stewart, Johnny Tillotson, Tongue & Groove, Bobby Vee, The Ventures, Sammy Walker, Andy Williams, Jesse Winchester.

Individual references to some of the respective albums can be found in *Rock Record*, written by Terry Hounsome and Tim Chambre, and published in Great Britain by Blandford Press.

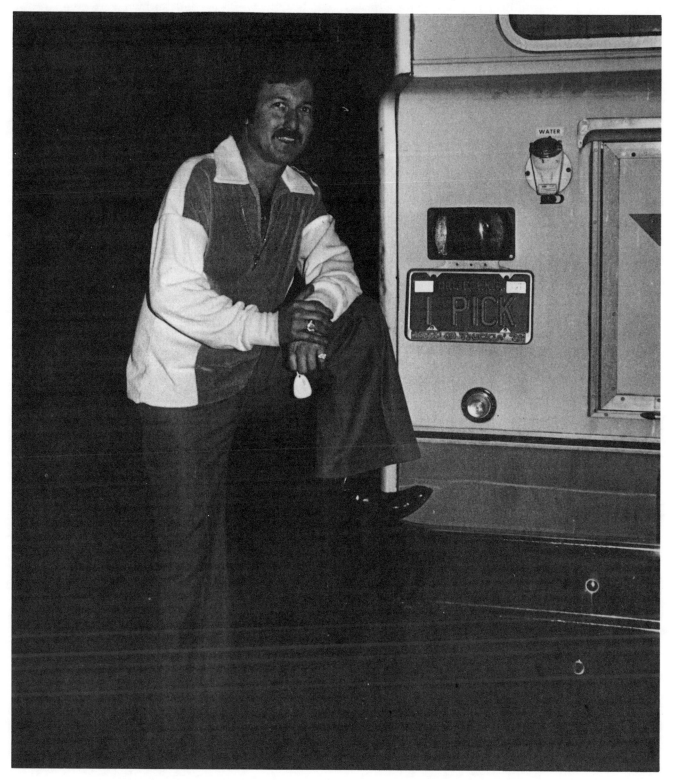

HANK B. MARVIN

To demonstrate to any potential unbelievers the importance of Hank B. Marvin, we must go back to 1977, when a TV commercial was screened showing a youth in his bedroom listening to a new album. After a cautious look around, he picked up a cricket bat and pretended to mime to the playing of the guitarist. The LP was *20 Golden Greats* by the Shadows, the guitarist being impersonated was Hank Marvin, and the album was the second biggest-selling LP of the year in Britain. Not bad for a group assumed to have been defunct by a large proportion of the British record-buying public . . .

Hank was born in Newcastle on 28 October 1941. His real name is Brian Marvin, his familiar epithet having been acquired at school. 'When I was in the first year at grammar school, I was one of several lads who hung around together, and four of us were called Brian, which meant that three of the four acquired nicknames, and I was called Hank although I don't think I ever knew the reason for the name. And the 'B.' is for Brian, of course, or sometimes Bridget, depending on the mood I'm in!'

A major milestone in the teenage Marvin's life was meeting Bruce Welch, who has played rhythm guitar to Marvin's lead for the majority of the past twenty-five years. 'Yes, it was obviously an important meeting. Bruce was very interested in music at school, and he had one of those metal-bodied guitars, Nationals, which I'd never seen before – he used to keep it in his locker at school and impress us all with the three or four chords he knew, and I think that was why we struck up a friendship, because we were both interested in music and especially guitar music. I'd gone through phases of traditional jazz, folk music and blues, which, I suppose led me to the guitar and banjo side of things.'

Hank's first instrument was a banjo, bought from a schoolmaster. 'Yes, and I've still got it somewhere. £2.10s (£2.50) it cost me, which I paid at the rate of 2/6 (12½p) per week, and that was when I was fifteen. It was a bit of a problem at first, because I wasn't able to obtain a book which clearly showed banjo chord symbols. I had a tutor, which was probably very good, but it was too complicated for me because all the chords were shown in note clusters, and there were only about three chords in three keys in chord notation form. So it took a while for me to get anywhere with the banjo until I got another tutor which I found much easier to understand. Then I shot ahead and learned lots of chords, and within a short time, I started playing with a couple of local jazz bands, playing the banjo and singing jazz songs. This was trad. jazz, and then, with the banjo, skiffle came along. Although I enjoyed Lonnie Donegan, I preferred what seemed to be more purist skiffle and folk/blues by people like Leadbelly and Big Bill Broonzy.

'Ken Colyer, the jazz trumpeter, had a skiffle group and I bought some of his records which I liked, perhaps because they weren't at all commercial – I was just trying to be totally the opposite of everyone else, so I learned some of the old folk and blues songs he recorded, and myself and some local lads formed a skiffle group and included these songs in our repertoire. Funnily enough, it was through doing one of them that we won a skiffle competition. We did a very bluesy version of "Stagger Lee' with a long banjo solo in it which I'd copied from a Ken Colyer record, and that intrigued the judges, I think, because it was probably the only attempt by anyone in any of the groups to try to play their instrument using single notes rather than just strumming chords. We won, the whole show was recorded, and we were given a copy each.'

It wasn't long before Hank moved from banjo to guitar and was actually given his first guitar as a present from his father on his sixteenth birthday.

That first skiffle group was called the Crescent City Skiffle Group, and did not include Bruce Welch, who was in another local skiffle band, the Railroaders. 'They were very successful locally, and they were very good and quite commercially orientated. Bruce was the main singer, a singer/guitarist, and they got a lot of work in working men's clubs and won prizes in competitions. It was run by a guy called George Williams, who changed from guitar to tea-chest bass, and also managed the group. He was a very go-ahead sort of guy, a bit of a hustler, and he got a lot of work for them, whereas my group was really just for fun, and we didn't have any thoughts of going to these clubs or anything. Bruce had heard me play, and mentioned me to George Williams, and they asked me if I'd like to join their group because they felt they needed a guitar player who could do solos and things, and I was just getting to the stage where I had the nerve to stand up and pretend I could play single note solos. So I left the group we had – as I said, it wasn't a money making concern and no one was upset – and went with Bruce's group and started doing a lot of work in working men's clubs.'

Marvin's early guitar influences were split between rock'n'roll players and jazz guitarists. 'When I first heard Django Reinhardt, I didn't know about his left hand being deformed, so I just appreciated his music, although I didn't really intend to sound like him at that stage. I liked his fluency and his tremendous freedom of expression appealed to me, and I maybe felt I could incorporate some of his little trills and runs into my style at a later date. Barney Kessel was probably the first modern jazz guitarist, and I heard an album of his and was totally overawed by all the chords he used, which I didn't know existed – I was very much into triads, majors and minors, as you would be at that age, and major 7ths and major 9ths and added 9ths and 13ths were like a whole new world to me, totally different from Reinhardt in style, sound and approach, but again with tremendous technique, and with a great ability for improvisation. Much later, I heard Wes Montgomery and I liked Wes' very tasty little riffs and the warm sound he got by playing with his thumb, much warmer than you get with a plectrum.'

The dilemma for anyone learning guitar in the 1950s was that it was considered very much more respectable to listen to jazz players, but teenage ears and sensibilities found rock'n'roll guitarists much more straightforwardly enjoyable, particularly Buddy Holly, James Burton, Bo Diddley and Chet Atkins.

'Indeed, and Scotty Moore, and Cliff Gallup, who played for Gene Vincent, and Al Casey, who did a tremendous record for Sanford Clark, "The Fool", which was built round this great guitar riff. Because I'd been brought up on trad. jazz, which is much more closely related to rock'n'roll in that both have an obvious heavy beat compared to modern jazz, which can sometimes be very subtle, I sometimes found it difficult to tap my toes to modern jazz, and the strong rhythmic beat of rock'n'roll immediately got through to me and to millions of young people.

'Rock'n'roll hit a different part of my awareness and I also loved the guitar sounds of the people we've mentioned, which I think come from a country music background, very heavily based on country music. I suppose it was early country/rock really, a fusion of country-influenced people like Presley and Jerry Lee Lewis with the black influence of Little Richard, Fats Domino and Bo Diddley, those guys that had been around for a while. They fused all that and got white rock'n'roll which I thought was great. The Railroaders had to start playing rock'n'roll at a dance we promoted because the other group didn't turn up – Bruce knew a lot of rock'n'roll songs, so we quickly learned them in half an hour and played the next set as a rock'n'roll band instead of a skiffle group, and after that, I started to listen to rock'n'roll and found it very enjoyable.'

In April 1958, Hank and Bruce decided to move to London, somewhat against their parents' wishes. 'Bruce and I weren't doing very well at school, because our interest in academic work had flagged, although it had soared as regards playing the guitar, staying out late at night in working men's clubs and not doing homework. Bruce, in fact, left school early, which I thought was absolutely right – I wasn't going to get any 'O' Levels at that rate, and I couldn't see myself pulling anything together, because it was too late and I wasn't at all motivated. Those were the days when things were starting to happen and people were being so-called discovered – Tommy Steele, Wee Willie Harris and so on – and there was always the possibility that something could happen, and the place where it was likely to happen was London.

'So I took my little record player, and we had a suitcase each, a guitar each, a tiny amplifier about the size of a cornflake packet, and went to London, and we were there for about six months before we met up with Cliff (Richard). It wasn't easy at the start – we mainly earned money playing at the 2I's coffee bar, in the small cellar there, into which they could

Young Hank and left: Flanking the boss – left to right: Bruce Welch, Cliff Richard, Hank

Early Shadows – left to right: Bruce Welch, Tony Meehan, Jet Harris, Hank B. Marvin

cram about two hundred people, and which had a very shallow stage at the end from which about five musicians could perform.

'They had a regular group of players who used to form makeshift groups, and Bruce and I very quickly got onto the scene there, along with Brian Locking, Brian Bennett, Tony Meehan and Jet Harris, who were all later in the Shadows, and a Country & Western singer called Rick Richards. Usually, five of us would form a group to play a repertoire of the latest rock'n'roll and pop hits. The favourites were Everly Brothers and Buddy Holly & the Crickets songs, early Gene Vincent and Presley material, anything by Little Richard, Fats Domino, things that were popular, even skiffle, so it was quite a variety of music, and we'd play down there as often as we could in order to pay the rent. Obviously our letters home said how wonderful it was in London, but we sometimes went very hungry, and I mean *very* – two days without eating.'

Another 2I's regular was Mickie Most, who, with Alex Wharton, comprised the Most Brothers. 'They both had blond hair, trying to do a British Everly Brothers, but their version of "Wake Up Little Suzie" was really bad and typical of British rock'n'roll of the time, very wooden and with an awful arrangement which lacked all the charm and country feel of the original. Then when we did the first tour with Cliff, the Most Brothers were also on that bill, and Jet (Harris) and I played for them as well as Cliff.'

Some months before meeting Cliff Richard, Hank and Bruce briefly joined their first London group, The Five Chesternuts, formed by one Peter Chester, son of comedian Charlie Chester. 'We made a single, which was the first one I'd played on, financed by Leslie Conn, who was managing the group at the time and was connected with an American label call-ed Carlton Records. He had a lot of faith in the group, what with Bruce and myself and Peter, who was quite a good songwriter, so we made this single of "Teenage Love" backed with "Jean Dorothy", which sounded like "Jean Darthy" with our pseudo-American accents, and we even got on 6.5 *Special*, which was fantastic.'

Although the Five Chesternuts lasted only a few months, Hank was in demand elsewhere, working with premier London skiffle group, the Vipers. 'That also came from the 2I's situation, although I can't recall exactly what happened except that Wally Whyton asked me to join the Vipers at a time when he was trying to revitalise the group, or perhaps resurrect would be a better word, and wanted someone to play lead guitar. He thought I could do the job, and I was cheap enough, I guess, and he also got Jet Harris and we worked with him for a week. After we got back to London, Wally was organising more work and asked me to carry on because he wanted a regular group, and by this time, it had been decided that the pseudo-drummer should leave and be replaced by a real drummer, Tony Meehan, who had appeared at the 2I's during the summer. Tony joined, but at virtually the same time, I left, because I decided I'd stick with Bruce and we'd try to carry on together, either with the Chesternuts again, or doing something else.'

At this point, things changed dramatically, when Cliff Richard, at the time an eighteen-year-old whose first single, 'Move It', had just been released, entered the lives of Hank and Bruce. 'First of all, we didn't meet Cliff, we met Johnny Foster who had been Cliff's manager but had become his road manager because he didn't have enough experience after Cliff got his recording contract. Johnny came to the 2I's looking for Tony Sheridan, who he'd heard was a good guitar player, and who he wanted because Cliff had his first big tour booked as a supporting act to the Kalin Twins. Sheridan wasn't there, but by chance I was down there with a country singer called Rick Richards, and Rick persuaded me to play for Johnny, who seemed fairly impressed, and asked if I'd like to do the tour with Cliff. As I was already doing it for the Most Brothers, that meant I'd be playing for two people on the tour which would be good money, so I agreed.

'As they were also short of another guitarist, I recommended Bruce, and we arranged to meet with John and Cliff, and then we all took the bus to Cliff's family house in Cheshunt to rehearse. We first met Cliff when he was being fitted for his now famous pink jacket, and he looked at us and sneered and we looked back at him and sneered. He obviously thought we were a couple of yobs, which is what we looked like, and he looked a bit the same, with a very greasy sort of 1958 hairstyle, tight black trousers and crêpe soles. But we got chatting on the bus and found we had a lot in common musically, which broke the ice, and when we got down to the nitty gritty of playing, we had a great afternoon going through the five songs he was going to play. Straight away, we realised he had talent, and a very appealing voice, young sounding as it was — we'd heard a lot of visitors coming down for one night and singing at the 2I's, and we immediately knew he was way ahead of all of them, with the movements as well as the singing.

'A few days later, we met the bus and went off up to the Midlands for our first concert, and that was it, really — a fantastic reception for Cliff. I'd never seen anything like it considering he was a brand new face at the bottom of the bill, but it was clear that the bulk of the audience were there to see him. "Move It" was in the Top Ten, and they'd seen him twice on *Oh*

Boy! where he'd made a big impact and that was why they were there. The reaction was fantastic — straight away, he was definitely the star of the show, and when we saw him work on stage, we thought "Wow, this guy's got something", because he just had them eating out of his hand. Obviously, he was totally inexperienced, but he just had that natural something and the audience responded so well — we were amazed, because we didn't expect anything like that, and we'd certainly never been in a situation with 2,000 people screaming non-stop.'

'Move It' was Cliff Richard's first record and first hit, recorded before Hank had joined the Drifters, as Cliff's backing group was called, while the same recording session produced the follow-up hit, 'High Class Baby'.

'After that, it was time for Cliff to record again, and Norrie Paramor, who produced the records, had seen us work on stage with Cliff and liked the sound, while Cliff also wanted to use us for recording because he felt we had an exciting sound and atmosphere which he wanted to use on the record. So Norrie booked us for Cliff's next session, but obviously, being very cautious and sensible, he also booked other musicians as well — Terry Smart was on drums, and he was in the group, and so was Jet Harris on bass guitar, but there was a guy called Frank Clark also booked for stand-up bass, then there was Bruce on rhythm guitar and myself on lead, but also on lead guitar a session player named Ernie Shear, who had played lead on "Move It".

'We did a number called "Livin' Lovin' Doll", and Norrie suggested that I virtually played rhythm and Ernie did all the lead work. Cliff wasn't too happy about that, and he had a point — he felt that Ernie wasn't really into rock'n'roll, and that while "Move It" was just right, "High Class Baby" didn't quite

Cliff and the Shads 1962/3 — left to right: Hank, Bruce (front), Cliff, Brian Bennett, Licorice Locking

*Left: the final 1960s Shadows line up –
left to right: Hank, John Rostill,
Bruce Welch, Brian Bennett
Below: Cliff and Hank*

happen guitar-wise and he felt that Ernie tended to do the same thing every time on a rock'n'roll record, and there wasn't really any variety. Anyway, Norrie wanted him, so he played a few fills and the solo and it was like "Move It" revisited. Cliff wasn't very happy and told Norrie he wanted me to play lead guitar, and eventually suggested that we each do a take, and that was what we did. After we did mine, Cliff said to me "I sang a lot better on this one" ... but as it happens, I think it was a better track anyway, because Ernie, who's a fine guitar player, just played the same sort of solo again, and I think my solo was a bit more original and had a different sort of sound. Cliff was much happier with my version, and because it was a better overall performance, Norrie agreed to take it. That was the last time Norrie ever booked any other musicians.' ... Not long afterwards, perhaps the most famous line-up of the Drifters was completed by the arrival of Tony Meehan on drums.

Marvin's ability as a guitarist in these early days was governed by the opportunities he was given in the material used by Cliff Richard. 'If we did someone else's song on stage, I might copy the solo out of admiration for the original guitar player, but when we did original material, I tried to be original and spontaneous in the studio – in those days, everything was recorded more or less live, and Cliff sang as we played. If Norrie the producer, said we'd done a great take, that was the record and we'd done it, so it had a great feel of spontaneity and nerves and everything, although I'm sure what I played was heavily influenced by those I admired. Playing fast was something I found a bit difficult, because I hardly ever practised – my only practice came when we actually played the numbers or rehearsed new ones.'

From providing a solo on 'Livin' Lovin' Doll', Marvin obviously continued to decorate Cliff's records with his distinctive solos, although the solo, of course, was not the main part of the record. 'It wasn't so much a question of how pleased I was with what I played, as how pleased Norrie was with the overall record, because he wasn't just recording me playing a guitar solo, he was making a complete record, so obviously Cliff's performance was of paramount importance.'

Cliff Richard and the Drifters' first LP, *Cliff*, was released in April 1959, inevitably becoming a major success, although it was not recorded in a conventional manner – while it sounded 'live', it was actually cut in EMI Studios.

'That was a very clever idea of Norrie's, and after seeing the shows and the response Cliff was getting, he had this idea of a totally unusual approach – instead of taking all the equipment to a concert and recording it, he decided to record within the reasonably controlled environment of a studio, but have an invited audience of about 350 people from the fan club, for whom a buffet would be provided. Studio 2 at Abbey Road has a long staircase leading up to the control room, so there was a stage built at the bottom of the stairs where Norrie could see us from upstairs. We worked on stage as though we were doing a normal concert, but we'd rehearsed all the numbers beforehand, so we were singing and playing in front of a live audience but with Norrie able to supervise. We did it for two nights, but on the first night, the barriers to keep the kids off the stage were too close to us, so there was rather too much screaming being picked up on the stage microphones. Then on the second night, the barriers were moved much further back so that there was a better balance between the screams and the music, but we had another problem because Cliff had laryngitis. It's terrible when you look back, and it could actually have ruined his career, but the studio and the session were booked,

HANK B. MARVIN

all the food was in and paid for and the kids had been invited, so EMI were determined to go ahead with it. It was a great pity, because if we'd done it a week or two later when he was singing normally again, it would have been a much better performance from Cliff. Although as it happens the public didn't seem to notice, and it was a monster seller in every territory where Cliff was selling records. People still refer back to that album and say it was fantastic . . . But it was live, no overdubs and a live audience.'

By this time, Cliff's backing group were no longer known as the Drifters, but as the Shadows, after objections from the better-known American group also known as the Drifters. 'Norrie approached us after a while and told us we had a problem, because we wouldn't be able to use the name in the States – and by that time we had our own recording contract as the Drifters, given us by Norrie – and suggested that we change the name to avoid further bother. All manner of names were thought up, some of which were pretty awful, and then one day Jet and I were out at Ruislip Lido with our motor scooters and Jet said, ''What do you reckon about the Shadows?'' It just seemed like the right name, with obvious connotations which people would immediately attach to it, but it sounded right, as if it had always been there as a name. Everybody else – Bruce, Cliff and Tony – all liked it, Norrie thought it was perfect, and that was it.'

Curiously, in view of what happened later, the first Drifters/Shadows single, 'Feelin' Fine', was a vocal record. 'Bruce and I used to sing harmonies and play guitars, and we didn't have any aspirations to be an instrumental group as such, although our second single, ''Jet Black'' and ''Driftin''', was a couple of instrumentals we'd written. We'd heard a few American instrumentals by people like Duane Eddy, who was becoming popular, and we were intrigued that people were having success with that type of thing, so we thought we could write something like those and do it ourselves, which would make a nice change from Cliff singing here and there – and I mean that in the nicest possible way! So we did those two numbers on Cliff's live album, and they got such a good reaction that Norrie suggested we record them again, without the screams and everything, as a single, which we did. We enjoyed rather better sales than with the first single, although we weren't sure whether that meant our audience was increasing or just that more people liked this record than the last one. The next step after we changed our name to the Shadows was another vocal single, ''Saturday Dance'', which we felt was the best thing we'd done, and in fact it only just missed the charts, so once again we'd reverted to being a vocal group.'

Although 'Saturday Dance' was not a hit, it is particularly significant as the first track on which Marvin used the guitar which has become his trademark, the Fender Stratocaster, although strangely he had acquired the instrument by mistake.

'Yes, that was probably the first record with the Strat – the earlier ones had been with the trusty Antoria or the Vega before that. But it's marvellous the way things sometimes happen by mistake and then turn out for the best. I'd talked with Cliff about getting a better guitar, because this Antoria had an interesting sound, but was awful to play. The neck was very bent and there was no way of straightening it, so that the further you moved up the fingerboard away from the nut, first of all the action got progressively higher and then gradually got lower again, and therefore the tuning wasn't very good because of that. We thought that the James Burton sound on Ricky Nelson records was a knockout, and we wanted to achieve something similar to the American rock'n'roll sound. We heard that he played a Fender, so Cliff's management wrote off to the Fender factory in the States and asked for a brochure. We pored through the brochure and discovered that the most expensive Fender guitar was the Stratocaster, with bird's eye maple neck, tremolo arm and gold-plated hardware, and we assumed that that must be the one James Burton used. It probably cost about £120, which is cheap by today's standards, and Cliff bought it for me because I couldn't afford it.

'It arrived in this magnificent tweed flat case with lovely plush red lining and this magnificent guitar lying in there. It looked a real treat – it was flamingo pink, with this lovely bird's eye maple fingerboard and neck, and of course all the gold-plated hardware looked fantastic. You didn't have to play it, you just had to hang it round your neck and the audience would be totally impressed.

'I already had an idea what tremolo arms did, because a few months before, on ''Living Doll'', which was Cliff's first number one, I played a copy of a Gretsch White Falcon which I borrowed from a guy called Tony Harvey, who later played with Johnny Halliday in France. It was a semi-acoustic f-holed cello guitar and the strings went onto a tailpiece, a little fishtailed piece of metalwork at the end of the body, and if you pressed that tailpiece, it acted like a tremolo arm, and that's how I got the tremolo effect on ''Living Doll''. I was disappointed when I found I couldn't bend the strings in the same way as James Burton. It took me years to find out that he used light gauge strings, while I was struggling with very heavy ones – I thought he must have Superman fingers! Several years later, I found out that he used a banjo string instead of a top string, then a first string instead of a second, second instead of third and so on, in order to get all those beautiful bendings he did. And the other thing, of course, was that he didn't use a Stratocaster at all – it was still a Fender, but he used the Telecaster.'

In July 1960, the Shadows really arrived in chart terms in their own right with the release of 'Apache', which topped the British charts. 'Jerry Lordan, who was on our British Tour, said he had an original instrumental which he'd written, which no one had released, and played it to us on the bus using his ukelele, which he used for writing songs, and we thought it was great and totally different from everything else that was happening, and we played it to Norrie, who thought it was marvellous. Norrie liked it a lot, but felt that the A-side of the record should be ''Quatermasster's Stores'', which he felt was obviously more commercial, but we didn't agree with him – we felt ''Apache'' was so different it had to be the A-side, and ''Quatermasster's Stores'' was a bit like Johnny & the Hurricanes and far less original. So he played both tracks around, and got a tremendous

49

reaction for "Apache", I'm glad to say, so he decided to release it.

'Every record we made was released in America, but there was no promotion, despite great write-ups in *Cashbox* and everything, which said "Britain's top teen orch come out with another surefire winner, hit all over Europe. Surely this one must make the charts". Nothing. It was a bit annoying, because when we worked in Europe, Americans often came to the shows and said it was a great show, but wondered why we hadn't made it in the States. We always considered live performances a very important part of our image, and everywhere we went, record sales rocketed after we'd appeared live, and I feel that might have been the key – if we'd gone to the States and maybe worked as support to some American act, I think we would have had the success, but we didn't, and that's the way the mop flops.'

One aspect of the Shadows which American audiences never experienced, but which became most popular in Britain was the celebrated 'Shadows' walk', which evolved as a result of seeing an American band who toured Britain in 1958, the Treniers. 'Bruce and myself and, as we later learned, Cliff, all went to see Jerry Lee Lewis at the Gaumont State on the third night of his tour and on the show with him was this American coloured band, the Treniers, who had several singers and used to perform very entertaining rhythm & blues type rock'n'roll. Their presentation involved a lot of concerted movement, and they'd do these little walks and things together which were great – we'd never seen anything like it before, and it seemed to be the essence of group rock'n'roll, which we thought was fantastic. Later on, about a year later, when we were with Cliff, we were chatting about how we could improve our presentation – up to then, we'd been very free in our movements, and we'd wander about the stage, lie on our backs, shake our legs in the air, kneel on the floor, all kinds of wild, abandoned rock'n'roll movements. We all harked back to the Treniers, and decided that it might be an idea if we could work out some little steps together – when it came to, say, a guitar solo, Cliff would step back into the band, and the four of us, Cliff, the bass and the two guitars, would start moving around together and do these movements. When we put this into the show for the first time, the audience loved it and thought it was absolutely fantastic, so we knew we were on to a winner, and kept it in.'

One curious feature of the late '50s and early '60s was the substantial popularity of instrumental records. As Marvin was significantly involved in this minor revolution, it seemed reasonable to ask whether he could explain the phenomenon.

'I'm tempted to say that there were so many bad singers around, but that's just not true, and I really don't know why that happened, and I don't think anyone does. Suddenly, instrumentals became tremendously popular – Russ Conway was having hits, Duane Eddy, us. Then there were other artists and groups popping up with one-off hits all the time in America, like the Fireballs and there was the Tornadoes here. I think it was Duane Eddy who started it all – he came out with a great new sound and made some good exciting records, and that's

why they were hits, and maybe because of that people became instrumentally conscious and therefore more open to buying and listening to instrumentals, that could be the reason for it all.'

After the enormous British success of 'Apache', the follow-up single by the Shadows was a double-sided hit, 'Man Of Mystery'/'The Stranger', the latter tune having probably stood the test of time better than the former, perhaps due to its comparative unfamiliarity. 'That was sent to us by a couple of writers, Bill Crompton and Morgan Jones, I think, and we thought it was excellent. It seemed to suit our style, and it had a slightly Western feel to the melody, probably influenced by "Apache".'

It was often the introductions to Shadows records which provided immediate appeal to record buyers, a perfect example being the third Shadows hit, 'FBI', which began with an intricate pattern played on the bottom three strings of the guitar, although not by Hank, but by Bruce Welch. 'Yes, Bruce plays that sort of little bass sound, and when we wrote it – and we did write it, despite what it may say on the record label – that was the basic feel from the rhythm guitar. I rather liked "FBI" because it got away from the acoustic sound we'd been having and the resulting rhythm guitar approach to a much more open, spacious sounding feel, where everything was quite clear.' The record also contains a pleasantly manic solo from Marvin ('I've never really been able to capture those manic days since then – I must have been high on EMI tea!'), which was just one facet of the highly-individual and instantly-recognisable Hank Marvin sound, which was produced, among other things, with the help of an echo device.

'I was first introduced to the echo box through Joe Brown, a fellow guitarist, who was doing one of those Jack Good TV shows in 1959. Joe took me to one side, and showed me this little box with a few knobs on the front, which he said was an echo box, and he gave me his Gibson and said "Play a few notes". I did, and there was this really great echo sound. I couldn't believe it, it was fantastic, and you could get that old rock'n'roll type echo. I'm not sure if we used it on "Saturday Dance", but it's definitely on "Apache". That sound happened accidentally really – it was the combination of the Fender Strat sound, the tremolo arm, the Vox amplifier which I had at the time and the echo box, and that sound, which people either love or hate, had arrived.'

The hits continued to mount up in 1961, the next two (the fourth and fifth for the group) being 'Frightened City' and 'Kon-Tiki'.

'"Frightened City" came from a film which starred a then quite young and totally unknown Sean Connery, and Norrie Paramor wrote the music for it. He felt it was a good piece of music, and we thought it was excellent and strong enough for a single, so we recorded it and it was another hit. "Kon-Tiki" was written by Michael Carr, who wrote "Man Of Mystery" and also "South Of The Border". Funnily enough, when "Kon-Tiki" was sent in as a demo, somebody told me that it was actually Joe Brown playing on it, but anyway, we liked it as soon as we heard it, and recorded it with a single in mind, and it got to number one.'

While it was obviously hits like 'Apache' and so on

which brought the Shadows to fame, a feeling existed among record-buyers of the time that in many cases, the Shadows provided something equally amusing and interesting on many of their B-sides, something which they shared with American acts like Buddy Holly and the Everly Brothers, neither of whom released anything remotely inferior as a B-side during their respective heydays. A couple of examples of the syndrome by the Shadows which stick in the memory are a straightforward instrumental, '36-24-36' (the flipside of 'Kon-Tiki') and 'Oh What A Lovely Tune', virtually a playlet with musical backing, which was the reverse of 'Guitar Tango', a top five hit in 1962.

'As far as "Oh What A Lovely Tune" goes, we have a bizarre sense of humour sometimes, and we'd try to get funny titles for our B-sides, and even for our A-sides if we'd written them, and now and again, we wanted to come up with something a little bit different. One day, we were fooling around when we were combining a writing session with rehearsing for a forthcoming session, and we were messing around with this silly piece of music which just appealed to all of us. Brian Bennett, our drummer, said something like "Oh, what a lovely tune", and we thought that would make a great title if we did the song as a novelty number. Which we did – we didn't think of it standing up as serious, although we felt we'd created a bit of atmosphere on it, this funny little song, almost like a Palm Court type thing, with Brian doing these odd interjections in this very suave voice.

'"36-24-36" was rather different, an attempt to do something in the nature of "Tequila", that hit by the Champs, but featuring this big bass riff that Jet played. Those things weren't just simple twelve-bar tunes with a solo – often, they were quite well thought out, or so we thought, and not simply vehicles for improvisation, although sometimes they may have appeared like that. We didn't record them with the feeling that they were trivial – they were valid pieces of music, and only inconsequential in the sense that because we never played most of them after they were recorded, they tend not to stick in our memories.'

For a guitar player who influenced innumerable younger players, it comes as a surprise to learn that Hank rarely practised his skill at this point in his career. 'The practice came from playing on stage and rehearsing for new numbers for records or stage shows, and I think that's why I didn't actually make much progress as a musician for quite a long time, because I was playing a lot of music over and over again and not practising. Many '60s musicians came up in an environment of the clubs, where two hour sets were played, particularly by the R&B bands, and that was a tremendous grounding for improving and improvising, but the sort of things we were doing were fairly limited, really. You can't improvise on "Apache" – if you do, the audience'll lynch you! Or "FBI" – you've got to do pretty much the same as the record. All right, on some of Cliff's numbers I could change the solos to a degree, but even then, I had to be careful because people would moan if it was too different from the record, write letters and ask why the solo had to be changed because it was great on the record, and that was what they had come to hear.

You have to be careful, otherwise you alienate the public, and they're the ones wot pay the rent!'

How then did Marvin see himself as a guitarist when the Shadows first became successful? 'I just felt that we were very lucky to have had the breaks we had. Obviously, we had a sound that was very appealing, otherwise people wouldn't buy the records, and we happened to be making the right records, but we also had a sound which had a very broad appeal and which stimulated and influenced a lot of other groups and copyists. And we had to be realistic about that – it was very flattering and made us feel good, but I still recognised my limitations as a guitar player. I wasn't as good as I'd have liked to be, but I didn't have the discipline to do much about it. Things were going along pretty well, we were writing a lot of successful songs, but there were only so many hours in a day, and there wasn't a lot of time left after the travelling, the writing and the recording to do what I should have been doing, which was practice.'

One important factor in the success of the Shadows, as Hank confirms, was their record producer Norrie Paramor. 'He was important because he had the wisdom to allow us to play the way we wanted, and to arrange all the music – we'd get together, Cliff and the Shads, and work out the new songs either that we'd written or that people had sent in, and we'd arrange them unless they came in with a particularly good arrangement. We'd arrange them, work the keys out ourselves and so on, and the first time Norrie would hear them would be in the studio. I think he felt that we had a raw feeling and an energy that he didn't want to inhibit in any way, so he let us get on with it – he felt that we were teenagers who knew best what we were trying to do because it came naturally to us. We just wanted to rock, and I think he felt that if he intruded too much musically, he might get in the way and iron out creases which should be left there, and I think he was quite correct there. Obviously if we were doing something a bit more complicated and there was a wrong note or chord somewhere, he'd suggest very tactfully that we could put a better one in – he'd just step in when he felt he could genuinely improve the music, but by and large, he just let us get on with it without allowing us a totally free rein. We were fairly disciplined in that we did about four tracks per session, and only once did he have to give us a talking to, and that was when we did "Dynamite", which in fact was a number one hit in Japan for about ten weeks, a monster.'

The first major change in the Shadows' line-up came during the autumn of 1961, when drummer Tony Meehan decided to leave the group, and was replaced by Brian Bennett.

'Tony leaving was traumatic for us to a degree, because we were just entering our second year of big success with record sales and everything going right for us in every area, and then one quarter of the group left. We were in a fortunate position, in that the public seemed to know us as individuals, which also helped our success – it was as if the group had four distinct personalities that were projecting to the audience in different ways, and the audience knew us all by name, even way before "Apache", when we were behind Cliff. I think that was all important, and we felt that one quarter of the group being removed might possibly have a bad effect on the group's popularity, although in the event, it didn't seem to . . . We knew Brian quite well, because we had played with him at the 2I's, and after that, Brian had been with Marty Wilde and also with Vince Taylor, although at the time we contacted Brian, he was working with Tommy Steele as Tommy's personal drummer, playing in the pit with an orchestra.'

Meehan's departure came soon after he had appeared in the first of the phenomenally successful series of films starring Cliff and the Shads, *The Young Ones*, although the film and its soundtrack LP did not emerge until several months after the change of drummer.

Despite their own great popularity, it seems possible that the Shadows might eventually have resented their position in Cliff Richard's shadow (pun unintentional), but Marvin emphatically denies it: 'We didn't resent it, because that's the way it was – we were five guys who were together a lot of the time, and we used to look upon ourselves as a five-man group. We knew that Cliff was a solo star and a big name and a big-selling recording artist, but at the same time, we worked together very closely and socially, and we felt we were a group, and that was the way Cliff looked at it too – he saw us as Cliff and the Shads. So there was never any bad feeling about the group being billed second to him. It was a bit like Fred Astaire and Ginger Rogers, or horses and carts – you go together.'

The third chart-topping single for the Shadows was probably, after 'Apache', the group's best remembered track, 'Wonderful Land', which remained at number one in Britain for no less than eight weeks.

'That was another Jerry Lordan composition, and one of which we thought very highly – it was very original, and different in that it had an unusual melody, an unusual chord sequence and the intervals were different. It was actually recorded when Tony was still in the group, and was then put in the can –we felt it was a potential single, but there seemed to be something missing, so we all thought about it, and then Norrie suggested overdubbing some strings. We had no objections, and when we heard what he'd done with the French horns and the strings, it really sounded wonderful, so we entitled it "Wonderful Land" as Jerry didn't have a title for it.'

One aspect of the track which separates it from many other Shadows' hits is Hank's string-deadening technique, which he achieved by touching the strings with the palm of his hand as he played them with his plectrum. 'That wasn't anything peculiar to me – it's a technique guitar players use. Les Paul used it on his old records, and country players often use it when they're damping the bass strings with the heel or the palm of their hand, and then picking the high strings open to get that damped bass effect. Bert Weedon uses it a lot too, but he gets it because he doesn't open his guitar case (laughs). It's a nice effect sometimes, and on that little piece of the melody, I used the echo – very cleverly, I thought at the time – with the damped effect to produce a nice sound behind the initial note of the guitar.'

A few months after Tony Meehan left the Shadows, bass player Jet Harris also decided to move on, and was replaced by a friend of Brian Bennett, Brian 'Licorice' Locking. 'Jet left in 1962, and of course he had quite a bit of record success, both alone, and particularly when he teamed up with Tony again, when they did things like "Diamonds" and "Scarlett O'Hara", both again written by our friend Jerry Lordan. Tony arranged those records, and I thought the arrangements were superb, and he also produced them. The difference between the Jet and Tony records and what they'd done in the Shadows was that Jet played six-string bass guitar playing the melody instead of the bass part, whereas in the Shadows, he'd been the bass guitarist playing bass and I'd played all the lead lines. He was actually playing the lead instrument, the six-string bass guitar, which has a slightly higher sound than a normal bass guitar, although in fact in terms of octaves, it reaches exactly the same. It just doesn't have the depth, and it's quite a good effect, and the public obviously thought so, because they bought a lot of their records.'

The arrival of Licorice Locking coincided with the Shadows gradually becoming those most heinous rock'n'roll criminals, family entertainers, although the two events may not have been connected. 'The change of direction wasn't conscious, just a gradual development of our talents, I think, due to the way the music scene was at the time – out-and-out rock-'n'roll wasn't doing very well at all, and the people who were lasting, or making it in a big way, were the ones who were developing from that. They might use rock'n'roll in their stage performances, as we'd done, and Cliff had done, but we were recording more melodic pieces of music. And we were attracting a wider audience, not just teenagers, but an older audience, almost a family audience. We'd always loved humour and been fans of the Goons and so on, and we used to stick a bit of humour into our act and fool around onstage. We didn't feel we were betraying rock'n'roll, because we were doing what we enjoyed, and why not? We still included rock'n'roll in our show, although not the Shadows so much as Cliff, because there weren't that many rock'n'roll instrumentals that we did, if you look back. Cliff still liked it, and we'd still keep putting rock'n'roll songs into his act, which gave us a little bit of rock'n'roll satisfaction – a little injection of it now and again keeps you going.'

After the success of 'Wonderful Land' came the first acoustic Shadows' single, 'Guitar Tango'. It was the only one of four singles by the group between March 1962 and March 1963 which failed to reach number one in the British chart. 'I even bought a flamenco guitar specially for that record, and I still have it. This was a piece of music sent to us by some French composer, and it had been recorded by a couple of artists as an LP track, but we just thought it had something, so we wanted to record it, and when we recorded it with the Spanish guitar, it seemed to work. In fact, we recorded it twice, first with Jet Harris, which wasn't very good – nothing to do with Jet, just the arrangement of it – and we re-recorded it with Licorice with a different routine and we felt that was a better version, a more commercial routine, and that was the one that was released as a single, and which became the hit. We were a little anxious about the outcome of that, because obviously it wasn't the accepted Shadows electric guitar sound – who knew it was the Shadows when hearing it for the first time? But I think it was a good piece of music and it sold very well, and most people seemed to applaud our courage, as they thought, in taking that step.'

Brian Locking, as it turned out, only stayed in the group for a comparatively brief period of eighteen months, leaving in October 1963. A potential replacement was John Paul Jones, who later found great fame as a member of Led Zeppelin, but at the time was passed over.

'John Paul was playing bass guitar with the Tony Meehan Band, and he also used to play keyboards as well, as he's apparently a very good organist. John Paul was a fine player, no doubt about it, but the others didn't feel that he was quite right for the band image-wise, so we were in a bit of a quandary because really the choice was between him and another person we'd seen working in a band called John Rostill and he got the gig, and poor old John Paul had to make do with Led Zeppelin, when he could have been playing ''Apache'' and doing all the steps! Brian Locking left because he had become a Jehovah's Witness while he was with the band. He'd been studying the Bible for some time before he joined us, and he made the decision to become a Jehovah's Witness and get baptised while he was with us. At that time, we were doing a tremendous amount of live work, which meant he could very rarely get to any meetings he wanted to attend, so he weighed up the decision and felt he had to leave and do something that would enable him to follow his beliefs more closely.

'All the bass players in the Shadows had totally different styles, which is interesting – Jet was a very driving, forceful player, Brian Locking not so driving or adventurous, but a very steady player, and then John Rostill, again quite driving and much more adventurous and much more of a virtuoso on the instrument, a very fine musician.'

One footnote to Brian Locking's time in the Shadows was that he seems to have influenced Marvin's own decision to become a Jehovah's Witness. 'The seeds, if you like, were planted by discussions I had with him, which made me look at the world and things in a different way, I think that probably started the ball rolling, although it was many years before I took it more seriously.'

The arrival on the scene of the Beatles in 1963 spelt the end for numerous acts, but curiously, the Shadows were less affected than many of their peers. 'Obviously, it must have affected us, but interestingly in the first year of so-called Beatlemania, 1963, we enjoyed one of our biggest record-selling years. Running concurrently with the success of the Beatles, we had ''Dance On'', ''Foot Tapper'', ''Atlantis'', ''Shindig'' and ''Geronimo'', two number ones, a number two and two top twenty hits during that year, so it was a big year for us, but clearly the Beatles were what everyone was waiting for. No one knew what form it would take, but the music scene after the early rock days had gone on to sweeter things, melody with a beat, and it was getting too

smooth, I think, and that included us and Cliff – we were starting to get too much the all-round entertainers – and along came a group who were very raw and had a raucous sound, but were writing great songs with good melodies. The whole music scene needed that injection of energy and vitality, and with these great songs, it was marvellous, a fantastic lift for the whole music business. To be honest, even if the Beatles hadn't come along I think we would have gradually lost ground on single record sales. It had to happen – I just couldn't see an instrumental group continuing year after year having the big hits we were having.'

This amounted to twenty consecutive big hits between July 1960 and August 1965, including five number ones. 'Yes, and we've had thirty-two top 50 hits altogether, and it's difficult for an instrumental group to sustain that kind of success. It's hard enough for a singer – the number of artists that have had that many hits can be counted on your fingers – so we recognised that at some point, things would change, but I don't think the Beatles necessarily hastened that end for us, I think that's just the way it would have gone anyway. We still had the odd big hit up to 1967, but by that time, we were in a situation where we decided to revert to being a vocal group, because that was the big thing, and we had a couple of hits with vocal records, which we enjoyed.'

Two of the last instrumental hits were particular favourites at the time when they were released, although the onset of Beatle-shaped success contrived to make them smaller hits than they perhaps deserved – 'The Rise And Fall Of Flingel Bunt' and 'Rhythm & Greens'.

'Both of those were made up in the studio. ''Flingel Bunt'' came up because of that opening riff which happened in the studio, and I suggested that we made a 12-bar type instrumental out of it. The time was right for that sort of instrumental, because R&B

Mid-1970s Shadows, Hank on the left

music, with the Rolling Stones and the Pretty Things, had become popular in 1964, and people were more attuned to that heavier type of 12-bar. Norrie felt it had potential as a single, and it was all done in one evening, from the concept to recording it, to the title, to being played to a couple of people who thought it was great. The title came about because we quite like titles with a bit of humour in them, or which make people think, or get them worried, and we'd seen a film called *The Rise And Fall Of Legs Diamond*, which was about a Chicago gangster, and we coupled that with the name Flingel Bunt, which comes from the actor Richard O'Sullivan, who's now a very famous TV actor. He was in a couple of the Cliff & the Shads films, and he used to have these two names of characters that he'd come out with, one of which was Flingel Bunt.'

This seems an appropriate point to list the films in which the Shadows appeared – *Expresso Bongo, The Young Ones, Summer Holiday, Wonderful Life* and *Finder's Keepers*, all of which starred Cliff Richard, plus *Rhythm & Greens*, a short film devoted solely to the Shadows.

'We were asked to do a half-hour comedy film about life on the beaches of Britain with four or five pieces of music, each supposed to be representing a period in history. So we wrote some things and recorded them, and the idea we had for the last piece, which was about life in the future, had people rocking on the beaches in their black leather kilts and dark glasses and all manner of weird things, like amplifiers with antennae on top, and we thought we'd do a send up of some of the rhythm & blues type things, with this 'yeah baby, ooh baby' sort of shout. We established what we'd do, which was just start and then play, just total improvisation with a few shouts thrown in, and then tacit at certain points, and a drum break. It was just complete improvisation, one take and that was it, and that was the atmosphere we wanted to create and capture, and we thought it might stand a chance of success, both because of the popularity of R&B and because it was a bit of a novelty record, a send-up, really. It was a top thirty hit, not as big as we'd have liked it to be, but let's face it – there was no melody there!'

The relationship between Cliff Richard and his trusty Shadows, like all good things, was eventually destined to come to an end. 'We stopped backing Cliff in October 1968, because we were doing a season of several weeks at the London Palladium and during that time Bruce decided to leave the Shadows. We were getting to a point where we'd all had enough of each other – we'd done such a lot of work together and been together so much socially that we felt the time had come for each of us to go out in different directions musically, perhaps, and be refreshed. At that point, the Shadows no longer existed as a group, so clearly we couldn't back Cliff any more.' In fact, singer and group did work together again, but their permanent relationship was terminated. For a 1969 Shadows LP, *Shades Of Rock*, keyboard player Alan Hawkshaw was recruited, and as well as helping to make the album, he also worked with Cliff and the Shadows on a Far Eastern tour which also spawned a live LP, *Live In Japan*, which Marvin describes as, 'awful – one of the worst

records that ever escaped from a record company.'

The next phase for Hank was a trio known as (Hank) Marvin, (Bruce) Welch, and (John) Farrar, which on paper looked to have every chance of being at least as successful as the Shadows, but in fact fell far short. 'I phoned Bruce and suggested that we write some songs together again, because we'd written well together previously, but not for some time, and perhaps we could write an album's worth of material and record it. He agreed, and he came up to Barnet in Hertfordshire where I lived at that time, and it was a lovely summer – we sat in the garden with our guitars and wrote virtually all the material for the first Marvin, Welch & Farrar album. I felt that to get the maximum potential we should have a third voice, because you can get far more interesting harmonies with three voices than with two, but we didn't really know anyone in Britain who might fit in, and then Bruce mentioned this guy John Farrar, whom he'd met in Australia and who had started playing because he liked the Shadows. We got on very well together, and went on holiday to Portugal to rehearse all the material, and John finished a couple of the songs which weren't complete. We recorded the album, got quite a lot of good acclaim from the press and from inside the business, but it didn't have the commercial success we'd hoped for. We carried on and did another album, then Bruce left due to personal difficulties with his love life with Olivia Newton-John, and we made another album called *Marvin & Farrar*, and then John left, and it was just Marvin!

'Then we got to the point where it was almost time to reform the Shadows. EMI, who'd been continually asking for the previous three or four years for some new Shadows recordings, asked us to do a new album. So we did a thing called *Rockin' With Curly Leads*, and included John Farrar as a member of the group. John Rostill had unfortunately died before this, and John Farrar and I were working together, and I didn't want to just ignore him while I did a Shads album. We were making a follow-up album when we were asked to represent Britain by way of a Paul Curtis song in the Eurovision Song Contest – clearly, they'd asked everybody else but nobody wanted to do it, and they'd got down to the letter 'S'! So we did it, got back together and did the contest, which was one of the things which prompted us to seriously reconsider reforming as the Shadows.'

The year when the Shadows were the British entry in the Eurovision Contest was 1975, and an associated LP, *Specs Appeal* (a pun on Marvin's trademark spectacles), was released. However, between the *Marvin & Farrar* LP, released in 1972, and *Specs Appeal* was a two-and-a-half-year period which Marvin spent in semi-retirement. 'I had a farm, and we lived in Devon, and I'm terrible when I get in places like that – I potter round, mending fences and chasing dogs who are savaging my sheep, that sort of thing, and I did a bit of songwriting. Once a month, John Farrar and I would play a club – we'd roar off to a cabaret club like Wakefield Theatre Club, Batley Variety Club or Lakeside Country Club, play for an hour and enjoy ourselves, get paid, try to write a few songs, and then I'd go back to the farm and potter again.'

This lack of activity was partially the result of the

poor public reception for the Marvin, Welch & Farrar and Marvin & Farrar projects. 'It was disappointing, because we felt that the material on those albums was good, and they were well recorded and well produced. We had more success in places like New Zealand and Holland, where they seemed to be less image-conscious, and could accept that we were trying to do something different, but in Britain, it was disappointing, particularly as we had so much response within the business, but that's the way life is, and you have to accept it and get on with something else.'

By 1977, the Shadows were back together, although perhaps not on a full-time basis, and recorded, in response to more requests from EMI, *Live At The Olympia* (a famous theatre in Paris).

'We'd done that *Live In Japan* album before, which as I said was awful for various reasons, whereas the one at the Olympia was much better. John Farrar was with us, and we did a few Marvin, Welch & Farrar songs, but mainly Shadows material, of course. After the Eurovision thing, we felt that we'd like to do a few concerts, and we did some here and some in France – it's a cheap way of making an album, because there's no studio time, and you just bang out a mobile and there's the show going on. I was very pleased with that album – I thought it was good, the singing and playing was good, and it was all live.'

1977 also saw the release of two further LPs involving Marvin, one the chart-topping *20 Golden Greats* by the Shadows, and the latter a solo LP, *The Hank Marvin Guitar Syndicate*.

'We were very surprised when we were approached by EMI for *20 Golden Greats*, and we wondered if they really knew what they were doing, but they'd just had a big success with the Beach Boys' *20 Golden Greats*, which I think was the first one they did, and the Beach Boys hadn't had the hits we'd had here. EMI had done market research, and they said the response was fantastic, and they had no doubt that it would be a number one hit album. So we said that if they felt that strongly – and they put up the money for TV promotion – who were we to argue? Even when they said that, we were still very pleasantly surprised when it got to number one, stayed there for six weeks, and sold a million and a quarter albums – it was marvellous, a great thrill.

'*The Hank Marvin Guitar Syndicate* was obviously different – the idea was to try to do a fairly modern version of something which had been done before, a guitar orchestra, really. We chose the material and had it arranged, and the band, all the ten guitarists, all played together, and it was live, except for my guitar parts, which were overdubbed because I was also producing. Also, I had to do some overdubs here and there when I found that the odd guitar was out of tune, and the more I heard it, the more it grated, so I had to replace it. Another thing I did now and again was double up on certain guitar parts by playing things an octave up, or slowing the tape machine down if I couldn't get an octave up any other way to give it real width. I'd double up their three parts and do three more parts, and then I'd put my lead parts on afterwards as overdubs, but all the guys in the band played it live. It was a tremendous experience,

A 1982 solo LP

and a real credit to their reading ability, to have all these parts stuck in front of them and read all the stuff off – you need a few rehearsals till you get more familiar with the music, like if I had some (note) bends written, I wanted them all to bend the same way, because there are different ways of bending, otherwise it sounds a bit messy. That's why it often sounds better when one guy does three parts himself, because he does it exactly the same, and it can be really tight. I was very pleased with the result of that album – it was aimed, really, at guitar players or people who are interested in guitar music, and I didn't really expect the general public to be too crazy about it.'

1977 was even busier for the Shadows, who embarked on a special British tour which was dubbed '20 Golden Dates' to reflect the title of their chart-topping LP.

'We had really felt like getting together again after the Eurovision thing, but then John Farrar decided to live in the States because of his connections with Olivia Newton-John – he was producing all her records, and she was living over there. So he left the group, which put back our plans, because we'd had plans for John being in the Shadows, which had to change. So everything was shelved, and then this business of *Golden Greats* came up, and because it was so successful, we reopened discussions about getting back together. We felt the least we could do for the fans was to do a tour and see how it went. It was so successful and we enjoyed it so much that we decided to stay together and do something similar every year, and off we went – we were back together and the ball was rolling again.'

By this time, of course, another personnel change had occurred – since John Farrar was no longer available, a new bass player had to be recruited in the shape of session musician Alan Jones. 'Alan's another of those guys who started playing because of the Shadows, and he was actually in a group that we

Hank, Brian and Bruce, 1981

knew years before, when he was at school, who won a Cliff and the Shadows lookalike competition. He's a tremendous player and one of the top session bass players, but he likes to do some live work now and again, so he works with us on all our live work and on our records. We use a keyboard player too – on the first of the recent tours, we used Francis Monkman, from Sky, but since then, we've used Cliff Hall, who's another great player.'

One personage who would appear to have been largely absent from Hank Marvin's story for most of the 1970s was Cliff Richard, although Cliff and the latterday Shadows were reunited for a season at the London Palladium in 1978, which also resulted in highly-successful live LP titled *Thank You Very Much.*

'I'd worked with Cliff on television quite a bit, and in the early '70s, John and myself went to Japan as Marvin & Farrar with Cliff, and we were part of his band – there was Alan Hawkshaw, Alan Tarney, Trevor Spencer and Brian Bennett as well as us, so we did play with Cliff, but under a different guise, not as the Shadows. So those two weeks at the Palladium were the first time we'd played with Cliff as the Shadows since 1968, and we didn't play with him again until the 1981 Royal Variety Show.'

In view of their somewhat contrasting religious beliefs (Cliff is a born-again Christian, and Hank a Jehovah's Witness), one wondered whether their separation was due to the virtual mutual exclusivity of their faiths. 'No, that doesn't enter into it. We've

had many discussions on that subject, but that isn't the reason at all why we rarely play together. Following the break-up, when there were no Shadows, Cliff was doing a lot of television, and he didn't need a live band, and when he did need live backing he used an orchestra, a big band, because some of his records at that time were orchestrated. When he started getting a band together, as I say, I was a member of it and we went abroad. And later on, when Bruce started producing Cliff, they used guys like Terry Britten and Alan Tarney and others on the sessions, and they were the basis of the live band that Cliff started to use when he began to revert towards the rock'n'roll scene with things like "Devil Woman". Cliff has his own band now, and I would never want to be touring as much as Cliff. I'm quite happy doing what we do, once a year – fine. Cliff hasn't got a family, he's off all over the place, but having a family and children, I wouldn't like to be away more than a couple of weeks at a time.'

More recently, the Shadows have begun to record tunes previously made famous by others, whereas at the start of their career, more than twenty years before, most Shadows recordings were of original material. According to Marvin, the change hasn't been as clear cut as it may appear. 'That cover version approach might not have worked for us twenty years ago – who can say? But as for something like "Don't Cry For Me Argentina", that was purely a stage number for us, which we did on tour in 1978 or whenever it was, and the audience response was absolutely fantastic, so that's why we recorded it, although we really didn't think it stood any chance of being a hit. "Cavatina", the theme from *The Deer Hunter*, again was a beautiful piece of music, and when we said we were going to release it as a follow-up, all the reps went mad, because they thought they had a possible hit on their hands, which they did. The one after that, "Riders In The Sky", came off our album called *A String Of Hits*. It was a slightly disco version, and again, it went very well on stage, and we just felt sure it had the potential to become a hit.'

As far as his preferred guitar goes, Hank Marvin will forever be associated with the Fender Stratocaster which has more or less become his trademark, and which he certainly has played for the majority of his twenty-five year plus career. However, there was a period during the 1960s when Marvin changed his allegiance.

'In 1963, we were doing a summer season at Blackpool, and we had a lot of trouble with the Strats we were using then – I wasn't using the original one, by the way, because that had been given back to Cliff, and we all had identically-coloured Fenders. Bruce and I had Strats, and Jet, and then Brian Locking, had a bass, but Bruce's guitar seemed to be awfully difficult to tune. We had a couple of new necks put on, but it seemed to make no difference, and we were informed by the importers, Vox, that there was a problem with the positioning of the frets, although I don't know whether or not that was true. Anyway, Bruce literally had a nervous breakdown because of this tuning problem, and towards the end of that summer, we approached Jimmy Burns with a view to seeing if he could make us guitars which would be the equivalent of a Stratocaster in terms of sound and vague appearance, but would have a good fingerboard and be in tune, and he came up with those original Burns-Marvin guitars, which was why we changed.

'I used those right up until 1970, I think it was, when I had five guitars stolen from a van, and by that time, my original Stratocaster had somehow come into Bruce's possession. After the robbery, I didn't have any guitars, so I borrowed that Strat and really enjoyed it, and used it for about six months. Then I bought another one, a black one, and gave the original one back to Bruce. I used the black one until 1980, when I bought a 1958 pink Stratocaster in Paris, which I've used on stage and on record ever since, and I've also got a Sunburst 1956 Stratocaster, which is actually the nicer of the two to play, although the pink one has a slightly warmer sound. They're both quite old, but age isn't necessarily a good thing in a guitar – it depends on how it's been treated and if it was a good one in the first place. The Sunburst one is in immaculate condition, it's really beautiful – some of the newer ones I've seen, the quality control hasn't been all it might have been, and I think that's the reason why some newer instruments aren't so good. Perhaps people took a bit more pride in the old days.'

There can be little doubt that Hank Marvin is comfortably placed financially and it would appear that, after a quarter of a century of being a star, there must be some special motivation in continuing to endure the pressures of rock stardom.

'The first thing is that we still enjoy it, apart from it being a source of income. The Shadows are now able to do concert tours as something we all enjoy – it's all very well recording and writing, but as a musician, one of the first motivations we had was actually playing in front of an audience, where you get an immediate feedback if you've done something good. If you're in the studio all the time, you're not going to get that, and it becomes a bit clinical, but with an audience, there's an atmosphere and an immediate response. Even if it's something you've played a thousand times before, like "Apache", you can still put something into it, because you know, as a performer, that the audience want to hear it and will enjoy it, because they haven't heard it a thousand times before, and we get something out of that, that buzz, that real feeling when the audience is really enjoying it, and it helps you when you play, and you put more into your music. So all that is enjoyable, and I think that stimulates us to want to record as a group, but we probably wouldn't have that motivation if we didn't do live work.'

One of the more bizarre episodes of the last few years also concerns the Shadows – after having recorded exclusively for EMI Records since 1958, it came as an enormous surprise to hear that in the early part of this decade, the group had signed with Polydor Records. The assumption was that EMI, for some unaccountable reason, had decided that the group were a luxury they could no longer afford. The truth was somewhat different . . .

'There was no problem about EMI renewing the contract. The problem lay in the fact that we had always been signed direct to EMI, which means that all the recordings we had made are owned by EMI, who can do what they like with them. There's another way of having a record contract, which is called a lease tape deal, where the artist is signed through a production company, and while it makes no difference to the records coming out and the

Still smiling – even after twenty-five years!

financial aspects, at the end of ten years, the tapes revert to the production company, which in our case is our own company. If the artist has had a great deal of success in those ten years, and the record company wants to release a *Greatest Hits* LP, the artist owns the tapes and can ask for an advance – if it's valid, the record company will do the deal, but at the end, the artist still owns the tapes. We felt that at our time of life, it was about time we owned our own tapes, and we approached EMI on that basis, but they had decided as company policy that they weren't going to do any more lease tape deals. Also, we only wanted to be with EMI for the UK and Holland, but they wouldn't have that – it was the whole world or nothing, so we couldn't reach any agreement, although we approached them several times to see if they'd changed their mind, but when they didn't, we talked with other companies. We felt that Polydor were offering us the best deal, so we went with them.'

In 1982, Hank Marvin remains the most familiar British rock guitarist there has ever been. He continues to record, both solo and with the Shadows, to great effect, and a final word concerns Marvin's alter ego, one Alec Galloway. 'He doesn't really exist, but what happened was that I once knew a person, who's now dead, a Scotsman called Alec Galloway. I just loved the name – it sounds like a Geordie name as well – and I mentioned it to Bruce, and during a promotional tour, which was for "20 Golden Greats", I think, we kept telling everybody that we were going to do an album with this non-existent Alec Galloway called *The Galloway Tapes*. We just had this idea that if we had time, we'd try to write some material, and do this album, but we never got around to it. This mystery singer . . . it wasn't a question of whether anyone would recognise me, it was just for the hell of doing it, doing something totally different. People wouldn't be limited to expecting it to be within a certain framework because it was me – if it was Alec Galloway, it could be anything really, couldn't it?' With all due respect, it seems unlikely that any appearance on record by Hank B. Marvin would be other than instantly recognisable, no matter what name was on the label – which is one of the main reasons for his inclusion in this book.

Hank B. Marvin Discography

	With the Shadows		
1961	*The Shadows*	1963	*When In Spain*
1962	*Out Of The Shadows*	1964	*Wonderful Life*
1963	*Shadows Greatest Hits*	1964	*Aladdin And His Wonderful Lamp*
1964	*Dance With The Shadows*	1965	*Cliff Richard*
1965	*Sound Of The Shadows*	1965	*More Hits By Cliff*
1965	*More Hits*	1965	*Love Is Forever*
1966	*Shadow Music*	1966	*Finders Keepers*
1967	*Jigsaw*	1967	*Cinderella*
1967	*From Hank, Bruce, Brian & John*	1968	*Established '58*
1969	*Somethin' Else*	1969	*Best Of Cliff*
1970	*Shades Of Rock*	1972	*Best Of Cliff Vol 2*
1970	*The Shadows*	1976	*The Cliff Richard Story*
1972	*Mustang*	1977	*40 Golden Greats*
1973	*Rockin' With Curly Leads*	1979	*Thank You Very Much*
1975	*Specs Appeal*	1981	*Love Songs*
1975	*Shadows Live At Paris Olympia*		
1976	*Rarities*		Marvin, Welch & Farrar
1977	*Tasty*	1971	*Marvin, Welch & Farrar*
1977	*20 Golden Greats*	1971	*Second Opinion*
1978	*Shadows At The Movies*		
1979	*String Of Hits*		Marvin & Farrar
1980	*Another String Of Hot Hits*	1973	*Marvin & Farrar*
1980	*Rock On With The Shadows*		
1980	*Change Of Address*		Solo LPs
1981	*Hits Right Up Your Street*	1969	*Hank Marvin*
1982	*Life In The Jungle/"Live" At Abbey Road*	1977	*Hank Marvin Guitar Syndicate*
		1982	*Words And Music*
	With Cliff Richard		
			Sessions
1959	*Cliff*	1976	*Evita* (original soundtrack)
1959	*Cliff Sings*	1977	*Roger Daltrey – One Of The Boys*
1960	*Me And My Shadows*	1979	*Paul McCartney – Back To The Egg*
1961	*Listen To Cliff*	1980	*Dennis Waterman – Waterman II*
1961	*21 Today*	1982	*B.E.F. – Music Of Quality and Distinction Volume I*
1962	*The Young Ones*		
1962	*32 Minutes and 17 Seconds With Cliff Richard*		
1963	*Summer Holiday*		
1963	*Cliff's Hit Album*		

ERIC CLAPTON

Out of the long list of potential candidates for this book, very few names were obvious and automatic choices, but one certainty for inclusion was Eric Clapton. It is very unfortunate therefore that we were unable to interview him. This happened despite an approach to his management about two years before our deadline, a time in which certain unforeseen and unavoidable circumstances prevented an interview taking place, which then culminated in our being informed by his manager that Eric could not be available for an interview due to contractual reasons. Nevertheless, his inclusion in this project was obligatory from our point of view – what follows is a profile of his history, compiled with as much care as possible, but without the benefit of his first-hand information.

Eric Clapton was born on 30 March 1945, in Ripley, Surrey. His childhood and early teenage years were of little account musically, and it was apparently not until 1961 that he first bought a guitar after hearing Chuck Berry records, Berry and Buddy Holly being his first musical heroes. This was during his period at art college, where he also began to listen to blues records by the likes of Muddy Waters, Big Bill Broonzy, Sonny Terry & Brownie McGhee and Sonny Boy Williamson. It seems that Eric took to the guitar immediately, becoming swiftly proficient on, so legend has it, a Hohner Kay, while there is an early reference to a group which purportedly included

Clapton, and who were known as the Muleskinners.

Describing himself as 'a blues aficionado with a guitar, attempting to sing', Eric recalled deputising for Mick Jagger as a singer at the celebrated Ealing Club (where most of the early British R&B bands of the pre-Beatles era played), before joining the Roosters, who could certainly claim seminal status, as the group had at one time included both Brian Jones, who moved on to the Rolling Stones, and Paul Jones (no relation, of course), later with Manfred Mann and currently with the Blues Band. The two Joneses had left the band by the time that Tom McGuinness, himself later in Manfred Mann and currently in the Blues Band, invited Clapton to join in January 1963, rescuing him from working on a building site, to which he had gravitated after being 'expelled' from art college, apparently on the basis that he had done too little work – no doubt he was concentrating more on his passion for music. During the middle of that year, the Yardbirds formed, and in October 1963, Clapton was invited to join after spending an abortive month (with McGuinness) as part of Casey Jones and the Engineers, whose leader was a Liverpudlian who had previously led a minor league Merseybeat band, Cass & the Casanovas.

Joining the Yardbirds was a significant step-up for Eric – the group followed the Rolling Stones into a residency at the Crawdaddy Club in Richmond where Eric soon became a guitar hero, earning the

Crew-cut Eric with the Yardbirds, mid-1960s. Left to right
(onstage): Paul Samwell-Smith, Keith Relf, Chris Dreja, Eric Clapton, Jim McCarty

epithet 'Slow hand'. This line-up of the Yardbirds (whose almost complete history can be pieced together in this book) was the first one to record, although the live LP, which was taped at the Craw-daddy with the band backing American bluesman Sonny Boy Williamson, did not appear for over two years, no doubt due to what was perceived as lack of commercial appeal.

However, Eric did participate in the group's first, and most commercially unsuccessful recordings, including their first three singles, an EP and the group's debut album, *Five Live Yardbirds*. This, as the title suggests, was recorded live at London's Marquee Club. The group's third single and first big hit, 'For Your Love', was the last on which Clapton appeared, and by the time of its release in March 1965, he had left the band – it is usually stated that this was because he felt that the Yardbirds had become too commercially oriented and were neglecting the blues, although others suggest that he left in a fit of pique when he was outvoted by the rest of the group concerning the choice of material for the third single, his being an Otis Redding song, while the band's was 'For Your Love'.

At this stage, Eric was said to have been very keen on the playing of B. B. King, although it is also reported that he broke many guitar strings in his efforts to emulate the master. . . . He also enjoyed the work of Freddie King, whom he also tried to copy, apparently being the only British guitarist of that era playing in Freddie King's style. On leaving the Yardbirds, he apparently stayed with a friend from the Roosters, piano player Ben Palmer, in Oxford, and nearly joined a group led by Mike O'Neill (formerly Nero of Nero & the Gladiators, and later a founder member of Heads, Hands & Feet with Albert Lee), before he was invited after two weeks of inactivity to join John Mayall's Bluesbreakers. Their ethnic credentials were more to Eric's liking as Mayall was then inflexibly committed to the blues. After eight-

een months with the Yardbirds, Eric should have been content to be playing with a successful blues band (the other members were John McVie, later of Fleetwood Mac, on bass, and Hughie Flint on drums, who went on to form McGuinness-Flint with Tom McGuinness), but after four months he suddenly decided to travel round the world with a group of friends, including Ben Palmer, none of whom were professional musicians. The jaunt ended in confusion after about three months – having got as far as Greece, the band began playing in a club, from which Eric eventually had to escape, returning home on the Orient Express.

Fortunately, Mayall was prepared to reinstate the errant guitarist in his band, and Eric remained with Mayall until mid-1966, placing the band on a higher plateau than that which they had previously enjoyed which was largely due to his mercurial guitar playing. Having gained a solid following as an excellent blues player with the Yardbirds, Clapton consolidated his reputation during the Mayall days, giving rise to one of the earliest and most celebrated examples of widespread wall graffiti, 'Clapton Is God'. With Mayall, he also made the first records which would begin to spread his reputation outside Britain, in particular the *Bluesbreakers* LP, whose sleeve shows Clapton reading a copy of the comic, the *Beano*. Still with Mayall, he recorded two further singles, one of which, 'I'm Your Witchdoctor'/'Telephone Blues', was produced by Jimmy Page. Page was also involved in an experimental jam session recorded apparently on a domestic tape recorder which was eventually released, much to the chagrin of those involved, on Immediate Records' 'Anthology Of British Blues', described at greater length in the chapter on Jimmy Page.

While Eric had been in Greece, a change of personnel had taken place among the Bluesbreakers with the temporary departure of John McVie who was replaced by Jack Bruce. By the time Eric returned, Bruce had joined Manfred Mann, but the end of Clapton's tenure with Mayall came when he was invited by Bruce and drummer Ginger Baker to form Cream, generally regarded as the first 'supergroup' (although perhaps not by the group's members themselves). Cream functioned between July 1966 and November 1968 with huge success, releasing three highly acclaimed albums during their existence, while at least another four (including two live LPs) were issued after their break-up. A measure of their success is that six of their first seven albums made the top 10 in Britain, and four made the top 5 in America, *Wheels Of Fire*, a double LP, topping the US charts in 1968, and *Goodbye Cream* achieving a similar position in Britain during 1969.

Cream disbanded at the peak of their popularity and Clapton and Baker went on to form yet another 'supergroup', Blind Faith, along with Stevie Winwood from Traffic, and the less well-known bass player Rick Grech, previously with Family. However, the pressures proved too much and after eleven months, during which the group recorded an LP, played an American tour and headlined a free concert in Hyde Park, Blind Faith dissolved. Winwood returned to Traffic and Baker and Grech remained together briefly in Baker's next band, Airforce.

Top: Blind Faith – left to right:
Steve Winwood, Rick Grech, Ginger Baker, Eric.
Right: Cream – Jack Bruce (left),
Ginger Baker (front) and Eric with their
military gear. Centre left: Bonnie (left) and
Delaney (centre) Bramlett with Eric (1969)
Below: Eric as Derek, leader of the Dominos

At the Rainbow Concert, 1973 – left to right: Ron Wood, Steve Winwood, Eric, Rick Grech

Clapton by this time had become much in demand as a journeyman guitarist – for instance he nominally fronted Powerhouse, a band assembled purely to record a few tracks for an Elektra Records compilation titled *What's Shakin'*. Powerhouse also included Bruce, Winwood, Ben Palmer and Paul Jones. Clapton had also been part of John Lennon's Plastic Ono Band which played at the Toronto Peace Festival in September 1969, by which time he was growing disenchanted with Blind Faith. Then, having become friendly with the support act on Blind Faith's American tour, the unwieldly but charismatic Delaney and Bonnie & Friends, Clapton guested with Delaney and Bonnie on their British tour. He was joined by a guitarist even more famous than he – at that time – George Harrison of the Beatles with whom Eric had become friendly in the late sixties when the two co-wrote a song on *Goodbye Cream* titled 'Badge' which was one of Cream's biggest hit singles, and on which Harrison also played. The tour took up the early part of 1970, and Clapton recorded his first solo album at that time with assistance from several of the Delaney and Bonnie band, including Leon Russell, Carl Radle and Bobby Whitlock, as well as Sonny Curtis and Jerry Allison from the Crickets, Buddy Holly's erstwhile group. The album was a reasonable success, making the top 20 in America and marking the first recordings by Clapton of 'After Midnight' and 'Blues Power', which became staples of his stage show. More importantly, it led to his next group, Derek and the Dominos, Eric being Derek, and the band being completed by Carl Radle on bass and Bobby Whitlock on keyboards from the Delaney and Bonnie band plus noted studio drummer Jim Gordon, who had also become part of the

'Friends'. Prior to making their own album, the group were used as a backing band by George Harrison for part of his remarkable *All Things Must Pass* triple album, which was produced by Phil Spector, and during the sessions for the album, Spector recorded with Derek and the Dominos, although only one track resulting from the collaboration, 'Tell The Truth', has ever been widely available.

The group then went to Florida, where Clapton was reunited with producer Tom Dowd, who had helped to supervise several of the Cream albums. The result was an excellent double LP, *Layla And Other Assorted Love Songs*, while the 'Layla' track itself ranks as one of the finest records on which Clapton has played. The song deals with unrequited love, ostensibly involving a Persian princess of folklore, but at the time Clapton himself was suffering a similar affliction, having fallen in love with George Harrison's wife, the former Patti Boyd. Aside from the obvious emotion contained in the track – falling in love with the wife of one of your best friends is never easy to handle – it became a musical tour-de-force due to the participation of American guitarist Duane Allman, whom Tom Dowd had introduced to Clapton.

While musically the Derek and the Dominos era was highly successful, the background to Eric Clapton's life was becoming more tragic by the day. He had become addicted to various drugs, notably heroin, in vain attempts to take his mind off his passion for Patti, and between 1971 and 1973/4, this addiction came close to bankrupting Eric, not to mention seriously endangering his life. He made occasional appearances, for example at the celebrated Concert For Bangla Desh organised by

Onstage with Yvonne Elliman, mid-1970s

Jeff Beck, John Cleese and Eric at the Amnesty International Concert, 1981

George Harrison, but it becomes obvious in retrospect that he came close to seeing both his career and his life end. Finally, of course, the drug habit was addressed and conquered by acupuncture treatment, this whole episode (along with other aspects of his life) being described in *Conversations With Eric Clapton* by Steve Turner (Abacus, 1976).

The years between the end of Cream in 1968 and his eventual return to health by 1974 must have been Eric Clapton's nadir – he rarely played his collection of guitars and was even reduced to selling his personal belongings to pay for more and more drugs, although Patti Harrison finally began to respond to his advances. The first steps towards a comeback came at the beginning of 1973, when Pete Townshend recruited an all-star band, including Stevie Winwood, Ron Wood, Rick Grech and himself, to back Eric at a special concert at London's Rainbow Theatre – the show was recorded and a record released towards the end of that year, but in truth is far from essential listening, although to judge the album on that level seems to be missing the point.

By the early months of 1974, Clapton, although seemingly not completely cured, was prevailed upon to try recording again. Returning to Miami, Florida, to the familiar control of producer Tom Dowd, a new band was formed from local musicians plus old friend Carl Radle and two of his associates, and a positive, if somewhat hesitant 'comeback' album, *461 Ocean Boulevard*, was cut, which included a substantial hit single, a version of Bob Marley's 'I Shot The Sheriff'. However, from this point on Clapton seemed reluctant to step out in front of a group of musicians as their leader, perhaps a throwback to his adopting the anonymous name of Derek and the Dominos for his band after the supergroup days with Cream and Blind Faith.

His confidence gradually began to return through the strength he felt from the musicians in the band, and Radle, drummer Jamie Oldaker and keyboard man Dick Sims remained with him until 1979 as the nucleus of a band which was joined and left by various other members, producing an album per year during the 1970s, including an excellent 1975 live LP, *E.C. Was Here*. This album contained a superb rearrangement of a traditional blues, 'Rambling On My Mind', in which Clapton shouts out key changes during an electrifying instrumental passage and is followed brilliantly by his band – Tom Dowd suggests that this stratagem was something which Clapton used to ensure that the rest of the band remained totally alert. The 1977 LP, *Slowhand*, was produced by Glyn Johns, and included a Clapton original of staggering quality, 'Wonderful Tonight', again addressed to Patti, who was now living with him, and who later became his wife.

During 1979, Eric recruited an entirely new band composed of British musicians who had been his peers, including guitarist Albert Lee (from Heads, Hands & Feet and Emmylou Harris's Hot Band), keyboard players Gary Brooker (ex-Procol Harum) and Chris Stainton (who came to fame working with Joe Cocker), and a rhythm section of Dave Markee on bass and Henry Spinetti on drums. With this new line-up, Clapton's confidence was boosted even further, and at the time of writing he continues to work with this most seasoned and experienced band, having cut another fine live double album, *Just One Night*, at the Budokan Theatre in Tokyo, as well as a further studio LP, *Another Ticket*.

1981 saw a hiatus in his career, caused by a stay in hospital due to the combined effects of a car accident in America and an ulcer, but 1982 has seen a return to health and a recording contract with Warner Brothers.

Slowhand

Apart from the main body of his work, as partially described above, Eric Clapton has been in almost constant demand to add his talent, although not always as a guitarist, to records made by others. During his early years, most of his 'guest performances' were on blues records, although one unlikely 1967 appearance was on *We're Only In It For The Money* by Frank Zappa's group, the Mothers Of Invention, and 1968 saw a cameo appearance on Aretha Franklin's *Lady Soul* LP. Among the 1969 sessions were the double 'white' LP by the Beatles, Eric playing the featured guitar part on George Harrison's 'While My Guitar Gently Weeps', on Jackie Lomax's *Is This What You Want?* album and on Billy Preston's *That's The Way God Planned It*. In 1970 he worked on the debut LPs of Stephen Stills and Leon Russell. 1971 saw a reunion with John Mayall for the latter's *Back To The Roots* LP, and work with Dr John and Yoko Ono (on her *Fly* LP). Further Beatle involvements came in 1972 when Eric appeared on John Lennon and Yoko's *Some Time In New York City*, and he also contributed, both as musician and as co-producer (with Tom Dowd), to an album featuring two black blues players, *Buddy Guy And Junior Wells Play The Blues*. In 1973 came a similar exercise, when Howlin' Wolf cut an album in London backed by assorted British stars who were his fans, although Eric was not involved in its production. He also attempted to revive the career of another early hero, Freddie King, in 1974. More recently, the number of sessions on which Eric has been prevailed upon to play has diminished, although he appears to

have contributed to at least one significant album (other than his own) each year, 1976's example being *Rotogravure* by Ringo Starr, and 1977's *Rough Mix*, the album on which Pete Townshend and Ronnie Lane collaborated. 1978 saw the release of two separate but special projects – *The Last Waltz*, a triple live album by The Band, whose final concert together saw a galaxy of stars, including Eric, making guest appearances, and *White Mansions*, an ambitious concept conceived by Paul Kennerly, and also including numerous guest artists. In 1979, the entire Clapton band of the time backed singer/songwriter Marc Benno (a sometime associate of Leon Russell), Eric and Albert Lee having previously (in 1976) appeared together on Joe Cocker's *Stingray* LP. A 1980s highlight was the first recorded appearance together of Clapton and Jeff Beck in the Amnesty International Benefit Concert known as 'The Secret Policeman's Other Ball'. Apart from appearing in such musical films as *Concert For Bangla Desh* and *The Last Waltz*, Eric played the part of the preacher in Ken Russell's bizarre film of Pete Townshend's *Tommy*. His apparent preference in guitars is for the Fender Stratocaster, which he is seen playing on the sleeve of *Slowhand*. We hope we may be forgiven for wondering why he apparently supports West Bromwich Albion Football Club. . . .

Eric Clapton Discography

With The Yardbirds
1965 *Sonny Boy Williamson with the Yardbirds* (recorded '63/4)
1964 *Five Live Yardbirds*

Yardbirds Compilations
1971 *Remember . . .*
1976 *The Yardbirds featuring Eric Clapton*
1977 *Shapes Of Things*
1982 *The Single Hits*
(the above albums were UK releases)
? *Greatest Hits*
1977 *Yardbirds Favourites*
(the above albums were US releases)

With John Mayall
1965 *Bluesbreakers*
Tracks recorded during this era also appear on
1969 *Anthology Of British Blues Volumes 1 & 2*
1978 *Blues Roots: British R&B*
1970 *The World Of John Mayall*
1971 *The World Of John Mayall Vol. 2*
1978 *Blues Roots: John Mayall*
1969 *Looking Back* (John Mayall)
1974 *Hard Up Heroes*
1967 *Raw Blues*
1966 *From New Orleans To Chicago* (Champion Jack Dupree)
1969 *The Blues World Of Eric Clapton*
1981 *Steppin' Out* (Eric Clapton)
N.B. Only the last two albums in this section feature Eric Clapton on every track

With Cream
1966 *Fresh Cream* (reissued as 'Full Cream')

1967 *Disraeli Gears*
1968 *Wheels Of Fire*
1969 *Goodbye*
1969 *Best Of Cream*
1970 *Live Cream*
1972 *Live Cream Vol. 2*
1973 *Heavy Cream*

Blind Faith
1969 *Blind Faith*

With Delaney and Bonnie & Friends
1970 *Delaney and Bonnie On Tour With Eric Clapton*

Derek and the Dominos
1970 *Layla And Other Assorted Love Songs*
1973 *In Concert*

Solo Albums
1970 *Eric Clapton*
1973 *Eric Clapton's Rainbow Concert*
1974 *461 Ocean Boulevard*
1975 *There's One In Every Crowd*
1975 *E.C. Was Here*
1976 *No Reason To Cry*
1977 *Slowhand*
1978 *Backless*
1980 *Just One Night*
1981 *Another Ticket*

Eric Clapton Compilation Albums
1972 *History Of Eric Clapton*
1973 *At His Best*
1982 *Time Pieces – the Best of Eric Clapton*

Sessions/Guest Appearances
For the sake of brevity, this list will merely give details of artist and title. The Band – *The Last Waltz*; Beatles – *The Beatles*; Marc Benno – *Lost In Austin*; Stephen Bishop – *Careless*; Joe Cocker – *Stingray*; King Curtis – *Get Ready*; Rick Danko – *Rick Danko*; Jesse Ed Davis – *Jesse Ed Davis*; Dr John – *The Sun Moon & Herbs*; Kinky Friedman – *Lasso From El Paso*; Buddy Guy & Junior Wells – *Play The Blues*; George Harrison – *Wonderwall, All Things Must Pass, Dark Horse, George Harrison*; Howlin' Wolf – *London Sessions*; Freddie King – *Burglar, Best Of Freddie King*; John Lennon – *Live Peace In Toronto, Some Time In New York City*; Jackie Lomax – *Is This What You Want?*; John Mayall – *Back To The Roots*; Mothers Of Invention – *We're Only In It For The Money*; Yoko Ono – *Fly*; Billy Preston – *That's The Way God Planned It*; Leon Russell – *Leon Russell*; Ringo Starr – *Rotogravure*; Stephen Stills – *Stephen Stills, 2*; Pete Townshend/Ronnie Lane – *Rough Mix*; Doris Troy – *Ain't That Cute*; Martha Velez – *Fiends & Angels*; Bobby Whitlock – *Bobby Whitlock, Raw Velvet*. Various Artists – *Music From Free Creek, Concert For Bangla Desh, What's Shakin'* (as Eric Clapton & the Powerhouse), *Tommy* (Original soundtrack), *White Mansions, The Secret Policeman's Other Ball*.

Despite its length, this list is probably incomplete, although it is believed to be accurate as far as it goes.

JEFF BECK

An American journalist once described Jeff Beck
as having an oversized heart and soul, which
elevates him above most other guitarists and compared him in the practice of his art in the same
league as Beethoven, Shakespeare, Da Vinci and
Chaplin. While such comparisons may seem over-
blown, and certainly Jeff himself would probably feel
that way, his guitar playing on an inspired day is
superior to that of any of his peers in this book.

Jeff was born on 24 June 1944, in Wallington, Surrey, where as a ten-year-old he sung in a church
choir. During the second half of the 1950s, he
acquired his first guitar – 'I borrowed if for an indefi
nite period of time, and when I'd got through the
strings that were on it by breaking them, and didn't
have the ten shillings to buy a new set, I restrung it
with some piano wire which I also used for flying a
model aeroplane. I had loads of the stuff, but of
course, all the strings were the same thickness,
which accounts for some of my tempers on the instrument since, about not being able to get a decent
sound . . . I think the first thing I learnt was the intro
to ''That'll Be The Day'', which sounded to me a bit
like a Winnie Atwell honky tonk piano phrase, and I
thought ''If I can do this, I'll be the King'', so I spent
about two or three days learning that intro, and that
was really where I started. As soon as I got hold of a
proper guitar, I waited for a couple of people to listen
to see if they recognised what I was playing, and
they said ''Hey, you can play!'', but that was all I
could do.'

Subsequently, Beck attempted on several occasions to build himself a guitar, although early results
were not conspicuously successful. 'The first one was
a cigar box, which probably took an afternoon to
make and failed miserably, but there must have been
some ingrained desire to make a guitar, because I
tried several times – I'd sussed out in my mind how to
make it without any plans, and I went to buy some
wood, which was about half-an-inch thick plywood,
so the front and the belly and the back were all half-
inch ply, making a total weight equivalent to about
six electric guitars. I just did it from a scaled up picture in my mind of how it should look, so it was about
fourteen feet long and ridiculously out of proportion,
but it was a start. It was a good thing to get hold of,
and wield about, and that's where it all started really,
with that one guitar – I used to prop it up in an arm-
chair, and just look at it more than play it, because I
loved the way guitars looked.

'The first date I ever played was at a fairground,
after I'd refused to play on the back of a float that was
part of something like a May Day parade – even then
I wanted things my own way, and I wanted an audience, so I teamed up with this other guy, who sang
Be Bop-A-Lula or something, and I just played a few
notes in the background. Believe it or not, people
were starting to talk about that one gig a couple of
weeks later – we thought it was terrible, and it was,
but there weren't many people doing that sort of
thing then, which was when I was about fourteen, I
think.'

By 1958, Jeff had acquired his early musical
influences, which he describes as 'All the greats who
still hold up to be the greats in my eyes – Buddy
Holly, Eddie Cochran, Gene Vincent, and it became
more Gene Vincent than anything because my sister
bought his album called *Gene Vincent & The Blue
Caps*, and from that point it was all over for my
schooling. I was much more into him than Elvis – the
talk at school was of this hip swivelling guy, and I
wasn't really interested in that kind of thing, I only
wanted to hear a guitar, so I had to wait awhile
before I got into Scotty Moore's playing because he
was associated with Presley. But with Vincent,
nobody knew anything about him, and all I could
hear was this raucous screaming electric guitar
which was on all the records, and there'd be three
guitar solos on some tracks, which was something
that I really loved, so I started copying all Cliff Gallup's licks. Chuck Berry came along a bit later.
''Sweet Little Sixteen'' was what got me going on
him – it was just the driving music, not so much the
separate guitar playing but the block sound that
Chuck Berry made that made me jump up and down.
And I was heavily influenced by James Burton with
Ricky Nelson – I used to put the needle back again
and again, slow it down a few times, and hear it
backwards and forwards and every way, just to learn
all the different ways it could be done, which is really
a good way of learning. After ''That'll Be The Day'',

the first solos I learnt note perfect were "My Babe" and "It's Late", which Burton played for Ricky Nelson, and "Twenty Flight Rock" by Eddie Cochran, which were all killers – short, but mind-blowing.'

On leaving school Jeff Beck managed to gain acceptance to Wimbledon Art College. It was there that he first met another notable young British guitarist, whose career would run somewhat parallel to his own – Jimmy Page. 'I was well into guitars at Wimbledon, and Pagey's name was being bandied around my house a lot, because my sister went to Epsom, where he went, and she kept telling me I should meet this guy – "You gotta see Jimmy, this weird thin guy playing a weird shaped guitar like yours". She was laughing at me all the time I was the only one, but as soon as she saw someone else, she urged me to meet him. We went over on the bus to see him, and he just knocked me out straight away, because he was far more into it than I was.'

Little has previously been recorded about how Jeff Beck spent his time between leaving Art College and joining a London R&B band called The Tridents, but Jeff was eager to deny the suggestion that he had never worked at anything but music. 'No, I was painting and decorating just to make a bit of money and pay for guitars and things after Art College, and then I drove a tractor on a golf course. That was so boring, and after thinking about what I could do, I somehow got back into paint again, spraying cars, and I also learnt a little about panel work as well as spraying, until I got really bored with that too. I was getting as good a finish as a guy who'd been there forty years, and I was getting twenty pence an hour while he was getting forty.' This particular apprenticeship was something which Jeff found very useful in later years, as much of his spare-time is spent renovating vintage American cars with a love bordering on the obsessive.

Prior to the Tridents, one of Jeff's early groups, in 1959/60 to the best of his recollection, was the Deltones. 'That was the hot item around our way. I used to see this van with "Deltones" written on it, and I loved the name, and they also had pink jackets, which I thought was great. Then I was asked to go down to see them, and this guy called Ian Duncan, who was fabulous, was leaving them, and I thought "My God, how am I going to fill his shoes?" He said "Look, I'll bugger off for a cup of tea, so you have a play and see how you get on", and from that moment on, I realised there was a job for me there, because I was playing the solos off pat, but that was what they wanted, solos like the record. If they'd asked what else I could play, I'd have been finished. . . . So I was knocked out, skipping home, and they said "You're playing at Putney Ballroom". It was great – you never forget moments like that, turning up in a Dormobile and getting all the gear out.

'I suppose I was in the Deltones for about a year, and afterwards there was a gap in the early sixties when nothing much was happening, because a lot of soppy pop records were coming out, and nobody wanted to be a part of that. No heavy rock band of those days wanted to copy records by Johnny Tillotson and Fabian and all that kind of crap – there was just no position for a guitarist like me, no way I could get off on it. And then there was the Twist, which

screwed me up for a while – I couldn't stand it. Then Chuck Berry came back with a few records and things looked good again, but then there was another big gap before R&B started to come on big, and Eel Pie Island started to happen, and I was asked to join a band called the Roosters.' Eel Pie Island is indeed an island, situated in the middle of the River Thames at Twickenham and in the early 1960s it became a centre for the burgeoning rhythm & blues movement, whose exponents would play in a vast barn surrounded by numerous bars which sold more varieties of beer than any of its patrons had ever seen. 'Although I considered it seriously, I finally blew the Roosters out. And then I had a request to play with John Mayall, but I didn't know anything about him. I was in a guitar shop in Charing Cross Road when I heard his name mentioned, and I asked who he was, and whether he was any good, and one of the guitar salesmen was saying "He's the guvnor, you'd better see him", but I never did get around to it, because I was still only fifteen or sixteen, I think, which is a bit young to be hanging around clubs. I carried on with this group called the Tridents, who were really my scene, because they were playing flat out R&B, like Jimmy Reed stuff, and we supercharged it all up and made it really rocky. I got off on that, even though it was only twelve bar blues.

'I made my first record with the Tridents, a demo – an agent got interested in us, so we were all hanging around his office waiting for lots of money, which never came, so he said "Let's make a record", and we were over the moon about making that first demo. I couldn't believe it when I heard it back – it sounded really great to me, and I thought "That's it! We've done it!", and of course the demo probably never went any further than his office. I can't really remember what the songs were, but I think one was like a half-assed blues thing with the words changed, which wasn't a very good thing to put out, and the B side was just us jamming.'

The part of Jeff's career between 1962 and 1965 is one which he finds difficult to recall with any accuracy – mention of a minor hit by a group known as the Mighty Avengers, on which he is supposed to have played, provokes denials. 'I used to do these weirdo sessions for Jim Page at a time when he was trying to muscle in on the production thing, and whenever he thought there was a suitable place for me to play, he rowed me in. I never really knew what was released.'

This explains a pair of double albums which have been repackaged many times in various forms, but were originally titled *Anthology Of British Blues Volumes I & II* on the Immediate label, for whom Jimmy Page was working as a producer, and from time to time would invite his friends to jam sessions, which would be recorded, albeit in a rather primitive manner. The participants were all somewhat surprised when these long-forgotten sessions appeared under credits which gave the impression that they were properly recorded. It is of interest to note some of the names that appear on the albums – Beck, Page, Eric Clapton, Nicky Hopkins, Jon Lord (Deep Purple), Albert Lee, Chris Farlowe, and various early members of Fleetwood Mac, few of whom can have been terribly pleased by their release. Much the

Yardbirds, mid-1960s.
Left to right: Chris Dreja, Jeff Beck, Jim McCarty, Keith Relf, Paul Samwell-Smith

same is true in Jeff's case of his appearance on an album titled 'Lord Sutch And Heavy Friends', again produced by Page, who, along with Beck, is one of the 'friends'. 'I was a fan of Sutch's band before I was a performer really, and I used to go to Wallington public hall and skulk around watching what was going on. I loved Lord Sutch's act – it was fabulous. But when that record came out with me on it, I was surprised and annoyed, although I don't know why, because I volunteered and I must have known what I was doing – when you're that age, you do anything and everything just to try to get on. I vaguely remember recording it, in some sleazy studio up a side alley.'

Rhythm & blues has been mentioned several times in general terms, but it was interesting to discover precisely what first turned Beck's head in the direction of that music, as opposed to straightforward rock'n'roll. 'The thing that shook me was an EP by Muddy Waters, which was taken from an album – the story goes that Earl Hooker was a slide guitarist based in Chicago, who had a crack at putting his own record out. He cut four sides, and because they didn't sell, Marshall Chess, who ran the record company, called the copies back and had Muddy Waters overdub some vocals on them, so you hear this huge voice with a guitar playing the same melody behind. One of the tracks was 'You Shook Me', which both Led Zeppelin and I ripped off and did it on our first

albums. That was one of the first records that got me going on the blues thing, and another was 'I'm A Kingbee' by Slim Harpo, and that kind of thing was exactly what we were doing with the Tridents. We were very popular around the Richmond area – we used to fill Eel Pie Island with about 800 people on a Sunday night. Then I dropped the rest of the group right in it, by leaving after I was invited to join the Yardbirds. Why I did it, I'll never know, because the Yardbirds didn't mean anything to me – as far as I was concerned, it was like joining another Tridents, and I think the real reason I did what I did was because the Yardbirds appeared to have good management, and seemed to be going places. It was the sort of story that was probably going on all over the place, groups splitting up and people hopping off.'

In fact, one item which may have swayed Jeff to join the Yardbirds was that the group had not only released a couple of records, but were on the verge of scoring a hit. 'That's right, I remember coming over the bridge of Eel Pie, and there was an old woman with a hot dog stand who had a crummy little transistor radio on, and as we got near, I was told that what I could hear was "Good Morning Little Schoolgirl" by the Yardbirds, who I'd just agreed to join, so I had to stifle my reaction.' Jeff became a Yardbird in March 1965, apparently at the recommendation of Jimmy Page, who had been offered the job himself, but declined.

Joining a band with an already established repertoire, and especially a band where you are replacing Eric Clapton, has to be one of the most intimidating experiences imaginable. 'Yeah, I didn't know what to do. I had to learn about fifteen bloody songs in four days because they had such tight schedules and I was quite frightened, to put it politely, because I knew I'd need to be on my mettle. It was a do or die thing really, but I played ''Beck's Boogie'' and got a ten minute ovation for it, so that was great, and it just nailed it all together for me. They had just released ''For Your Love'', and we used to rehearse at the Marquee and play there as well. One morning, Bill Relf, Keith's father (Keith Relf was lead singer of the Yardbirds) came in and said the group was in the charts. Great – it wasn't me on the record, but what the hell? The next thing I knew, I was on planes all over the place, going here and there, filming this, that and the other, ''Top Of The Pops''.'

Jeff's early impression that his position in the Yardbirds was not especially secure is confirmed by other reports which suggest that it was not until he made a special contribution during the recording of the group's follow-up single to ''For Your Love'', ''Heart Full Of Soul'', that he was accepted as permanent. An Indian sitar player had been specially flown in to play on the record by Yardbirds' manager, Giorgio Gomelski – 'That's right – Ravi Shankar was coming over a lot and doing concerts, and all the people who had ever dabbled in sitar came out of the wood, out of their little bed-sitters, and these two guys who looked like they'd come out of a seedy Indian market started playing a riff. I was late for the session, of course, and they'd already muscled in on the sitar and tablas, so I thought maybe I'd got the boot and these two guys were going to join. But they couldn't get the timing. They just couldn't play that riff in four, and they were going all over the place. The tabla player was a joke, and he couldn't play, so I said ''Giorgio, why don't you just let me play it?'', and I got the old fuzz box out with my (Fender) Esquire. I played on middle G, and on the octave as well, two notes together, and it sounded better than the sitar because it was more conducive to the record, so the poor guys were told to go away. From then on, I started getting interested in inventing things, getting by using a guitar instead of somebody else doing something.'

The mention of the Fender Esquire provoked a story about the way Jeff acquired the instrument – having previously played a Fender Telecaster, he purchased the Esquire from John Walker of the Walker Brothers.

'We did a UK tour – the Yardbirds, the Walker Brothers and Manfred Mann, and we were all so keen, with everybody watching each other's act. It was really good in those days, no snobbery at all unless somebody played up – the first two or three nights of a new tour was all ''Have you heard what they're doing?'', and it was great and so competitive, and I couldn't believe these Americans. The closest I'd come to America was this American, John Walker, playing my favourite guitar, the Esquire, and after the tour, I told him I'd like a guitar like his. He said I could buy his for £70, and he ripped me off, because it wasn't worth it – it had been battered

about, and he'd shaved the back off to make it a contour body like the Strat, but I bought it anyway, and used it right through my time with the Yardbirds. Fender, you see, used to cater for poor student types and make an economy model of everything, and this was the economy Telecaster, with one pick up fixed in by the bridge, so there was very little tonal quality variation. It had a great rock sound, but you couldn't really get a jazzy rhythm out of it because of the positioning of the pick up. It was just a chunk of wood with a neck on it, really, but a great shape that still looks good even now. Same with the Strat – those two guitars are the definitive rock guitars.'

The Yardbirds, although they were never rated particularly highly in Britain, have become one of the most well-respected British groups of the 1960s, largely because the group was connected at various times with such a trio of guitarists as Beck, Clapton and Jimmy Page, but also as a result of the early machinations of Giorgio Gomelski, the group's first manager. 'Giorgio wanted to see something exciting coming out of just blues – progressive blues would be the word, I think – and just good blues based pop records coming out. If you think about it, that Gregorian chant, ''Still I'm Sad'', has a blues lilt to it, even though it was a Greek Gregorian chant, I believe. He was into anything that was bizarre and passable as a pop record, which I agreed with all the way, because it's so much more fun to be part of something new and exciting, than merely good at something millions of people can do well.'

Beck was only rarely on especially amicable terms with the other members of the group, as he and they appeared to have different priorities. 'In the end I became alienated from them because of the way the records were produced. I'd just sit around and be moody and play the most godawful row over what they'd done, and somehow it worked.

'There were a few things that were supposed to be my projects, like ''The Nazz Are Blue'', which I sang on, and ''Beck's Bolero'' – to keep me quiet, they said ''Right, if you promise to play and do what you're told in this band, we'll let you have some studio time, and maybe, who knows, you could put this track together with that and have your own album'', and I thought ''Oh, great''. Those tracks were just that – the ''Bolero'' was towards my own album, and I had to sing ''The Nazz'' because they said it couldn't all be instrumental.'

The Yardbirds, and in particular, Beck, were pioneers in several ways – apart from including a feeding back guitar on a track titled ''What Do You Want'', Jeff would also play the solo in ''I'm A Man'' one-handed and behind his head. 'We were using feedback all the time. You had no choice, because the amplifiers would feed back anyway, but to use it was a good way of getting out of it. It would start whistling and singing, then you found that you could probably handle it, and make quite an interesting trumpeting noise with it, and with an echo, all sorts of mysteries started to happen and it would sound really bizarre. Playing one-handed behind my head was something I used to do every night, just to show off. It's quite easy, or at least it's easy to play that badly, and it's a little trick you can pull off that looks amazing and that's half the theatrics of it.'

Analysing the above, it would appear that Jeff regarded the studio as a necessary evil which sometimes prevented him from playing live, although two occasions on which the studio may have seemed more appealing occurred when the Yardbirds recorded at both the legendary Sun studio in Memphis, where Elvis Presley had started recording, and the Chess studio in Chicago, where the likes of Muddy Waters and Chuck Berry worked.

'Obviously, touring and the live thing was what I wanted to do, and I'd get out of the studio and do all the things I'd been hemmed in from doing before, but it's still the same now – if things go really well in the studio, and you know that something you really like is going on tape, it's a good feeling, and if it's not like that, it's terrible. At Chess, of course, everything was a mindblower for me – everything I wanted was happening, and being in the studio where the actual big men had been was just too much to handle.

'It was hard selling the idea of a white English progressive blues/rock band to a hardened Chicago producer and engineer, but as soon as we cranked up, they realised they'd better sit up and listen – if you listen to the bass drum on 'Shapes Of Things' and 'I'm A Man', that is serious, and I don't think there's a disco that could handle the bass drum on those tracks, because it would just blow the speakers to smithereens.

'Sun was another mindblower – there I was, in Sam Phillips' studio wandering round in a dream, because you have this strong imagination when you want something really badly. I'd been thinking since I was ten that I'd never get to America, and then all of a sudden I was there, and wanted to do everything at once. But it was a great experience.

'We did "Train Kept A-Rollin'" there, and he couldn't believe that these spotty-faced oiks from England were doing one of his favourite songs. He taught me a lot, just in the two or three days we were there – he said, "You don't have to be powerful, because I'll make you powerful, so just play, and don't worry about how loud you are. Just play as loud as I tell you and freak out, do what you want, because I'll make you sound big". And boy, when he played some of those tracks back, I just couldn't believe the sound that was coming out.'

By June 1966, the Yardbirds were definitely thriving, having scored five top ten singles in Britain. Bass guitarist Paul Samwell-Smith then decided to leave the band for a career in record production at which, incidentally, he was fairly successful for some time. To avert the potential crisis, it was Jeff's idea to draft in Jimmy Page as a replacement.

'I suddenly realised that one of the key figures in the Yardbirds' sound was going to leave, and that left us with quite a problem on our hands. I really didn't want the group to fold, because I loved America and wanted to tour there more, and I thought about who we could get – I decided to start with the big boys, and thought of Jimmy straight away. Not only did he have a good reputation, he also looked pretty good and fitted in perfectly, and he was a good friend, which was a bonus. The original idea was for him to replace Samwell-Smith on bass, but we all knew it wouldn't be too long before Chris (Dreja) was taken off rhythm guitar and put on bass, and when that

A rare picture of the Yardbirds'
twin guitar line up – left to right: Jimmy Page, Chris Dreja, Jeff Beck, Keith Relf, Jim McCarty

happened, Jimmy took over on rhythm, and eventually on dual lead.'

The period during which both Beck and Page played together in the Yardbirds was to be brief, five months to be precise. It was during this time that the Yardbirds appeared in a somewhat celebrated film of the "swinging sixties", Antonioni's *Blow Up*, in which Jeff destroyed a guitar in a bloodcurdling manner. 'They wanted me to break a vintage Les Paul '54 gold top, and I said "On your bike! Can't you use another guitar?", and he eventually said that would be OK, provided it was exactly identical – he was a real stickler for that, and for one film, he painted the bloody desert red, used about five million gallons of paint and sprayed it. Finally we agreed, and I said I'd do it provided I could smash up someone else's guitar, and all the time I was feeling that they should have got Townshend to do it, even perhaps with the Yardbirds, but in the end I thought that I couldn't really afford to turn the money down, and I just merrily smashed away for a couple of days, and destroyed five or six guitars. It was great, they had this representative from Vox or Hofner down, and he brought this bloody great tea chest full of crappy guitars all wrapped up in cellophane, ready for the shop window display, and after we had a take that was accepted, he said "Great, eh?" and I said "Well, I'm smashing your guitars up", and he said "Yeah, but it sounds great". He was all for it – only a British guy could be over the moon about their guitars being smashed instead of played.

'The song we played in the film was called "Stroll On", although it was actually our version of "Train Kept A-Rollin'", and that was what I wanted to do originally. Antonioni wanted the most exciting thing we could do, so we played "Smokestack Lightnin'", but he didn't like that, even though we had this incredible build-up in the middle which was just "Pow!". I thought it was perfect, and it would have been a better song, but he wanted an up-tempo thing, and that was the only double-fast thing we had, so we changed the lyrics on, I suspect, the recommendation of Giorgio, because of the money – it's amazing how the song was ruined by changing the words.'

Perhaps more important in the overall scheme of things were two other tracks (the only other two) on which Beck and Page were both involved, 'Happenings Ten Years Time Ago' and 'Psycho Daisies'.

'I think those tracks have become important to me. They were pretty wild for those days, but at the time, I suppose you just think you've made a weird kind of record during the complete whirlwind of excitement that was happening, but when you look back, "Happenings Ten Years Time Ago" is a pretty good record which reflects quite accurately the confusion of the sixties. It was played a lot on Los Angeles radio, and I couldn't understand how they'd singled that one out when there was a whole other bunch of ordinary straight up and down rock'n'rollers, and then all of a sudden our record. And there was an accident in it – we simulated a car crash or something in the middle of it for no reason at all, and it was just a chaotic record. Actually, when I made that, I'd just recovered from meningitis or something and couldn't go on the road, so they said "Right, you've got to prove your goodwill and that you're going to play in the band by recording, and they had me in the studio while the lads were all off doing their thing. I think they were playing live without me, and Pagey was taking over on lead and enjoying every minute of it, but I was brewing up these weird solos in the studio that he didn't know about. He wasn't in the studio when I played on "Happenings", but when they came back, they were delighted with the two tracks and I was in good stead again. "Psycho Daisies" was one of the few tracks I've ever sung on, and Mary Hughes, who's mentioned in the song, was a girl I used to go out with, and who I was strong on for a while. The lyrics to the song were written by the manager, because he knew that I'd sing them if they had her name in them, otherwise I'd have flatly refused.'

Before the end of 1966, Jeff had left the Yardbirds. 'I realised I couldn't handle the strain of touring, and I devised this dreadful throat complaint, which turned out to be real. My throat was totally choked, the glands were swollen – it was dreadful. The tonsils came out while they were infected, would you believe, and my throat's still not really right. I think I went back to LA and hung around there by the pool for a while and then went home expecting the Yardbirds to fold, but Page was on form and people started freaking over him, so they were all right. In fact, Mickie Most somehow came into the picture while I was off the scene and there was one last bid to put the group back together, but by that time I'd blown the whole idea.'

Jeff's thoughts about his time with the Yardbirds, who subsequently have come to be regarded as almost legendary, are worth capturing: 'I didn't regret leaving them when I did, although I suppose it would have been nice to have had things on a different footing, like a good management. I'm not making any apologies, the management was the real reason that group broke up. There would be pressures on any band that was doing well, but in the States, where we had a really good crack at it, we could have been enormous. If we'd hung together for

just another year, we'd have spanned into the '67 period when you got acts like Sly and the Family Stone, and I think that if the Yardbirds had had enough solid financial backing that we would have been all right, but we were limited by management, and the gigs were wrongly chosen. By the time Jimmy Page took over completely on guitar, the wind had gone down, and it wasn't blowing them anywhere – the ideas were going and I don't think Jim really did the number on the group like perhaps he should have. I would have liked to see them develop a bit more, and that's the regret I have, but physically, I couldn't wait to get out of that band.'

Following his departure from the group, Jeff confirmed that he didn't pick up a guitar for six months, and the only thing which made him return to music was acute financial embarassment. 'Yeah, I was well skint – I never had any money then. After I'd sat around for that six months, wasting my life away, I realised that I had to get back and do something a bit serious, and I thought that if I was starting with a clean sheet, who would I get on drums? Right, Keith Moon for a start – he had the most vicious drum sound and the wildest personality. So we rang him up, expecting to get the blank, but he said "Yeah, I'll be there tomorrow" and he turned up! At that point, he wasn't turning up for Who sessions, so I thought that with a little wheeling and dealing, I could sneak him away. That's when "Beck's Bolero" was done, and I was so knocked out with the way that turned out – I thought he might wind up being my drummer, and if we'd been able to apply the right pressure, I think he might have been, but it didn't work out, of course. That was probably the first Led Zeppelin band – not with that name, but that kind of thing – with John Paul Jones on bass, and Jimmy and me and Keith. Moony was the only hooligan who could play properly and Pagey was on 12-string by the way, on rhythm. I thought "This is it!" – you could feel the excitement, not knowing what you were going to play, but just whoosh! It was great and there were all these things going on, but nothing really happened afterwards, because Moony couldn't leave The Who. He got out of the cab at IBC Studios in Langham Place wearing dark glasses and a Russian cossack hat so that nobody could see him being naughty with another session. He told me in a club that he was sick of the Who, and I'm sure that would have been the first Led Zeppelin if Moony had been able to join, but nothing really took off.'

Curiously enough, although Jeff didn't mention it, what that particular dream band would have obviously lacked was a singer, and it was when a singer was found that Jeff's new career began to take off, although this was not achieved without some hiccoughs. 'I had to start thinking about forming my own band, because I couldn't stand being in other bands and doing what their manager thought was right and what they wanted to do, which is where Rod Stewart came in, because I knew I'd have to find a singer. I thought about who I liked and straight away, without bothering to see or hear anyone else, I thought of Rod.

'I first saw him playing with Steampacket – I think the Yardbirds may have been playing the same gig, or perhaps it was a Festival, but I was totally blown

The first Jeff Beck Group – left to right: Jeff, could this be Rod the Mod Stewart with a borrowed beard? Mickey Waller, Ron Wood

away with him and Julie Driscoll. The next thing I know, I'm in the Cromwellian Club, which was a hot spot, and there's this forlorn character sitting nodding his head to Pete Green, and I said "Hey, that stuff's happening – it's great, Buddy Guy, the blues. Why don't we just form a band and do that?" He sort of looked at me and asked if I was joking, and I said "Oh, sorry, forget it", but then he asked if I was serious, and when I said I was, he said I should prove it by ringing him the next day, which I did. We met somewhere in a museum, some bizarre war museum, and walked around, not looking at anything, but talking about blues, and the next thing, we had a rehearsal set up.'

Eventually, Ronnie Wood became the group's bass player, later going on to stardom as a member of the Faces and the Rolling Stones. 'Before the friendship between Rod and Ronnie cemented, everything was great and we were all over the moon about what was happening. Then they started acting like a couple of girls together, and I couldn't handle that idiot kind of girl guide humour – we were all self-destructing then, and I didn't want to go on much longer with those silly vibes.' A further problem arose when the new band began to record. 'After we had the outlines of what would be the Jeff Beck Group, I said "Look, I've got this bloke Mickie Most, so we'll make a record", and we all went up there to RAK Records, and we're sitting outside, all four of us, thinking we're all going to be treated like a group. Then it was "Jeff, come in", and the others were left outside and never even saw Mickie, and I thought "Oh no, this is going to upset them". Mickie said "Now look, never mind those faces out there" – and they could hear everything – "You're the name, you're the person I'm interested in." I said "OK, but I'll tell you something – I'm not singing". He goes "There's the door", and I thought "Aaah". That's what it virtually amounted to, although he didn't say it quite like that. It was more like "I have the right to make you do whatever I want on this contract, and if you want to make a hit record, we'll do it my way", so

I agreed, and out came the demos, and "Hi Ho Silver Lining" was the one I had to sing, and I was saying to Rod "There's the record, mate", and Rod and all of us learnt it, but Most wouldn't wear it, and insisted I sing it.

'So we did that, and grudgingly, Rod did as he was told. It was a mis-identity right from the start – I was going out plugging "Hi Ho Silver Lining", one song out of the hour we used to play, and Stewart was wondering what the hell he was doing there, because the audiences only wanted to hear the single. That was what was really wrong in the first place with that band, Mickie Most not really being cool enough to get Rod singing, and gradually I was beginning to think about forgetting it all. Then his partner, Peter Grant, saw that there was more in it, and rather than lose the whole thing, said he'd fix up an American tour, and that was just the one thread left that we were hanging on to. Anyway we made it to New York, and blew the town apart completely, smashed it wide open with one performance, and we had an identity as a band right there, and that cemented it all for eighteen months. I still think "Hi Ho Silver Lining" is trash really, but if people like it as much as they seem to, then let them go ahead and like it. The people I'm associated with don't even know about it, or wouldn't want to know about it, or poke fun at me about it, and other people swear it's the best pop record ever made.

'"Tallyman" was the next one, and that was contractual recording again, the "do it or I'll sue you" sort of thing that was Most's policy then, and then "Love Is Blue" was just going from bad to worse – it was almost as though he was planning the next worst record in order of terribleness! The actual melody I started playing sharp or something on purpose – at least, I hope it was intentional – but I don't think he was actually very astute with that one. Most of the decisions Mickie's made have been winners, but I think it was stupid to get me to play that bloody French song, a five minute wonder. It was coming out of every jukebox and every toilet in every hotel, and I thought "Is this me, chaps?" No, it wasn't. And it was even a Eurovision song – Beck on a Eurovision song! But I survived it.'

Fortunately, the band did survive, and stayed together to make two albums, the first of which *Truth*, is conceivably one of the finest pop albums (with heavy rock credibility) ever made. There are many excellent tracks on *Truth* – a Yardbirds remake in 'Shapes Of Things', a couple of Rod Stewart written songs, and a number of cover versions, three of which stand out particularly, Tim Rose's 'Morning Dew' and two classic R&B items, 'I Ain't Superstitious' and 'You Shook Me'.

'There was a series of concerts at the Saville Theatre, and that was a hot place to be – kind of an underground gig, but it was better than the Marquee because everyone was seated. We saw Tim Rose there, and loved that song, because it was played in all kinds of nightclubs really loud and it sounded great. I told Rod that he should sing that, and he agreed and said he really liked it – we didn't care what we played as long as we felt like that. We used to do "Loving You Is Sweeter Than Ever" by the Four Tops, just because it was great fun to play and a really well-constructed tune. That bagpipe noise at the end of "Morning Dew" was just a whim when I was convincing Rod that we should record the song. He said "I want bagpipes", because he loves bagpipes, and so we got this bagpipe player in who was dreadful, which you can hear – he's just shocking, slightly sharp and all the rest of it. It was kind of a really corny way of illustrating mist and the Scottish highlands and that sort of thing. Great eh? "I Aint Superstitious" was the kind of song the Yardbirds might have done. I was still heavily influenced by them because they used to choose some really good blues things to play, and everyone was fumbling around for material. When you're forming a band at that age, you say "What else can we play?" and you're so quick and pick up something in ten seconds and modify it – it was a very fertile period.'

The name of the highly successful Led Zeppelin, a quartet led by Jimmy Page, has already been mentioned, and it has been noted more than once that Led Zeppelin may conceivably have owed their inspiration to the Jeff Beck Group.

'That's probably fair to say, and old Jim was around quite a lot – after he heard *Truth* and saw us, he actually came to America with Mickie Most when we went there. Some people say he came because he wanted to see what was going on, some people say he came to look for a record deal and musicians, but nobody really knew, and he was hanging around an awful lot, staying at the same hotels and having an ear, you know, listening. I think it was in New York when I heard his demo of "You Shook Me" – this was after we'd done it, of course – and he said "Listen to this, listen to Bonzo, this guy called John Bonham that I've got", so I said I would, and my heart just sank when I heard "You Shook Me". I looked at him and said "Jim, what?", and the tears were coming out with anger. I thought "This is a piss-take, it's got to be" – I mean, there's *Truth* still spinning on everybody's turntable, and this turkey's come out with another version. Oh boy . . . Then I realised it was serious, and he did have this heavyweight drummer, and I thought "Here we go again" – pipped at the post kind of thing. A lot of people that I talk to still say that the first album's the best one Led Zeppelin ever did.'

Truth remains a milestone, although the same cannot be said of the band's second (and final) album, *Beck-Ola*, which was curiously sub-titled *Cosa Nostra*.

'That *Cosa Nostra* thing means "our cause". I talked to Mickie about it, and he said "Why don't you call it *Cosa Nostra*, because there's like an evil overtone to it, and it's kind of underhanded. It suits you, it suits the band's music, it's evil and it's a great title for an album". The record company didn't like the name at all, didn't want to know about it, so they put it in smaller letters. My nickname was Beckola – for some reason, they had this habit of calling everybody "igi" or "ola", some kind of Italian connection, although I don't know – and Peter Grant used to call me Beckola after the Rockola jukeboxes, and I thought "The name's there and it fits, so why not use that for the title?". He still calls me Beckola on the phone. We just did that album – it was as close to rock as we could get, with a funked up, kind of Vanilla Fudge-y

type heavy heavy backbeat to things like *All Shook Up*. It was all right, and if you listen to it now, it sounds more hip than anything else I did because it's just Elvis-type vocals.'

One particular criticism of the album relates to Mickie Most's production, which is untypically messy sounding. 'He didn't understand anything like that. He didn't understand what the hell was going on with progressive rock, because he'd never meddled with it – it was all chunk chunk stuff, Lulu and Donovan, easy stuff, where he could walk into the session and take over and say "That's too loud, I want more acoustic guitar, Donovan louder and you softer". But with our stuff, nobody knew what was going on, there was noise and feedback, and it was just confusion in that era, never mind just that record. You couldn't really expect Mickie to suddenly rally round, and he got worried because he came out to the States to see what was really happening on the music scene, and he was quite shocked when he found out how big the crowds there were. I'd say to him here and now that he thought the whole world existed round RAK Records and that office, so he didn't need to go out. But then he realised he'd never seen so many people, and instantly the businessman started working, but he still didn't want to know too much about heavy rock. He couldn't stand cymbals – you ask him now. He hates cymbals, but he likes the drums, because they're beat, while he considers cymbals jazz.'

Another task undertaken by the Beck group at this point was making a single as Donovan's backing group, both artists being produced at the time by Mickie Most. 'Donovan was reported to be on a sticky wicket at the time, and he needed some beefing up. He wasn't making it very big on that airy-fairy butterfly stuff he was singing, and Mickie thought it would be bizarre to have a wild heavy rock band behind this Donovan. "Barabajagal" was made up very quickly – I think Donovan wrote it on the back of a bus ticket – and he sang us the riff. Tony (Newman) was straight in there, because he was a session drummer, and within a hour, we had it down. It seemed great, and I liked the song, and still do – Madeleine Bell singing a few soulful licks in the background.'

During 1969, the Jeff Beck Group finally disbanded as a result of the many tensions which seemed to be continually afflicting it. 'The pressure was getting silly, and I mentioned earlier about me not liking Rod too much – not having him as a friend any more was a bummer. Really, these things sound silly, but when you spend your whole bloody life with a bunch of guys, they've got to be all right guys. So we blew that out, and Rod made plans to join the Faces.'

In fact, a prior plan had been for Jeff and Rod Stewart to team up with Tim Bogert and Carmine Appice, the rhythm section of Vanilla Fudge. 'I wanted a beefy rhythm section, and they were the two perfect guys – what with them and Rod, it had to be a winner, but Rod didn't think he'd be able to front a band like that. He thought he'd be the underdog again, and he probably would have been, but he never even gave it a chance, and lo and behold, now his drummer's Carmine. Anyway, it never happened,

73

Early '70s Jeff Beck Group – left to right:
Clive Chaman, Bobby Tench, Cozy Powell, Jeff, Max Middleton

because I had a serious car smash, although nobody believed it. Peter Grant came to the hospital with Mickie Most, and they all thought they were going to find an empty bed, but I was there, all bandaged up, and they realised it was for real. So they sent a cable to Timmy and Carmine telling them, but then they didn't believe it and formed Cactus, so I was lumbered and out of work again, and Rod had buggered off with the remains of the Small Faces.'

The start of 1970 saw Jeff attempting to recruit a new band. 'I went all over England with this ex-roadie of mine who's really a good friend, and was prepared to help me look for a drummer. We drove all over the place, and it was depressing – every place I went, people were asking when I was going to play again, and I said I'd be playing as soon as I'd found a drummer. Eventually, the only way we were going to get a drummer was by advertising and holding an audition, which we did in Hampstead – I've never seen anything like it, there were group vans a mile long with drum kits. I walked in and there were twenty or thirty guys there, and Peter Grant's secretary came over to me and said "Don't worry about those guys. We've got the right one and he's in the back room having a cup of tea". It was Cozy (Powell) and I saw him and straight away there was this understanding, telepathy thing. He said he'd come back another day because I had to hear all these other blokes, and I said "No", so he said he wanted to play first. He played and I thought "This is it!", and I just told all the other guys to pack up, which was quite silly really, because some of them might have been great players, but it just felt so good playing with Cozy, because we both dug the same things.'

The search for musicians to complete a new group involved numerous candidates, including Elton John

(shortly before the latter achieved stardom) and a group of American session players at Tamla Motown. 'I went through managers like a dose of salts at that time, and one of them put me on to Elton, and took me down to the Speakeasy to see him play. I first of all thought it wasn't right – a guy fronting a band as a pianist, singing these kind of wistful songs. But then he wound up with a couple of heavy ass-kicking rockers and I got a bit more interested, but nothing happened immediately. A couple of weeks later, this manager persisted about us getting together, and said that he thought he could get Elton's bass player and drummer out, and Cozy and I in with Elton and a great bass player. So we went for a rehearsal at Hampstead Town Hall, but I turned up late and he gave me a terrible roasting, which made me think it wasn't such a good idea – it actually wasn't my fault, because my car had broken down – and here I was, playing lead guitar for a band that was already complete, because Elton didn't want to change his rhythm section. I thought the next thing would be that he'd have me wearing a tie or something. . . .'

Eventually, it became essential to make a new record, and without really finding the type of musicians he wanted, Beck put together a new band, including singer Alex Ligertwood (replaced soon afterwards by Bobby Tench), bass player Clive Chaman and Max Middleton on keyboards. 'I made myself a rule about seeing everybody I got for the band perform before I even considered them, but I never did it. I never saw any of those people in that band before they were in the band. And I'm still saying I won't have anybody until I've seen them play, but I never do see them. Maybe it's fate – you may be put off your stroke a bit if they're doing something that isn't quite what you like, so you miss their potential. But the two albums I did with that band were at a time when I was looking for something. I don't know what it was, but I didn't want to sound like me anymore because – and I have to say this – I was so sick of listening to guitarists that sounded like they were ripping me off. It seemed to me that everybody sounded like me, all these groups that were on the way up, and that's the way I felt for a long time, so I tried to change, tried to bring a bit of class into rock. Those albums show it a bit, but they weren't fully realised by the production, because I didn't have a clue what I was doing. Strangely enough, there's a kind of medley on the first of those albums, *Rough And Ready*, which is "New Ways" and "Train Train", and the Stray Cats used to play that. I just met them recently and they freaked out when I said I dug their music, and they said they used to play all my licks. Of all people, they were the last I'd have expected to say that.'

Rough And Ready used a vocal sound, courtesy of Bobby Tench, which sounded very similar to the style of Curtis Mayfield. 'Yeah, but I feel really terrible about that time – Ligertwood wasn't right, and I realised I'd wasted a fortune, trying to get him to sound right, and had to kick him out, which must have disappointed him a lot. Then Tench came along, and he really didn't know what the hell was going on – I just told him to write some songs quickly, because I'd buggered about long enough. He just went home, perhaps the one and only time he's ever done it like that, and came back with these lyrics which at the time sounded passable, and off we went. Some people in the States like that album a lot, which makes me feel better about it, but for my part, I wish I hadn't gone through with it, and waited until I got the right guys.'

Which makes it seem all the more odd that he should go on to make another LP with the same line-up, although this time produced by Steve Cropper, legendary guitarist with Booker T & the MGs. 'I'm not going to put Steve down in any way, because I really like him and I think he's great – he was one of the major influences in the early '60s with "Green Onions" and that sort of thing – but he wasn't really a producer. It was a new toy for him – he had TMI Studios in Memphis, and all these local people in clubs and bars used to ask me what I was doing there, and when I said I was working with Steve, they were really uncomplimentary. I'd say things about Booker T and they'd ask me about Rod – it was like my world was crumbling. . . . So I figured we'd just see how the record sounded, and at the time, everybody was jumping about it, until *Rolling Stone* said that it was a large piece of junk – "Another Cropper failure, a mistake". I didn't think it could be that bad, and it wasn't, it was a pretty good record with some nice things on it, but once again, it was lacking in concept and direction and strong sound, which were all vital ingredients it needed.'

Two tracks on the album (which was simply titled *Jeff Beck Group*, although it is often referred to as *Orange*, because a fruit of that type is shown on the sleeve) stand out – 'Can't Give Back The Love I Feel For You' and 'Definitely Maybe', which would lead to a momentous decision eventually. . . .

'Those tracks are just more me. It was those sort of

things that made me think "They go down well, so why don't I just say goodbye to singers, and try and make instrumental albums?". And that's been more or less like that ever since – after Rod, who was the best voice for my guitar, plus the best singer around at that time, apart from Wilson Pickett, who I was never going to be able to get, it was a question of "If I can't get a guy like that, what do I do?" I could get a smooth voice, but that's not conducive to my playing, and finally I got pissed off with looking around for singers. I believe what people tell me to my face, but thank God, the scales are heavily on the favourable side. What creamed it for me was playing with Stevie Wonder, which was a real feather in my cap, and when José Feliciano told me he liked my playing – that was in front of my old lady as well, and she was thrilled, because we both love José Feliciano.'

Stevie Wonder entered Beck's story about this time, apparently as a result of Jeff's record company trying to find an inspiring collaborator for him. 'There was a time when I was pretty bored with my music, and I think somebody at CBS asked me what I wanted to do. I said I loved Stevie's stuff, so they quietly broke it to him that I was interested in doing something together, and he was really receptive. The original agreement was that he'd write me a song, and in return, I'd play on his album, and that's where "Superstition" came in. He basically wrote it for me, but the story goes that he loved it a bit too much – no, he played it to Motown, and they said "No way is Beck getting this song, it's too good", and as they had the right to say what Stevie released at that time, I lost the song as an original. Apart from that, I did some sessions for the *Talking Book* album – "Looking For Another Love" was one track that was released, and I think another one we did was "Tuesday Heartbreak", although there were others. I wanted to express my guitar playing through Stevie, who I admired and enjoyed, and he was one guy I would have played lead guitar for.'

Another potential collaboration at this time was with Sly Stone, whom Jeff had seen as a major force in the late '60s. 'That would have been trying to pick up the pieces of a failed recording session in London, and it was pretty diabolical, because we couldn't get the right drum sound – to me, that means there's no point in going on, because half the balls came from the drums, and if they sounded like cornflake packets, it wasn't worth the aggravation. By that time, I'd got to know Tim Bogert and Carmine Appice again, but nothing happened for a while, until they rang me up at four in the morning with Sly Stone on the phone. "Hey, Beckola, got a surprise for you – Sly Stone's here", and I didn't believe them, but then this voice came oozing out of the phone – great! He was quite coherent, but he gradually broke down and I couldn't understand a word, because he was just waffling. It wasn't costing me any money, but I asked to speak to Carmine again, and he said "Man, things are jumping – we've got Sly and he's going to sing and help produce the albums we're all going to do together", and it all seemed like the end of a bad run of trouble. I went out to Sausalito and saw the bay and a few boats, counted a few bricks in the Holiday Inn wall, but nothing much happened, except that I wasted two weeks and realised I wasn't

Beck (centre), Bogert (right) and Appice (left)

a negro, and didn't want to be part of all that black power thing.'

This abortive episode was intended to result in a second LP from Beck, Bogert & Appice, a band which should have had the potential to be world beaters, although things, as often happen, didn't quite turn out like that. Initially, Max Middleton from Jeff's previous band was included to make the band a quartet, while there was also a brief dalliance with a lead singer, Kim Milford.

'All sorts of crap went on, probably because I hadn't put enough thought into what I wanted to do. It would've been so easy if I'd thought it out like a businessman, but I dream a lot – I'm just not practical. At the time, we were supposed to be the ultimate heavy trio, but not heavy in today's sense of heavy metal, which I gather is just loud music with a simple backbeat and really gutsy riffs. We had all that, but we also had a precision and a funk thing which heavy metal lacks – there was New York funk going on, plus a sort of super Motown bass, and we had all the ingredients, but they weren't fully realised. We had this singer at the start, Kim Milford, but he got booed off the stage. He probably wouldn't now with his long blond hair – he was a real pretty boy, and a great guy, but they didn't want to know, they just wanted to see us burn. And we did – we burned him off the stage every night.'

One track on the album which did emerge was the previously mentioned 'Superstition', which tends to pale in comparison with Stevie Wonder's own version of the song. 'Yeah, but don't forget that when we got hold of it, we didn't know Stevie was going to put it out. We all freaked when we heard he'd released it, but on the other side we were delighted because his was a great record and a worldwide smash, and the credit went where it was due, because he wrote it.'

The reliance on outside material was a major factor in the dissolution of BB&A. 'That was the main reason, but equally, there were too many managers

hanging around. They had their New York based manager, and I had my English manager, and there's no way it could have worked for long with two managers, not when you're trying to push something. If it's already there, and there's millions of dollars involved, then you can work out a deal, but when everything's on a knife edge, there's no way it can work. They were both positive thinking managers, but tugging in opposite directions, and that led to lots of mistakes, and you're in a forest of confusion as to who to approach to put you on the right road.'

In fact, BB&A did record a second album live in Japan, but Japan was the only territory in which it was ever released. Following this disappointment, Jeff once again entered a period of comparative inactivity, broken only by his work as a guest on other people's records, one about which he recalls little being by an offshoot of Yes known as Badger, and another with a hitherto unknown trio called Upp.

By 1975, Jeff had resolved to return to making albums on his own account, for which he called initially on Max Middleton, who had worked on the two LPs prior to BB&A, and was originally going to be a member of the latter band as well. 'Max is cool in every way, he understands. He helped me no end with that next album, *Blow By Blow*, writing some of the material and getting other players. He just dug out these session men that were most suited to what I wanted to do, like Richard Bailey, who's a superb drummer. He was about eighteen years old, and to play like that was unbelievable. They were all into the idea of a totally instrumental guitar album, the sort of thing that had probably been bandied around by a million guitarists but never actually done, and there was a sort of chemistry about it that seemed to happen.'

'I'd also started to be influenced by Jan Hammer, and I was starting to become more fruitful musically. I wasn't as afraid of my playing as I had been, because I couldn't stand the sound of my own playing at one point, because it started sounding like the guitarists I'd been complaining about copying me, and I was like a copy of a copy. But then I heard Jan, who's such a positive player and so prolific and brilliant in every way that my ears were soaking it all up, and I suddenly realised there was more in me than heavy rock, or whatever it was called at the time. Another thing about *Blow By Blow* was that George Martin was the producer. That happened through a process of elimination, from guys wandering round with a joint in one hand and a Samsonite case to look important in the other, and doing the mashed potato during the session, which was what one of them did. Eventually, all we wanted was a level-headed staid sort of guy to say when he thought the playing was awful and that he liked this and didn't like that. I wanted somebody positive, a guy I could respect without any bullshit, to put it crudely, and when I met George at a preliminary meeting, I just loved him straight away because he's such a great guy, even though he was way off the beam as regards the musical direction, because he didn't know what I was going to play. He said "Jeffrey, I think we ought to have some material and then I'll know better what you want", and straight away he was willing to listen to something he'd never heard. He hadn't decided what sort of record it would be, and nobody knew what was going to happen, almost until the time they printed the sleeve.'

This was also the LP on which Jeff first used the voice tube, which, in simple terms, is a method of intercepting the sound from a speaker and distorting it vocally so that the impression is given of a synthesised voice. 'I started using that in '71 or '72, and finally dropped it because it's only a trick or a toy, and I didn't want to be labelled as the guy that makes that funny noise with the tube in his mouth. It's a mind-blowing sound when you've never heard it before, and it gets people's attention for a few seconds. I'd thought it was just for use with keyboards, but then I found it could be used with anything, and I used it right up to the time of *Blow By Blow*, when I remembered that I hadn't used it on record. So I thought it would be a great little novelty to use it on those few lines in the middle of "She's A Woman".'

Two other notable tracks on the LP, which was certainly Jeff's bestseller of the 1970s, and peaked at number 4 in the American LP chart, are 'You Know What I Mean' and 'Cause We've Ended Now As Lovers', which is dedicated to another guitar player, Roy Buchanan.

'That other one, "You Know What I Mean", the title speaks for itself, and covers the whole concept of the album, which was a blow, all musicians playing together in the studio, and it was like a kind of spectrum, which was also the title of an album which was the kind of thing I wanted to do. Apart from one or two specifically written pieces of music, it's all blowing on the album, soloing, but so good that it sounds like it was written out.'

Around this time, an oblique approach to Beck was made by the Rolling Stones, who were attempting to replace the departing Mick Taylor, a position which was eventually filled by Ron Wood, who ironically had been Jeff's bass player in the *Truth* days, but had subsequently discarded his bass in favour of a six-string guitar.

'I'd just done a double headliner tour with John McLaughlin, which was most enjoyable, then I had this bizarre request to play on the new Stones album. For some reason, I was going through a period where I could hear "Brown Sugar" a lot in my head, and that encouraged me to think about playing stuff like that, and gave me this image of what I might sound like playing with the Stones, but not really thinking for a minute that they might ask me to join — well, perhaps deep down at the back of my mind — but they did. After I got to Holland, which was where they were, we didn't do anything for two days. The road manager was drinking Glenlivet and getting plastered at lunchtime, and I was waiting to play, but nothing was happening. Mick (Jagger) was moodying it somewhere else, and they were all stuffed away in this hotel, with all these oiks hanging around outside, saying "You new Stone, eh?", these Dutch people, and I was going "What? No, no". Then I was summoned up to the bar where Stu, the road manager, was oiled up, and he said "I don't know if you realise what's going on, but we're going to be recording" and I said I knew that, and let's get on with it, and he said "But on top of that, you prat, they want

you to play for real, in the Stones", and I thought "Oh boy!". Now this is in no way disrespectful to the Stones, because I really like them, but for the next few hours, the sudden realisation that I might be a Rolling Stone frightened the hell out of me. So Alan, my accomplice, and I spent three hours compiling this letter to pop politely under the door, and we got the next plane out after having played. I was a bit annoyed, because when we actually did play, there were all kinds of people wandering around with weird looking wires and tape recorders and things, and about 6,000 guitar cases all stacked up, which I thought must all be Keith's, and there were about fifty guys hovering about and a guy with an American accent, and I thought "Oh, Jesus, I'm auditioning for a job in the Rolling Stones".'

The mention of Stu, in formal terms, Ian Stewart, prompted the memory that this worthy had been the man responsible for introducing Jeff to the bottleneck. 'That's true. I used to know about the old bluesmen who had a piece of broken bottle, the neck, and they'd file down the broken edge and run it up and down the strings, but I only thought they did it with acoustic guitars. Stewart had acquired this Elmore James record, which had some slide (bottleneck) guitar on it, which he played through a Vox AC30, and just plastered me all over the room with it. And that was it really — straight away, I realised that the bottleneck had to play a part in what I was doing.

A fruitful union took place with bass player Stanley Clarke, over a period of several years. 'On that tour with McLaughlin, Stanley heard I was using a song of his called "Power" as an encore, and it used to go down a treat because everyone got to jam on it, including McLaughlin, and it floored people. So Stanley came down one night — I couldn't believe that all these people I admired enjoyed my playing — and then I went to his house on Long Island. We got on pretty well, and before I knew it, he was asking me to play on his album, which was all very well, but wasn't getting me any further towards what I wanted, and that was "Journey To Love", where I play a solo. Then, much more recently, between the end of 1977 and the end of 1979, I did two more, one he wrote called "Hello Jeff" which is all me, and also "Rock'n'Roll Jelly". He knew just what he wanted, which is just as well, because I'm not experienced at playing for someone else, and I only know how I'd want to play it. And then there's a live album which also includes "Rock'n'Roll Jelly", but that's his guitarist playing it, not me, although there's a track on there that isn't live that I'm on, "Jamaican Boy", which was left over from the previous album, from the same session as the "Rock'n'Roll Jelly" I'm on. So he eked me out over three albums.'

An earlier interesting collaboration was with David Bowie on a television show. 'They filmed it at Hammersmith, and I think I was tricked into playing with him. It turned out that Mick Ronson (Bowie's guitarist) idolised my playing, but even before that, we mysteriously got two backstage passes for Bowie's Show at Croydon, which I went to and enjoyed, and it was Bowie's birthday that night, and he gave me this stuffed puppet, an effigy of myself, which I thought was a really weird present – I've still got it somewhere. This was at the time when Bowie was doing the *Ziggy Stardust* thing, and by the time they got to doing Hammersmith, it was Ronson's birthday, and Ronson said to me, "I've always dug your stuff", but I couldn't see what was going on at all. I knew Bowie was a hot act at the time, and I remembered him when he was Bowie and the Buzz or something and used to play the Marquee a lot, and then he asked me if I'd play that night. Apparently, Ronson had this one track thing about wanting to play live with me on stage, and Bowie was trying to disguise the fact that it was more of a present to Ronson than anything – "I can get Jeff up here, no problem". Bowie told me I was being respectfully included because he'd liked "I'm A Man" so much he'd made "Jean Genie" out of it, like he was inspired by the Yardbirds, and that sounded feasible to me at the time – if he'd said to me, "Look, my guitarist freaks when you play, so can you play with us?", I'd have said "No way".'

Following the success of *Blow By Blow*, Jeff once again used George Martin to produce his next album, *Wired*, released in 1976, which actually was closer to a jazz LP than anything else. 'I suppose even *Blow By Blow* was really, but I've never been one to categorise things – I just treat what I play as music, and I know what I like to hear. Even if a threadbare piece of music is played to me, I can hear things I'd like to add to it. It's just the way you're influenced at the time, and on reflection, when you listen to *Blow By Blow*, there is quite a lot of true jazz there, although I didn't hear it that way at the time – it just seemed to me like we were playing and blowing. With *Wired*, we lost George even further, and he said to me, "I had to stand on tiptoe to understand what you were trying to do". But then he's the guy who was responsible for the Beatles, and that's why I wanted him, because he was so open to new things, and they were reported to be the most creative band ever.'

The personnel on *Wired* was slightly altered from *Blow By Blow* – still including Max Middleton and Richard Bailey, it also featured Jan Hammer and John McLaughlin alumnus Narada Michael Walden. 'Michael was Billy Cobham's replacement

Playing at 'The Secret Policeman's Other Ball' – left to right, Eric Clapton, Sting, Jeff Beck

in the Mahavishnu Orchestra, and we were introduced by Harvey Goldsmith, the promoter, who's largely responsible for me being into that kind of wild avant garde jazz rock – at that time, there was a realness, a reality, about the music I was listening to, whereas before it was just way off. Michael wrote a track on *Wired* called "Love Is Green" – he used to psych me out from the side of the stage when my band was doing its set at the time when he was with McLaughlin, and he'd grab me and say "You're just a softie", and I'd say "Piss off, I'm not – I'm tough", and he'd tell me I was soft, and that he was going to write me a beautiful melody, and he'd go off into all this greasy stuff. ... But you have to love him because he's a great all round musician who can play great drums, great clavinet when that was popular and good old honky tonk piano.'

While Jeff admired Jan Hammer's playing, Hammer tended to dominate everything when he appeared on Jeff's records, although one track on *Wired* where Hammer was happily absent was the Charlie Mingus song, 'Goodbye Porkpie Hat'.

'Cozy (Powell) gave me a tape of that played by McLaughlin on an acoustic guitar, with him overdubbed over himself on this knockout tune, a really classic blues thing. I was noddling around with it, playing the melody, and Max asked what it was. When I told him it was Mingus, he couldn't believe it, because he loves all that. Then he sneaked off and learned the chords without me knowing, and asked me to play the melody – it was one of my favourite blues songs, because it had that very strong melody and very expansive chord sounds, but still had an open solo you could just blow on.'

Immediately after the release of *Wired* in June 1976, Jeff embarked on a tour with Jan Hammer's group which eventually lasted a year, predominantly work-

*All my own work – Jeff at home in Kent with one
of his collection of rebuilt hot rods*

ing in the United States. This was the only lengthy period of time when Jeff has lived outside Britain – those who have accused him of being a tax exile are confusing tax avoidance with a low profile . . . Even so, the combination eventually turned out not to have been conceived in Heaven. 'I had to make some money, so I went to America to make it – Jan had a band but no market, and I had a market but no musicians, so it should have worked out really well, but it was a total balls up really. We got away with it in terms of shows, but I couldn't believe how I'd mis-judged the role he was to play. Not musically, because his playing's superb, and if he fell on his arse on a piano, it would come out a magnificent chord, because he's that sort of bloke, but I couldn't believe how he wanted to grab the whole show. It started with him opening for me, doing two numbers to warm up, one to balance the PA and the other a real steamer, then I'd come on, and one of his songs, "Darkness", would lead into my thing, which was a nice opening for the show. And every night, it was a little bit more until he had fifty minutes, and people were saying "What's going on? Is Jeff playing or what?" When you've got an irate Beck freak in the first six rows, you've got bad trouble, and it was embarrassing because there was this amazing music, but nobody wanted to hear it, and about half the time, they couldn't handle it and wanted me right away, but Jan would go waddling about with his bloody electronic stick, and nobody could talk to him. Then one day we had to have a meeting and tell him that he could do what he liked in his half hour at the start, but after that, he had to back me, but I'm afraid he'd been given this toy which was like a guitar, but with keys on it . . . Later, we had a mother and father of a row, and he realised it was all going to be over, although he wanted the tour to go on for the

whole year, so we completely revamped the whole set with a lot more of my stuff, and after that it was great.'

One more permanent momento of the tour was a live album recorded towards the end of the tour, and while all true Beck fans will inevitably own a copy, this is possibly the least essential of Jeff's albums. Jeff began to work on his next LP in 1978 although it would not be released until 1980. 'I was looking for players again, and Jan Hammer was one of the first people, because despite that fight we had, I still couldn't get away from his influence, because I was so impressed with the way he plays his Moog. When I didn't hate him any more, he asked if we could play together again, but I told him I couldn't go on the road again until I had an album out, so he wrote me four tunes, and sent them over to me on a cassette. At least two of them were knockout, "Star Cycle" and "You Never Know", which are both favourite stage numbers, but we really had to force it recording them, because Simon (Phillips, Jeff's latest drummer) wasn't happening on those at all at the beginning, although eventually it began to get much better – you have to understand the way Jan writes to under-stand the whole thing as an entity. Jan came over to record with Simon and I, and we had a whole album, about seven or eight tunes, but I decided against doing that on principle after what he'd done to me, because they were all his. So we just took the best three, and then had the problem of finding other material, which took a long time.

'Meanwhile, I toured Europe and Japan with Stan-ley and Simon and Tony Hymas, who I found through old Uncle Max (Middleton) again.' Tony Hymas had played, unpredictably enough, with the Ballet Rambert, had also worked previously with Simon Phillips on a Jack Bruce album, and even more incongruously, had helped to write the theme music for the TV cartoon series, *The Mister Men*.

'When I found that out, I nearly ... Then I was whistling it while I was working on my car. Bloody tune! I'm going to do a heavy metal version of that. But after I'd got Tony, I was then stuck for material and also for a bass player – if we could get a guy from the States to come over, they only wanted to come for a day or two, so eventually we got Mo Foster in to finish the album, and it was a pleasure to work with him, so that he also came on the last tour, when I played in Britain for the first time in eight years. That was very worrying beforehand, but it thrilled me the way the audiences listened – you could hear a pin drop in between numbers.'

The album in question, *There And Back*, was certainly Jeff's best for some time – while one side contained predominantly material written by and incorporating Jan Hammer, the most intriguing track on the album is 'The Final Peace', a duet between Jeff and Tony Hymas with no other instruments save guitar and keyboards.

'That's a freak, a complete and utter freak. Tony's got a keyboard synthesiser which he can programme to sound like a really superfine orchestra, and when you get that without anybody else there, just one guy, you get a totally different feel. He was playing it in my front room one day, and he said, "Look, I've got this lament type thing that you could play on, but I'm not going to tell you the melody, because I just want you to listen to the chords and blow all over them", which was what I did. We started to put it together, but when it started to sound really good, he insisted that we stop and leave it until we got into the studio. And that's what happened – we did it in one take. The thing is, you've got no restrictions with a bass and drums and other people in the band. It was just a locked in mental thing between us, and I had no idea what he was playing or what key he was in – I just followed him, and he'd pick up from a phrase I'd finished with and we went on like that.'

Such an explanation could never do justice to the quality of the track ... Equally good, although in a very different way, is 'Space Boogie' where Jeff's playing verges on the demented (a compliment, by the way). 'I had about fifty tries at soloing over that, probably because the track was just bass and drums, and when you play that high-speed stuff, you have to be totally involved, and the sound has to be around you. You can't just play to a couple of dumb looking speakers, although I had to in the end, but you need to be in the mood for that kind of stuff, be angry, get that kind of naughtiness going and then let it out. I generally feel fulfilled after I've let off steam that way, but sometimes, you don't get enough out, and you have to beat somebody up or get drunk – I'd have been locked up long ago if I hadn't had a guitar!'

Which seems an appropriate point to pause in this highly-revealing look at a guitarist who, perhaps more than any of the others in this book, is capable of generating excitement on a level of which others only dream. We say 'Pause', because there is a very definite feeling in our minds that for Jeff Beck the best is yet to come. . . .

Jeff Beck Discography

With The Yardbirds
Jeff Beck was a Yardbird for eighteen months during 1965/6, and while all the group's original albums are long deleted, several compilations remain available, to the best of our knowledge.

1977 *Shape Of Things* (UK)
1977 *Yardbirds Favourites* (US)
1982 *The Singles Hits* (UK)
(Titles of original Yardbirds LPs, all long since deleted, were as follows: *Having A Rave Up With The Yardbirds* (1966 – US), *Yardbirds* (1966 – UK), *Over Under Sideways Down* (1966 – US), plus *Greatest Hits* (1967 – US))

Jeff Beck Group
1968 *Truth*
1969 *Beck-Ola*
1970 *The Best Of Jeff Beck* (European compilation)
1971 *Rough And Ready*
1972 *Jeff Beck Group* (Orange)
1973 *Beck, Bogert & Appice*
1975 *BB&A Live In Japan* (only released in Far East)
1975 *Blow By Blow*
1976 *Wired*
1977 *Jeff Beck With The Jan Hammer Group*
1980 *There And Back*

Sessions
2 tracks on *Anthology Of British Blues* (1969), reissued as *Immediate Blues* (1980)
1 track on *Lord Sutch & Heavy Friends* (1970)
2 tracks on Donovan's *Barabajagal* (1968)
1 track on Badger's *White Lady* (1974)
1 track (with Yardbirds) on *Blow Up* soundtrack (1967)
1 track on Stevie Wonder's *Talking Book* (1972), plus possibly more with Wonder
Production and playing on *Upp* (1975), plus 1 track on *This Way* by Upp (1976)
Various items with Stanley Clarke
2 tracks on Cozy Powell's *Tilt* (1981)
3 tracks with Eric Clapton and 1 track with The Secret Police on *The Secret Policeman's Other Ball – The Music* (1982)
3 tracks on Murray Head's *How Many Ways* (1982)

PETE TOWNSHEND

Pete Townshend needs little introduction – he is, although he would perhaps reject the term, a celebrity. Pete was born on 19 May 1945, in London, to a musical family – his father was a musician, of which Pete was very proud and he enjoyed going to see his father play.

'It was mainly what I'd call post-war dance music, highly arranged big band stuff, with over twenty pieces, with a bit of Dixieland jazz thrown in and mainstream jazz when he had the opportunity, plus a wide variety of session work, sometimes playing bass clarinet on symphonic works, and at other times, playing bass or baritone sax for a rock album. But we didn't have much music at home, apart from when he was practising or when he had a jam session with a few friends. We never had a piano in the house, and I don't think my parents have got a decent record player even now – I think there are quite a few musicians like that, who don't necessarily live in an atmosphere of music, because I suppose they don't always want to take their work home with them.'

No pressure was applied to Pete to make him learn an instrument, and his first musical attempts involved playing the mouth organ in the bath. 'I did think about playing clarinet at one point, but I couldn't get the embouchure right to make a note, so I waited until I was eleven or twelve and could get hold of a guitar and eventually my grandmother gave me one for Christmas which I think cost her three quid – she was robbed! It was a bit of a disappointment, because it was much harder than I thought, and because it was such a poor instrument, it was really difficult to play. I think a lot of learners suffer from being told that they'll be bought a better instrument when they've shown they have a bit of flair, but the irony is that if you pay a lot of money for a good instrument and the kid doesn't work out well on it, you can always sell it for more than you paid for it, because good instruments hold their value, whereas rubbish instruments don't. Obviously, a lot of people can't afford to pay £60 for a good learning instrument, but it's worth doing, because I think it's very hard to gauge your potential on a bad instrument. So I mucked about for two years, not achieving very much and sitting in my bedroom playing a few chords, and it took me two years before I got a plectrum and a chord book. The first decent instrument I had was a banjo, so my guitar playing style developed for about 18 months around almost a Dixieland banjo style, and there are still traces of it in my playing today, that rhythmic, chordal approach.'

During the late 1950s, Townshend was in fact a member of a traditional jazz band. 'John Entwistle and I had a band with a couple of schoolfriends, but we were more interested in the glamour of rock, and trad. was about to die – a lot of the musicians were getting old and losing their energy, and the Acker Bilks, Kenny Balls and Ken Colyers were obviously just about to move into cabaret. There was still a small cult following for jazz as a result of the Aldermaston marches and so on, but it was in its dying years, and we could sense the rock revolution coming up on the horizon, through Elvis and Bill Haley, and to a lesser extent, through bands like the Shadows. Once the Shadows were established, that was all we wanted to do, so John chucked away his trumpet and built a bass guitar, and although I still play the banjo to this day, I concentrated much harder on guitar – I literally shut myself away for three or four years and learnt properly.'

Historically, soon after rock music supplanted traditional jazz, rock itself became somewhat uninspiring, only being rescued by the Beatles and their ilk, although Pete, it seems, was unconcerned. 'I didn't care, because I had none of the aspirations then to do what I have done, and I wasn't interested in songwriting. Remember, my dad was a member of a band, and guitar players then had few courses of action. They could play in a small combo doing clubs and hope that one day they might get into a rock band, but then I always thought of myself as a rhythm player, and had no aspirations to be like Hank Marvin. I never wanted to front a band or sing, I just wanted to play rhythm, which fitted in very much with my status within the group of friends I had at the time, because I wasn't in any way a charismatic part of the team of geezers I hung around with then. I was the shortest and probably the least significant, and that was the way I was thinking – it was only later on, under great pressure from record companies, that I started to write and take a slightly more aggressive role.'

Aggression certainly appeared to be a major Townshend characteristic at one point during the Who's early career – was it due to pressure, or simply the discovery of a burning ambition? 'I don't know, but I think a lot of it came from the way Roger (Daltrey) led his life during the early days of the Who, when we were called the Detours. He was a very challenging guy – not freely aggressive, but he knew what he wanted and how to get it, and in a sense, he taught me how to fight for what I wanted, and as I started to improve and become more positive and forceful about what I was doing, he readily allowed me to take over from him as lead guitarist in the group, and at that time, of course, we didn't have a rhythm player, and I just played lead. We were one of the first bands to use that trio line up, loosely modelled on Johnny Kidd & the Pirates, whose guitarist, Mick Green, forged that particular guitar style later used by me and Hendrix and Eric Clapton and Wilko Johnson.

'I got an early introduction to rhythm & blues music through an American friend who went to the same college as I did – that was when I was sixteen, so I got into stuff like (John Lee) Hooker, Jimmy Reed and B. B. King before anyone else, and the only other people who were as clued up with records were the Stones, and in fact, we had virtually identical record collections, although it later emerged that quite a few other people were fairly well educated in the blues, but at the time, it was a bit of a plus.'

Like so many notable British musicians from the '60s, Townshend attended art college. 'It's because rock is art, and I don't think you can argue with that anymore. I think a lot of art college people were trying to do the kind of art which they had a preconception about, and they suddenly realised, and were actually told by people like Peter Blake, one of the great pop artists of that period and still a good friend of mine, that rock or pop music was a new art form, although not necessarily one that had to be taken incredibly seriously.'

Townshend's guitar technique was not the result of lessons. 'My father got me started, but tended to leave me to my own devices, although he was very encouraging, and told me to learn some basic musical principles, which I did, concentrating mainly on chords and harmony rather than sight reading.' It's often suggested that too much formal training detracts from a player's individuality . . . 'I'm not sure about that − it's potentially a problem because you learn using exactly the same procedure, sitting the same way and practising exactly the same scales as the other people you're competing against, and virtuosity becomes the premier attraction, but let's also remember that in classical music, it's interpretation that's important. Like Rodrigo's Guitar Concerto, which has been recorded now by about eight players, who play exactly the same part, but interpret it all very differently.'

His own group, the Detours, who started around 1961/2, were together for about four years. 'That band went through a few changes, so many, in fact, that it would be boring to note them all, because Peter Vernon Kell, who now runs a record label and a production company, was the only one who ever did anything else musically, and he played guitar with us for about two months. There was a drummer, a couple of singers, a couple of keyboard players and a couple of other guitarists, but they were just people who passed through the band. We got a hell of a lot of work, and we were good at copying other people's music, but the aims of a small band playing at the White Hart, Acton, are quite modest, and our idea was really to have a good time. The atmosphere then was very similar to how it is today, with a lot of young people walking around saying that the end of the world is nigh, and they might as well get it while they can, so we weren't willing to wait for success. So for us, a good time was maybe a season at Butlin's, where we could spend six months in the summer knocking off birds, getting drunk and being paid for the privilege, sunbathing during the day, and doing Cliff Richard impersonations every night − but we failed the audition.'

However, despite this somewhat unambitious approach to a career, the Detours were making experimental moves musically. 'The R&B records I mentioned included a lot of music I had never come across before, like I'd never heard Ray Charles doing R&B, only his smoochy stuff, and Howlin' Wolf, and Jimmy Smith's organ playing . . . Roger started to get very interested in R&B, and we started to introduce it more and more − I found this music much more a vehicle for the expression I felt akin to. Once I wrote a song, it really freed the band and me a lot to start developing our own image, our own stance, and to talk about our own lifestyle and environment and who we were. The fact that blues singers sang about

There's an innocent face . . .

real life was quite important, and affected Roger and I and eventually the whole band.

'Then we got Keith Moon, who was an enormous catalyst for the sound of the band, because his style never changed − right through his life, it was always that incredibly fluid, rumbustious, extravagant style, but still very musical. He had an incredible intuitive response, so you could sound like you were going bananas, but in actual fact be playing quite disciplined stuff. He was like the missing link, and we only worked with him for six months before we were "discovered". Then came the scenes with our first manager, a local Jewish entrepreneur, who introduced us to Pete Meaden, and then Kit Lambert arriving and finally taking over the management, which all happened within about two months.'

During the first half of 1964, the group briefly changed their name to the High Numbers and released a single, the only one they made under that name, 'I'm The Face', which was not a success, despite the climate apparently being perfect.

'I think only 300 records were pressed, and the rumour is that Pete Meaden's mum bought them all! Pete was a very deep influence on the band − apart from some of his image-grooming maybe appearing to be trite, he actually made us very conscious of the audience, and aware of the idea of reflecting their feelings rather than just ramming music down their throat.'

It has been said that the Townshend visual style was partially to compensate for his lack of musical ability on guitar and Pete himself agrees. 'I was tremendously frustrated because I wasn't moving ahead fast enough, and I was in an arena of incredible guitar players, like Eric (Clapton), who didn't start until he was seventeen or eighteen, and a year later was blowing people's minds in the Yardbirds, whereas I'd been struggling along since I was eleven, so there was some frustration there, things I felt I should be able to do which I couldn't do, and I compensated with visual things. I found it was easier to get more effect from the things I could do, and that's still the case today, where I can get the audience screaming and cheering as though Bruce Springsteen had just walked on by simply smashing a guitar. Not everybody could do that, but I can do it and get an audience on their feet, and I could spend two hours trying to play clever guitar solos and have to work bloody hard to get anything like that kind of theatrical effect, because rock, to me, in live performances is still a theatrical event, and its pointless to ignore that.

'And that's what's so unique about the guitar, as a new instrument – it has new qualities which are still fairly fresh, and can do so many different things, like on Jeff Beck's last album, where it sounds like a violin, with that expressive quality, or it can sound incredibly angry and incredibly sweet, and it's still available in its original form, a classical guitar with nylon strings, or in country & western hybrids or folk hybrids. All these styles and types of sound are still available, but the main thing is that it's an instrument you can stand up with on stage, wear round your neck, hold like a machine gun and turn up bloody loud! It's a perfect theatrical tool.'

So what about the idea that the guitar was on the point of being made extinct by the synthesiser? 'I think that people in the music business always believe, in a visionary sense, in technology always advancing at exactly the same rate, but I tend to disagree, because I think we're already in a situation where synthesiser development is running too fast for musicians to keep up – only now, for example, is the mini-Moog being used properly and expressively.'

We returned to talking about the Who's ability to reflect the feelings of their audience, many of whom, in the early years, were 'mods'. 'I don't think we exactly performed that function – they could relate to us in several different ways, partly through the songs we wrote and archetypically through ''My Generation'', and the first three Who singles, ''Can't Explain'', ''Anyway, Anyhow, Anywhere'' and ''My Generation'', were the ones where I tried hardest, and were overtly aimed at trying to reflect street level frustration, because there was something happening at that time. The atmosphere was very doomy – there was Bertrand Russell standing on a podium with an audience of 20,000 in Trafalgar Square, everybody saying that he was a genius, a doctor of this and that with sixteen degrees, and he said that the world was going to end in two years. The old bugger was 82 years old, and we're still here, but he gave us all a bit of a fright, and I think one did walk around in a bolshie mood. Later, I think we tended to use more subtle devices, and it wasn't always by dressing the same as the audience or anything like that – really, the Who discovered a technique and we don't quite know how it works, and it's evident to me that Springsteen has discovered the same technique. It's quite interesting that the first rock concert he saw had the Who performing, and he saw something we had that other bands didn't have. We weren't a band with a figurehead, like the Stones with Jagger in front, we didn't have a particularly powerful image, and we didn't make particularly wonderful records, but there was just something there, some trick. If you talk to early Who fans, they'll tell you it was more than the music, it was a magic, and I think that was something we learned to get back from the audience, something to do with audience/performer awareness.'

Once Pete had discovered the ability to write, he seemed to become very prolific very quickly, with which he agreed. Was, for example, 'Anyway, Anyhow, Anywhere' written quickly?

'Yeah. I actually wrote that song about Charlie Parker, when I was listening to one of his solos, and I just scribbled those three words on a piece of paper because I thought that was how he sounded, so free and liberated. Roger helped to write the final lyric – he wanted it to be more about the street, and we finished the lyrics off together.'

One aspect of the Who's early recordings which many found appealing (perhaps a very early foretaste of the punk rock movement of ten or more years later?) was the roughness of their quality. Was this intentional, either on the part of the group, or of their producer, Shel Talmy? 'Shel was sort of a factory producer, a good hard worker who wanted to make records as efficiently and economically as possible, and wanted hits but didn't want to spend too much time messing about with what the artist wanted, so often we were very unsatisfied. Later on, when we really tried hard and spent a long time in the studio with Kit (Lambert), we ended up with results that weren't always better anyway, and I think Shel's skill was in using studio set ups and mikes and things to their best advantage, like the use of the early limiter/compressors and stuff like that, which nowadays everybody raves about – can they get hold of an old valve limiter/compressor so that they can get that old horrible sound? (Laughs). Even that was in its infancy then – a limiter/compressor wasn't something you used for effect, you used it for control. We made our first album, My Generation, in two days, two four hour sessions, all the tracks and all the vocals and everything.'

As a songwriter who was also a guitarist, was there a tendency for Pete to write in a way which catered for his own style of playing? 'I did start to get a little bit in a rut – there was always a feedback passage where I could go ''Yaggadang!'', and I still tend to do that to some extent. Yes, of course I write for the style I play in – even if I write on acoustic guitar, I tend to leave myself room, and I hope on my next solo album to include more straight up guitar solos, but then again, you have to concentrate on what you're best at, because everybody's evolving in such acutely different directions.'

Was Pete prone to experimentation in those early days, for example, with feedback? 'I started to get into really rough-sounding guitar through listening to John Lee Hooker records, and I suppose his sound was rough because he had a rough guitar, and probably a tiny amplifier, so it was very distorted. John Entwistle used the first 4×12 cabinet that Jim Marshall made, and the first Marshall amp, and I really liked the sound of that. It was developed for

This track really swings!

bass originally, and I asked him to build me a speaker cabinet for guitar, which I drove with a Fender amp, and used at ear level, so I'd literally get the whole force of the thing blowing my head off. Before that, people put their amps on the ground, or at most on a chair, but I decided I wanted it higher, and thus it was also blasting right into the guitar pick ups, and I got feedback immediately, which at first I dealt with as a problem, but I quickly began to realise that it could be controlled musically, and once I'd got my semi-acoustic Rickenbacker, I could actually play songs on one note on feedback, just picking out the harmonics by moving the angle of the guitar, and I got really good at it. I was never interested in outboard equipment, like echo effects or wah wahs – I used to leave those to other people to muck about with.'

We have already mentioned the fact that Pete was world famous for destroying his guitars, but how did it actually start? 'It happened initially by accident, and a few pretty girls in the audience laughed, so I decided to make it look deliberate, and I'd luckily just got myself a spare guitar – I broke a Rickenbacker 6-string, and I'd just bought a 12-string – so I finished it off, and they rapidly stopped laughing, and I think I emptied the hall, but it filled up again the next week. In the end, it reached the daily papers and stories were printed about it, and it just got out of control. Once Keith realised he was getting left out, he started smashing his stuff up, and it developed from there, and eventually became less of a spontaneously jumped on gimmick than a potential outlet for frustration and a great theatrical device we could use when things weren't going too well. And we also liked the fact that when we decided the show was over, it was over, and there was no way the promoter was going to tell us that we hadn't played long enough, or that we were going to get any of this encore rubbish, which occasionally used to happen.'

One of the Who's strongest aspects has been their often superb (and frequently lengthy) live performances, although Townshend, for one, has more recently disclosed that he enjoys playing on stage

less and less as time goes on. 'I don't know whether I've ever really enjoyed it that much – I've always had reservations about it, but I think I both enjoy and abhor it to the same extent now as I did then. Roger and I both find it very difficult being rock musicians carrying a large past, apart from simply getting older and finding it physically difficult to sustain stamina over a long period of time, although that's one of the easy bits, and after a week of touring, you're usually in incredible shape . . . with the Who, anyway. But it's really the fact that a player like B. B. King has a certain dignity which I don't think I'll ever have. I'll probably still occasionally want to get up and play when I'm his age, but his material isn't really concerned with youth and youth subjects as so much of mine has been for such a long time – I wrote *Quadrophenia* when I was twenty-nine, so I was middle-aged by then, and I was still writing about Brighton beach and punch-ups and popping pills.'

Advancing age seems always to have been one of Pete Townshend's major concerns, and still seemingly worries him greatly. 'I think it does more than I let on, actually, even though I let on quite a lot, because I really enjoy the company of younger people more than I should, and although this may be heresy to a few of my mates, I'd almost prefer to see the Original Mirrors than Bruce Springsteen.'

During 1967/8, the Who were making hit records, yet, for a highly-successful band, they seemed to be suffering financial embarassment. 'Yeah, we were really broke, partly because of the guitar smashing, but also because having hit records in Britain didn't make you a lot of money. I used to do better than the rest of the band, because I wrote the stuff, and towards the end, John used to write the B-sides, so he had an income from that period, and then we started to share the B-sides out among the guys in the band, but even if you sell 100,000 singles, you don't make much money, and we were trying to run a very hard touring band who were over-equipped hardware-wise compared to other bands at the time, with a much larger PA, much larger amplification and lots of spare equipment, which was necessary. Eventually, everything we put out seemed to peak at eight or ten or twelve, then we'd get a brief period of successful touring in Britain and Europe, and then the record would slide out again, and we'd have to climb the same mountain again, and I got really sick of it. I'd kept "I Can See For Miles" back for about eighteen months or two years as a kind of ace in the hole, and we finally stuck it out and I thought it would be the Who's first real number one record, but it didn't do at all well, and was one of our least successful records, which wasn't through lack of play. I was bitterly disappointed and disillusioned, and I just decided to go for broke and do something completely mad, and started work at that point on "Tommy", which took easily a couple of years. It didn't start off as work on "Tommy" – I started on two other things, one of which was called "Rael", a full blown rock opera thing which didn't get completed, and turned up as a cameo track on one of our albums. We must have started "Tommy" in early '68, because it took ages and ages to finish – not because we spent a lot of time in the studio, although we did decide that we were going to spend a lot of money on

A mod soundtrack – left to right: John Entwistle, Roger Daltrey, Pete Townshend, Keith Moon

it, but mainly because we kept having new ideas, so we'd go back and re-record tracks, because we wanted to include a theme from another song. That was a drawn out period of recording.'

'Tommy' is generally regarded as the Who's finest hour, or at least their most ambitious and successful project. How does Pete feel about it more than ten years later, as it certainly appeared from the outside to have become a millstone around his neck at one time?

'In my life, it probably still is, because I'm still involved with the publishing, the follow-ups, the amateur dramatics, the touring productions, the West End production and everything else, but from the band's point of view, I think we're well over it now. It really was a millstone during the Woodstock period – we played Woodstock, and after a long quiet period, the *Woodstock* film came out and the record went back up the charts, so we had to play ''Tommy'' for another nine months on the road in America, when our tours were just exploitative. But equally, it sold more than probably any Who record ever made, and helped us significantly financially, and gave us a lot of credibility with American audiences, more than some of the other bands who had benefited from Woodstock, like Ten Years After, because it was considered a very serious work, even though half of it was tongue in cheek, and it was the record that finally broke us once and for all in the States.'

Another facet of Pete Townshend's life has been his patronage of other promising musicians, and in 1969, Joe Walsh was the recipient of encouragement

above and beyond the call of duty, his band of the time, the James Gang, being invited to support the Who on tour.

'Yeah, when the Who first played alongside the James Gang, I immediately recognised Joe as a very important player. His style was lyrical and flowing, but his chord work, both on keyboards and on acoustic guitar, was very much a derivation of my work, which made me feel flattered – I felt he was a great synthesis of the American lazy, Hendrix-y kind of guitar style and the more English sound, and I really liked him because of that, and I also really liked their first record at the time, so I gave them a plug wherever I could'.

This was the era of the huge open air festivals, and as well as Woodstock, the Who played the 1969 and 1970 Isle Of Wight extravaganzas – how did he feel the two compared? 'The Isle Of Wight was very different, and I enjoyed it much more than Woodstock, which I didn't enjoy at all. Both the Isle Of Wight festivals were wonderful – when Rikki Farr first came round to tell me that Dylan was going to play the 1969 festival, I didn't believe him, because the last time Dylan had played in England, he'd been booed off stage at the Albert Hall, but when it all came together, I was really pleased. I enjoyed both years, and they were great festivals.'

No profile of Pete Townshend would be complete without some reference to Meher Baba, his 'guru', an Indian mystic whose memory Pete has kept very much alive since Baba's 'bodily demise' in 1969, only a couple of years after Townshend had learnt of his teachings. 'I discovered Baba in 1967, or at least

End of the '60s Who – left to right: Keith, Pete, Roger, John

definitely before *Tommy*, because I was really conscious of trying to write that in the Sufi tradition, to have a multi-layered story which could be read either as a series of rock songs, or just a story, or a story with religious overtones, or a spiritual tale, or what you will. I wasn't exactly sure what he was about at the time, and it's probably taken me to the present day to fathom what he really is all about and what he was really saying, and what he was doing when he was living in India, although I've obviously been very deeply and personally involved in the work of disseminating books and films and stuff to anybody that wants to know, as one of the only people with enough spare cash to do it really. Initially, Baba affected me deeply, and it was manifested most instantly on *Tommy* – there's a credit on *Tommy* which reads ''Avatar, Meher Baba''. My interest started when I stopped using drugs, which was a very sudden, immediate, impetuous decision. All my friends and the people in the music business were very druggy people – narcotics weren't common, but hallucinogenics, marijuana, LSD and stuff like that – and I just decided after the Monterey Pop Festival in 1967, which was the first big festival we played in America, that I'd had enough of it. I looked at all these hippies walking round in California, and thought, ''This has got nothing to do with Shepherd's

Bush; I've had enough of it''. As soon as I stopped, I realised that I'd been replacing with drugs an important vacuum of experience and knowledge-gathering and feeling and emotion-gathering that needed filling, and I started to read and search, and looked fairly light-heartedly at certain sort of mystical things.'

The next subject we discussed was about the possibility of the Who ceasing to perform live, and just how they coped with the problem of playing lengthy sets, and what material they included from the vast catalogue of songs accumulated during a career taking in nearly two decades.

'There would be debates, but we tended to end up playing what was obvious. If we do any long shows again – although they may not necessarily be long tours – they'll inevitably include lots of the songs we're still doing, that we can't leave out, like ''Won't Get Fooled Again'', ''Baba O'Riley'', ''Substitute'', classic standout tracks which don't necessarily have any stigma attached to them and haven't been analysed as deeply as the ''Tommy'' things or ''My Generation''. They're just really great rock songs which get everybody at it, so we'd inevitably use them, and we don't change the way we play them much at all, because for twelve or thirteen years, we'd been using exactly the same line-up – the biggest change

A typical Townshend trick?

How much does fatigue have to be taken into account by Townshend, as a rhythm player who has to drive the show along, acting almost like a dynamo – does he have to go into training for a tour, and how does it affect his hands and the way he plays? 'Since I've been slightly less brutal on my hands, my playing has improved a bit – funnily enough, it improved after an extremely childish, brutal event where I punched a wall and broke a finger, and had to do the last American tour with a cast. It changed the way that I held the pick, and turned out to be an advantage, because I used to hold it very loosely – it almost used to float in mid-air and I'd keep catching it, to get that fluid, percussive fast rhythm sound. I started holding it a lot harder, and a lot of modern players are discovering that the harder the pick you can afford to play with, the more fluid your solo style becomes. But yes, I used to not only psych myself up physically but mentally as well, and almost start to withdraw two weeks before a tour or an important show. Sometimes I ran a bit, but never a hell of a lot, because it was just nervous energy. I've always been naturally fit, although I've never looked it, which I think has been one of the great things about being on stage with the Who – I always looked like a corpse, but to act like an athlete is kind of an anathema – dichotomy, rather.'

The familiar image of Pete Townshend on stage is of him swinging his arm in a huge circle as he strikes a chord, something which he adopted after seeing

that ever happened in the career of the Who was when we brought in a keyboard player. We did attempt it once before, when we were working on *Who Are You?*, and Nicky Hopkins came over from the States to work with us, but he's a very frail guy, and he was really sick, so we decided not to drag him round the world on the road, although we did rehearse with him. Then we dropped the idea for a long time, but when Keith (Moon) died, I pushed very hard to get a keyboard player in, or another guitar player. We had routined a couple of tracks with Rabbit (John Bundrick) when Keith was alive for recording, and I'd liked the way he played and we used him, but I suppose it was me wanting someone to play against – I felt I'd always been caught into providing the rhythm, the backbone, particularly on the earlier material, and I wanted to be free to play solos and one note lines, and sometimes just not play at all. The other element was that songs like "I Can See For Miles" and "Dr. Jimmy & Mr. Jim" from *Quadrophenia* are very complex harmonically and use juxtaposing chords on different instruments to get a particular effect, and sometimes even more complicated than that, like taking the left hand of the piano and playing it on the guitar, and there were things like that which we just couldn't do – we couldn't get the fullness of sound that we wanted in sections like "See Me, Feel Me" in *Tommy*, which needs a good sustained sound behind it, and I felt it would really help a lot, so I'm glad we've done it, and I think the keyboard is the right thing with which to augment the Who.'

New York, 1979 – a third guitar?

87

Onstage in New York City

Keith Richard play. 'Yeah, it was in '63, when we were called the Detours, and we played with the Stones when they'd just started at St Mary's Ballroom, Putney, and he was literally limbering up as the curtains opened, and I just copied what he was doing. He did it once, and I did it forever . . . He's always been my favourite player, and the Stones have always been my favourite band.'

The guitars on which Townshend performs, unlike his style, have gone through several changes . . . 'The first decent one I had was an Epiphone which Roger gave to me, a solid guitar with quite a small body and little black pick-ups on it – Epiphone was about to merge with Gibson at that time, I think. Later on, I flogged that and got my first Rickenbacker, and I used Rickenbackers up to about '66, I suppose, and then I got fed up with how weak they were strengthwise, and they were also very hard to get and very overpriced – I hadn't helped because I'd been using them, and the Beatles hadn't helped because they had too, and they were very striking-looking guitars.'

But don't guitar makers form a queue to make instruments for someone like Townshend? 'To some extent, I suppose – the custom-makers line up because they want the money, as there are very few people that can afford to pay £2,000 for a guitar, which is what a really excellent instrument costs, and that's because the wood is so expensive, because the pick-ups are so carefully wound, because so much craftsmanship goes into it, and because there aren't factories doing it, but just small companies, hundreds of people. The large companies pursue you for endorsements, which I've never given, so I've almost always had to pay for my guitars – I turn them down because I don't want kids to think I can get something for nothing and they can't. . . . After Rickenbackers, I went on to Gibson SGs, with a small solid body, which I used for about another three years, then I started using Fender Strats and Telecasters during Hendrix's reign. Then I went back to Gibsons, Les Pauls, and after that, I tried all kinds of things – I used a guitar called a Coral once, but not their sitar/guitar, and all kinds of cheap guitars which I liked the sound of – the Coral had a Danelectro pick-up – and then I went back to Fenders for a short period, and then I used a Les Paul De Luxe, which has very small pick-ups on it, but they're too heavy, and as I got older, I found that I'd get this incredible pain across my collar bone just from the weight of the guitar across the strap, and I think it buggered up my collar bone. So I looked for guitars with lighter bodies, and in the end, I got them made, first by an American company called Scheckle, and finally by an English company, Giffin, who make all my guitars now, and they're not too expensive either.'

One of Pete's 'extra-curricular' activities during the late 1960s was working with a group he championed, Thunderclap Newman, and on several of whose records he played bass using a pseudonym of Bijou Drains. 'The name didn't really mean anything, but what was most interesting about that was that I played the bass while engineering the record, going from two track Revox to two track Revox.' But wasn't he disappointed that, after scoring a number one hit with 'Something In The Air', the band achieved little else?'

'No, not really – I think it would have sustained had Kit Lambert taken over the production and management of the band properly, but also it was really a lack of follow-through in the band. Speedy Keen was the drummer and writer, and I was very much his mentor, in the same way that Kit Lambert was my mentor. Once we'd finished the album, which was

Helping Eric Clapton's comeback at the Rainbow, 1973 – left to right: Ron Wood, Eric Clapton, Rick Grech, Pete Townshend

meant to be a very light-hearted homespun affair, the Who went out on a massive American tour, and when we got back, it was all finished. They'd tried to put out three singles from the album, but the album really wasn't singles material. They would have done better to wait, and they also made the mistake of trying to do live appearances, which were a disaster.'

At this point, we turned the clock back to influences – 'Syd Barrett was an influence because I used to love early Floyd, and I think Roger Waters was a bit of an influence as well, although to a lesser extent. Syd influenced Eric (Clapton) as well – we went to see the Floyd at the UFO Club a couple of times together, and I went to see them every time they played there. They were just unbelievable, one of the most literally frightening bands I'd ever seen, and it wasn't just because everybody was doing LSD. They were frightening when I saw them at Alexandra Palace and I was stone cold sober, which may have been the worst way to see them. They were spine-chilling – Syd was just manic, and everything went through dozens of echo units, and you couldn't tell the beginning from the middle from the end. I listened to John Fahey a lot and still do, and to another player called Robbie Basho, who incidentally shares my interest in Meher Baba, and was on John Fahey's label, Takoma. What I get from Fahey's playing is almost the same as I get from listening to a Terry Riley record, cyclic electronic music, and it has a similar kind of round quality.'

Which leads to the 1971 album, *Who's Next*, on which Townshend used synthesisers in the style of Terry Riley, even calling one track 'Baba O'Riley'.

'That was an interesting period for me – that John Fahey type guitar playing, the constant bashing away fingerpicking style was similar to the electronic music of someone like Terry Riley or (John) Cage, certain things they did. I was introduced to that whole kind of area of electronic music by Tim Souster, who also introduced me to the synthesiser. I got a great big ARP synthesiser and started to work on a film script, which is called *Lifehouse*, and which I'm still working on today. It examines the whole theory of music, where it comes from, how it affects you, and all that kind of thing, and I used that kind of mood as a backdrop for Who music.'

Surely making *Who's Next* must have somehow changed Pete's approach to guitar playing? 'Maybe it did a bit – remember, this was also the first album since the very early days that we'd done with Glyn Johns, and it was our first album that he'd produced. Kit Lambert had done an incredible amount of preparatory work on the album, taken us to New York, where we re-recorded all the tracks I'd done as demos, and routined and rehearsed them before we went in with Glyn. Joe Walsh had just given me a really great Gretsch guitar, the kind that Neil Young once used, and is currently used by the Stray Cats, and I really got into solo playing quite a lot. Nicky Hopkins did a lot of keyboard work on that album,

The Who with Townshend in full flight

and most of the tracks were done live, just with piano, guitar, drums and bass. What I was doing was overdubbing the rhythm guitar, and putting the solo guitar on while we were doing the tracks, which was a complete reversal, and was Glyn's idea, which I thought was brilliant at the time.'

Was the fact that the Who didn't like some of Townshend's songs part of the reason for him doing the *Who Came First* album, which many consider to be his first solo album? 'I don't really think of that as a solo album, because I used a song by Ronnie Lane and a song by Billy Nicholls on it, and I had very little to do with those apart from the fact that they were recorded in my studio. It was more of a devotional album, really, which we did together in reaction to the fact that the Meher Baba limited edition albums that we'd put together, of which there were only 2,000 copies printed, had sold so well, and there was tremendous demand for the material. I offered it to my record label in America, and they said they'd donate the funds to a Meher Baba charity, and I thought it was worth doing.' The authors have always considered one track on the album 'Sheraton Gibson' most attractive. 'I loved that track – "Sheraton Gibson" – I think it's sweet, and I like the fact that it was the first time I ever played the Chet Atkins guitar style, which I used to play when I was a kid. I studied his playing – he

played with a thumb pick, and that was the first time I ever managed to pull it off on a record and have it sound like anything.'

Who Came First was a completed project, but having already mentioned the *Lifehouse* project, were there other items which were in the course of completion which related to Pete? 'Because I've always had a studio at home, and always had fairly free access to studios – at the moment, I'm lucky enough to have three studios operational, all at various levels of technical excellence – I tend to get a tremendous backlog of material, not only of my own stuff but of bands that I've worked with or people that I know. For example, before Roy Harper went over to the States he was going through a troublesome scene with his record label, and just didn't have the money to record, so I lent him a machine, and I presume he churned out a few songs . . . and I've always had that – if I ever feel like doing anything, I do it, so I've got a tremendous amount of stuff, some of it unfinished, some of it off on a tangent because I do it purely for pleasure, and some of it experimental, but a lot of it's complete and just not very good.'

Following the enormous success of *Tommy*, the world seemed to be waiting for a similar Townshend extravaganza, which eventually appeared, although perhaps with less striking results, as *Quadrophenia*.

*Why should Roger
look so cool
when I'm so hot?*

'That was actually a very quick project – I started writing it on holiday in France in May or June, 1973, and it was out in November, and we were on the road with it immediately. It was very quick, and while we were recording it, the Who also built Ramport recording studio. *Quadrophenia* was a slightly weird project for me, because perhaps I was moving a bit too fast for the band, but I wrote the story and then the music, and I took in a batch of demos that fitted together like a jigsaw. Very unlike *Tommy*, where there were just five or six songs to start with, and we talked about it, and John and Keith would come in with ideas – for example, at the end of the story of *Tommy*, I wanted to have some kind of church affair, some kind of nutty cathedral at the end, and Keith suggested that it should be a holiday camp, so there was a lot of exchange there. *Quadrophenia* was completely intractable – if you changed any part of it, it wouldn't work, so there wasn't room for an exchange of ideas, and although the band were very pleased with what they did on it, they did feel a bit cornered, particularly as it was a double album.'

Shortly after the release of *Quadrophenia*, the Who's career seemed to enter a hiatus, the next four years providing little in the way of new material other than a rather strange collection of old tracks whose title, *Odds And Sods*, was all too appropriate, and an equally disappointing new LP, *The Who By Numbers*. 'Yes, but there were two factors involved in that. One was that our management had fallen apart – Kit Lambert had moved out of the picture because it was becoming impossible for him to work with the group, because the group was still really quite disciplined and he'd become very undisciplined. And the other factor, of course, was the bloody *Tommy* film, which occupied a massive chunk of time, and in fact went right through that whole period.'

Despite its taking up so much of Pete's time, the *Tommy* project, and particularly the film, had made him a good deal of money. Does being rich affect his creative output? 'I've found that if I've ever been lucky enough to have a lot of money in the bank, I've always been able to think about something to do with it very quickly, either to pour it back into some fairly massive creative project or some business scheme, or else there'll be something that I need, like some musical instrument I can't live without, or a new mixing desk. *Tommy* did make a lot of money for the band, which we spent almost exclusively on buying Shepperton Studios, or about a third or a quarter of it, and putting together a big PA company, so that our roadies had something to do with their lives. So it wasn't as though we were walking around with wads of money, not feeling as though we had to work, but then I don't think it's ever been money that's driven us.'

Pete had always seemed to be the member of the Who to take the major responsibilities on his shoulders . . . 'I don't know that that's entirely true – each individual in the band took as much responsibility as I would allow them to share, and with *Quadrophenia*, I took the whole project on my shoulders and wouldn't let anybody else in. It wasn't a question of them not wanting to. I still suffer from that to a great extent today, and I'm very closeted not only with creative things, but with anything involving emotion – I like to keep it private until I feel it's been sufficiently edited to unleash on the unwitting public. I think I'm an extrovert, but I do oscillate – sometimes I feel very extrovert, sometimes I don't, and I definitely get very maudlin and moody occasionally, but then if you can get really high naturally, then you can expect to get really low naturally too, and everybody goes through that, but not everybody lives their life under a microscope.'

Duetting with John Williams for Amnesty International, 1979

In 1977, Townshend was involved in an album titled *Rough Mix*, on which he shared the billing with Ronnie Lane. 'That was really spontaneous – Ronnie wasn't getting taken seriously by his record company, and he told me that he reckoned that they'd take him a bit more seriously if I agreed to produce the record that he was about to make. I told him I really couldn't do that, despite the fact that I'd recorded a lot with him at home, and we were very close at the time, because it would be awful if he ended up seeing me like Glyn Johns or something, walking away at the end of the sessions saying "I don't want to see him for another two months, because he's told me some horrible truths, like I was singing flat and it was a crappy song". So I agreed to play on a record with Ronnie, if he could get Glyn to produce it, and Glyn agreed immediately, so we did it. It didn't turn out to be a creative collaboration as much as a three-week party, and it was great fun.'

1978 saw the untimely death of Keith Moon, whose last work for the Who was on the *Who Are You* LP, a record which to some gave the impression that it had been created largely for the American market. 'That's very true – the backdrop to that album was the punk movement in this country, which initially alienated all the established musicians because it was so incredibly aggressive towards them, despite the fact that a lot of people quietly welcomed it. I welcomed it loudly, but it didn't help, and they still called me rude names, and one tended to feel that Britain was going through an explosive situation, and we should look to where we could manage to survive for a bit longer, so we were more conscious of the American market than we had been up to that point. It's just starting to happen in America, but of course not with the same venom, and there's quite an interesting band called the Dead Kennedys, who've got the same kind of venom as the Sex Pistols, but

none of the genius. As the Talking Heads said, "I'm still waiting for the music revolution to happen", and I think it hasn't happened there because a lot of America is so staid and middle class, and how spread out it is. It could possibly have succeeded in New York, but even New York's incredibly cosmopolitan, and the white teenage situation in New York is a minority, whereas in London, it's a landslide.'

During 1979, Pete Townshend played several public shows which were, to say the least, out of the ordinary. One was for Amnesty International, where he and John Williams, the noted classical guitarist, duetted on Pete's 'Won't Get Fooled Again'. 'The first day of that went on for ever, and seriously, I think I fell asleep on stage in the middle of the song and actually came round, but everybody in the audience was doing it too, because the show went on for nearly four hours, and everybody was sitting there after their big dinners and two bottles of wine. I enjoyed doing it, but most of all, I enjoyed meeting John, because he's not the kind of man I expected. I've been a great admirer of his classical playing, and although I don't much like Sky, his rock band, I admire him for that as well, that distilling of styles, which is an idea I like, and I'm sure I'd enjoy them live.'

The Who also appeared during a series of charity concerts for the benefit of the people of Kampuchea, which were held at London's Hammersmith Odeon, and Pete also played as part of Paul McCartney's huge 'Rockestra', although he claims not to have been too happy about it. Far more serious were his appearances at various 'Rock Against Racism' concerts – does Pete feel that, as a rock music personality, he should be involved in politics?

'When I started, I felt that it was beyond our scope to effect any changes whatsoever, because we weren't really respected as human beings – which I think goes for the rest of the band as well – and we only wanted to talk to our particular audience, although not necessarily just our generation. In later years, we realised that we were getting the respect of people outside the rock field, so then it means slightly more to say what you think and do things rather than just talking. I obviously did the Rock Against Racism things because I identify with the motives of the people involved, but I got very severe on the subject a long time before, after the altercation with Abbie Hoffman at Woodstock, where he tried to use the Who's performance – right in the middle of *Tommy* – as a platform for some diatribe about the Chicago Seven trials and John Sinclair being in jail. For a long time, I just stood back and whenever a political issue came up, I tried to keep out of it, because that really tainted it for me, and I don't think I became more open again until the Rock Against Racism thing – it seemed that fascism was getting a foothold against a backcloth of unease in this country, and I didn't like the look of that at all. We've learnt our lesson once in Europe, and it just seemed a waste of time to go through it all again, and I felt I couldn't sit in my shell for ever, and say it was nothing to do with me or that my money would get me out of it, like in the last war, when all the singers and artists and film directors got out of Germany the first day there was a sign of a jackboot, and were all over in Hollywood. That's all very well, but there were a lot of people left behind who couldn't move. So I've changed quite a bit, and the band's attitude to playing for charity has changed, because initially, we played charity shows, but didn't let anyone know we were doing it. It's our business whether or not we give our money away, so for a long time the Who ran a charity, the Double O Charity, which still gives a lot of its earnings away to charity. I think it was formed about the time of *The Who By Numbers*, and we were giving away quite phenomenal amounts of money, and nobody knew, which I suppose made us feel fairly smug, but when somebody says "Why don't you do a charity concert, you filthy rich pig?", you eventually have to tell them what you've been doing, and people realise that you're receptive to doing charity work, or concerts for no money, and they descend like hawks.'

In 1980, Pete Townshend finally released a solo LP, the excellent *Empty Glass*. One of the more popular tracks included was 'Let My Love Open The Door' . . . 'Yes, it's got three chords in it, hasn't it? When I was getting the songs together for a gig I did recently, I realised that all the songs I wanted to play had the same three chords in them, the old kind of "Pure And Easy" thing . . . but that song was very spontaneous, and I did it on a computerised organ machine, and then decided to put a vocal on it, just singing the first thing that came into my head, and that's what came out. I did the same thing with another song on *Empty Glass*, "Little Is Enough" – a computerised organ performance, doing it all in one go with the drums and the bass, and then made up the vocal as I went along, and I had to think fast for that one. "Little Is Enough" is a much better song, and about my favourite song at the moment, because I think it's the way I feel about life – a little has to be enough in this day and age, not just of money and

food, but of love too, because there isn't enough to go round, it seems, and you grab the little bit you can get and try to make it last.'

1980 also saw what was termed by the press as a 'Mod revival', echoing the attitudes and especially the fashions of the first half of the 1960s, when the Who were the favourite 'Mod' band. Had Pete considered that a genuine revival might happen? 'No, but I think there was a revival of sorts, which was absolutely, directly, specifically tied up with a modest little English outfit called the Jam – I think they started it, and I think they'll finish it. When the Jam move on to something else and evolve, which they inevitably will, because Paul Weller's too clever to stand still for ever, and too agitated, and so are the other members of the band, I think they'll take their fans with them. A lot of the kids that you see riding around wearing parkas with The Who written on them don't even know who the Who are – they're Jam fans who've seen Paul wearing a Who badge, although some of them may have investigated Who records. When the first Who album was reissued by Virgin, it sold well, and probably not exclusively to Who collectors, but also to that bunch of kids who follow the Jam – when you think that the Jam's singles go directly to number one sometimes, and sell 400,000 copies in three weeks, they've got a pretty significant following in Britain among the twelve to eighteen age group. It made me feel good when Paul stuck one of my early songs, "Disguises", on the B-side of one of his singles.'

Apart from the Jam, who does Pete rate among the current crop of bands? 'I like the Original Mirrors, U2 and New Order in the new rash, and with the more decorative outfits, I think Richard Burgess is a genius, who's very clever, and I think he'll prove himself a brilliant film maker. He's got such a visual sense which he seems to sum up musically, so I like the bands he's involved with, like Landscape and Ultravox, and I like some of the pop bands that are around, like Duran Duran, who make great sounding records. But ultimately, I think I'll keep coming back to slightly more earthy things – I like odd dabbles in electronic music and stuff like that, but eventually, when it comes down to what I listen to in the car, at the moment it's very much U2 who sound a bit like certain early Who mixed with the Byrds mixed with the Beatles. It's difficult to explain, but it's just a sound that very much appeals to me. It's not that it's old fashioned, but it's the kind of music I relate to a lot at the moment, and I relate to the words as well. What's really difficult for me – and this is why people think I'm a pretentious old bugger when I say I like new bands – is that I've got an incredibly wide taste, and while all this new stuff is happening, which I sincerely enjoy, I still listen to all the old stuff, and also to jazz and classical music. I don't even mind middle of the road music, although I'm not saying I listen to it, because I was brought up on it with my dad playing in a dance band, and it doesn't offend me to hear Frank Sinatra or Ella Fitzgerald, or even Max Bygraves – they're the easiest people in the world to take the piss out of when they're doing their scat singing, but it doesn't offend or annoy me.'

So did any of these disparate influences play a part in the 1981 Who album, *Face Dances*? 'That was a very peculiar album, one of the most peculiar we've made – I think we've got a real job ahead of us to re-establish a direction, and the Who might really go back to square one for the next record. I'll probably continue in the direction that *Face Dances* established after *Empty Glass*, but which it didn't really follow through properly, on my next (solo) album, and try to get that out of my system, but I think the next Who album will be much more basic guitar/bass/drums and much simpler songs.'

At the time this interview was conducted, Pete was preparing to start recording his next solo LP, which eventually turned out to be *Chinese Eyes*. This was what he said about the album some months before it was released: 'It won't be anything like *Face Dances*, at least superficially, and not much like *Empty Glass*, I don't think. I'm still concerned with the art, the craft of writing, essentially, but I'm making incredible departures at the moment. Let me just say that when I played the demos to the record company in New York, they all went into shock, and they wanted me to go straight to a psychiatrist and have him play me AC/DC records, which are selling very well in America. So it's about as far from heavy metal as you can get, but I don't want to say too much, because I don't really know yet. I've written about twenty-five songs which I think are possible for the album – that's a single album, by the way, and you need fifty songs for a double . . .'

Although Pete Townshend is not a frequent player on other people's records, some of his sessions have been with interesting people, such as David Bowie, on the latter's 1980 LP, *Scary Monsters*. 'He didn't let me do much, but we really enjoy one another's company, and we see each other so rarely and I think he really invited me over for a natter. I saw him in New York when I went over there to play my new stuff to the record company, and we went out on two occasions – I like him because he's very intelligent, but he's also very relaxed and easy company, not the glamorous distant figure some of his fans imagine him to be. He took me to this Japanese restaurant, and I went into shock when he ordered the food in Japanese!' Other session credits include those for Billy Nicholls and Mike Heron; one of Heron's solo LPs has backing on one track provided by 'Tommy & the Bijoux'.

Two other involvements were on an Yvonne Elliman LP, and on the sound track for the film *Mahoney's Last Stand* . . . 'With Yvonne Elliman, I was just invited to play because she was covering one of my songs (in fact, "I Can't Explain"), and I didn't mind, although I don't think I added anything new. *Mahoney's Last Stand* was just showing up in the studio to see Ronnie Lane, and him saying "Pick up a guitar and play". It's the uncredited work that I've done on Rolling Stones' albums that's really interesting – I'll write a book about that one day, but I'm not going to say any more about it now, because it was uncredited for a reason.'

Finally we asked Pete Townshend, after this fractured and incomplete journey through his past, how long did he reckon he'd carry on writing songs and playing music? 'I don't really know how long I'll be in a group, but I suppose I'll always have to play with other musicians, unless I become a Stevie Win-

The Pete Townshend we'd like to see all the time

wood type. But I've worked at home on my own for so long, played the drums and the bass and anything else I can get my hands on, so now I enjoy playing with other good musicians, particularly as I can now command probably the best musicians in the world to play with, command them and pay them! In the rock frame, in the way I've been working for a long time, I think on my next album I'll have already started to change direction, to move away from the Who fans' conception of what rock'n'roll is about. I've changed my stance in the past several times, with great success, so I feel I could possibly do it again without too much trouble. I did it once on *Tommy* and once on our third album, *The Who Sell Out*, and those were radical musical departures for the band, away from the traditional sound that we still produce, but sometimes to get that needle a little bit off centre, you have to go a long way to left or right – it might feel very awkward to you, but from the outside, it can often look like very little is happening. So I want to create some major changes in the way I work now – not because I'm particularly worried about age, but I do think it's very difficult to age creatively. Some people look young forever, like Cliff Richard – I've looked forty since I was nineteen! But to age creatively with dignity is really difficult in heavy metal full frontal rock, because you can end up looking a complete prat, whereas in classical music or jazz, you can age with dignity. I think to some extent it's the high critique which surrounds rock and is always trying to bring it back down to earth, yet at the same time, by definition, high critique means it's worthy of high critique, and therefore must be art. It's difficult to live with the schizophrenia of being in the rock business, but I'm determined to find a route, perhaps less as a musician and performer and more as a writer. I'm going to have to concentrate on what I have to give, and try to develop it, hopefully in the company of a lot of other people and musicians that I enjoy playing with and being with, and to have it appreciated by some audience somewhere. Whether it's going to be as big as the audience I've enjoyed in the past, I don't really care anymore.'

Pete Townshend Discography

It should be noted that the details below refer to
British releases, which in a few cases, differ from
albums released in the United States.

The Who
1965 *My Generation* (reissued 1980)
1966 *A Quick One*
1967 *The Who Sell Out*
1969 *Tommy*
1969 *Direct Hits* (compilation)
1970 *Live At Leeds*
1971 *Who's Next*
1971 *Meaty, Beaty, Big & Bouncy* (compilation)
1972 *Tommy* (Stage Version)
1973 *Quadrophenia*
1974 *Odds & Sods*
1975 *The Who By Numbers*
1975 *Tommy* (Film Soundtrack)
1976 *The Story Of The Who* (compilation)
1978 *Who Are You*
1979 *The Kids Are Alright* (Film Soundtrack)
1979 *Quadrophenia* (Film Soundtrack)
1981 *Face Dances*
1982 *It's Hard*

Solo & Other Albums
1972 *Who Came First*
1977 *Rough Mix* (Pete Townshend & Ronnie Lane)
1980 *Empty Glass*
1982 *Chinese Eyes*

Sessions
Thunderclap Newman
1970 *Hollywood Dream*

Mike Heron
1971 *Smiling Men With Bad Reputations*

Eric Clapton
1973 *Eric Clapton's Rainbow Concerts*

Yvonne Elliman
1973 *Food Of Love*

The Crickets
1973 *Bubblegum, Bop, Ballads & Boogies*

John Otway & Wild Willy Barrett
1974 *John Otway & Wild Willy Barrett*

Ron Wood/Ronnie Lane
1976 *Mahoney's Last Stand* (Soundtrack)

Various Artists
1979 *The Secret Policeman's Ball*

David Bowie
1980 *Scary Monsters*

JIMMY PAGE

There are certain guitar players without whom this book could not claim to approach completeness, and, of course, one of our criteria for inclusion was that the players should all be alive, which accounts for the omission of Jimi Hendrix, Duane Allman, Mike Bloomfield etc. Actually contacting some of our subjects was next to impossible, but in general, as soon as one of our choices was fully acquainted with the nature of this project, he immediately agreed to co-operate. One of the very difficult people to whom our message had to be passed was Jimmy Page, who was particularly vital as the leader of Led Zeppelin, arguably the most popular band in the World during the first half of the '70s.

It would be misleading to suggest that our time spent talking with Jimmy was completely straightforward – the part of his career prior to the formation of Zeppelin presented few problems, but on the subject of his work since the group's formation in 1968, Jimmy was understandably suspicious of the motives behind certain questions and topics, the band having suffered extensively at the hands of the media. Perhaps the equation reads as follows – critic, for whatever reason, dislikes LP, feels aggrieved when his request for an interview is refused, and decides to vent his pique in a blast of innuendo which often claims rumour as fact. Whether or not this is the fault of the critic or of the band is, of course, a moot point, but when Jimmy reads this, let us reassure him at the start that there has never been any intention to create controversy where none exists, save where it has significantly affected his music.

Jimmy Page was born in Heston, West London, on 9 January 1944, and moved with his family to nearby Feltham during his infancy, finally spending his formative years in Epsom, Surrey, from around the age of eight. For such an inventive and mercurial player, it is strange to note that he made no moves towards the guitar until his fifteenth year.

'Some friends had given a Spanish style guitar, but with steel strings, to my parents, and it lay around the house until I equated it with everything that was going on with rock'n'roll, and picked it up. I didn't manage to do anything with it, of course, until I learned how to tune it, so things started very slowly. In those days, you'd find that a sort of grapevine of record collectors would spring up, and it was the same with guitarists – someone at school who later became a friend showed me how to tune it. I remember going onto the playing fields one day and seeing this great throng crowded around this figure playing guitar and singing some skiffle song of the time, and I wondered how he did it. He showed me how to tune it, and it went on from there, going to guitar shops, hanging around watching what people were doing, until in the end, it was going the other way, and people were watching you.'

What? No *Play In A Day* by Bert Weedon? 'I've got to be honest – I did get that, but more out of curiosity. Most guitar tutors fell flat when it came to the point of the dots, because I was far too impatient, and all the records you heard and were totally absorbed

with at the time just weren't matched by the songs in the tutors, which is why one took the approach of learning to play by ear. Solos which affected me could send a shiver up my spine, and I'd spend hours and in some cases days trying to get them off. The first ones were Buddy Holly chord solos, like "Peggy Sue", but the next step was definitely James Burton on Ricky Nelson records, which was when it started to get difficult, although the particular record which first made me get interested in playing was "Baby Let's Play House" by Elvis Presley, because it was so infectious. It was only later that I realised it was just acoustic and electric guitars and bass, but the excitement and energy just grabbed me, and I wanted to be part of it. Of course, I'd heard rock'n'roll records before, but Bill Haley didn't affect me the same way. I knew Frannie Beecher (Haley's guitarist) was a fine player, but that wasn't the style of guitar that really hit me – he played in more of a country/swing style, which I should think Albert Lee got straight into, and they were jolly intricate solos, but it was the bending string style of solo that really got me going, and that's James Burton. That was where the problem came, because it took a dimwit like me about a year to realise that you had to remove your traditionally coated third string and replace it with an uncoated one, because it was physically impossible to bend otherwise.'

Two significant encounters during these early years were with Jeff Beck and Glyn Johns. 'I think I met Jeff through his sister – he came round to my house with a home-made guitar and played the James Burton solo from Ricky Nelson's "My Babe" and we were immediately like blood brothers, and we're still friends, of course. Things are a bit cloudy as far as Glyn goes – I remember meeting him at Epsom station and chatting, at a point where I was playing in a local hall and he'd started work as an apprentice engineer, but it wasn't until later that we worked together on a business basis.'

Jimmy's own instruments changed frequently at the start of his career, starting with a Grazioso as his first electric guitar. 'I did a paper round and got a Hofner Senator, which was really so that I could hear myself, and after increasing the paper round, I got an electric pick-up for it, but obviously, what I always wanted was a proper electric guitar, which to me was one with a solid body. It was a question of economics, and the Grazioso was the first one of that type that I had – it looked similar to a guitar that came out sometime later called a Futurama, basically a Stratocaster idea, but that shouldn't be thought of in today's terms where you see copies of Strats or Les Pauls, which are dead copies. This one had its own identity – it's like Hank Marvin with his Antoria. I had the Grazioso for about eighteen months, and then I think I got an orange-coloured Gretsch Chet Atkins for most of my period playing with Neil Christian.'

Neil Christian's Crusaders was the first semi-notable band in which Jimmy played, a later graduate of the Christian guitarist school being Ritchie

Blackmore. 'I played at the local Epsom dancehall, where a lot of really good bands came through, the best of which was Chris Farlowe and the Thunderbirds, whose first guitarist, Bobby Taylor, had the other Stratocaster that came into England – Hank Marvin had the first one – and he made a great impression on me. The Dave Clark Five also played there, but this was before "Glad All Over", and I played in the support band, just auditioning, really, and the night we auditioned, Neil Christian was there. He was actually managing Red Lewis & the Redcaps, a Gene Vincent style group, and we started to chat, and he asked whether I'd like to play in London, which of course I did. He had to talk to my parents first, which was quite a courteous thing to do – I was tailored in the mould to do what all young lads do, which was to go through school and pass exams, which was what I was doing – certainly, being a rock'n'roll musician wasn't the choicest of professions, but he reassured my parents and said he'd keep a watchful eye on this young lad, and anyway, the gigs were at weekends.'

Somewhat surprisingly (or so it now appears), Jimmy was not immediately invited to play on Christian's records. 'Auditions are a story in themselves – I remember going to the BBC for an audition with Neil Christian, and the blokes told us that Chris Farlowe had just failed his, which gave us the horrors, because in my estimation, they were the best band in the south. When we went to EMI, it was a very different situation from today, which is one thing the Beatles did for everybody, opening the door for groups with their own material – not that we did, but that was the way it was. The singer recorded and the band got the chop, and the producer who was assigned would get his mates who were songwriters to supply the material, and session musicians would back the singer, while the band weren't even invited to the session – but that was how it was in those days, and we were quite happy that Neil Christian was making a record. Looking back, you can be pretty cynical about that, but at the time, we just thought we weren't good enough, although I think I was on one of his records later on.'

To some extent, destiny finally struck when Jimmy became very ill as a result of the rather irregular life he was leading. 'Eventually I said I couldn't go on, and curiously enough, at that point, Cyril Davies, who had just broken away from Alexis Korner, and was the one who turned everybody on to the electric harmonica, asked me to join his band. I thought it would be awful to go with him and really start enjoying it, and then start getting ill again, but I did in fact play with them a bit, and the band was basically the nucleus of Screaming Lord Sutch's band. I think Neil Christian felt I wanted to go with Cyril Davies, but I was being perfectly honest in telling him that I couldn't carry on – I couldn't understand why I was getting ill all the time, and I just retreated to the only other thing I could do, which was a pretty grim prospect. It was painting, and I went to art college at Sutton, although I was also accepted by Croydon – I don't know how, because I was a terrible draughtsman. The Cyril Davies thing was quite interesting – he had what was known as an interval band which played at the Marquee. We never

actually rehearsed, but we were allowed to play the interval spot, which was all right, but the most terrifying night of all was when they had a big blues package over, with Muddy Waters and a guy called Matthew Murphy, who, believe me, was some guitarist. I'd always had this theory that Murphy had played on some Chuck Berry records, and in fact he had, on things like "Sweet Sixteen", the B. B. King song.'

From this point, Jimmy, to some extent due to his poor health, became involved in playing as a session guitarist – the 'Hired gun' who could play in most styles and was available in case the guitarist with a new recording group was found to be unsuitable by a producer. In fact, his first session was for a hit record, 'Diamonds' by Jet Harris and Tony Meehan, who had shortly before departed from the Shadows.

'Glyn (Johns) introduced me to the session world, although that was a long time before I did the work which everything stemmed from. What went wrong there was that they stuck a row of dots in front of me, which looked like crows on telegraph wires, which was awful. I could have played it so easily, and it was so simple when another chap came and did it – I realised what had to be done, but that wasn't the game. I'd never bothered or tried to read music, because it just didn't come into the pattern of things at that time, so they said I'd better play the acoustic bit, and when the other chap played this simple sort of riff, I gave myself hell for it. It wasn't so much a matter of a lost opportunity as a matter of pride – I felt really stupid.

'Then, some time later, I was invited to do a session after one of those Thursday nights at the Marquee, and that was my first proper session, which was for Carter-Lewis & the Southerners [later better known as the Ivy League] and that record, which was called "Your Mama's Out Of Town", made a dent in the charts, and it was at a point when the Beatles and the Stones were really coming on strong in the charts – groups were burning like dynamos all over the country, and as far as the session world went, there were just two young guitarists, Big Jim Sullivan and Vic Flick, but Jim seemed to be the only one in tune with what was happening, so they also pulled me out by the scruff of my neck, and gave me an opportunity to have a go . . .

'I was in on a lot of sessions for Decca artists at the start, and some were hits, although not because of the guitar playing. Nevertheless, I'd been allowed into the whole sort of impenetrable brotherhood, and it was great fun and games to start with, although it had its embarrassing moments, such as recording with Van Morrison and Them. This wasn't when he was being produced by Bert Berns, because those sessions were fantastic, but one particular time, I'd been booked as a guitarist with a group, and often, there'd be a drummer, and bit by bit, as the evening went on, another session musician would appear, one sitting next to the bass player, another sitting next to the keyboards, so in the end, it was just Van Morrison, session players and the group, but the session players were just duplicating the group. You can imagine the tension, and what these chaps from Ulster must have thought – it was so embarrassing that you just had to look at the floor and play because they were glaring. It could have been the end of their musical career in one evening' – Jimmy played on several famous tracks by Them, 'Baby Please Don't Go', 'Gloria' and 'Here Comes The Night'. However, there presumably came a time when an endless round of sessions, although lucrative, left something to be desired in terms of ambition fulfillment . . .

'For the first eighteen months, it was really enjoyable, and I'd come to terms a lot more with the technical side of it and having to read music. Although I could never read music in the same way that I could read a newspaper, I could scan through a sheet of music and know it by the time they counted the song in. So I never actually learned to read, although I wish I had . . . As the situation and mood of the music scene changed, and say, the Stax sound came in with saxophones, the guitar was still riffing in the background at that point, but then orchestras would be reintroduced, and the guitar would go even further into the background to such a degree that whereas I'd initially been there doing all the hot licks, so to speak, now I'd be doing, for example, a session with Tubby Hayes, the jazz saxophonist, then something with Petula Clark, and to follow that, anything from rock'n'roll to a jingle to a folk session, so I was really having to stretch my musical resources and knowledge without even realising it, which was really good, as far as discipline and an education went.

'So at the start and for some time afterwards, it was really good, until the day I was booked to do a muzak session, and then it really came down hard as to what it was all about. The way they do these things is you have a sheet of music which looks like a magazine or something, and you just keep turning over and over, and they don't stop – for someone who was having a bit of trouble with reading music, it was terrifying. The whole thing wasn't enjoyable any more, and putting that side by side with the fact that I was getting booked on muzak sessions, I just wanted to leave, and after that, I tried to find out what I'd been booked on, and I actually turned things down if I thought it would be a waste of everybody's time.'

Among the other more notable artists for whom Jimmy played sessions were Billy Fury, Joe Cocker (under his early alias of Vance Arnold and the Avengers) and the Kinks, the last of which at one point became a controversial topic. Jimmy confirmed that he hadn't played on the group's first hit, 'You Really Got Me', but was certainly on several later singles and an album, playing both lead and rhythm guitar. 'That's like the Van Morrison business – I never mentioned to anyone that I was on Kinks records, but it was mentioned to me later. Certainly, in the early days of Led Zeppelin, I wasn't telling people that I'd played on this, that and the other, which might have gained us some mileage, but a lot of people knew about it and were doing it on my behalf, which I guess was a drag as far as Ray Davies was concerned, but the thing was that he didn't straighten the situation out beforehand.'

In 1965, Jimmy released a solo single, 'She Just Satisfies'/'Keep Moving', which may have been the very first time on which a noted session player was invited to make a record under his own name. 'Possibly so . . . I was just asked to do it. They probably hoped for a lot more than they got – it was just a drummer, Bobby Graham, and myself, and initially a

bass player, but eventually I did the bass and everything else but the drums. It really sounds funny now when you listen to it. "Keep Moving" has a lot of harmonica on it – you had to play harmonica as part of the blues thing, and once you'd heard these great players like Little Walter, which was such a rude sound, and realised the mechanics of the thing, even though you played badly, it was really fun to do, so I just played it a bit, and every now and then, I got the chance to play it on a record.' Other harmonica sessions were for Mickey Finn & the Blue Men, whose leader later played in the Heavy Metal Kids, and for Cliff Richard, while Jimmy was also used on an early David Bowie release, when Bowie and his group were known as Davy Jones & the Lower Third, plus sessions for Dave Berry and also for the Everly Brothers.

Both the Kinks and David Bowie sessions had been with Glyn Johns engineering and Shel Talmy producing, while another act using this team was the Who, at this point just starting their recording career with their first single, 'I Can't Explain'/'Bald Headed Woman' on which Jimmy says that he was 'basically riffing. OK, I was there, and I think there's a couple of phrases on the B-side, but what the heck? The next one, they did on their own, and obviously, as it was the same producers, Townshend must have said that he could handle it.'

Another unlikely liaison was with American singer/songwriter Jackie De Shannon, with whom Jimmy had what was described as 'a whirlwind romance' in 1964. Ms De Shannon was in England, having been invited to cross the Atlantic by the Beatles, who had previously asked her to be their support act on tour.

'She was over here recording this single, "Don't Turn Your Back On Me, Babe", which was good, actually, and she said "It's like this". I did it, and she said "That's fast – it usually takes them a long time to get it off in the States", although I don't know whether or not that was true. We wrote about eight songs together – well, she certainly wrote the lyrics, and I probably came up with a title or a line, because she was really a writer.'

Several of these songs were recorded by artists of the calibre of Marianne Faithfull, among others.

A slightly more substantial part of rock history came in the form of Immediate Records, which was in operation for the second half of the 1960s, and with which Page was involved in various guises for the first part of its existence. One of his first jobs for Immediate was working with German chanteuse Nico (this is prior to her more celebrated period as a member of the Velvet Underground), for whom he produced a single released on Immediate, 'I'm Not Saying'/'The Last Mile', also writing the latter song.

'Andrew Oldham [who launched the label, concurrently also managing the Rolling Stones] had a remarkable ear and was totally vibed into anything that was going on anywhere. He was really sensitive, a remarkable intuitive man, who could always put his finger on the pulse here, there and everywhere.' Page also produced a single for a band named Fleur De Lys, 'Moondreams', and another for a band known as Fifth Avenue, 'Bells Of Rhymney'.

Page's most famous production for Immediate was

of a single by Eric Clapton and John Mayall, 'I'm Your Witchdoctor'/'Telephone Blues'. 'I'm glad you said that, because I was just starting to wonder what I had done – I knew Mayall from the Marquee, and Eric and I had been mates there as well. I first met Eric when I was booked to do a session and he'd just been recording in the same studio beforehand, and we met up in the lobby. He said "They tell me you play a bit of Matt Murphy" and I said "Well, I have a shot", but I didn't hear him play at that time – it was a fantastic shock when I did, because he's a tremendous player. I did four tracks altogether with Mayall and Eric – the other two were "Sitting On Top Of The World" and "Double Crossing Time", and that last one came out on the *Bluesbreakers* album on Decca, or at least a very similar recording.'

Which leads to what was arguably the largest blot on Immediate's escutcheon, a series of sub-standard recordings released in many different forms with several different titles, the best known of which is probably *Anthology Of British Blues, Volumes I & II*. Had it not been for the fact that these albums 'featured' Jimmy, Eric Clapton, Jeff Beck, Nicky Hopkins, John Mayall, Cyril Davies, Albert Lee, several members of Fleetwood Mac and other almost equally famous names besides, the records would have been forgotten, although in fact three of the very few good tracks are those by Mayall and Clapton produced by Page, the omitted item of the four mentioned above being 'Double Crossing Time'. A number of other tracks are credited to 'Eric Clapton with Jimmy Page', and it has been rumoured that these were in fact sections of a single 45 minute jam session recorded informally at Jimmy's home, which were later claimed as being the property of Immediate Records.

'That wasn't Andrew Oldham personally, by the way – there were other parties in that company – but it was claimed that at the time we made the recordings, Eric was signed to Immediate, and they wanted to put the tapes out as they were, which was ludicrous. But as they were going to do it anyway, I asked if some extra instruments could be added, and so Mick Jagger played harmonica on some of it, and Stu from the Stones played piano, and Charlie (Watts) and Bill (Wyman), but really it was pretty much the same theme of blues, but with those extra musicians. I actually thought they were only going to use one track – when one of the things that was just a jam at the end of the session came out as a B-side, I hit the roof, but there wasn't much I could do about it, being pretty green at the time. Then this *Anthology Of British Blues* came out just as Immediate was folding, so there was really nothing to be done, but the whole thing was just an experiment, and it wasn't done in the way in which it finally appeared – I think everybody was cheated at the end of the day on that.'

At this stage in his career, Page began to achieve greater public visibility when he joined the legendary British R&B band the Yardbirds in June 1966, although not initially as lead guitarist, Jeff Beck still holding that position in the band, but as bass player. 'It was fate that brought that Yardbirds opportunity around – Jeff and I were the greatest of friends, and I'd been going with him to a number of Yardbirds gigs, and he had always said it would be great if we

Yardbirds 1966 – left to right: Jeff Beck, Jimmy Page, Chris Dreja (front), Keith Relf, Jim McCarty

could play together, which I never thought would be possible. Then one night they did a gig at Oxford University, and Keith (Relf, the group's singer) saw all these chaps in the audience dressed like penguins, and let them know what he thought of them, but the bass player, Paul Samwell-Smith, didn't really like that too much. He said he was leaving the band, and I think he suggested to Jim McCarty, the drummer, that he should do the same, but Jim didn't. I guess they thought Paul would change his mind the next day, as I did – I thought it was a bit of a joke – but then Jeff called me and said he'd definitely left the band, and I said I'd play with them if they wanted, because I'd certainly been listening to what they were doing. Mind you, Samwell-Smith's was a big position to fill, because he was a noted bass player, and although I may have played bass before, I'd never played it in that role, but the thing was that we hoped we could get Chris (Dreja, rhythm guitarist) to play the bass parts, and then Jeff and I would be doing a sort of dual lead thing, which really could have started a whole new thing going. Viewed that way, the rest of the band seemed really keen on it, so I picked up the bass, and when we played the Marquee, which was one of their strongholds, I was terrified, having to fill Samwell-Smith's role, but fortunately it went OK. Eventually, we did the dual lead thing, although there aren't that many recordings of that line up, which is a great shame; just "Stroll On", a commercial for American radio, "Happenings Ten Years Time Ago" and "Psycho Daisies", but it was already starting to get into solo projects – Keith had already done his first one before I joined, and Jeff was going to do his, which was when the "Bolero" was done.'

In fact, 'Stroll On' was a curious mutation of the Johnny Burnette song, 'Train Kept A-Rollin', whose title was changed apparently in order that a financial advantage should be gained as regards publishing royalties, and was featured in the Antonioni film, *Blow Up*. A recent showing of the film on television reinforced an original impression that the brief scene featuring the Yardbirds, in which Jeff Beck destroys a guitar, seems contrived.

'The curious thing was that nobody in the film

crew seemed to know what the film was about when we asked them, which sounds ridiculous, but it's absolutely true – when you see the film, you know it's about photography, and what I've just said seems totally off the wall, but that's how it came to me at the time, and we didn't know what the film was about. I suppose it was put together to be a statement of a particular point in time, and maybe Antonioni felt that whole issue there was relevant, but our bit is rather a sore thumb, isn't it? The club in which we were supposedly playing was supposed to be the Ricky Tick at Windsor – I never went there, but the other lads said it was identical, cobweb for cobweb.'

'Beck's Bolero' was mentioned as one of the solo projects which members of the Yardbirds were involved in . . . 'There was a plan for Jim (McCarty) to do a comedy record, and his humour was amazing, so as weird as that might sound, it could have been really good. Jeff's solo project was to be instrumental, although it could have been vocal, and this thing was cooked up, the "Bolero". I was mainly instrumental in getting it together, I think – Jeff obviously added lyrical parts to it, and he also put a riff in the middle of it, but the major part of it was mine, and I did arrange it up to the middle point where the riff comes in. The other side to that occasion was that the band which played on "Beck's Bolero" might have turned into the first Led Zeppelin, because Keith Moon was on drums, John Entwistle was going to do the session, but something else cropped up, and John Paul Jones actually did it, and Nicky Hopkins was on piano, and there was a lot of talk afterwards of actually getting a band together – Keith was really keen on doing it, but there were certain politics involved – and singers were approached, but suddenly, it got a bit hairy and everyone backed off. Steve Winwood and Steve Marriott were the two immediate names that were thought of – Rod Stewart didn't come up until later – and it was a dream at the time.'

Encouraged by the 'Bolero', Jeff Beck soon afterwards left the Yardbirds. 'That was really a shame, because we'd just got it going. There was about six months of the twin guitar thing, I suppose – we did a tour with the Stones, and then there was a tour of the States which was thirty-three dates, I think, and of those thirty-three, twenty-five or something were doubles! You'd think a double (two shows in one night) would be in the same town, but it wasn't, it was in two different towns – the show was in two halves, and as the first half finished and there was an interval, that lot would be in the coach driving to the next venue while the second half went on, and they in turn carried on to the next place when they'd finished. Jeff stood about four days of that, and then knocked it on the head – he had really bad tonsils, and I think the whole thing made him ill, but we carried on.'

The impression gained of the morale of the Yardbirds during their final period, following Beck's departure, was of a somewhat discontented quartet, particularly with regard to their recordings. 'It wasn't the happiest period, and it must have been very depressing for the founder members of the band, because they'd lived through songs that I hadn't, like "Heart Full Of Soul" and "Shapes Of Things", think-

ing back. The first thing we did was "Little Games", which was at the point where we were two separate entities, and Jeff did "Love Is Blue", although we were still mates and we told each other what we were doing. We were allocated "Little Games", but it didn't do anything. I think the straw that broke the camel's back was one particular song, "Goodnight Sweet Josephine", which we didn't want to record, because we weren't at all keen on it. We knew it wasn't anything like the sort of thing we were moving towards, because by this time the band had started to feel itself as a four piece unit, and I'd managed to get some identity into it with new material and new directions for some of the things that they'd done before – not songs like "Shapes Of Things", which were done pretty much like the original, but "Smokestack Lightnin'" and things like that – and this number was put to us. We knew it wasn't right, but we decided to try it to see if it worked, but it didn't work, and unfortunately it came out – in the States, not in Britain – and it was really upsetting. In Mickie Most's defence, he must have believed in it, because he obviously wouldn't release if he didn't, but it didn't do anything and everyone was upset at the end of the day.'

To revert to the guitars which Jimmy used, he had played a Gretsch Chet Atkins during his days with Neil Christian, which he changed eventually for a Gibson Stereo, which he owned very briefly indeed. 'It wasn't really a case of it not being right, but rather that I saw a Les Paul Custom, which I'd never seen before, just after I bought the other one, so I traded it in for the Les Paul, which was called both the Black Beauty and the fretless wonder, and was just the most magnificent guitar I'd ever seen. The frets were actually filed down to produce a very smooth playing action – in fact, at a later stage I had it fretted in a standard manner, but it just sounded so pure and fantastic . . . plus at that time, I was over the top with Les Paul anyway, as a player, so it all followed.'

It was presumably on the Les Paul that Jimmy first attempted an effect for which he later became famous, using a violin bow across the strings of the guitar. The first definitely identifiable occasion where this effect can be heard on record was on a late Yardbirds B-side, 'Tinker, Tailor, Soldier, Sailor'.

'I had used it on a session many years before, but I can't remember what it was, because it wasn't my idea – one of the violinists suggested that I try it to see what would happen.' This technique would assume far greater proportions after Led Zeppelin was formed.

Almost the final episode in the career of the Yardbirds was the recording of a live LP in New York, which has appeared for sale briefly on a couple of occasions, before injunctions have removed it from the market – the album's title was/is *Live Yardbirds featuring Jimmy Page*.

During 1968, the Yardbirds finally threw in the towel, but somewhat strangely (or so it seemed until it was explained), the newest member of the band, i.e. Jimmy, owned the copyright to the name 'Yardbirds'. 'That sounds really ghastly, doesn't it? What happened was that I was trying to keep the band together – when I think about it now, I can see exactly why Keith and Jim wanted to leave, but at the time, I couldn't. It was wanting to do something different, and I thought that no matter what it might be – Mr Big Head, who'd done it all in the studio! – we could try it and maybe get it together, but Keith came out with it and said "The magic died for me when Eric left the band", which seemed most peculiar to me, because I thought the best stuff they'd done had been with Jeff, but if you think about it, you can see that those were the days that were more important to him, as opposed to the way we see it. He said "If you want the name, you can have it" – I don't know where there's any copyright thing, and I certainly haven't put my name on any piece of paper, but he said I could keep the name if I wanted it.'

Page played considerably fewer outside sessions during his time with the Yardbirds than he had previously, although some were with notable artists, including Johnny Halliday, maybe the only French rock'n'roll artist to gain any credibility outside France, Donovan and Ian Whitcomb. However, the two biggest hit records on which he played during the second half of the 1960s were Chris Farlowe's "Out Of Time" and Joe Cocker's "With A Little Help From My Friends", which both topped the British chart. Of the Cocker record, Jimmy recalls 'That session was fantastic to do, just one big smile, with such a warm feeling going round the studio. It was one of those things where it deserved to be heard elsewhere, and you hoped it would be – you could sometimes tell that a record was going to be a big hit, but more often, you knew that they weren't.'

After the Yardbirds, Page and Chris Dreja, along with manager Peter Grant, who had been involved with the group during their death throes, were left to make new plans. And what Jimmy did, of course, was form Led Zeppelin. It has been suggested elsewhere that a possible projected line up might have been Jimmy on guitar, Chris Dreja from the Yardbirds on bass, Terry Reid singing and B. J. Wilson (from Procul Harum) on drums.

'I was mainly going after Terry Reid, who had really impressed me during a Yardbirds tour when Jeff was with me in the band, and we toured with the Stones. I remembered him from that, but as fate would have it, he'd signed to Mickie Most. But he recommended Robert (Plant) and I went to see Robert and was gassed out, because he was really great. It seemed really strange to me that somebody that good hadn't emerged before, but it always seems that at the end of the day, someone who's good will come through, a classic example of that being Albert Lee. I wasn't sure about who to use as a drummer. B. J. Wilson was somebody I'd worked with on the Cocker sessions and he was really good – as far as I can remember, he called me up, but I wasn't absolutely sure, because it was something where you had to really work out the chemistry to make sure it matched before the first rehearsal, or else it would be a total disaster and might spoil three elements out of four. Robert suggested Bonzo (John Bonham), and obviously, when I saw him, there couldn't be anybody else as our drummer. At that point, as far as I can remember, there were some outstanding contracts to be fulfilled with the Yardbirds, and Chris was still there, but then John Paul Jones, who I'd met through studio work, rang up – he was getting into sessions about halfway through the period that I was doing them, and he was firmly established by the time I decided to get out. He was doing arranging as well, and he'd done stuff for Andrew Oldham on the Stones records, and for Mickie Most, the Donovan things – and said "I hear you're getting a group together and I'd like to be part of it", and when that happened, Chris told me to go ahead, and suddenly there it was – four guys that could go into a rehearsal room and know it was going to be dynamite.'

Led Zeppelin were rumoured to have been recommended to their record company, Atlantic, by one of the label's very few British acts prior to Zeppelin, Dusty Springfield, but Jimmy thinks this is unlikely, although he is more willing to concede that his band may have been the first British group to be signed directly to an American label, rather than via a UK subsidiary. 'As far as I know, we were the first white band on Atlantic, because all the earlier white bands had been on Atco. At the time, we said we'd really like to be on Atlantic as opposed to Atco, because it was the first true independent label that had really sailed through and done it well.'

So what did Jimmy intend to do with Led Zeppelin when he first conceived of the band that would be different from the groups with which he'd be competing? 'I think it's all there on the first LP, but personally speaking, I was trying to explore the different avenues of the guitar, establishing that we could play acoustically (as well as with electric instruments) right from the start so that it didn't make any difference come the third LP, when there was more of a leaning towards acoustic numbers than before – in fact, acoustic playing figured on the first album. Apart from that, I wanted the band to come through with something that was hard hitting dynamite that other musicians would respect as well, but would be so good that everyone in the band would feel committed to it, which was how it went, in fact, and what was great was that such a respect was built up between the four of us for each other.

'We rehearsed quite a lot within the framework of the numbers, but the full construction – the embellishments, the overdubs, and certain lyrics, like the verses on "Communication Breakdown", where there had just been a chorus – was added. We had numbers from the Yardbirds that we called free form, like "Smokestack Lightnin'", where I'd come up with my own riffs and things, and obviously I wasn't going to throw all that away, as they hadn't been recorded, so I remodelled those riffs and used them again, so the bowing on "How Many More Times" and "Good Times, Bad Times" was an extension of what I'd been working on with the Yardbirds, although I'd never had that much chance to go to town with it, and to see how far one could stretch the bowing technique on record, and obviously for anyone who saw the band, it became quite a little showpiece in itself. It was really enjoyable to do, and people used to remark on it, so obviously they enjoyed watching it, and it was also musical as well – some of the sounds that came out of it were just incredible, and sometimes it would sound like that "Hiroshima" piece by Penderecki, and other times, it would have the depth of a cello. "Good Times, Bad Times", as usual, came

*An early Led Zeppelin shot – left to right:
John Bonham, Robert Plant, Jimmy Page, John Paul Jones*

out of a riff with a great deal of John Paul Jones on bass, and it really knocked everybody sideways when they heard the bass drum pattern, because I think everyone was laying bets that Bonzo was using two bass drums, but he only had one.

'"Dazed And Confused" came from the Yardbirds, and that was my showcase, show-off bit with the bow, and that was one example, I guess, of how everything but the kitchen sink was in that first album from my end – I think that was something I did consciously, because I started off all the numbers on that LP, and I did a lot of different things with diffe-rent instruments, leaning heavily on some of the ideas that I'd developed with the Yardbirds because I knew they were things I'd come up with myself rather than riffs that Eric or Jeff had done. I'd always been interested in every facet of and approach to guitar playing, from flamenco to classical to early '50s rock'n'roll – it's always intrigued me, because the tonal quality of the approach to classical guitar is totally different in its finger style from say, folk guitar, and the way the fingers have to shape on the right hand to attack is quite different, and the tones are absolutely stunning, and from that, you can get to Django Reinhardt's beautiful tone and emotive feeling.

'I just love every aspect of guitar playing, and I try and play a little bit of everything. On "Babe I'm Gonna Leave You", which was pretty original as far as it went, and I don't think anything like that had been done before, I tried putting on a pedal steel guitar, which I'd had, but never known the legiti-mate tuning of, so the only thing I could really play

on it was the sort of instrumental thing that Chuck Berry had done, things like "Deep Feeling". I'd heard those and read afterwards that they'd been done on a pedal steel that was sitting in the studio, and the full extent of my knowledge on pedal steel was finding a tuning that emulated those slow blues instrumentals which Chuck Berry did, but anyhow, out it came, and it was OK on "Babe I'm Gonna Leave You", but on "Your Time Is Gonna Come", the intonation was extremely suspect, and that one tried to get a bit too ambitious.

'The idea of "Communication Breakdown" was to have a really raw hard hitting number. It's hard to describe the feeling of playing those numbers at the time, but it was so exciting and electrifying to be part of it, and that one was always so good to play, so staccato – just a knockout to do.'

Led Zeppelin was made at high speed, which Jimmy explains was partly due to the fact that the band had previously played some live dates, and was engineered by Glyn Johns, who claimed he also pro-duced it, although Jimmy, who was credited with the production, feels that the credit was correct, although it was in fact the first complete LP he had ever produced.

'What happened afterwards came as a massive surprise, that success, and to be perfectly truthful, the shock didn't hit me until a number of years later. We were touring until the day when we were pre-sented with a gold record – I thought "My goodness! A gold record!".'

Both the first and last months of 1969 saw Led Zep-pelin albums released. *Led Zeppelin II* obviously differed from the first album in that the material was not as well-established before recording. 'We were extending the repertoire at that point, and recording it at the same time, so we were pretty much working all the time, and looking back, it seemed like a 24-hour commitment every day. There were so many overdubs applied to the numbers that some of them actually changed their format. On the first LP, we had benefitted by having played some of the songs before going into the studio, but I can remember during that time around the end of the second LP, we started to work on "Since I've Been Loving You", which we recorded on the third LP, and that was one we got used to playing onstage, but it was the hardest one to actually record. That was at the point where we were getting very self-critical. Anyway, the second album was recorded while we were touring, so it was recorded partly in London, partly in Los Angeles, some was done in New York, and a vocal overdub was even done in an 8-track studio in Vancouver, and that's how it was done until the mixing, which was all done in New York. Contrary to rumour, I was quite happy with the album, because I thought it had the energy that was totally relevant to what was happening onstage at that point.'

The best known track from *Led Zeppelin II* is undoubtedly 'Whole Lotta Love', which for some years was used, although not as recorded by Zeppelin, as the theme tune for 'Top Of The Pops'. The riff used in the song was instantly memorable.

'The riff came from me, but don't ask me where it came from before that, because it just came out of thin air, as nearly all riffs do. It was pretty infectious, I suppose, although its being on 'Top Of The Pops' every week killed it over here, which was a drag.'

Another interesting aspect of the recording of 'Whole Lotta Love' is that on it, Jimmy plays a somewhat obscure instrument known as a theremin. 'The theremin was something that came out of France in the '30s, an oscillator, where the closer you get to the aerial, the higher the pitch goes. I saw one being used by Spirit, but I don't remember what they did with it – they were quite readily available in music shops, although they're far rarer now, and I remember having a lot of trouble getting it going at Knebworth.'

Another standout track, especially from Jimmy's point of view, was 'Heartbreaker', in the second half of which he plays an excellent guitar part. 'That song's pretty much in two sections – it stops and there's a whole guitar bit before it moves into the solo, like changing gears into overdrive. It was fairly similar to the sort of thing that was coming out in live performances – I wish there was more material recorded live, apart from that film soundtrack (see below), but as far as that heavy metal label we were given, it wasn't that, because it wasn't just like hitting a riff and going on and on at it at the same intensity, it was a question of light and shade and dynamics, and it would be really loud one minute, and so soft that a pin could drop and be heard the next.'

Equally significant was the large part Robert Plant was taking in lyric composition. 'In the early days, I was writing the lyrics as well as the music, because Robert hadn't written before, and it took a lot of rib-

The rustic Page, early 1970s

bing and teasing to actually get him into writing, which was funny. And then, on the second LP, he wrote the words of "Thank You" – he said "I'd like to have a crack at this and write it for my wife".'

Between the recording of their second and third LPs, Jimmy and Robert Plant went to India, where they spent some time in a local recording studio. 'The intention was always to do a complete world tour, at the same time recording in places like Cairo, Bangkok and Bombay, and involving local musicians as well. It was just an experiment to see how well we would get on, so we recorded two tracks in India, "Friends" and "Four Sticks", just to see how it would go, and it was tremendous. It would have been lovely to do that with the group, but we never got around to it, and those two tracks never came out in that form.'

They were, however, included on *Led Zeppelin III* and the untitled fourth LP, respectively, but in more straightforward studio recordings and by the complete band. The third LP was released in October, 1970, and received a mixed critical reaction. 'We went and stayed in a cottage in Wales, and wrote some songs which fitted in with the mood there, so obviously one recorded them – our albums were mostly a statement of where we were at the time we recorded them. But after the second LP, which had a lot of hard-hitting rock, it was interpreted as us mellowing and losing all our power.'

From this point on, a noticeable and perhaps understandable reluctance on Page's part to respond to a substantial percentage of our questions became noticeable, thus a good deal of what follows is rather sketchy. *Led Zeppelin III* topped the LP charts around the world, as had *II* before it, but, as noted, critical reaction was muted. The critical flak led directly to some basic rethinking for the fourth album, which was released in 1971, but lacked a title, and in fact lacked words of any sort on the sleeve, apart from those dimly visible on an Oxfam poster photographed as part of an urban landscape.

Onstage at Bath, 1970

'The band came under a lot of attack from the press after the third LP – the musical press attitude is that you're God one minute and shit the next, and you've got no right to be recognised by anyone else and become successful or whatever – so on the fourth LP, we decided to release it with nothing on whatsoever, no name of the band, but just the runes (symbols apparently relating to each individual band member), and just saying "This is us – you don't have to buy the LP, so don't, if that's the way it is". That was a hell of a legal battle – I remember sitting in the office for a whole afternoon and being told it had to have this, that and the other written on it, and I said "Well, it doesn't, and if it does. . . ." You have to make certain stands at times – afterwards, it may seem totally ridiculous, but at the time, the band were totally in agreement, so it was worth doing.'

A postscript to the third LP concerns the track 'Celebration Day' – 'The beginning of that track actually got wiped (erased) by an assistant engineer, who made a terrible mistake, so we lost the first part of it. The bloke just ran out, in case he was going to get killed! Between "Friends" and "Celebration Day", there's this drone that brings the track in, there's part of the vocal, and then it comes into the rhythm, and I put that together as a salvage job after having lost it.'

Reverting to the fourth LP, which became popularly known as either the 'runes' album, or 'Four Symbols', the four curious shapes were referred to as 'artistic symbols chosen by the band'. 'Initially, it was just going to be one symbol, but then it was down to one each, so everyone had a shot'. Page's own symbol seems to read 'Zoso' . . . 'That's not the pronunciation, it's just a doodle, and although it looks more like writing than the other three, that wasn't the intention.'

During the recording of the LP, several interesting occurrences took place – Peter Grant, the group's manager, attempted without success to organise live concerts in central London for them, first at Waterloo Station (which would have been a remarkable coup) and also at the headquarters of Surrey Cricket Club, Kennington Oval. However, one venture which did come off during 1971 was a tour of small clubs around Britain, including such venues as London's Marquee Club.

During July 1971, the group were inadvertently involved in a major riot in a stadium in Milan, Italy. 'When we went in, we could see these riot police – to which we're now accustomed, but at that time, we hadn't seen anything like that. We saw a few of them in a van, but as we started to play in this football stadium, which was oval shaped with a catwalk round the top, we could see movement round the catwalk, and all these riot police coming in. We just carried on playing, and there was smoke at the far end of the outdoor arena, and the promoters ran onstage and said would we tell them to stop lighting fires. So Robert asked them, we carried on playing, and there was a bit more smoke, and suddenly there was smoke by the front of the stage, and it was tear gas! The statement in the press the next day said that a bottle had been thrown at the police, which obviously was true by the end, because there had been quite a few of these puffs of smoke going on over a period of time, and it was about fifteen minutes before it hit the stage. But the police were

Onstage, wearing his 'symbol'

just provoking the audience, and suddenly it went off like you couldn't believe. It was just pandemonium, and nowhere was immune from this blasted tear gas, including us. I was terribly upset afterwards – I couldn't believe that we'd be used as the instrument for a political demonstration like that.'

Concurrent with several major British concerts, whose atmosphere was far happier, during November 1971 came the release of the fourth LP, the first track of which was titled 'Black Dog'. 'I didn't have a black dog, but there was one at Headley Grange, where we recorded the album. Another track reworked at Headley Grange, recording with a mobile truck, was "The Battle Of Evermore", and there was a mandolin there, which actually belonged to John Paul Jones. I don't think there was anything going on at one point, and I just picked up this mandolin and started playing a sequence, which probably consisted of the most basic chords on a mandolin, but from that, I worked out the sequence to that song. Listening to it now, it seems strange that it was really the first time I'd ever played a mandolin, although as I say, it's probably pretty basic chords, but the end result was really great.'

Another notable track on the LP, which is arguably the group's finest moment, was 'Four Sticks', which had been previously attempted during Jimmy and Robert's Indian trip. 'We tried a different way of approaching it, because it wasn't four sticks to begin with at all, it was two sticks. Bonzo was playing with two sticks, and the idea was to get this kind of abstract number, but then he had a Double Diamond, picked up four sticks, and we did it again, and it was magic, one take, and the whole thing had suddenly been made.'

An album with many high points, but the highest of all was certainly 'Stairway To Heaven'. 'That really sums it all up – it's just a glittering thing, and it was put together in such a way as to bring in all the fine points, musically, of the band in its construction.

When it came to the point of running it down with Robert, there's actually a first rehearsal tape of it, and sixty per cent of those lyrics, he came in with off the cuff, which was quite something, just by running through and coming in with the first thing – that was amazing. When we were recording it, there were little bits, little sections that I'd done, getting reference pieces down on cassette, and sometimes I referred back to them if I felt there was something that seemed right that could be included. I wanted to try this whole idea musically, this build towards a climax, with John Bonham coming in at a later point, an idea which I'd used before, to give it that extra kick. Then there's this fanfare towards the solo, and Robert comes in after that with this tremendous vocal thing. At the time, there were quite a few guitars overlaid on that, and I must admit I thought – I knew – it was going to be very difficult to do it on stage, but we had to do it, we really wanted to do it, and I got a double necked guitar to approach it. We were doing a tour in the States, and we'd worked this song in, and I remember we did it in LA and got a standing ovation at the end of it.'

It might appear odd that Led Zeppelin never released a single in Britain, while very few were released in the United States, and those primarily for promotional purposes. 'Stairway To Heaven' was one obvious possibility for single release, but making it available in that form would have necessitated, as Jimmy put it, 'Breaking the continuity of that album'. Of the song, Jimmy finally said that he regarded it as the pinnacle of the band's achievements, which he considered tragic 'because we haven't got the opportunity to explore any more'.

Almost eighteen months later, in March 1973, a fifth LP, *Houses Of The Holy*, was released, again with no writing on the sleeve. Probably the classic track on the album is 'The Rain Song', which Jimmy recalled had also been difficult to play on stage initially. 'It was hard until we got the feel of it, but it became a classic in the end. It was one of those cases of keeping going at it, especially as we had initially played all the instruments ourselves and it was a matter of sorting out which overdubs were the least important, or maybe inserting a new phrase.' Although the album predictably enough topped charts everywhere, it seemed to be generally accepted that it was by no means the group's most instantly accessible record. The group, however, were starting to work on other projects – shooting began on a film featuring them, the Swan Song record label, owned by the band, was launched during 1974, and during 1975 came the first Zeppelin release on Swan Song, the double album, *Physical Graffiti*.

As well as many new tracks, the fifteen songs included several items recorded some time before, but for various reasons not included on previous albums. The track from the album generally singled out for praise was 'Kashmir'.

'Along with "Stairway", that's probably the one that most people would think of if we were mentioned, although they were totally different numbers in terms of content. The intensity of "Kashmir" was such that when we'd done it, we knew that it was something that was so magnetic within itself, and

Latterday Led Zep – left to right: John Paul Jones, John Bonham, Robert Plant, Jimmy Page

you couldn't really describe what the quality was. It was just Bonzo and myself at Headley Grange at the start of that one – he started the drums, and I did the riff and the overdubs, which in fact get duplicated by an orchestra at the end, which brought it even more to life, and it seemed so sort of ominous and had a particular quality to it. It's nice to go for an actual mood and know that you've pulled it off.

'Physical Graffiti' was the longest album to make, because we had about three sides of new material recorded, and it seemed to be a good idea to put on some of the numbers that had been left off previous LPs at that stage, because there had been quite a few out by that point, and obviously there was a period of going through, listening to the different tracks and adding things if they were necessary. There would usually be a guitar solo needed, which I'd do, and I'd usually add other parts as well, and at other times, Jonesy would do bits. You'd have the overall idea of what it was going to be like, especially once the vocal lines and phrasing were sorted out, because then you'd know where not to play, which was as important as knowing when you should play. With "In The Light", for instance, we knew exactly what its construction was going to be, but nevertheless, I had no idea at the time that John Paul Jones was going to come up with such an amazing synthesiser intro, plus there's all the bowed guitars at the beginning as well, to give the overall drone effect. We did quite a few things with drones on, like "In The Evening" and all that, but when he did that start for "In The Light", it was just unbelievable.'

The first of two 1976 LPs was *Presence*, which was

recorded in three weeks, a particularly impressive statistic considering that Robert Plant had been involved in a very serious car accident, which was made worse by the fact that he was unable, due to tax problems, to recuperate at his own home, or to be with his wife, who had also been injured in the accident. One of the tracks on *Presence* not only relates to this problem, but also illustrates a further problem which Jimmy encountered during recording.

'When we were doing *Presence*, we made an attempt at a blues that was called "Tea For One", about ultimate loneliness in a hotel room, which was Robert's title, and a really good one, and which had a really laid-back feel to it. It was basically a 12-bar, and there were two verses to do as solos on guitar, and it suddenly hit me at that point that everybody has played a blues number, and there are so many musicians whose forte it is, like Eric (Clapton), so what was I going to do? It was one of the last solos to go on, because I'd feared it a bit, and it had this atmosphere to it, which I knew was there, and when I heard it back, I was really pleased with it.'

The second Zeppelin album of 1976 (the only year other than 1969, when the first and second albums had appeared, when the group would release more than one record during a year) was the double soundtrack LP of the film which had been in preparation since 1973, and was finally premiered in October 1976, accompanied by the album whose title it shared, *The Song Remains The Same*. Following this, there was a lengthy silence from Led Zeppelin as far as newly recorded material went, this being partly explained by the tragic death of Robert Plant's five-year-old son in July 1977. By mid-1978, the group began preparations for what was to be their final album – 1979 saw them fully active again, releasing the LP, *In Through The Out Door*, and also playing to a vast crowd at the Knebworth Festival in Hertfordshire. A subsequent international tour seemed to indicate that the group were gearing up for further work, but on 25 September 1980, John Bonham was found dead in Jimmy Page's house, the coroner's verdict being accidental death.

After a period when it was uncertain whether or not Bonham would be replaced, the remaining members of Led Zeppelin finally decided that they would prefer not to relaunch the group with a new member, and instead, the three survivors went their separate ways, although, of course, there may come a time in the future when more than one ex-member of the group will appear on a stage simultaneously.

After a lengthy gap, Jimmy Page released his first solo project during 1982, this being his soundtrack to a film starring Charles Bronson, *Death Wish II*.

'I went to see the film at the director's house, and he asked me if I liked it. I said I thought it would be a challenge, and he correctly presumed that I wanted to take it on, and told me that I had eight weeks to do it. I walked out of his house after having had a very pleasant afternoon, feeling like a sledgehammer had hit me over the head. I had eight weeks to do forty-five minutes of music – that's collectively, the longest section was two and a half minutes, and most of the bits were 17 seconds or 45 seconds. I worked from videocassettes with timing on them, and realised that whatever I'd done before with films, I knew nothing whatsoever about how to really do it properly. I was working mainly to action, making the music synchronise with the action, even if it hadn't really been called for, because it would still be good and acceptable if it worked like that, although there were obviously a lot of sections which did need to be totally in synch. I'd find a metronome count where particular movements would coincide on the beat, which might be a dissipated beat, but would have a sort of tempo, and then count the bars from it and work on, being totally confident that something would be dead on the nail. I wrote everything from scratch that way, apart from one riff that I'd had from before – the rest of it was off the cuff, and it was an absolutely incredible exercise in discipline, which was terrifying, but I just about made the deadline. The only unfortunate thing was that it was a mono soundtrack that was needed, and the music had to be remixed in stereo for the LP, but none of the tracks were re-recorded.'

One particularly interesting aspect of the *Death Wish II* LP concerns Page's personal use of synthesisers, something for which he was not previously well known. Did he, like some of our other subjects, suspect that the age of the guitar was nearly over?

'The thing is that technology changes so fast within every six months that you see so many developments in every area. I must admit that guitar synthesisers had stimulated my imagination for quite a long time, but before the one I am using now, none of those available would track properly. You'd play, and it would be late, or it would just stop tracking, and the pitch to voltage would go wrong, and it would make a horrible squeak. But this particular

Jimmy Page today

machine is the works, and it finally gives a guitarist a chance to compete with keyboard players, purely because in the past it just wasn't technically possible. Now it is, and they're getting extra units so that you can have memory banks and at the push of a button, the sound will totally change. It's got great new scope for that for somebody like myself, who can't play a keyboard with two hands! On *Death Wish II*, I did some keyboard synthesis, but when it came down to needing a proficient player, I got Dave Lawson. Nevertheless, this has really opened up a new world, and as we see now with new groups, synthesisers really are a big part of what's going on. The guitar synthesiser that's been in any way comparable to the keyboard has been a long time coming, but it's here now, and I think we're going to hear a lot more of it. So you'll still see me with something that looks like a guitar – I might have some strange sounds coming out of it, and I may not be using the bow to do it, but I'll still be there.'

With the twin-necked guitar

Jimmy Page Discography

Early session work
As there is a great deal of this, and presumably the vast majority of it was recorded in the form of singles rather than albums, and since Jimmy was rarely, if ever, credited, it would probably be misleading to provide a list.

	Miscellaneous work pre-Led Zeppelin		Led Zeppelin
1969	*Anthology Of British Blues Volumes I & II* (These tracks have been released in many different forms under several titles)	1969	*Led Zeppelin*
		1969	*Led Zeppelin II*
		1970	*Led Zeppelin III*
1967(?)	*Little Games – Yardbirds* (only released in USA)	1971	Untitled fourth LP (*Runes* LP or *Four Symbols*)
		1973	*Houses Of The Holy*
1969	*With A Little Help From My Friends* (Joe Cocker)	1975	*Physical Graffiti*
		1976	*Presence*
1969	*A Way Of Life* (Family Dogg)	1976	*The Song Remains The Same* (soundtrack)
1969	*Love Chronicles* (Al Stewart)	1979	*In Through The Out Door*
1969	*Three Week Hero* (P. J. Proby: on which all four Led Zep members appear as session musicians)	1982	*Coda*
			Post Led Zeppelin
1976(?)	*Jimmy Page & Sonny Boy Williamson & Brian Auger* (material recorded during mid-1960s)	1982	*Death Wish II* (original soundtrack)

RY COODER

It may be that American readers of this book may wonder why? And even perhaps, who? It is an unfortunate fact that Ry Cooder, a Los Angelean born on 15 March 1947, remains under-appreciated in his native land, while a measure of his success in Europe, and in particular in Britain, is that at the start of 1982, he was able to sell out no less than eight consecutive nights at London's Hammersmith Odeon, thereby improving on the 'record' set a few weeks earlier by Status Quo, a band whose appeal is much easier to fathom. Although it might not be accurate to describe his family as musical, Ry was introduced to music by his parents: 'They had music everywhere in the house, and still listen to it all the time, and my dad used to play the guitar somewhat and sing, which is where I first heard guitar when I was a tiny kid.' Ry's first instrument was a four-string guitar which he acquired at the age of three or four. 'Somebody gave it to my father, and after a while, I asked him to show me how it was done. I had big hands, and I guess I could play a little, enough to enjoy it – if you make a sound you like, you make another one, so it's pretty simple.'

The next milestone for Ry was being given a Josh White record, which to some extent was instrumental in shaping his musical tastes. 'My parents had a lot of friends who were interested in politics, and in those days left-wing politics and certain music went together – a social statement, social condition type of thing – and in that genre, you had people like Josh White, (Pete) Seeger, Woody Guthrie, of course, and a whole collection of folks in some way involved in making that statement, and what it turned out in retrospect to be was bringing some kind of folk, or traditional unprogrammed music, to white middle class people who would never have heard it otherwise, which was an interesting by product. Of course, once I heard those records, I was fascinated, because I could tell this music was strange, from some other place, and that was why I liked it.'

Acquiring his first guitar at the age of ten, Ry gradually taught himself to play, with, as he says, 'A lot of help from various people. There were no particular guitar teachers in those days for that kind of music, but I got around some folks who could play, and they would show me things, and I had lessons when I could, but I worked at it all the time.' So when would he estimate that he became proficient? 'Proficiency's hard to define – I could play a song right through at any point, but getting to where you're playing what you want to play is another story, and that didn't begin to happen until I was in my teens, and it's just a matter of co-ordination and experience.'

At the age of thirteen, having already discovered the 'protest' end of folk music, Ry became aware of another type of American ethnic music, bluegrass. 'The wave hit LA, which was ripe for something like that, and it arrived as a good-time, happy-faced kind of music that was white, which meant that people could get behind it more easily than they could any kind of black music – it suggested that there might be a carefree, simple-minded world beyond all the stress and strain of Los Angeles, and that people could wear cowboy hats and boots and play banjos and be cowboys, which was a silly notion, but of

Onstage in California

course, everybody dug it. I liked the singing, and still do – bluegrass harmony is really pretty, especially the gospel stuff, but I don't play it anymore, because I can't stand the sound of the banjo, because it's too loud. There weren't many acts that I heard in those days – Bill Monroe, Flatt & Scruggs, the Stanley Brothers, who were my favourites, the Country Gentlemen – but these were guys who were still very good, and really in their prime, and it was a whole rich vein that was tapped. It was quite a thrill to see Bill Monroe who I even played with, and see the Stanley Brothers doing their stuff, and then look at them, check them out, and realise that these were strange folks, weird, who don't like black people and don't understand why they can't shoot off guns in a nightclub if they feel like it, and get drunk. It was more of a study of folks than anything else, and it all died out, although you still have banjo players in LA or New York, but it's not the same anymore – now it's pizza parlour music, and it's degraded itself.'

Another ethnic influence on Ry were the country/ blues players. 'I came across those people as they were re-recorded and rediscovered and generally made available, which was accomplished by the folk wave. Lightnin' Hopkins became a folk hero all of a sudden – he'd been a very successful recording artist in his own way in Texas, but when he became a folk hero, suddenly his records appeared on the Folkways label, and he was a person of importance whose records you could buy, and the same happened with Brownie McGhee and Sonny Terry, who came out after having had long careers to become important folk performers.'

This was, of course, prior to the domination of popular music by the Beatles. 'The Beatles took care of everything else, and brought it all to a screeching halt, although by that time, the blues revival had really flowed and the craze had hit pretty big – Howlin' Wolf came to town, Muddy Waters, Sleepy John Estes, Son House, and it was really amazing, and that happened through the energies of people like John Fahey, who were trying to get these guys like John Hurt out again. But then the Beatles came along, and nobody cared about this stuff anymore, and almost overnight the whole thing evaporated.'

Did Ry learn a lot from these blues players? 'Yeah, it was tremendous. You absorb by watching a guy and you learn where it's coming from. Not so much how it's played, because who knows how anybody plays anything, but you get a feeling of what kind of energy's in it, and what the people look like and how they move around, which was very illuminating. People like Gary Davis were fantastic. . .' Apparently, Ry had paid Davis to show him how to play certain things. . . 'That's what you did, it's a simple thing, You give the guy some money – what are you going to do, not give him money? It comes down to a question of what the rewards are for folks like that, who have been poor beyond your wildest imagination for their whole life, and still were that poor, except that they happened to be playing for middle class white kids like me, which doesn't change the fact that they're still poor beyond your wildest imagination. So you just say "Here's five bucks – how do you play that song?", and it seems like the right thing to do, money being about the only way you can show any kind of appreciation to such people. One by one, these guys died poor – John Estes, they had to borrow dirt to bury him, and Gary Davis and everyone died so destitute. . . But there was nothing that anybody could have done to change that anywhere along the line – that was never even a question. What could you do – buy Gary Davis a new car or a new suit? Later on, there was the thing about money being made from this stuff when people in pop music recorded the songs, and major labels, publishing, the whole trick. But it had never changed – on one side, you've got a group of people indulging their sensibilities in the warm bath of ethnic purity, and on the other, you've got the guys who actually do it, but who can't afford firewood, and that creates a certain kind of ambivalence that you can never resolve.'

Curiously enough, despite watching these veteran blues players, Cooder developed his celebrated bottleneck technique elsewhere – it is also of interest that he actually uses the neck of a bottle rather than a cylindrical piece of metal for this style of playing. 'I found out how to use a bottleneck by asking John Fahey, who had covered the territory looking for records and thus had been down there a lot, what it was that those guys were up to when they made that sound, and he showed me that all you needed was a bottleneck, to tune the guitar in a certain way, and then to go for it, sliding it up and down. Now, how you do it is another story which you have to work out for yourself, but I didn't understand what was actually going on there – the question was about Blind Willie Johnson, primarily, because the records

were so beat up and scratchy and unclear, yet the whole thing was so magical sounding, and I just couldn't straighten it out until it was explained, and then, when I saw somebody like Son House, it was pretty obvious what was going on, and after that, it's a matter of going out for yourself and trying to learn to do it. I use glass bottlenecks because I like the weight and I like the glass against the steel string, which makes a nice sound. Fred McDowell used polished soup bones every now and then, but that's a matter of preference. . . It makes a tremendous difference in sound if you use a metal bottleneck – metal on metal makes one kind of sound, while glass, being less dense and less heavy, or more porous, anyway, and with a different surface, makes another kind of sound.'

The Beatles hit America at the start of 1964, and this seems to have been about the time when Ry first began to play in public, although these early appearances were sporadic. His first documented professional appearance was with Jackie De Shannon, a notable songwriter/performer, although there had apparently been previous occasions on which he had mounted the stage. 'That was around the time that I was proficient enough to play something, and I was a pretty good accompanist, even in those days, and I could always play behind someone singing, because I could concentrate and listen to what they were doing and follow them, which I liked doing more than anything. I had some jobs very early on, while I was in High School, and then I went with Jackie into the recording studios here and there, and I saw what that was, and it was pretty interesting. I didn't know studios were there, and I often wondered where records were made – was it on street corners, or in barbershops?

'Jackie De Shannon had the idea that she wanted to be a folk performer, which wasn't a bad idea – it didn't quite go over, but there was something to it, and we got some blues and country tunes together, some pretty interesting songs, but it was a little too late, although it was good, and showed me something about what you do with a song to make it appealing to somebody who knows nothing about it. In other words, how you present things, which is really the heart of all this, and it's vital, because if the presentation's wrong, everybody misses the point, which was what happened with her in some cases – she just didn't know what the audience was going to be receptive to, so maybe she miscalculated, but at other times, it was right on the money, and the lesson of it all for me was that if you're going to do what you want to do and enforce that on people, you have to figure out how to get there with it. I was with her for about a year, on and off, but I've been thinking about presentation ever since.'

During 1965, Ry was in a semi-legendary band, the Rising Sons, which at various times also included Taj Mahal, Ed Cassidy (later of Spirit) and Kevin Kelly, who subsequently briefly joined the Byrds. The group did record fairly extensively, although little was ever released other than on posthumous bootlegs, but these sessions were where Ry met Terry Melcher, a notable Los Angeles record producer and incidentally the son of Doris Day. 'He produced the Rising Sons by default – the poor guy was given the job of producing this group that wasn't a group, with material they didn't have. He tried his best, and I got to be friendly with him because we got along, and then he called me to work on real sessions that he was doing with other artists like Paul Revere and the Raiders, and that was great. Terry had the idea, since folk/rock was happening, to integrate certain instruments that hadn't been tried before into a normal Hollywood rock session band, and he was very smart about that. The question was how you made the leap from some sort of folk club with your dulcimer into the rock'n'roll studio, and what you did with mandolins and things, but that was the fun of it then, trying to make all that up and make it work. Nobody knew what to do – he said "Play something", so I played'.

The next item of major importance, and probably the first occasion on which the name of Ry Cooder was visible to British audiences, was when, probably at some point during 1965/6, he joined Captain Beefheart & the Magic Band. 'There was all kinds of stuff in between, actually. I had this business with Taj (Mahal), where we used to play in bars' (Ry played on much of Taj Mahal's eponymous debut LP) 'and Beefheart used to come around, because he was having trouble with his guitar player at the time, who was suffering from nervous strain, which was brought about by Captain Beefheart! He had this record deal with Buddah Records, and they needed a little organisational assistance. He's an imposing figure, and what happened was that I started messing around with him, at his invitation, only to discover that it was like a hornet's nest, although he had great musical ideas, and that was kind of interesting. I still think that *Safe As Milk* (on which Ry played) is a good record – what's really good is the master tape, because I think it was badly mixed.'

Interesting or not, the alliance between Ry and the Captain was destined to be brief. 'The Monterey Pop Festival was pending, and it's worth naming names, because it's funny, and Bob Krasnow, who was an executive at Buddah – and God knows what Buddah really was, and I'm not even going to speculate – had this idea that Monterey Pop was going to be a big deal, which he turned out to be very right about, so he said to me "Now you've finished this record with Beefheart, I want the band to go to Monterey Pop and blow the roof off that thing". I told him that the band was in no shape to do that, but he said "Oh yeah, you can do it – you've got to get them ready, rehearse and work them and make it happen", so I said I'd try, but I didn't think the band should go into a venue like that cold, because people were liable to be good up there, and things might be very competitive. So he said he'd get us on at this little festival in Berkeley the next weekend, which seemed like a pretty good idea. The band rehearsed a little, and we flew up to San Francisco, and on the way from the airport to Berkeley, Beefheart started to hyperventilate and get nervous – he's a hypochondriac, there's always something wrong with this guy. "Oh, I can't breathe, something's wrong, stop the car, I think I'm sick, I think I'm really sick". "We can't stop, Don, we have to get to the show, because they're waiting. We're only going to get there and drive right up to the stage, and it has to be this way". (This passage

has to be heard to be really appreciated – Ry Cooder, should he ever decide to stop playing guitar, has a potentially sparkling career ahead of him as an impressionist). "No I can't, I can't. What did they put in my coffee on the airplane? I think they're trying to poison me. Oh God, I can't go on". He went grey and white, and he turned all these colours, which was one thing he could really do, one of his things. So we got up there, and it's hot, and there's dogs, and the whole stupid outdoor concert trip – chaos, you know? It was an acid trip, funky Bay Area acid bands making noise, and I thought we didn't belong there, but we were there. So they introduced us, and we hit the stage and started into one of these insane numbers, and people are walking around playing frisbee – it was real ... dumb. Beefheart starts this song and gets through it, and then, during the next one he's singing, he starts to teeter towards the edge of the stage, holding his chest. He stops singing, looks around, turns to me and comes walking back – "I'm going to fall down, I can't do it, I've got to get out of here", and he falls off the stage into the grass on his face and just lies there! The people are cheering, because they can dig that, and the band's left on stage, trying to play instrumentally, which is just gobbledegook, nonsense.He wouldn't come back, so we did another tune instrumentally, and he wouldn't get up, claimed he had a heart seizure or whatever. He dramatised it, and said it was something that had happened to him, and that was the end of the performance. Krasnow was mad at me, and I was mad because I was embarrassed – I'd anticipated something like this, but you never know – so I told him to give me the keys to the rentacar, because I was getting out of there. The next week, back in LA, I told Krasnow that he could forget Monterey Pop, because there was no way a situation like that could be controlled, and it would be awful, and he lay there, fanning himself on his couch, saying how could I do this to him, and finally I said, "I quit, and I'm walking away from this, because it's too much for me."

By this time, Ry had got to know notable Los Angeles music personality Jack Nitzsche, and reinvolved himself in session work. 'Nitzsche used to arrange for Melcher and (Phil) Spector, so I met him when I was working for Melcher. Nitzsche really had good insight into things and he could organise, so when he did dates as producer, I worked for him, and he'd call me if he did dates as an arranger – it was all good training. Then he did this film thing, soundtracks, which was really good, because I began to learn about that. Also, he worked for Warner Brothers (Records), where they had a collection of artists who were a cut above the average major label, people like the Everly Brothers, who were really interesting and fun to mess around with. I wasn't doing sessions every day – if I got a call maybe once a week, I thought I was doing OK – and I lived at home with my folks, and then I went away to school, which seemed like a good idea, and used to fly back down to Hollywood to do this kind of work. Pretty soon, I realised it was what had never seemed possible – all the musicians I had seen were so poor, and nobody seemed to make any money – but here was this land of opportunity, and after a time, I started to do more work and make some money.'

Above: Electric
Right: Acoustic,
Below: 'Come here and say that!'

By 1970, Ry had become a fully fledged recording artist in his own right, making records for Warner Brothers. Twelve years later, this can obviously be seen as an inspired arrangement, although at the time, Ry was far from the most obviously commercial act around. 'In those days, they seemed to sign a lot of artists, the scattershot technique, and see what surfaced, although they've reversed that policy now and sign very few, but in those days, they were beefing up the roster and they signed me along with lots of others. Lenny Waronker, the producer there, had a lot to do with it, because I'd done a lot of studio work for him and he had some idea that I could make a good record of some sort, and I agreed, although whether it might be commercial was something nobody was sure about in those days. It's much more organised now, but in those days it was loose – there was more access to the public, there was freeform radio, and FM radio was really viable, whereas it's not now. There was a whole college market that's been homogenised into the mainstream now, so it was more relaxed in some ways. A guy like me wouldn't get signed now, without a doubt – I wouldn't have a shot if I came along from nowhere now, not being a writer and not being an obvious upfront type of cat. When I made the first album, I suppose I wanted to take songs that I liked and put my own stamp on them, which is an awful tough thing to do.'

The album contains eleven tracks, some by names already mentioned like Woody Guthrie, John Estes and Willie Johnson, plus a few more modern items by the likes of Randy Newman, but commercially, it was hardly a huge success. Had Ry been happy with it when it was released? 'Of course not. I don't like my records too much, but in those days, it was quite a feat to make a record, so I respected the fact that I'd made it, held it in my hand, and thought "Uh huh – here's a record", and since that day, I haven't had that feeling just exactly, so there was a moment when it became obvious that my record existed, which was pretty thrilling. I don't know if I liked it so much musically, but at least I had it.'

Ry's interest in Woody Guthrie was also to some extent consolidated in 1970 when he performed at a 'Tribute to Woody Guthrie' concert at the Hollywood Bowl, along with many notable folk performers, the results being released on record. Woody Guthrie, rightly or wrongly, has almost always been cited as perhaps the greatest influence on Ry Cooder's music, particularly with regard to those songs Guthrie and others wrote about the American Depression.

Why did Guthrie's work have such a strong appeal for Ry? 'What's music for? Music like that is like dialogue, a discussion among people, and it's very realistic and visual, and has a lot of power because it comes from real experiences, thoughts and problems, and Woody was one of the great communicators in that way. The simple man with the guitar sang a lot of heavy things, and that has a lot of power as music – whether you're in the dustbowl (an area of 150,000 square miles comprising parts of Kansas, Colorado, New Mexico, Oklahoma and Texas, where lack of crop rotation rendered the topsoil useless – dust) or out of it, you can feel that stuff, and it carries a lot of weight. I always liked playing those songs –

the words are great, the melodies are traditional and they come back at you all the time.'

Ry's second LP, *Into The Purple Valley*, contained a Guthrie song, 'Vigilante Man' – what were the circumstances behind its subject matter? 'A lot of people came west, because they had no homes any more after the banks foreclosed on them. The banks had bought up all the notes (mortgages) on the small farms in a wide-ranging conspiracy to consolidate farmland – the banks took the opportunity to eliminate small farmers and to become major property owners, with the co-operation of some agro-business conglomerates. Once the folks were off the farms where they'd lived, they went west, because it was known that in California there was a year long picking season which never stopped – you picked peaches, then lettuce, then tomatoes, then you harvested grapes, and you could work all the year round. Picture postcards proclaimed that it was a sunny, happy, wonderful place, but what they didn't bargain for was that it was also a tight scene, that agro-business was entrenched there and the institutional order was very complete, so there were no small farms. California had always been a state full of big farms, and agro-business was running the government in that state, so when these poor Okies and Arkies came out, they found this tight block, with scab prices being paid. They couldn't support themselves, and were caught in a mesh of being manipulated as cheap labour against each other, and to keep order, the corrupt local police departments deputised vigilantes, who were just hired thugs wearing badges, to carry out the will of the big farm conglomerates. They would bust everybody up now and then, keep them terrorised and keep them scattered and prevent them from getting together, because the one thing agro-business in California feared was a farmworkers' union, since cheap labour's only cheap and able to be manipulated when it's not organised. Wherever I sang that song, especially in the '60s,

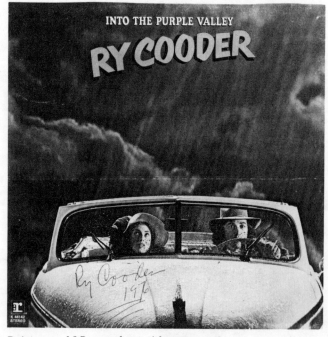

Ry's second LP complete with autograph

when Vietnam was a problem, the dope culture was staking its claim and the youth culture was stating its case, it was well received, like any song that's about the revolt against institutional order. Those songs have a life because of that, and I still get a lot of requests for that song today, because there's always someone who's the vigilante, and someone else who's getting their head beat open, wherever you may be.'

This full explanation of a song's origins may give some clue as to the seriousness with which Cooder researches his subject, something which does not always pay off in sales terms, although the album which includes 'Vigilante Man', *Into The Purple Valley*, was an improvement in terms of public acceptance, perhaps to some extent because of its sleeve. 'A fair amount of money was spent on that album in terms of promotion, which resulted in a lot more visibility, but that presented certain problems, because you can't forge a career based on social type music in an era when that music is becoming less and less current, and less interesting to people. But I still thought it was the sort of stuff I should do, and I still think it's good, but it got to be a little cryptic after a while.'

The title of Ry's third LP was *Boomer's Story*, and on one track, 'President Kennedy', the song's writer, Sleepy John Estes (by this time extremely old and in decline) played and sang, although the idea was not purely to be charitable. 'Jim Dickinson (co-producer and participant on the LP) lived in Tennessee near where John lived, and I said to Jim "Suppose we get Sleepy John down here – something might take place", so he came by one night. We got out a tape machine, and sat up all night playing, and that was the best and most coherent one we recorded, although there was some other good stuff. It was quite a nice time – I played mandolin, Dickinson played piano, and Sleepy John sang and played guitar – it was kind of like old Sleepy John records, which was a big thrill for me. He was a great guy, a funny old cat, like some kind of man on a mountain somewhere.'

Ry's 1974 LP *Paradise And Lunch*, seemed to mark the point where the process of 'meeting the public halfway' appeared to come properly into operation, and he was perhaps coming to terms with what might be more generally acceptable. 'I suppose that's so, but as I said, working out a style that I could use indicated certain things that were worth doing that worked better on record, and you try to eliminate what's not working, and concentrate on what seems to make great records so that the album isn't just a collection of songs. That album isn't too different from the others, it just sounds more coherent because the style is better worked out. That was the album where I used some (male) singers for the first time, and I really began to realise that that was one of the main handles to put on all this stuff, getting that background singing to work. I'd used girl singers before, but unsuccessfully – I can't stand girl singers, although I don't mean personally, but black male voices on that kind of material are still strongest and most appropriate for me, and they also do a lot for a tune rhythmically'. So it was pure coincidence that *Paradise And Lunch* contained such comparatively well known tracks as 'It's All Over Now' and 'Mexi-can Divorce', and not any conscious decision to use songs that were more widely familiar? 'Yes, it's pure coincidence – I'd known "It's All Over Now" for a long time, but I loved the Valentinos' version so much that I wouldn't touch it until I realised that it was almost like a reggae song, very close to Jimmy Cliff, so that was my excuse for doing that, and Dan Penn suggested I try "Mexican Divorce", and I was very grateful.'

Of the previous type of Cooder material, a stand-out track on *Paradise* is 'Tamp 'Em Up Solid'. 'That's an old railroad song I heard from Josh White. One of the gospel singers on the record, Bill Johnson, knew it – I asked him if he knew it, he said he did, and I wondered how we ought to do it, so he said "You do it like this, then you play this, so and so sings that, and that's how it's done". You learn from people like that – all of a sudden you find you're learning a whole great big thing about arrangements which stays with you, although it doesn't happen very often.' In fact, these 'gospel singers', as Ry describes them, have become a vital part of his sound, particularly in a concert situation, so how did he meet them? 'I met one, then another, and once I began looking for them, I met a whole lot of them, and then I started meeting the real heavy cats who had come to LA over the years, because that was where all the work was, and the record business was there, so a lot of guys had drifted in, and it's like a community, a whole network of folks.' The singer whom Ry has most used over the years has been Bobby King, who has an exceptional voice. 'He's exceptional, period – in this day and age, the guy's practically unique, as good as he is and as experienced as he is. He could sing anything, he's fantastic, and we're real good friends at this point – I've known him for a long time, and he understands my attitude, and what's to be done.'

A further guest on *Paradise And Lunch* was veteran pianist Earl Hines. 'I heard he was in town, and I thought "How can I lose?", so I called him up. He wasn't doing anything that day, so although he didn't know me, I asked him to come down, and he said he had a song we could play, which was "Ditty Wa Ditty". He was fine, an agreeable guy, and it was just one of those crazy things – we never did hardly any more recording, but that was lucky, it was correct and a good idea, which you have every now and again.'

After *Paradise And Lunch* there was a lengthy hiatus in Ry's recording career, from which he finally emerged with the remarkable *Chicken Skin Music* LP. 'I was driving in the car one day, listening to this Mexican radio station, and I heard this accordion band, which was really different from all the usual nightclub music, and I wondered what it could be, because it was beautiful, bar music, almost like R&B. Since I couldn't understand what they were singing about, or who it was, I called up Chris Strachwitz of Arhoolie Records in Berkeley, who knows about these things, and it turned out that he was working on a project to document that music, which was Tex/Mex, Norteno music. It's music made by the people who live on the border between Texas and Mexico, along the Rio Grande, which was a cultural region of North Mexico before Texas was a state, but since

A little night music . . .

there was a border there, half of them live on the Texas side and half on the Mexican side. During the last century, German people started moving into Texas from certain areas of Bavaria, and carried on as they always did, and they brought accordions and played polkas and waltzes, after which the Nortenos took it up, and incorporated it into their own melodic structures.

'So I flew up to Chris Strachwitz, because this thing in the car had really hit me, and I felt I had to hear some more of it, and he had this amazing collection of records. I went crazy and said I had to see these people playing, and he and Les Blank were about to start work on a documentary film about this music, so I went with them. My idea was to find someone I could play with in that style, who would be compatible and interested, and most of them weren't, but I met Flaco Jimenez, who had worked with Doug Sahm (of Sir Douglas Quintet), and had been introduced to the world of white folks. Also, he could speak English, and he could hear another form of music combining with his – he's a very good player and a nice man, so we started working together and had a pretty good time.'

While part of the album is devoted to Tex/Mex music, two other tracks feature a pair of Hawaiian musicians, Gabby Pahinui and Atta Isaacs. 'That was the same sort of thing but in a stranger way. I had spent a lot of time with these Hawaiian guys because of their music, and it was a tremendous education. I liked them so much that I wanted to record with them because I thought it'd be fun, and once I did that, I decided to stick to it on the album. Gabby Pahinui plays what they call "slack key" guitar, which is their way of saying they tune it to a chord, which is what I do anyway, and they call it "slack" because they're tuning it down from concert (pitch) – their whole theory seemed to be that they'd tune the guitar low and sing high, in that Hawaiian falsetto, so you get this interesting spread . . . Gabby made a big impression on me, and I don't expect to meet a better musician or a more complete talent than him. He knew what music was and where it was coming

from, and he could make it from there every time, drunk, sober or whatever – he's one of the guys who's going to magically insert himself right into the microphone, through the wires and on to the tape, and then on to the record, which is a very hard thing to do, and that's besides being an utterly fantastic guitar player with a very wide range. He could play Django Reinhardt music, Count Basie music, he knew it all.'

Ry himself plays an instrument on one of the Hawaiian tracks on *Chicken Skin Music* called a tiple, among several unusual musical devices. 'A tiple is a Colombian instrument primarily, which became popular in a ukelele format in the '20s as a collegiate kind of instrument, but is still used and played in Hawaii. Playing with a lot of different instruments is perhaps a bit risky, because people need to hear coherency and have a focus, but I have to be pardoned for doing it, because it seemed like a good idea. It's always a guess – if I hear something I think I should do, I go on and do it, but since that time, I've recognised that it isn't always too easy for the listener to follow along, and they may wonder unconsciously what's happening.'

Chicken Skin Music was perhaps the start of the polarisation between Europe and America regarding Ry's popularity – 'The Dutch and the English liked it, but that was about it, and in the United States, it totally fell on deaf ears'. However, following its release, Ry took a band of Tex/Mex musicians on the road fronted by himself and a gospel trio for a tour which in Britain at least was riotously successful.

Anyone who saw any of the concerts by Ry with the *Chicken Skin* band will not be likely to forget them in a hurry, especially as a live LP, *Showtime*, is available. One aspect of Ry's own performance is that some of the time, he allows his backing singers to be lead vocalists, especially on the live LP's stand out track, 'Dark End Of The Street'. Is this democracy at work? 'I'm grateful when they sing, I'm telling you – as I said, I enjoy accompanying people, and to have to play and sing is a hard job, so if somebody's going to sing a tune, I get to rest and relax, which I appreciate, because that's the fun part for me.' So you don't really feel cut out to be a front man? 'Probably not . . . I feel ill suited to it, although I know I can sort of do it, and sometimes it's gratifying, because I know it has to be me doing it to make it right.'

Equally odd is the feeling that on some of Ry's records, there is less upfront guitar than might be expected. 'That's a matter of preference, and I do what I think's appropriate. The guitar's part of the group, and what we're striving for is the group sound – whatever the level of the instruments, or the dynamics, it's about a unit in which there are no soloists. I think orchestrally, even with a small band, and that develops something which becomes a whole lot deeper and more interesting. On stage, it's different – somebody has to do something, and you have the chance to stretch out and play solos. I don't know what I'm going to play – if I feel good, I'll play well, and if I don't, I won't – but at least the moment's there and the energy, and you do what you can.'

1978 saw the release of the album which we were a little surprised to discover Ry loathes – titled *Jazz*. It attempts to explore the connections between tradi-

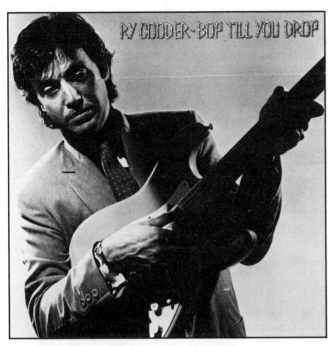

Bop Till You Drop – 1979 LP

tional jazz and the music of the Caribbean, although such a brief description perhaps does scant justice to the concept, which included reworkings of songs attributed to legendary trumpeter Bix Beiderbecke and Bahamian guitarist Joseph Spence. 'I regard that album as a wretched mistake, a brief ugly interlude. It was not directional, nor was it even well-considered or well-executed, and I hate it, but having done the damned thing, I was stuck with it, and I had to accept full responsibility, which I did, and take everybody's barbs and criticisms, which were all justified, I'm sure, and get on, because that damned thing was a dead end if ever there was one.'

After this failed experiment, Ry's 1979 LP, *Bop Till You Drop*, returned to more familiar musical pastures. 'Yes, things I knew I could do, which was to sing something like music that's in a continuity, to include some soul and some blues, which are all part of the same thing, as far as I'm concerned, but in this case, what makes the record what it is is the musicians – getting the right guys in the room at the right time is so often the measure of it all. With a record like this one, it's not so much the songs as what they sound like, although it is a good selection of songs, and we played them well.' Certainly, the players involved on the album – David Lindley, Jim Keltner, Tim Drummond, Milt Holland and a choice selection of backing singers headed by Bobby King – were among the most respected session musicians of the time, so was this any kind of ideal band for Ry?

'There's no ideal one – that group was great in the studio for those sessions, and you could hardly get anyone better, but I wouldn't call it totally ideal. I should have had Jim Dickinson there, and I realised my mistake later on, because that record's a little stiff for me, and a little thin here and there, but that's just part of working it up and trying to get it right.'

One of the nicest tracks on the album is an instrumental version of Ike & Tina Turner's 'It's Gonna Work Out Fine', while also included is a track on which Ry vocally duets with Chaka Khan, ex lead voice of Rufus. 'I copped the idea of the instrumental version from Otis Rush, I think it was, who did the same thing. He had that vibrato, tremolo effect that he did, but I thought about it as a bottleneck tune, which seemed like a good idea, and I think it's a real pretty song. With Chaka Khan, I know her – she had just had a baby and was bored staying home, so I asked her to sing with me. I'd thought that someday it might be good to do a duet of that song, "Don't You Mess Up A Good Thing", which was by Fontella Bass and Bobby McClure, and Chaka's certainly an extra good singer at that kind of stuff.'

Another aspect of *Bop Till You Drop* was that it utilised the revolutionary digital recording process. Was Ry's use of it in some way pioneering? 'No, I was just a guinea pig, a subject for somebody's carpet-bagger engineering notions, I'm afraid. I hate digital. However, it will come to be a good thing, when we stop having to transfer to analog disc form, because digital does not transfer. It makes other digitals all right, but if you mix them up, it's apples and oranges, and you end up with practically nothing, which nobody bothered to explain to me at the time.'

Nevertheless, *Bop Till You Drop* was a reasonably satisfying album, if less challenging, at least on the face of it, than Ry's next LP, the soundtrack to *The Long Riders,* a film directed by Walter Hill dealing with the celebrated gang led by Jesse James. It was the first soundtrack Ry had conceived on his own, although his previous work on similar projects with Jack Nitzsche had given him an appreciation of the mechanics of creating film music. 'I didn't find it difficult, and it was just a matter of understanding with Walter Hill how it was going to sound. He had a very good idea of what he wanted, and he was right, and he was easy to work with, so it was a matter of learning the film, knowing what it is and isn't, then trying to get the music together and getting people who could play it. People like Bill Bryson and Tom Sauber are veterans of the country music days in LA who still work and are adept, and Arkansas music has, or used to have, a certain sound, so if you want an Arkansas fiddle player, you call so and so. LA is amazing in that way – you can get anybody you want, and it's the perfect town in which to construct something like that.'

One rather odd aspect of the music was that while its subject matter concerned turn of the century America, one prominent musician was Rastafarian percussionist Ras Baboo Pierre. 'I couldn't resist that – in the film, somebody sings "Rally Round The Flag", which was written to be a rallying song at a time when the Union Army was losing the war, but if you bend the lyrics a little bit and write them from the point of view of the emancipated slave, you have a whole different kind of song. In other words, everything's going to be OK, we're out of it now, we're headed North and this and that, and the expectations are that life will open up. But the historical irony is that life clamped down for the emancipated slaves.'

Shortly after the release of *The Long Riders* came a conventional Ry Cooder album, on which he was assisted by the somewhat unlikely figure of John Hiatt, a singer/guitarist in his own right who had been making LPs of his own for several years. 'I was looking for contemporary songs like I always do, and a friend of mine recommended that I should listen to Hiatt. So I got some Hiatt demos from his publishers, and my first thought was that he could sing really well, and that the songs were interesting and complex, with rhythms that I like and with chords that refer to soul music. There was a lot going on in them, but there wasn't anything I thought I could do, but I thought there was something to this guy, so I invited him over, and it turns out that he's a really nice guy, a very sweet, very smart, serious minded cat, and we became friends.'

The album on which Hiatt first assisted was *Borderline,* and the title track, a Cooder original, is a good example of Ry's attitude to playing, where the ensemble sound is of greater importance than individual virtuosity. 'That's a cute little song – it doesn't mean anything to anybody, but I always thought it was a pleasant little dance tune. See, people aren't used to us – they're used to hearing the guitar player who steps forward, puts his foot up on the monitor cabinet and blasts away for 84 bars, so because they're conditioned to music played that way, they just don't know that anything else is real unless they hear it. That's a relatively recent development, and where I'm coming from, you're listening to what's happening between players, what line the group takes, how it works, what it feels like, and what the chord inversions are doing, which is a much more sensitive thing . . . but people like to see the actor, the guy who gets up and blows his brains out – it's a popular form of entertainment, like a bullfight, and I can't do that, because it's not part of my thinking and it doesn't mean anything to me. I can dig the guy who can take the solo, but it can get awful dull in a hurry, unless he's awful good – even Django Reinhardt would only solo for a good reason, not just to take up space.'

After a tour by the *Borderline* band, a live EP was released of four tracks recorded variously in London and San Francisco. 'The record company thought that since they weren't getting much airplay out of the album, they might do better if people heard something like what they heard at the shows. It was a marketing gesture, and in the States, it was strictly a promotional item which wasn't for sale. I had to listen to all this stuff and choose the tracks that were decent, and I realised that it wasn't what I'd hoped it would be, but not so bad as to not let it happen.' While the live tracks, Ry asserts, are not to showcase his live guitar playing – although he plays rather more solos than on studio recordings – but rather to 'bring up the idea that there'd been this great big lively stage show, and here was a lively little record, because one of my problems, and one which I don't know how to get around, is that the records and the stage show don't sound enough alike', one outstanding cut on the EP is 'Crazy 'Bout An Automobile' which Ry heard on a record by Sam the Sham (see below), who in turn got it from Billy 'The Kid' Emerson.

The start of 1982 saw two new Ry Cooder LP releases, one being another film soundtrack, to a film starring Jack Nicholson, *The Border,* which provided the opportunity for somewhat more modern music than that called for in *The Long Riders.* The sound-

A recent portrait

track was put together with the help of Flaco Jimenez again, as 'Musical Consultant', and included contributions from Tex/Mex superstar Freddy Fender, and from Sam Samudio, better known as Sam the Sham, of 'Wooly Bully' fame. 'I talk to Flaco all the time, and for this project, it was pretty obvious that something of that generic sound was needed, because it's a border story. So I put him together with other people from that general area, like Freddy and Sam, who each represent a different piece of the pie down there, and it worked out really well. Sam has a boat these days out in the Gulf of Mexico – he pilots a launch that services the big oil derricks off the coast of Louisiana, and he does some fishing. I think he'd like to get back more into music, but he probably doesn't know quite what to do because he's afraid they're going to make him wear a turban again – and he's probably right! But he's a great talent, and I've been looking for years for an excuse to get him into town, and this was the kind of story he could certainly identify with. He used to be famous for carrying guns, but I found him very pacific, and he's married with a child now, although he's an eccentric character still, but very smart and very positive.'

For once, Ry himself wasn't featured on any track as lead singer – was that modesty? 'I didn't want to sing, I wanted to listen, to make sure it was right and watch the movie while they were playing and keep track of it, because it wasn't written down. I think it's a great job writing for films, and I'd always wanted to do it after working with Jack Nitzsche because it's very liberating, and it's abstract – the music has a different structure and it's not just another three or four minute song. There are some of those, but you can also have lots of sounds and nice textures, and it's doing a job of work for the film, a craft occupation. It pays well, I enjoy it, and I can stay home and do it – you can't argue with that.'

Most recently, coinciding with the triumphant eight nights at Hammersmith in London, came *The Slide Area,* a title which is hardly self-explanatory. 'There's an English fellow named Gavin Lambert, a screen writer and novelist, who lived near where I lived, on the beach in LA, for a while, and while he was there, he wrote a book called *The Slide Area,* which was a series of character studies, the idea being that in LA, you have mudslides, earthquakes, deluge rains, fires, floods, everything happens, and he says that all these natural phenomena contribute to the insanity of the place. So he wrote about this collection of people, whom he obviously knew – he created all these characters from life, all of them very peripheral and eccentric – and it's set in the locale in that way, the slide area being where things move around all the time and are perpetually about to give way. The idea appealed to me, and I liked the book, and you could obviously also say that there's some kind of pun about slide guitar in there, but I related to it and thought it would be something to call the record, because who knows what you should call a record?'

The album is a milestone for Ry in that it is the first of his records, other than the soundtrack albums, where he has written or co-written the majority of the material. Was this a new talent he had suddenly discovered? 'I had to do it for the films – I'd been hired, so I couldn't tell them I can't write – and I'm not saying I discovered how to do it, but I discovered a way of making up something that could be called a song. I have ideas, but it's a matter of the format, and having worked with other people's songs for so long, rewriting them and editing, you learn about song structure and what you like and what you don't like.'

An impression gained from listening to Ry's music over the years is that he wouldn't undertake something – songwriting, for example – unless he could do it properly; was that what had held him back? 'Probably, although I wouldn't put it quite like that. I can tell if I'm not writing anything that's good, but I realised during the making of *The Border* that some of the stuff was OK, so I'd put myself in that frame of mind by looking at the film and seeing what was needed, and I just tried to do the same thing, but without the film, put my brain in the same sort of working order. I'm not saying I'm a songwriter, but it's something I think I can do and maybe have good results with.'

All right – what inspired another of your songs, 'UFO Has Landed In The Ghetto Land', then? 'Believe me, that's strictly from walking my dog. I walked round the block in the dark, and after about 500 feet I heard this little rhythm that my dog had, so

I added some chords to it, and recorded it without knowing what it was. Then you're faced with the problem of what to do with it, so I tried to imagine what it would be about, and got a picture of hurtling through space and hearing this soul music on the satellite transmission, and going towards where it was coming from – it's a cartoon – and landing, then cruising up the street in this tiny spaceship, and people wanting to dance because there's a sort of tradition about this spaceman that teaches everybody a new dance step. It's just a nice little idea.'

In 1982, Ry Cooder is in an interesting position: he can sell out eight nights in London, but his appeal on the other side of the Atlantic is negligible in comparison, although he is unsure about why this situation came about in Europe. Incidentally, the observant Cooder-watcher will detect the omission of any discussion of Ry's period with the Rolling Stones, an episode upon which he did not wish to elaborate.

Finally, a few words from Ry on his chosen instruments. 'I've got about fifty guitars at home, and my favourites seem to be the ones which produce certain types of sounds. I've got a couple of Stratocasters that are real good heavy beefy guitars, which take the abuse and have a lot of presence, because there's a lot of mass to them. I've got another electric, a little Supro with steel guitar pickups that Lindley gave me, but unfortunately, it has so little mass and it's so light that it's hard to project off the stage – I have to play it hard, and I knock it out of tune, but it's a great recording guitar, and most of the good sounds on the records are made with that. It was made in the late '50s/early '60s, and marketed to be sold in places like Sears & Roebuck, and by mail order – a junk guitar, a poor man's Les Paul, but the pick-ups have a real vibrant fat sound. When stage lights hit the circuits, though, it makes all this noise, and there's nothing you can do about it. Then I've got a sort of Japanese surf guitar that has a really beautiful sound, but it's so underpowered it can't be heard when I play it on stage. The guitar question's a problem, because to get one built now, I'd have to find a guy who could get that sound, but make it loud and tough to take road abuse, and most people who build electric guitars build them for different purposes, for loud lead solos with a lot of distortion, or something of that nature.'

Ry claims to be able to play any fretted instrument – 'you hand me one, and I'll figure out how to play it' – but one of his rarest instruments is a Vox 12-string guitar with a short neck, which looks rather like an electric mandolin. 'They marketed those in the '60s, although I can't imagine why they did it.' That assertion is somehow typical of Ry Cooder – he's intelligent but uncomplicated, musically brilliant but modest (and not falsely so), and a man who has pursued a path which perhaps no other player would have been sufficiently patient to follow. It is to the credit of Europe in general and Britain in particular that his genius is recognised here – let us hope that his own country soon comes into line.

Ry Cooder Discography

With Captain Beefheart
1967 *Safe As Milk* (reissued as *Dropout Boogie*)

Solo Albums
1970 *Ry Cooder*
1971 *Into The Purple Valley*
1972 *Boomer's Story*
1974 *Paradise And Lunch*
1976 *Chicken Skin Music*
1977 *Showtime*
1978 *Jazz*
1979 *Bop Till You Drop*
1980 *The Long Riders* (Original Soundtrack)
1980 *Borderline*
1982 *The Border* (Original Soundtrack)
1982 *The Slide Area*

Miscellaneous
1972 *A Tribute To Woody Guthrie Parts 1 & 2*

Sessions
Taj Mahal
1967 *Taj Mahal*

Arlo Guthrie
1969 *Running Down The Road*

Gentle Soul
1969 *Gentle Soul*

Phil Ochs
1970 *Greatest Hits*

Randy Newman
1970 *12 Songs*

Longbranch/Pennywhistle
1970 *Longbranch/Pennywhistle*

Ron Nagle
1970 *Bad Rice*

Marc Benno
1970 *Marc Beno*

Original Soundtrack
1970 *Performance*

David Blue
1971 *Stories*

Buffy St. Marie
1971 *She Used To Want To Be A Ballerina*

Little Feat
1971 *Little Feat*

Don Everly
1971 *Don Everly*

Rolling Stones
1971 *Sticky Fingers*

Crazy Horse
1971 *Crazy Horse*

Rita Coolidge
1971 *Rita Coolidge*

Randy Newman
1972 *Sail Away*

Everly Brothers
1972 *Stories We Could Tell*

Various Artists
1972 *Jammin' With Edward*

Rod Taylor
1973 *Rod Taylor*

Clarence White
1973 *Why You Been Gone So Long?*

Brenda Patterson
1973 *Brenda Patterson*

Arlo Guthrie
1973 *Last Of The Brooklyn Cowboys*

Maria Muldaur
1973 *Maria Muldaur*

Claudia Lennear
1973 *Phew!*

Randy Newman
1974 *Good Ol' Boys*

Terry Melcher
1974 *Terry Melcher*

Arlo Guthrie
1974 *Arlo Guthrie*

Johnny Cash
1974 *John R. Cash*

John Sebastian
1974 *Tarzana Kid*

Doobie Brothers
1975 *Stampede*

Randy Newman
1977 *Little Criminals*

Original Soundtrack
1978 *Blue Collar*

Rodney Crowell
1978 *Ain't Living Long Like This*

Van Morrison
1979 *Into The Music*

This is probably but a fraction of the sessions on which Ry has played, but the size of the list and its scope and quality illustrate just how much in demand he was before 1975.

RITCHIE BLACKMORE

One reason for the selection of ace heavy metal guitarist Ritchie Blackmore as one of our subjects relates to a previous, slimmer and somewhat inferior volume on guitarists which was written some years ago by John Tobler in which the choice of the players was not his. Little or no correspondence ensued following the book's publication, the only letters received all being from puzzled readers enquiring how it was that Ritchie Blackmore had been omitted. During the ensuing years, Ritchie's standing has become substantially greater and now records by his band, Rainbow, are guaranteed huge sellers, while tickets for his rare British concerts are oversubscribed at great speed. Aside from that, he possesses the ultimate qualification for inclusion – he is undeniably a great guitarist.

Blackmore was born on 14 April 1945, in Weston-super-Mare – 'No, it was 1950!' (laughs) – and his first memory of a guitar came, as he puts it, 'at the stage of puberty. Maybe it was because it was like a woman in shape, so I loved it. It was an acoustic 6-string guitar, and I became interested in the gloss and the sheen and the way it was made. It was a very fine instrument, and I wanted to play it. So I persuaded my father to buy a guitar for me which cost seven guineas, and it went from there – he said that if I was going to play this thing, he would either have someone teach me to play it properly, or he'd smash me over the head with it. So I took classical lessons for a year, which got me onto the right footing, using all the fingers and the right strokes of the plectrum. I think when you first go into an instrument, you need to be set in the right direction, otherwise you can pick up very bad habits. That first guitar was a Framus, a Spanish guitar made in Germany, and I kept adding pick-ups to it, and as I was into electrical wiring at that time, I ended up with loads of switches to the point where I wasn't sure quite what they were doing, but they looked good. I'd like to see that guitar now, but I sold it to buy a Hofner three years later, which was 32 guineas, a lot of money in those days.'

Blackmore's early influences included Duane Eddy, 'Big' Jim Sullivan, who was Britain's premier session guitar player during the 1960s, and who apparently gave Ritchie some instruction, Hank B. Marvin and Buddy Holly, while later on, at sixteen, his father insisted that Ritchie listen to Les Paul as well as to his current favourite, Chet Atkins.

'Les Paul was much more refined, not the type of player you recognise when you first take up the guitar – there's always some sort of novelty you look for, and Hank B. Marvin had the tremolo arm and the very straightforward melodies which I could pick up, whereas Les Paul was very difficult to emulate. I left him till later, and even now I couldn't copy half of what he's put down.'

Ritchie joined his first group around the age of thirteen, although not playing guitar. 'I was playing what was called the "dog box" – a tea chest with a piece of string and a broom handle, and you can play any note on it and sound vaguely in tune. I started

that after hearing Lonnie Donegan, and after three years, I started to play rhythm guitar.' This first group was known as the 21s Junior Skiffle Group, although Ritchie was too young to ever visit this haven of British popular music, having to console himself with once standing outside. 'Being at school, we had about twenty-five guitarists on stage playing in the band. None of us could really play, but it looked good, and we played in the school concert. We did three numbers, of which "Rebel Rouser", I think, was one, and when we started it, the audience started clapping, and because the amplifiers weren't very loud, they drowned the sound out, and all the twenty-five guitarists just went into oblivion. I suppose that group lasted just one day – we had a rehearsal that afternoon in the school, and I plugged my guitar straight into the mains, which wasn't too bright, and it blew up the entire lights of the school for fifteen minutes.'

Blackmore's first serious group came when he was fourteen-years-old, and was named, oddly enough, after an amplifier. 'Watkins, the people who make amplifiers and tape recorders, had an amplifier called the Dominator, and I thought that the Dominators was a good name for a group. That amp cost me 22 guineas, and I remember it looked fantastic, a kind of triangle effect with speakers going in different directions. The first one I bought blew up, and the next week, I travelled by underground from Hounslow West to Piccadilly Circus, where they were located, to take it back, and they gave me a replacement, which I took all the way back home on the train. The curtains opened on our first performance, and that amplifier also blew up. I took it back to the shop, and this happened six times – I said that there must be something wrong with them, but they said there couldn't be, and they suggested that I tried the amplifier out there in the shop. I agreed and blew it up in the shop, which they couldn't believe, so they gave me a different amplifier, which they wouldn't let me try out, and they told me to go away and said they never wanted to see me again. Fortunately, that amplifier they gave me, which was a Fenton-Weill, lasted for a long time, but the Dominators, the group, folded after about six months – they were just school-friends.'

Ritchie's scholastic career was hardly a major success story, and he in fact left school when he was fifteen. 'I couldn't wait to leave, but the headmaster tried to persuade me to stay, even though I was always in trouble, always getting caned for talking in class and being naughty. It was quite funny – in the mornings, I'd be awarded medals for throwing the javelin, and the headmaster would say that the school was proud of me, and in the afternoon, I'd be seeing him to be caned and being threatened with expulsion, which I found quite ironic, because he was such a hypocrite.'

On leaving school, Blackmore worked as an apprentice radio mechanic at nearby London Airport, before joining a professional group, Mike Dee & the Jaywalkers, who gigged three or four nights per

Ritchie today

week. 'We had gigs all over the place, a hundred miles away and more, and we had a Bedford van whose door wouldn't shut – those are the things you remember for a long time, and they're roots, part of growing up, I suppose. We played basically copy material, Shadows stuff, and all the steps that went with it, and the suits and ties. I was trying to be Hank Marvin, although I didn't have the horn-rimmed glasses or the physique he did, but I was playing lead. I was with them for about six months again, until they became known as the Condors, but I can't remember much about that time, because it was so long ago. Then Screaming Lord Sutch saw me, and wanted me to audition for his band – I went, and passed the audition, and I think Pete Townshend also went, but strangely enough, he failed. I was thrown in the deep end really with that band, because they were very professional, touring everywhere, very good musicians, and I had to learn quickly. I used to play through an echo chamber, and the first thing they said to me was that I had to get rid of it, and that I had to move around like Elvis Presley – we had these hip movements which we had to do in unison, which takes some doing for three-quarters of an hour at a time. But Sutch taught me a lot – I had a habit of disappearing off the side of the stage, because I was so shy, and all the people, especially my relatives and so on, would look for me, and all they could see was this guitar sticking out of the wings. But Dave

Sutch took me out on stage and started throwing me about – I thought he was totally crazy, and I'm still not sure whether he is or not, coming out of coffins and dressing up in loincloths.'

'In '62, '63, we were into a very heavy kind of basic hard rock, like Johnny Kidd & the Pirates, with a rhythm & blues base, and then the Beatles came out, and the Hollies, and it was all harmonising, and one had to sing. I didn't sing, in fact I could hardly talk at the time, and I was just into playing the guitar and very hard rock'n'roll and distorting guitar solos, which were out of vogue then – it was all pleasant vocal harmonies, and that lasted about four years until Hendrix and Cream came along. As for the Stones, I didn't think they were good enough musically. I thought the Beatles had it musically, but the Stones didn't impress me at all, and I still don't see it to this day. A good rhythm section, I suppose, but I don't think there was an outstanding musician in the band that I liked – I always look for one person in a band to like rather than just a conglomeration of guys moving backwards and forwards and not getting anywhere.'

Ritchie joined Screaming Lord Sutch in May 1962, and by the October of that year, had joined the Outlaws, whose lead singer, Mike Berry, had decided to leave the group. 'The Savages (Sutch's group) actually kicked me out because I wasn't good enough. They'd had some really brilliant lead guitarists, and then the drummer and the bass player were going to join Cyril Davies and the All Stars, and I was just left to get on with something else. So Joe Meek (famed British record producer, often cited as the nearest UK equivalent to Phil Spector) heard about this, and asked me to join his band, the Outlaws, which sounded good to me, because the Outlaws were better known than the Savages. I was quite pleased, and about two weeks after I joined the Outlaws, Carlo Little, the Savages' drummer came back from Cyril Davies' lot, and asked if I'd like to rejoin, because they'd had second thoughts, and I said I couldn't, because by now I was obligated to the Outlaws.

'We recorded a lot as the Outlaws – there was a point in time when I'd put the radio on, and out of every ten records I heard, there must have been six where the Outlaws were doing the backing, and I'd always feel that I'd heard things somewhere before, and then suddenly realise that it was me on the record, but with somebody else singing who hadn't been present at the time we did the session, but had been dubbed on later. I think that session work with a session band like the Outlaws can be good discipline, as long as you don't take it too far. I did it for about a year, which is long enough, because you start to get a little clinical – even now, I find I'm a little bit clinical, and I get into a studio and think I'm doing a session and everything has to be perfect, and then the atmosphere goes, whereas someone like Hendrix just went in and was always like having a party going on, which is the right way to do it really.'

During this period as a member of the Outlaws, Blackmore played on numerous records as a backing musician for Joe Meek's productions, although he is unsure of precise titles and artists. 'I must have performed on a good 400 records, with artists like

The Outlaws, with Chas Hodges (left), Ken Lundgren, Mick Underwood (at drums) and Ritchie (right)

Michael Cox, Danny Rivers, Freddie Starr, Heinz, even Tom Jones. Joe Meek's studio was a very small room, ten feet by eight, I think, with another room joined to it with all the electrical equipment in it, and that was six feet by six. Joe was very secretive about the things he did, and he'd often tell me that he'd been speaking to Buddy Holly who told him that he must do this record, which was ''Tribute To Buddy Holly'', and all the Mike Berry things. He actually thought he could communicate with Buddy Holly, and other people like that.' The period to which Ritchie is referring was from 1962 to 1964, and Buddy Holly, of course, died on 3 February 1959. Meek was certainly fixated about Holly, and it may be no coincidence that on the eighth anniversary of Holly's death, Meek blew his own brains out with a shotgun. 'Being with Sutch and then working with Joe, I feel probably accounts for the way I am today, completely schizo – being thrown in at the deep end with these people, after having led a really sheltered life up to that point.'

While the Outlaws were highly rated musically among their peers, and even backed such notable American rockers as Jerry Lee Lewis and Gene Vincent on several tours, their reputation was less than spotless on a personal basis – Blackmore himself was at one point, apparently, 'deadly with a flour bomb'.

'That's right – we had this habit when we were travelling in the van of buying four pound bags of flour which we split open, along with eggs and tomatoes, and we'd throw these things at people we saw on the way, preferably old women in wheelchairs. But it got out of hand, and we became very cocky and started throwing them at policemen and all sorts of people. It was great fun, but it got us into a lot of trouble, until nearly every week when we'd be doing a session at Joe's, Joe would say that there was a policeman downstairs, and it would nearly always be me he was looking for, to the point where Chas Hodges had to cover for me. On one occasion, I could have been put away for three months, because somebody had complained that they'd been seriously injured by a flour bag, so Chas said that he'd thrown

it and pleaded guilty in court. Luckily, it was his first offence, but it would have been my twentieth. It was a very strange period when I wrecked a lot of things, although I still don't know why – I used to have grave doubts about myself between the ages of seventeen and twenty-one, because I just wanted to smash things up and cause as much trouble as possible. To me, it was very funny, and I couldn't see why people couldn't see the funny side of it, but we were banned from nearly everywhere because we ruined so many things, and that was why we had to disband, because we couldn't get any work as a band – when we were throwing these flour bags and doing all this nonsense, we had our telephone number in big letters above the van, saying ''Please call the Outlaws'', with a North London telephone number, so of course the police did, and that's why we were caught so often.'

Having been an Outlaw in more than one sense of the word, Ritchie next became a Wild Boy, the name of the group backing Heinz Burt being the Wild Boys. Heinz was initially part of the Tornadoes, another Meek-produced act and possibly the most celebrated part of Meek's stable due to their enormous worldwide hit, 'Telstar', after which Heinz left the group for a solo career, although by the time Ritchie joined him, Heinz' greatest successes were behind him.

'As the Outlaws, we provided the backing for his biggest hits – ''Just Like Eddie'', ''Country Boy'' and ''You Were There'' were the first and biggest, I think – but the Outlaws didn't go on the road with him, and when I left the Outlaws, he asked me to form the Wild Boys with him, which lasted for about a year, although it was a terrible band. We did a three months summer season at Rhyl with Arthur Askey, or Mr Big Head, as he calls himself, and we got into a lot of trouble again. There was a 12-piece pit orchestra, and when they went home at night, I'd add notes to the trumpeter's part, and things like that, and the next day there would be this couple of bars of awful trumpet solo, which didn't go down too well.'

Despite this somewhat rowdy life, Blackmore was still determined to improve his guitar-playing ability. 'I used to practise for about five hours a day, because I loved playing and felt that I had to improve, even though the band I was in wasn't very musical. They could hardly play their instruments at all, I felt, so I was in this weird position of playing three chord music and trying to extemporise in a way which I thought was quite good at the time. I thought the audience might have picked up on that, and wondered why I was in this band who were speeding up and slowing down and playing the wrong chords, and then there'd be a very good solo.'

At the start of 1965, Blackmore joined another semi-legendary seminal British beat group, Neil Christian's Crusaders, a band which, like Lord Sutch's Savages, at various times included many of today's notable musicians, including Jimmy Page. 'At the time I joined, Neil Christian had his only big hit, ''That's Nice'', in the hit parade, and the band were going out on that success. I went along with people saying to me that they liked the guitar introduction that I played on the record, although it wasn't me, it was actually Joe Moretti.'

Ian Gillan (left) and Ritchie

The period from the start of 1965 until the latter part of 1967 is particularly confusing – Blackmore spent part of this time in Germany, admitting to marrying and divorcing two German girls, several spells with Neil Christian, occasional returns to Lord Sutch (one of whose bands included four saxophonists as well as Blackmore), and a solo single of 'Getaway'/'Little Brown Jug'. 'That was produced by Derek Lawrence, and in the band, I think, were Nicky Hopkins on piano, Carlo Little on drums, and Cliff Barton, who was a fantastic bass player. I'd always been kind of on the shy side, and I thought it was going a bit too far to call that the Ritchie Blackmore Orchestra, but that was the way Derek wanted it. I don't really rate that single – I played through a three inch speaker which I'd kicked in to give a fuzz box effect. Jimmy Page had the only fuzz box around, but with this three inch speaker being overloaded by 30 watts, it gave a similar kind of fuzzy effect.'

Shortly afterwards, Blackmore returned to Germany with bass player Avid Anderson and drummer Jimmy 'Tornado' Evans, who were known as the Three Musketeers. 'I was a little bit disillusioned with England, and I wanted to be somewhere else, anywhere, and I loved Germany. So I found this backer who was prepared to put up some money, and we became the Three Musketeers, dressing up as musketeers, coming on stage sword fencing as the drummer played two bass drums which was unheard of in those days, and only being a three piece, which was also unusual. I have fond memories of that period, because the band was excellent, but it was far too advanced for the German public, because we used to play very fast instrumentals. They couldn't dance to it, and they couldn't understand what we were doing, coming on stage fencing and then going into an incredibly fast Django Reinhardt number or something like that – I don't think they were too

The classic Deep Purple – left to right:
Ritchie, Ian Gillan, Roger Glover, Jon Lord, Ian Paice

pleased on the whole . . . I wish I had some recordings of that time, because I'd like to hear how I was playing in that period.

'After that, I came back to England, and back to Neil Christian – there were only certain groups before 1967 that would have pure guitarists like myself, who refused to sing or get involved in harmonies, but just played lead, so it was actually quite difficult getting gigs, because everybody wanted someone who could also sing. One of Sutch's bands that I joined was called the Roman Empire, and we used to dress up as Roman soldiers. For a publicity stunt, we marched through Oxford Street dressed like that, and held up a bus, much to the dismay of a policeman who arrested us, or tried to.'

Following this mayhem, Blackmore formed a shortlived band called Mandrake Root, which in itself was of little note, save for the fact that it led almost directly to the formation of the band which initially made Blackmore a superstar, Deep Purple.

The early origins of Deep Purple are complicated, to say the least. The group seems initially to have been the brainchild of ex-Searchers drummer Chris Curtis, who convinced a financial backer, Tony Edwards, that a group could be formed around him. Among the other musicians he contacted to recruit members for the group was Blackmore. 'Chris Curtis, who I'd met back in 1963 at the Star Club in Hamburg, sent me about a hundred telegrams to invite

me to join his new group, which was first going to be called the Light, which lasted about one day, and then Roundabout. It's a strange story – I asked him who else was going to be in the band, and presumed that he'd be playing drums, and he said he was, and that he would also be playing lead guitar. So I asked what I'd be playing, and he said I would be number two, second guitarist, and I must always remember that he was number one and I was number two. I said OK, and asked who'd be playing bass, to get off the subject, and who'd be singing, and he said he'd be doing all the singing, and we wouldn't need a bass player, so in actual fact, it was just the two of us, and he was playing every instrument, including lead guitar, but I had to remember that he was number one guitarist. And I hope he takes this in the spirit it's meant, because it was funny, although I couldn't quite understand it at the time. He was always saying to me ''I'm number one, what are you?'' and I'd go ''I'm number two''. It was a very strange set up, but he did get one other player, Jon Lord, who was an excellent organist, and whose playing really interested me. We talked about it, and Jon was very interested in my playing, although he wasn't very sure about Chris either.

'Prior to getting together with Chris, I'd been stuck in Germany, living off immoral earnings. This woman was helping me out, and I stayed there for about a year, practising about six or seven hours a

Deep Purple, late 1973 – left to right: Jon Lord, Glenn Hughes, David Coverdale, Ian Paice, Ritchie Blackmore

day, which was all I could do – there was nothing to do but practise and drink. At the end of that year, I saw Ian Paice at the Star Club drumming with the Maze, and I offered him a job with my band. He asked what the name of the band was, and who else was in it, and I told him that there was nobody else in the band, so he asked me how he could join. I told him he was the first member, and that we'd get some really good players, so he told me to let him know when I had the other members together, which I did, about a year later.

'I think it was the backer's wife who was really more interested in Chris Curtis than Tony Edwards was, and in about two weeks, we all saw where it was going, and I got Ian Paice involved, and then we had the semblance of a band, with Dave Curtis on bass first, and then Nicky Simper, and it sounded very good, with Jon on organ, Ian on drums and me on guitar. It was a really happening thing, and Tony Edwards saw this, and Chris Curtis seemed to fade out. I think he went back to Liverpool, and I haven't seen him since, but he was the first one to get Deep Purple together.'

With Lord, Paice, Simper and Blackmore himself, the only ingredient missing was a singer, a position finally filled by Rod Evans, who had also been in the Maze with Ian Paice. Deep Purple were an astonishingly popular group, almost from their first formation in March 1968 until their final dissolution almost exactly eight years later (after myriad personnel changes). However, their early records gave little clue to the fact that, within a few months of their debut, they would become one of the heaviest hard rock bands of all, one example from their first LP, *Shades Of Deep Purple*, being the choice of a Neil Diamond song, 'Kentucky Woman', to cover. Hardly the obvious type of material, Ritchie?

'I was quite happy playing it, because I just had no direction at the time and was very happy to be in a band with some financial backing behind us. We were living in a haunted chateau in St Albans, and I think "Kentucky Woman" was Jon Lord's suggestion, putting it to the type of beat which Mitch Ryder & the Detroit Wheels would have used. And it worked – I think it got quite high in the charts in America, as our second single.' In fact, it was hardly a triumph, reaching number thirty-eight, a respectable, but hardly overwhelming position, especially as it followed 'Hush', the group's debut 45, which peaked at number four in the USA, bringing almost instant stardom to the group.

'"Hush" was more my idea – I really liked the song, which I'd heard sung by Joe South, who had a small hit with it, and I couldn't understand why we had the hit with our version. It helped us a hell of a lot in America, but in England, we weren't known at all – we were playing a festival at Sunbury or Plumpton, and we were due on at seven o'clock and Joe Cocker was on after us, and the papers said that the show started with Joe Cocker, and that was the kind of press we were getting.'

After three LPs, all of which were substantially more successful in America than in Britain, Deep Purple experienced some personnel changes, which saw the departure of Rod Evans and Nick Simper, who were replaced by Ian Gillan and Roger Glover,

respectively. 'I could tell that the fashion was going to be for screamers with depth and an overall blues feel, which is why we got Ian – he had a scream, but also had a way of singing which was, and still is today, very different. He's got a lot of identity there, and you always know when it's Ian singing.'

This line up of the band, widely known as Deep Purple Mark II, is regarded by an overwhelming majority of Purple fans as the ultimate permutation of the band, with which Ritchie wholeheartedly agrees. 'There was a chemistry, and basically, we were all very enthusiastic, plus the band was very musically inclined, I thought. Roger is an excellent catalyst who's very good at putting things together, Ian was a very good showman and a good looking guy who had an incredible voice, Jon was a very good arranger and a very good musician in the old school form, who could put it down on paper, and I was the mad irritable guitarist, I suppose, who certain people could relate to, and I thought I also played quite well. I worked on that image, because Jon had this gentleman image, Mr Nice Guy, and I wanted to be the opposite, which is in my nature. I think you have to be yourself, otherwise the public sees through it, but I was embellishing it, blowing it out a lot, and I suppose that's why today a lot of people still think of me as the moody guitarist. Which I am, and I'm proud of it.'

Strangely enough, the first album released by the new line up was hardly the type of thing which a 'moody guitarist' would enjoy, a slightly bombastic item composed by Jon Lord and entitled *Concerto For Group And Orchestra*. 'I didn't like that at all – I thought it was a total gimmick, and I told Jon that I'd be prepared to try it, but that I had a lot of heavy rock numbers that I wanted to put together on an LP, and that we'd see which one took off. I didn't want to be involved with the *Concerto* because of the novelty effect and the press we were getting out of it because of playing it at the Royal Albert Hall and all this business, but I said that if the next LP, about which I had some very firm ideas, and which was *Deep Purple In Rock*, didn't take off, that I was prepared to play with orchestras for the rest of my life. So we agreed to see which way the public wanted us to go, and the *Concerto* was a success to most people, but when we did *In Rock*, they went really crazy, thankfully, because that was the music I was into.'

With the release of *Deep Purple In Rock*, the tide had totally changed for the group in Britain. It became the group's first UK chart album, closely following the success a few weeks before of the single which would prove to be the group's biggest hit 45, 'Black Night'/'Speed King', which reached number two. 'Black Night' was a total rip-off – I stole the riff from Ricky Nelson's record of "Summertime" (the George Gershwin song). The lead guitar playing on "Summertime", which was by James Burton, is the intro to "Hey Joe", and then a bass figure comes in which became "Black Night". As soon as I heard "Hey Joe", I thought if Jimi Hendrix can take that lead guitar line, I'll take the bass line, and consequently we both had hits with them, which is quite nice really, although poor old Ricky Nelson didn't get anything. "Speed King" also had Hendrix connections, because it was based around "Stone Free".

Pretentious? Moi?

Roger wrote most of that actual riff, I think, and that was the first hard heavy metal rock'n'roll track that we'd written, and we were very pleased with it, although there are some parts which sound similar to "Stone Free". We wanted to incorporate that type of thing, and Ian (Gillan) wrote some innocent lyrics really, which the Americans interpreted as being about drugs, whereas in fact the song's just about a fast driver.'

A most interesting facet of the group's songwriting ability was that a backing track would be completely recorded, after which it became Ian Gillan's job to construct lyrics and subject matter, often without a title. 'Led Zeppelin used to do the same thing to Robert Plant, he told me, but that was the way it was – we would always write the backing track and not even think about what was going to be sung over it. The fact that it was a good backing track was good enough for the band, and if Ian couldn't sing anything over it, it was just too bad and meant that he was inferior, so he had to sing around these certain riffs, which must have been very difficult sometimes. Hearing these things in retrospect, people would say that it was very clever how the voice suddenly stopped and the guitar took over with a riff, but really it was just that it was an awkward riff to sing over, and that's how those things came about. I know it dispels the myth of working together, but we would go in for

one purely instrumental day, and Ian would be in the studio for the next day to put the vocal down.'

Although they were tremendously successful during the nearly four years they were together, Deep Purple Mark II worked under a good deal of pressure. 'We were working all the time, either on stage or in the studio, and we had about a week off each year, at the most, in between dates. I went down with hepatitis, and so did Ian, and I even had a bit of a nervous breakdown in '69 because I didn't want to go to America – I loathed America, and I didn't want to have anything to do with it. I wanted to stay in Europe and just go around quite merrily doing Germany, France and England, but the managers were always saying that we must break America, which is true, I suppose.'

Nearly ten years later, how does Ritchie view the work of Deep Purple Mark II? 'I can't really say that I've heard any of it recently, because I'm very bad at collecting and listening to what I've done, and I don't get off on what I've played, except for a few tracks that I consider to be very good and very emotional, but I didn't consider a lot of the Deep Purple material that I was on to be very good, now or even then. I could see that the public bought the records, and that it was commercial, but I really didn't like half the stuff we did. But there again, I think that was me being me, just being bloody moody and saying I was tired of a song within an hour of playing the riff, and by the time that I heard the end result, I hated the whole thing. It may sound strange, but I just didn't like most of what we put down, which is probably what keeps turning me on now, keeps pushing me on to believe that one day, I'll be able to play something that I actually like.'

One song which Ritchie will admit to liking from his Deep Purple years is 'Smoke On The Water' from the 1972 LP, *Machine Head*. 'Yes, there's a story behind that, which was that we went to see Frank Zappa playing in Montreux, where we were recording, and somebody shot a flare gun off which set the roof on fire, and the whole place went up and was gutted within two hours. Everybody was running out of the place, but I didn't know why – I thought it was an intermission or something, because I had got tired of Frank Zappa within the first ten minutes, and I was more interested in this girl who was quite well endowed. I took her outside and was talking to her, and all these people were running past me with white faces, and I presumed it must be an intermission and that they were going to get ice creams until I saw the smoke coming out and realised something was wrong. It's a good job I realised it, because otherwise I'd have been with this certain young lady somewhere, in some kind of cupboard, up to some sort of mischief, and I would have been burnt down with the place, because it was a habit of mine to disappear into cellars and places. . . . We had already recorded the backing track before the fire, and we did it in about four takes because we had to – the police were banging on the door, and we knew it was the police, but we had such a good sound in this hall that we were waking up the neighbours about five miles away because the sound was echoing through the mountains. We had just finished it when the police burst in and said we had to stop, and since we'd finished it, we did. Then Ian wrote the words after the fire – he probably didn't have anything else to write about (laughs).'

Not long after this, the newest members of the band, Ian Gillan and Roger Glover, decided to leave the band, Gillan to form his own group, and Glover, initially, to become a producer. How had Blackmore and the remaining members of the band felt about the split? 'I guess there's two answers to that, the professional one and the honest one, and the professional one is that we were stunned, as they say. But really, it had been coming for quite a time – I wasn't getting on with Ian too well, and it had been three years or more, which was long enough for me to get on with anybody, so I more or less said that I wanted to leave in 1973, at the same time as Ian Gillan, and form my own band, which was going to be with Ian Paice and Phil Lynott. It was suggested that it would be better if I stayed because of all the financial things involved, and I said I would stay, but that if Ian was going, I thought we should probably replace Roger, and the band decided that they would rather have me in the band and get another bass player. So I was the cause of Roger being asked to leave, which I wasn't particularly pleased about, because he's such a hard worker and a nice guy and a very good musician, but I thought his ideas were a little too commercial. I was dying to get into some blues, some very heavy stuff, like Bad Company were playing, but Roger was into a lot of vocal backings and the fairy dust effect which thankfully sells records. He always puts a glossy sheen on things, and I liked the more earthy side of music, he was more into pop, and I was more into non-selling rock. I suppose that I considered myself a heavy metal guitarist, although people often say I'm not because I have finesse and I play with subtleties and ups and downs, but I don't care what people call me as long as nobody calls me a folk guitarist.'

The replacements for the two outgoing members of the group were singer David Coverdale and bass player Glenn Hughes, but it seemed to take very little time before Blackmore discovered that he had probably been better off with the members who had left. 'I under-estimated Ian's talent and the way he sang, so I was definitely wrong there. I didn't like the way he sang after a couple of years of listening to it, but on reflection, it was much better than when we got the other two in – which is not putting them down, but just saying that I didn't like what they did. I didn't stay much longer, because it started to become a soul type band with the *Stormbringer* album. It became very, very funky and it wasn't a rock'n'roll band anymore – to me, it's either classical music or rock'n'roll, it's black or white, and I don't like funk music or soul music, which I think Ian Paice and Jon are still into to this day.'

On this occasion, there was no attempt to convince Ritchie to stay in Deep Purple. 'I left because I'd met up with Ronnie Dio, and he was so easy to work with. He was originally just going to do one track of a solo LP, but we ended up doing the whole LP in three weeks, which I was very excited about. It wasn't that I found Ronnie Dio and that I was into this band Rainbow, it was that I was determined to leave Purple; because I no longer respected their music.

An early loon-panted Rainbow with Ritchie (centre) and Cozy Powell (second right)

So in May 1975, Ritchie Blackmore finally left Deep Purple, although there has been constant pressure ever since for the group, and preferably the Mark II version, to reform, if only for a brief tour and album. Will it ever happen? 'The longer it goes on, the more I doubt it.'

This major change in Ritchie's career seemed a good point to discuss matters such as practise, choice of guitars, technique and so on. 'I practise more mentally, which is an easy way out of that one, and means in other words, that I'm lazy and don't practise at all, which is what everyone means when they say they practise mentally. I practise for an hour or two every day, especially when I have time off.

'When it comes to new guitars, I'm very unadventurous. I play a Fender with my own special concave wood effect on the neck, and I'm very satisfied with it, and the same goes for amplifiers. People offer to let me try things, but I don't, which is probably detrimental to me – I hear certain sounds, like phasing and things like that, which I should really try, but I never do – for some reason, I'm too busy either practising or just thinking. I don't experiment enough with my life in general, and that goes for music, food and a lot of other things, although I'm starting to experiment with hotels, and I now stay in as many places of historical interest as I can find, much to the regret of our road manager, who has to check me into castles and weird haunted places all over Scotland.

'During my time with Deep Purple, I'm sure my guitar technique improved, because I'd never played to so many people, and for once in all the years, I could see an actual point in all the practising. I mean I practise just because I love to practise, but then I saw that there was this other avenue where there were actually people willing to listen. Then I thought it was maybe because I'd practised so much. I'm certainly no better than most guitarists, it's just that I've practised a lot more, so if I have a faster right hand, it's just that I'm always shaking it around in practice. I think technically, but I think I lack a lot of mental innovation, and in that way, I'm not as creative as I'd like to be. I'm not pitch perfect and I don't have a very good musical memory, so most of what comes out in my practising is enthusiasm. I never particularly wanted to be distinctive as a guitarist – I'd rather be distinctive as a person – and the guitar was the thing I could do better than anything else.'

Reverting to Rainbow, the band Ritchie formed after leaving Deep Purple, one of the most outstanding features of the band, aside from its music, has been an almost constant spate of personnel changes – during the seven years of the band's existence, no less than seventeen musicians, aside from Blackmore himself, had played in the band, which never exceeded a five man line-up at any time.

'I think the problem is that they don't like me (laughs). Really, when I was with Purple, I was so confined with those five players, and we had our limitations within the band, which weren't that many, but they were there, and I was conscious of them, so that when I got a new band together, I didn't want any limitations whatsoever, which, the more I get into it, is actually impossible. Every band has to have limitations, but I find that very hard to accept, which is why I keep changing members.'

It would be pointless to list all the comings and goings which occurred within Rainbow, and for the purposes of the radio version of this series, we chose a number of tracks from the various Rainbow LPs, and asked Ritchie to talk about them. From the 1977 Live LP, *On Stage* came the simply titled 'Blues' . . . 'Playing the blues is a challenge on guitar, because you're so limited within the minor mode of the blues, and if you start to go off into majors and diminished scales, it doesn't sound right, so you limit it to about six notes, and certain people can pull it off, although I don't know who they are at the moment – there must be somebody! But it's very difficult within the blues frame to come up with something that's different, and that's what I find a challenge with the blues – it's a case of slowing down and playing three or four notes very well with a very good vibrato, which is a lot more difficult than it would seem on the surface. To contradict myself, blues can be very easy if you're totally relaxed and you've been drinking, and then it's very hard to produce edge music, music with any sort of intensity, nervous adrenalin type music, and I find that side of things fascinating – it's hard to live with it, because you're continually nervous, but I wouldn't change it for the world, because I like being on the edge of the Rainbow.'

Next, 'Kill The King', which can be found on the 1978 LP, *Long Live Rock'n'Roll*. 'I have no idea what the lyrics to that song are about, because with Ronnie (Dio), I didn't know too much about the lyrics, and they were very abstract, most of them talking about demons and devils. The riff was just a very fast one which is my typical type of block chord in G sort of riff – I must stop writing in the key of G – and it's just a very frantic, upfront, no nonsense number, which you either love or hate, and I knew that when we were playing it. We recorded that particular number in a château in France that had been haunted by Chopin, and it seemed very weird that we were doing this out-and-out rocker when we should have been full of melodic content and playing in a very sympathetic way in sympathy with the environment of the château, whereas we were crashing out "Kill The King" and disturbing all the local residents, but it's still a very interesting song.'

Rainbow's greatest successes in the British singles chart came after Ronnie Dio had been replaced as vocalist by Graham Bonnet, the first hit for this combination being 'Since You've Been Gone', which reached number five during the autumn of 1979. Unlike the vast majority of the tracks recorded by Rainbow, this song was a cover version which had been recorded several times before, and had been written by Russ Ballard. 'I first heard that at my manager's house, and he asked me what I thought of the song. I said it was a hit, and wanted to do it, and he was quite surprised. We did it in about two takes, because Cozy (Powell, Rainbow's drummer for five years) hated it. It was released and it was a hit, which we knew all along it would be, and it was kind of a way of getting our foot in the door and getting a broader public, but at the same time we weren't letting the side down. "I Surrender" (a number three hit in Britain at the start of 1981) is a similar type of song, and I'll always stand by those songs, because they're great songs – people say "How can you do that? How can you sell out? You're a heavy metal guitarist and known to be uncommercial", but that's rubbish, and I'll play anything. If it has a good melody, that's all that matters, even if it's "Over The Rainbow" by Judy Garland (which has been used to close the Rainbow live show). I did "Since You've Been Gone" because I thought it was an extremely good melody, and I can listen to it now and feel quite proud of it – I'm more proud of that song than I am of some of the Deep Purple songs which were kind of underground hits, like "Woman From Tokyo". I can't stand things like that.'

For many listeners, 'Since You've Been Gone' was 'made' by a typically attacking Blackmore solo which came at the end of the track, almost like an afterthought. Was it a conscious decision on Blackmore's part to tack on a guitar solo at the end of what had been a heavily vocal-dominated track? 'I wasn't conscious that I had to put it in. I didn't want to put a solo on the end, but everybody insisted that I should kind of put my mark on it, but I felt that I didn't want to ruin the song, because it was perfectly good enough as it was, and stood up as a great song, so why should I have to start improvising at the end of it? But at the same time, because I have a lot of self-confidence in certain respects, I felt that it didn't matter whether or not I put on a guitar solo, so I just played over the ending, and they kept it in.'

Graham Bonnet's sojourn as Rainbow's vocalist was brief, and for the 1981 LP, *Difficult To Cure*, he was replaced by Joe Lynn Turner. Turner, however, was not featured on the LP's title track, which was actually largely derived from Beethoven's Ninth Symphony. 'I remember watching a football match during the 1970s between Germany and Holland, where they had 90,000 people singing this tune, which sent shivers up my spine. Ever since that day, I've really loved that particular melody, although I don't especially like Beethoven. I know it's very easy to cop a tune like that, but again, it had the melodic content, and I used to throw it in as a kind of added bonus on stage.'

Although Ritchie's name has appeared quite frequently on songwriting credits, he refuses to consider himself as a songwriter. 'I'm a riff merchant – I export and import riffs and chord progressions and vague melodies, but when it comes to lyrics, I don't have much to do with it. I'll often think of a theme, like "All Night Long", which was about seeing a girl off the side of the stage when you're playing live, and she looks quite nice, so you want to get to know her, and that song was loosely based around that. I had some lyrics for that which I gave to Roger Glover (yes, the same Roger Glover whom Ritchie had caused to leave Deep Purple, but who became Rainbow's bass player/record producer in 1979, since which time the group have experienced their greatest success commercially), and which he changed around a lot, but I don't usually come up with lyrics at all – I concentrate on construction and I always have a vague melody in my mind.'

So had he ever thought about taking a leaf out of Jeff Beck's book, and making completely instrumental albums? 'I've thought about it, but not in the Jeff Beck jazz/rock style, and even though several of my influences were guitar-based trios, like Jimi Hendrix, I wouldn't front a trio, because it's too much of a strain. Not on myself, because I've been in several three-piece groups, but on the audience, because I think it's too much for them to take for an hour and ten minutes, with just the lead guitarist taking the breaks. That gets too monotonous for me – I could handle it, but it doesn't appeal to me, and even with Hendrix, I always thought that there were

'What's going on over there?'

only so many solos he could take before you wanted another instrument to come in, even if it was a trombone, just to change the atmosphere a bit.'

It's difficult to sum up Ritchie Blackmore tidily – it would be easy to suggest that his guitar does his talking for him, but perhaps his answer to a question about the future should remain his epitaph, at least in this volume.

What a shocking chord!

'I shall remain as stubborn as I've always been and given enough time and patience, I might come out with something worthwhile somewhere along the line. I have the ambition of a slug, and I'm not interested in goals of any sort, and that's why I don't hang out in the right places and talk to the right people and do the right things, probably. The only way I can do certain things that appear to be right is because I feel that it's inside me – I love playing the guitar, but I don't like being involved in everything else that goes with the business. I don't really understand myself, and my parents certainly don't understand me, but in a way, I like to leave it like that, because I'm never bored with myself. I'm often very confused with myself, but never bored.'

Ritchie Blackmore Discography

Early years
Prior to joining Deep Purple, Ritchie played on numerous sessions, most of them overseen by Joe Meek, but as it is unclear which records by which artists he was actually involved in, it seems safe to only list the following:

Various Artists
1979 *The Joe Meek Story* (all tracks from 1960s)

Heinz
1980 *Remembering* (all tracks from 1960s)

Heinz/The Tornados
1982 *Heinz/The Tornados* (all tracks from 1960s)

Deep Purple
Blackmore was with Deep Purple for seven years (1968–1975). While he played on many of their LPs as listed below during those years, the group's immense popularity resulted in several 'posthumous' albums being released.

1968 *Shades Of Deep Purple*	Rainbow
1969 *Book Of Taliesyn*	1975 *Ritchie Blackmore's Rainbow*
1969 *Deep Purple*	1976 *Rainbow Rising*
1970 *Concerto For Group & Orchestra*	1977 *On Stage*
1970 *Deep Purple In Rock*	1978 *Long Live Rock'n'Roll*
1971 *Fireball*	1979 *Down To Earth*
1972 *Machine Head*	1981 *Difficult To Cure*
1972 *Made In Japan*	1981 *The Best Of Rainbow*
1973 *Who Do We Think We Are*	1982 *Straight Between The Eyes*
1974 *Burn*	
1974 *Stormbringer*	
1975 *24 Carat Purple* (recorded 1970–1973)	
1976 *Made In Europe* (recorded 1975)	
1978 *Powerhouse* (recorded 1969–1972)	
1978 *Deep Purple Singles A's & B's* (recorded 1968–1971)	
1978 *The Mark Two Purple Singles* (recorded 1971–1973)	
1980 *Deepest Purple* (recorded 1970–1974)	
1980 *Deep Purple In Concert* (recorded 1970–1972)	
1982 *Deep Purple Live In London* (recorded 1974)	

STEVE MILLER

When we met Steve Miller in the Seattle studio where he mostly works these days, he was planning to make more than one album – not unreasonable since he hadn't had an original LP released for over four years. Seattle, being at the extreme north-western tip of the United States, is a place where a substantially low profile can easily be adopted, and Miller was pleased to note that he can walk down the street there without anyone looking at him twice, something which was not the case when he lived in California and scored a series of huge hits during the mid- to late 1970s.

Steve Miller was born in Dallas, Texas, on 10 October 1943, the son of a doctor who was also very interested in music. 'My dad loved music, especially jazz, and as a child, I knew Charles Mingus, Red Norvo, Tal Farlow – these people would come by the house all the time – and Les Paul and Mary Ford were real close friends of my parents. Mary Ford showed me my first chords, electric guitars were around all the time, and my dad made a plexiglass pick guard for Les Paul's guitar. I was able to see these people perform at the age of four and five, and I just thought, "Well, it's a lot neater than work!" I had a natural talent for singing from my mother, so I was really exposed to all of this at an incredibly early age. And that includes the recording process – I knew about multi-track recording in the '40s.'

Certainly, one item which has characterised Steve Miller's recording career is his devotion to technology and the use of sound effects to decorate his music, although from time to time, his technique has been unorthodox. We knew, for example, that at one fairly recent point in his career, he had played a left-handed guitar right-handed, or upside down, and the idea occurred that perhaps he had always played in this manner, because the guitar given to him by his uncle had been a left-handed instrument. The reality was quite different: 'Yes, that was kind of peculiar. I did have a couple of left-handed guitars, but that's not the way I play my guitar all the time, that was more of an experiment. I'd watched Hendrix play a Stratocaster upside down, and I decided there were some distinct advantages to playing with the controls on the top of the guitar, rather than always having to reach down, adjust, and then come back up to play – it could save quarters of seconds and things by having everything closer and then being able to make down strokes, so I tried that for three or four years, but now I'm back to the other way. Anyway, the strings weren't upside down – it was strung in the normal way for a right-handed guitar. It was just to get to the controls quicker and have a vibrato bar on the top instead of the bottom.

Steve Miller formed his first band, The Marksmen Combo, at the age of twelve. At thirteen or fourteen he was playing at college parties, and as soon as they could drive his group moved into the clubs. Another member of the band who also made his name in the rock world was Boz Scaggs, who was connected with Miller on and off until the seventies.

'We played through high school, and when I left to go to college, to the University of Wisconsin, it began to seem as though everywhere I went I was involved in the first rock'n'roll band. We basically did a lot of blues, Delta blues – Jimmy Reed, Bill Doggett and T. Bone Walker were really the people who influenced me.'

The band formed by Miller (and Scaggs again) at the University of Wisconsin was known us the Ardells. Whatever else it may have been, the Ardells was Miller's first band to record – after a fashion. 'We didn't make any albums or anything – we made tape recordings, and tried to record, but I never even thought of myself as ever making a serious attempt at recording. That always seemed to be something that happened to somebody else, guys like Fabian or Frankie Avalon – we just didn't even consider ourselves in the same league, as the same kind of people, or as the same kind of entertainment. It never seemed that we would be able to make a living doing what we were doing, because all we were doing basically was playing fraternity parties for a bunch of drunken students. It was more a party than serious art. That band came to an end because I was getting pretty tired of the University. I spent a year in Denmark at the University of Copenhagen, and that pretty much put it all together for me – when I came back, I was really being drawn to Chicago. I wanted to go to Chicago to play music – I didn't want a Doctor's degree or a Master's degree in Literature or something like that, which was no longer of any interest to me.

'It was when I moved to Chicago that I started to see that I was going to get a recording contract and I was going to be able to make records – this was the time that the Beatles were just appearing, and Simon and Garfunkel, and all of a sudden, people were beginning to say that there might be something in all this, and I began to realise that I might be able to make a record.'

Miller's first band in Chicago was called the World War Three Blues Band... 'Yes, that was aptly named. We were working in the Mafia-controlled neighbourhood of Chicago, and in fact, the band got shut down on its opening night because some guy got up on the roof and cut the power, as part of a little Mafia war that was going on at the time about who was going to run this nightclub we were playing in. But that was an interesting band, and then, when Barry Goldberg joined, we changed. Barry had the manager and all that stuff, and I had the band, so we got together. Barry and I really enjoyed playing together – he was probably one of the more creative people I've ever worked with – and we were really able to do a lot.'

The Goldberg/Miller Blues Band, as this aggregation became known, recorded a few tracks in 1966 which have been released on obscure compilation LPs, although the most readily obtainable example of Goldberg and Miller playing together on record is a deservedly under-rated double album titled *Word Of Mouth* by one Neil Merryweather.

At the end of 1966, Steve Miller moved to San Francisco, where he first made a significant impression as a musician. 'Everything was drying up in Chicago – it had been a very creative centre for about two years, and it was really exciting there, then, all of a sudden, just as fast as it started, it began to go away. Dylan was beginning to happen, bands were starting to tour, and things were beginning to catch up in America to what had already become established as an English rock'n'roll scene. English bands like the Stones and the Beatles had been touring, and Americans were beginning to understand the concept – 'Hey, you know, touring, right? This can become something' – and it was really up to the English to show us, and then when we saw what they were doing, people started doing it here, and everybody left Chicago to go to work. The whole scene was put together with (Paul) Butterfield, Muddy Waters, Junior Wells and Buddy Guy, Otis Spann, Otis Rush, Barry and myself and a couple of other groups, and everybody left to go on the road and the whole thing collapsed – everybody left town, and it was gone.

'What was starting to happen in California was that they were beginning to develop the first signs of the psychedelic revolution, and the venues that were available started to attract bigger gatherings. So I went to California to see what was actually happening.

'It was a completely different situation, and what I found was a social revolution, a phenomenon going on led by bands, by personalities like Jerry Garcia, a fascinating guy on stage and to talk to – Captain Trips, you know – and the Jefferson Airplane, who had learned the manipulation side of working with an audience, and the star personality side of it, which was something I had never even thought about or paid attention to. So what I saw when I got out there was these hordes of adoring fans, and lots of production, lots of lights, light shows and all this kind of stuff, with really pretty atrocious bands playing very loudly, but not very well.'

It requires little imagination to recount what happened next – faced with an almost total lack of musical expertise, Miller, who had by this time been playing in a band for eleven years, was able to acquire his coveted recording contract with remarkable ease.

Around this time came the first recording Miller undertook in San Francisco, on which he and his band backed the legendary Chuck Berry at a live concert. 'That was just another thing that happened in the scene. Chuck Berry, as you know by now, plays (concerts) but doesn't have a band, so when they wanted to bring him to the Fillmore, they needed a band, and they obviously had to have us because we were the only guys who were able to back him. The other bands wouldn't have been able to do it, and it was just decided that we were going to back Chuck Berry, so we rehearsed with him for three days, and we had this absolutely great set, and we really felt good about it. Then, on the night of the show, he walked out onstage and was really weird – "turn that down, don't do that" – but we did this show, and it was recorded and an album made out of it, which I think was mixed in an afternoon. It was another real fast "Let's get right in there" record – the whole scene was surrounded by record companies, and the first time we played, I think I had fourteen contract offers after one gig in San Francisco. Guys were coming out of the walls wanting us to do this and that, and on that occasion, I said yes, because I thought that working with Chuck would be a good project, although eventually, I didn't really think much of the record.'

The first Steve Miller Band was a quartet, comprising, apart from Miller himself, two friends from Madison, drummer Tim Davis and guitarist/singer James 'Curley' Cooke, and bass player Lonnie Turner, whom Miller had met in San Francisco, and it was this line-up which backed Chuck Berry for the live album, whose title, *Chuck Berry Live At The Fillmore Auditorium* is only marginally less inspired than its content. The band was also involved in a film about the burgeoning San Francisco scene, *Revolution*, although the so-called soundtrack album, like so many 'original motion picture soundtrack' records, was in fact recorded some time later.

During 1967, the Miller band first expanded with the addition of bass player Jim Peterman, and then, shortly before Miller signed to Capitol Records, an arrangement which continues, at least in the United States, to this day, another change occurred when 'Curley' Cooke left to form his own band, and was replaced by Miller's old cohort, William Royce 'Boz' Scaggs.

Despite having been pursued by virtually every major record company, Steve Miller chose to sign with Capitol Records during the latter half of 1967, and elected to record his all-important first album in Britain. 'We had had such a bad experience trying to record in the States – we had all the best intentions, but we always found ourselves in an adversary posi-

The Steve Miller Band, 1968 – left to right: Boz Scaggs, Jim Peterman, Steve Miller, Lonnie Turner, Tim Davis

tion as far as the record companies went. So then we just packed up and went to London, because we knew it was going to be better in London, and that's where we ran into Glyn Johns. I was thinking about working with George Martin, and we discussed some things and played him some tapes and showed him some ideas, but although he seemed kind of interested, he was a little tied-up, and he wanted a lot of money. So we looked around and then we heard about Glyn and started working with him. We spent two or three months in London recording, and it turned out to be great because when we got there, everybody liked what we were doing – they liked loud guitars, and they knew how to record the amplifiers for us. The first sessions I'd done here (in America), the engineers had just finished doing the "Sunday Picnic Polka", and they hated us, they were really down on us as people – it was a bad time to be trying to do what we were doing, but in London, we had a lot of freedom, and it was good.'

Steve Miller's first album was called *Children Of The Future,* and when it was released in the spring of 1968, it was widely acclaimed as adventurous and interesting, although it is difficult, listening to the record nearly fifteen years later, to discover quite what the critics saw in it, particularly with the advantage of having heard Miller's later work. 'To tell you the truth, I don't think that album's stood up very well, and when I hear it, I hear a lot of problems and a lot of things that could have been improved, but it was our first album. We were still learning about the studio, and we were going through head changes while we were recording – maybe there are a few tunes on the album that were OK, like perhaps "Stepping Stone", although the first side was supposed to be a concept.'

Miller's second album, released only a few months after *Children*, was a significant improvement. One of the items which contributed to the superior quality of the later LP, *Sailor*, was the use of evocative sound effects – although there had been traces of these on the first album, they came to the fore for the second.

'I don't really know when it all started, but I've always loved sound effects – as a child, I used to listen to "Bozo Goes To The Circus" records, and "Murder Mysteries" on the radio. We have a great

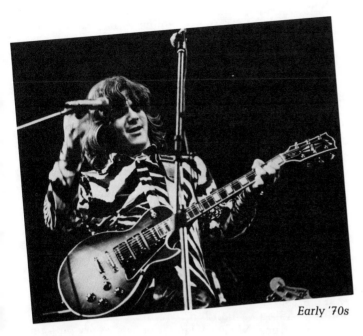

Early '70s

tradition of drama on the radio, much better than our television drama, and on the radio they have all these great murder plays, and things with sound effects and cars and ''The Shadow Knows'' and all these characters. As a child, I was fascinated by all that, and when I got my hands on a tape recorder, it seemed quite natural to record sound effects and electronic music. I was also fascinated by Stockhausen in the early '60s, and it was just something I was going to do if I got the chance. It was really difficult at first with Glyn, because I wanted to do a lot of sound effects on the first record, and it was a huge fight from day one. Here we were, we'd gone through all these years of work to get to this point, and when we get in the studio, the engineer does not want to do any sound effects. Finally, towards the end of *Children Of The Future,* we got to do the sound effects – we went to the BBC and used their mellotron, which is somewhere in the dusty rooms in that place, and it had chickens at dawn, birds at sunset, people arguing upstairs, screams, thugs in the alley and whatever, and we started working with all these sound effects and the subway trains and all that. To me, it just seemed real natural, and now I do all kinds of sound effects. I've been experimenting, and I've had two years of nothing but sound effects fun lately, and it's really been good.'

Sailor is such a classic LP that we prevailed upon Steve to go into some detail about why certain songs were chosen and how they were recorded, one being 'Gangster Of Love', the first in a series of 'personae' which Miller has adopted, others being the 'Space Cowboy', 'Maurice' and most famous of all, 'The Joker'. '''Gangster Of Love'' is just one of those great tunes. I have a list of songs, and it's nice to see that people have started really going back and going through all this material, because there's a wealth of that sort of stuff, like ''Gangster Of Love'', which is an old Johnny ''Guitar'' Watson tune we used to do in high school. It's just a great song, and when I got the chance to record it, I did.' 'Living In The USA' is another superb track, and was, we thought, Steve's first hit single. . . 'It really wasn't a hit, but people

have always talked about it as if it were a hit. Apparently it captured a lot of imaginations, but didn't capture so many dollars – a strange record. When it was released, it didn't do very well at the time – the album did much better – and then it would do things like fourteen months later, it would sell 100,000 copies in Cleveland, and then disappear again, and then it would show up in Florida, and they'd need to press some more. I guess that was the first single we did that got us airplay, and it was just a tune we were doing at the time – I think I was actually more into playing harmonica on it than guitar.'

Another track which deserves some explanation from its creator is 'Song For Our Ancestors', which opens the album, and with its array of varied sound effects, becomes an audio delight with few equals. 'That was a tune I'd written a long long time before – I wrote that in 1964 during a period when I left Chicago and there was nothing going on, I didn't have a band or anything, and I was beginning to do multi-track recording on quarter track tape recorders, and fiddling around with tuning and stuff, so I put this little tune together, but the sound effects was all Glyn Johns – that's a perfect example of the kind of producer Glyn Johns is. When we started *Children Of The Future,* he didn't want anything to do with sound effects but by the next album, old Glyn was the guy who made us stay in the studio for forty-eight hours or something – you wouldn't believe the stuff we had to go through to make that track. It was before synthesisers, so the string sections in that record are vocal tape loops, where you hold a note until you pass out, and then the tape is cut and a loop made. Four chords out of that, and then the tape recorders are run at different speeds – it took forty-eight hours and we didn't stop. We just started and something like four days later, we got the fog horns from the Golden Gate Bridge – that was real, the fog horn was real – all the other business was created in the studio, but you could never get something like that fog horn except underneath that bridge, and that was pretty exciting. Now, in my studio at home, I've got five synthesisers right next to the control board, and it's great – sound effects city!'

Rarely has the written word been proved so inadequate as in the description of 'Songs For Our Ancestors', and in fact of the entire *Sailor* LP. Despite its lack of remarkable guitar solos, Miller's intention was not to showcase his virtuosity on the instrument. 'I didn't regard myself as specifically a guitar player, I thought in terms of myself as a band leader, with all the things that entails – getting the people together, getting the material together, getting the singing done, working out the arrangements – so the guitar work was just one aspect of it. I didn't consider myself a particularly terrific soloist or a virtuoso by any means, and so I've always tried to pretty much hold back on my guitar playing, and not put too much on a record, so I certainly wasn't looking to present myself as a guitar player at that particular time. There's always been a big difference of course between on the road and in the studio. In the studio, I would sing five parts – I did most of the singing on all the records, just about everything. Boz was the only other singer really, although Peterman sang a little and Davis sang a little at the beginning, but on the more recent records I've done all the vocal work in the studio.' The band became a trio shortly after the release of *Sailor*, when both Peterman and Scaggs decided to leave.

'Boz and I had been together for a long period of time, and we were changing both as people and in our musical directions. His influences and mine were really different, and he wanted to do some different things, and he didn't want to do some of the things that I wanted to do. I was sorry to see him go on one hand, yet on the other, I was free to do the things I wanted without somebody being critical of what I was doing – I was always into a lot of vocal harmony, and Boz became real tired of that.'

Even so, it must have come as something of a surprise to both Steve's audience and to his record company when they came to see him in concert, and found the band unable to reproduce with any real fidelity much of the albums which had attracted them to Miller in the first place. 'Well, the record company people never came on the road anyway, so they didn't know, but we used to have really good shows – at that time, people were knocked out that there was a show in town they could go to. Because we were making this business up. I was thinking about that the other day – we said "Look, we're going to start playing live", and then we said, "Now we're going to start playing in coliseums" and "Now we're going to make coliseum shows like you've never seen them before – we've got a better idea for PA systems, we've got a better idea for lights" and we made up lasers and took them in there, and we made up dry-ice machines. All the stuff that everybody today says is just another group, just another show, we were making it up at that time – it had never been done before, so all you had to do was be there.

'I find technology fascinating, and that applies to every aspect of what I do. At the start, there weren't very many professional people involved, and because I had a lot of knowledge about a lot of those things, I saw a lot of mistakes being made, and I was able to save myself a lot of problems. You saw people build PA systems that were absurd, and took three days to set up, and the whole business that we now accept as being normal was being developed, and it seemed to me like we were sort of passing it back and forth between Britain and the United States – the British would see what was going on, would become very objective about what was happening, and would select the best of all these things and come over with these fabulous productions from your fifteen hundred years of theatre, and we would see that, and kind of say "Yes, but we've got all this technical stuff, and we can make this lighter, smaller, faster, cleaner, bigger, neater," whatever, and it's been trading off back and forth. It's been a real productive situation as it's all happened, and as I'm fascinated with PA technology, for instance, I'm always trying to figure out some way of building a stage twice the size of the Pink Floyd's that fits in a suitcase and is inflatable!

'It's similar with guitars – guitar technology has come a long way now, and the instruments are much better, the amplifiers are much better, although I still have the original amp that I had in high school, that little Bassman over there, which still sounds real good. I got that one when I was sixteen, but the basis of it has pretty much stayed the same – it's like the Stratocaster or something, which is about as clean a design as you can get, and it'll look good two hundred years from now, but the equipment and the sound quality and the outboard gear, the echo devices, the equalisation, we've learned a lot about that stuff, and now it's easy. I remember when we first used to make records, we'd go into the studio and get the best sound we could in those dead rooms – you'd start playing and your guitar would sound the size of a pea, and it was real tough, but now it's easy.'

Steve Miller's third LP, released in June 1969 in America, was titled *Brave New World*. The remaining trio of Miller, Lonnie Turner and Tim Davis were augmented for the making of the album by various friends, including ex-Ardell Ben Sidran and star session pianist Nicky Hopkins, with even producer Glyn Johns lending a hand on guitar and percussion, while one track 'My Dark Hour', boasts a very famous musician indeed playing under an alias.

'I was in London mixing that album, and Glyn was working with the Beatles, who were doing *Let It Be* at that time, and Glyn invited me over to one of their sessions. Then I was invited to another session, apparently because I behaved well and didn't say a word to anyone the first time. So I went to this second session, which was on a Sunday, and Ringo didn't show up – he was going to do some drums, but he didn't make it, so all the equipment was there, everybody else was there, and the engineers were ready, but there was no drummer. So we sat around for two or three hours just chatting about this and that, and finally George decided he was going to play a little bit, and he invited me to do a little jamming with him. Then George took off, and there was just Paul left, and he wanted to play some more, and he'd been playing drums. After George left, Paul and I really hit if off, and I told him about this tune I had which we started playing, and Glyn, being very clever, said "Well, why don't we just record this?" like an engineer would, and he turned on the machine. We worked on it for about seven hours, and Paul played bass and did some background vocals, and I did some too, and we got a pedal steel guitar out, did some different things, and recorded this little tune. As Paul was leaving, I said, "Hey, we've written this song together, you know – what do you want to do about the publishing and that sort of thing?", and he said, "Oh, just call me Paul Ramon, and don't worry about it", and I said "OK, whatever you like", and that's what I did. He was great.'

Yet another appearance of the 'persona' aspect of Steve Miller comes with 'Space Cowboy' – having side-stepped the previous enquiry about 'Gangster Of Love', Steve was much more forthcoming about his second 'alias'. 'You're right, I have side-stepped these things, and my thoughts about this topic are these. First of all, out of the hundred or so songs that I've recorded, about four or five have characters in them – Maurice, the Gangster Of Love, the Space Cowboy and whatever the others are. I've always felt that records should somewhere have a sense of humour in them – you can't be serious about every-

Rehearsing at the Rainbow in London, 1973

Johns, is 'Little Girl', and this, coincidentally, was recorded in a manner which would be repeated in the future. 'That was just a neat little tune we did, where I was able to spend some time on my guitar work, and that was where I began to develop my guitar sound. That song was done with an American engineer over in San Francisco at home, where I had time to relax and work on some things, and it helped me develop a much more comfortable way of working. I think I did all the vocals in the control room – we were really breaking the rules and doing whatever we wanted. After that, I wanted to work with other producers and try some other things. For the next album, which was *Number 5,* we went to Nashville and made it in eleven days, and I realised that there were different ways of working in the studio, and other engineers, and that there were other people in America – things were getting a lot better and it was becoming easier to work here, and whereas before we'd really needed Glyn, as I was growing up, I didn't need his help so much any more. Down in Nashville I think we cut our first tune in the first fifteen minutes we were there – just sat down, shook hands, the earphone system was already balanced, the echoes already on. They hadn't changed anything in twelve years, nobody had vacuumed in there, they just didn't touch anything, and it was just perfect, so all we had to do was just go in and play.'

While it paled in comparison with *Sailor, Number 5* did have its moments, in particular a fine track titled 'Tokin's'. 'Tim Davis wrote that song, and I guess it was one of his fantasies, just about his life. The song was recorded with Wayne (Moss) and Tim and some other Nashville musicians – we were there, and we wanted to record with these guys. We'd never let anybody record with us before, but we did it, and it came off great. They learned the song in seven minutes and sat down and recorded it, and when it was done, it sounded better than anything else on the record, and we said "Well, that's how pros do it!" It was real funny being in a situation like that, working with guys who were such great musicians, but whose records didn't sell because they weren't popular, and that was another real learning process that went on, between Wayne and his friends and us – they explained to us how they did what they did, and we explained how the hell we did what we did, and it turned out to be a real fruitful relationship.'

Just as well, because a somewhat lengthy hiatus occurred in Miller's career following the album's release in mid-1970, at which time Tim Davis, the only other remaining member of the original Miller band, left to embark on a solo career, and it was somewhat more than a year before Miller was able to pick up the reins of his career.

'Everything got really weird. I was going through some serious changes – I got married, then got divorced, and I'd been on the road for so long. I look back on this period of my life, and I was just on the road, twelve months a year, for years – seven days a week just working, working, working all the time. I got back to San Francisco and started recording, and I think most of that next album, *Rock Love*, was recorded in a little studio on the second floor of a house belonging to a friend of mine. I was tired, but the record company just leaned all over me for a new

thing all the time, and I've always been sort of a class clown kind of person – and these tracks were really unthought out, very quickly done without much thought given to them at all, and usually done out of boredom in the studio during overdubbing. If you get some echo on your voice, it can make you sound like somebody else – it's proven me right in that people remember and really like these characters, and they're something that sticks in people's memories a lot more. I also did what I would now call a 'feeder' article, now that I understand better how press coverage works, with a friend of mine a few years ago. This friend, Tim Cahill, writes for *Rolling Stone,* and he said they wanted to do a piece on me, but I said, "Look, I'm tired of all these boring things. Can't we do something interesting?" So he started talking about Maurice, and we got talking about the characters, and put together this article. It was the first national article that came out on me in '76, when I came back after a long rest and started doing things again, and newspapers all over the world took that one article, shaped it the way they wanted to, and talked about those characters, and I thought "Wow, does it really happen like that?" I'd heard people discuss those kind of things but it almost overwhelmed me when I found that everywhere I went, people were saying, "Oh, tell us about the Space Cowboy" – and all I can tell you about it was it was written in twenty minutes in 1967, while we were eating ribs or something. I don't remember much about it, because I didn't know I was going to live with it!'

One of the best tracks on *Your Saving Grace,* Miller's fourth album and the last to be produced by Glyn

Steve Miller Band, mid-1970s, with Steve on the right

record – they picked that record up at four-thirty in the morning after the first mix, and cut it immediately. I sort of succumbed to their pressure, but I learned a lot by doing that. Everybody was leaning on me, my band was changing and I had different musicians, and there was a lot of pressure, which I had to deal with as best I could, because, of course, at that time I didn't know I could just stop when the pressure got too much.'

One aspect of the pressure revolved around Miller's lack of solid commercial success up to this point – although his albums had sold respectably, without a major hit single, his sales pattern was static. 'Yeah, and there were some real reasons for that – number one was that there was no real central figure developing out of the band, as a personality to write about, or whatever. Number two was that our singles weren't that good, they weren't commercial in the same way as what was being played on the air. I purposely avoided a lot of personal publicity – I saw it happening to other people, and I didn't want it, because I really wanted to make my living on my music. I wanted to have hit singles and be successful and commercial, but I wanted to do it on my own terms, and I began to find out that most of the really successful people had extremely powerful managers, heavy connections, lots of money being spent telling the public why this person was so great, and I didn't

have any of that. I was just cruising along, but able to hold my own, because I was selling a large amount of albums at the time, and this was due to the fact that we were performing every night, somewhere in the United States, doing sold out concert dates. The *Number 5* album caught my record company flat – it sold three hundred thousand copies in six weeks, and they didn't have any records for the next six because there weren't any more sleeves, *Rock Love* was a bad album and just didn't work, but it had to be just a matter of time before I hit something that my record company could comprehend.'

The 1972 album, *Recall The Beginning: A Journey From Eden,* was unfortunately less impressive musically than its imposing title, and was for Steve Miller what he later referred to as 'the end of a cycle'. 'Yes, pretty much – that just sort or wrapped it up from *Children Of The Future* to that point. *Journey From Eden* was the end of that period, in which I learned a lot, and a lot of my dreams had changed. I had come to understand the pressures of living in the real world, and somehow putting that together with the fantasy world of music. When I finally finished that record, that was the last fight I was ever going to have with a producer. Ben Sidran produced that album, and I felt like he ruined it. A few years later, as he started his own career, he came to me and said, ''I don't know how I ever did the things that I did to you in the studio, but I'm really sorry", so I said, "We've all got to learn this kind of stuff, and I just figured at the time that if it was our friendship or the album, that the album was expendable". That's when I finally decided that from that point on, I was going to be responsible for album budgets and for everything – it was a frightening thing to walk in and say "I'm going to spend sixty thousand dollars, and I'll be responsible for it". I didn't really want that responsibility, but I finally got to the point where I had to. *Journey From Eden* was the point where that started – the end of producers, the end of games and fantasies, the end of rock'n'roll stars.'

It would be eighteen months before the next Steve Miller record, a period when many things affected and afflicted him, to a large extent the result of his playing no less than 220 concerts during 1972. 'I got sick, and caught hepatitis while I was touring, and I also had a hairline fracture in my neck. I was on a forty-city tour, and I almost killed myself, although I didn't know it – I was drinking like a fish because my neck was killing me, and this hairline fracture made me really stiff, and when I went to see a doctor, he diagnosed a bad case of 'flu, so I carried on with the tour. I was really ill for about eight months – I had no energy, I couldn't do anything and it was frightening. I finally decided to make it real simple, and take it easy, and *The Joker* was a big change.'

The Joker, released in the autumn of 1973, was indeed a big change commercially, the album selling prodigiously, and the title track topping the American charts when it was released as a single. 'That was the first big commercial success that I had, although I didn't really conceive it as such – the conception revolved around me stopping this 'genius' trip that I had kept putting myself through when I made records, and making the simplest album I could. It was a big humbling experience before I went into the studio – I said to myself, "I'll never be Eric Clapton on the guitar, I'll never be the writer that Paul McCartney is, I'll never be B. B. King, I'll just be Steve Miller, with a lot of limitations, but I'm just going to accept them and I'm through complaining, I'm through trying to convince my record company they should do anything. If they don't do what I think they should do, then that's their business – it's not my business to make them do anything, and I'm just going to take care of myself". So I went in the studio and made a very simple album, I spent nineteen days doing it – done, mixed, finished, and I had no idea that 'The Joker' was a hit single. I liked a tune called "Sugar Babe", which I felt was a neater tune, although I've come to realise that while it was a good tune, it wasn't mixed very well.'

Anyone listening to FM radio in America during late 1973 and early 1974 could not have failed to hear 'The Joker', a track which boasted instantly recognisable guitar sounds which were irresistible to American audiences, although curiously the track was not a commercial success in Britain, despite achieving far greater airplay than many genuine hits. So how was that guitar sound achieved?

'It was just a special sound that I wanted, and I knew exactly what it was. A slide guitar with a few different parts and pieces and a little experimentation in the studio to get that fat, big, clear sound. It

The Joker

also had to be a real simple track, and this was the first time that everybody had to do what I said – if the drummer didn't do what I wanted, he was not the drummer, and we'd bring in a session drummer like Jim Keltner, and if Jim Keltner wouldn't do it, then we'd bring in someone else. I got to call the shots the way I wanted and I wasn't arguing with people about anything and I cut a very simple (backing) track – I spent a little time looking for the guitar tone, but the engineer was really patient and helpful, and we just got it, and I played it.'

Millerophiles were excited on seeing the sleeve of *The Joker* on the basis that it was assumed to be the almost legendary 'Hallowe'en' album, one of at least four special 'project' albums, the others being an album of Christmas carols, a jazz LP with the celebrated Adderley Brothers – Nat and Cannonball – and a concept album detailing the fate of the American Indian. 'Well, none of those ideas have ever been finished, but I can understand why people thought it might be the Hallowe'en record because probably the pictures would make it seem that way. In fact, that picture was quite unplanned – I went to see the art director at the record company, and told him about this new cowboy hat I'd got, which I felt I'd really like to wear in a picture. He said, "Great, let's go over to Norman Seeff, who's a great photographer, and I want you to meet him". Normally, I just freeze when anybody has a camera – it's terrible. But Norman told me that things weren't right, and in the meantime, I had found this mask on the wall, which I put on because I didn't want to have my picture taken, I was real uncomfortable, and Norman said that we should get together again the next day. We came back the next day, and he'd gone out and found all these masks, which was perfect, it was so easy – I just put on the masks.

'I had to meet the guys at Capitol who were twenty-five years old and wanted to work, and tell them that I wanted to work too, and suggest that we work together, and ask them what they thought of the

139

Late '70s

music. And it blew them away – "What? Somebody's here who isn't demanding caviare and a limo?" I don't know exactly what it was, but we sat down, and they decided that 'The Joker' was the single – some kid just said, "That's the single right there. That's what we should go with", and everybody stood up in the room like they do in a Hollywood musical, and walked out of the door.

'Then it got crazy, because it was on every radio station three times an hour, twenty-four hours a day, for half a year or something. It just went on and on, because we'd started touring and just finished up a hundred and some cities when it all happened, and we tried to go back out and do another thirty-two concerts in forty-two days, or something like that, and after that, I was totally blown out. I decided I was going to take a year's holiday, just not doing anything, because I couldn't do anything.

'So the band went off and played with other people, and I went back to California and remodelled a house I'd found and put a little studio in it. I relaxed

and took it easy. After I had got the house together, I started writing (songs) again, and I began to feel real good, and then this thing came up where we went to London in the summer of 1975. It was put together really casually, a real lightweight thing, which was a good way to do something like that – I called these guys up, we rehearsed twice in my living room, got on a plane to London, played for 100,000 people at Knebworth, and then we were on vacation.

'Then I came back and finished off the next two albums, *Fly Like An Eagle* and *Book Of Dreams,* because I'd learned from *The Joker* that if I was going to go out and tour and do all that stuff again, I really needed to have a couple of albums in the can, because I wasn't going to be able to stop in the middle and start writing again. The Beatles gave everybody such a huge goal to try to equal, but everybody forgets that they didn't do many concerts – they only played sixty-four concerts or something after they became famous, so they didn't have that pressure of being on the road all the time. The road really, truly, wiped me out.'

The idea of making two separate albums at the same time is, of course, rather novel, as most artists find it difficult enough to complete one LP successfully. . .

'The majority of the work was done in one eight- or nine-month period, and when *Fly Like An Eagle* came out, I knew what the first tune on *Book Of Dreams* was, because I purposely held it off *Fly Like An Eagle* so that there would be something good to follow it. I knew I was making two records, and I felt really confident that *Fly Like An Eagle* was going to be a very successful album. I thought it would sell four and a half million copies – I just had that number in my head – and that's what I thought would happen, but I didn't know it was going to take a year, which made it quite a while before we could release the next record.'

One aspect of *Fly Like An Eagle* which some found disconcerting was its substantial use of synthesisers. 'You guys are doing this series about guitar players, but soon it'll be a series on synthesiser players. I think the synthesiser is the instrument of the future. I had a great interest in them at the time we're talking about (1976), and I kept finding that the people who played them were way too complex, and could never remember how they got their sounds or anything. So I went to a little local music store and asked them if they had an idiot synthesiser, one with a stop that says "flute" or "French horn" or whatever, and they said they had just what I needed, and showed me this very simple synthesiser that none of the players would ever be seen with – it really hurt my keyboard player to have to use it, because he didn't want the other guys to see him with it. I took it home and started fooling around with it, and got all these sounds – it was very easy to use, and there were no problems with it, and from that point, all of a sudden it was "Wow, we've got to have synthesisers on stage now, and we need polyphonic synthesisers", and we really got into it.'

The *Fly Like An Eagle* album produced three hit singles in the title track, a comparatively 'modern' sounding piece with synths to the fore, and two more traditional items in 'Take The Money And Run' and

Playing a left-handed Stratocaster

'Rock'n Me'. The former was of particular interest in that it used a device to be found on many classic rock'n'roll records of the 1950s, handclaps. '"Take The Money" is just a real simple tune, a good rock-'n'roll track with a simple little story. I just wanted to get something going so that I could sing it; a lot of the time, some of the better songs I write are done that way, because I want to hear the harmony parts. I hear everything like that, all my ideas, I can hear everything in harmony, so I just want to get the track going so that the background vocals can be put on. As for the handclaps, I just tried them out one day, and it seemed to work, so we left them. Then "Rock'n Me" was the one that got all the airplay and seemed to be the big hit, but "Fly Like An Eagle" itself sold a lot more copies. I came within a quarter of an inch of throwing "Rock'n Me" off the record, because I didn't think it was a very good tune. I spend a lot of time sequencing my records, or at least a lot more time than it would seem it would take. Days, months, thinking about what should follow what. It seemed to work where it was, so I left it on, and after it came out everybody said, "Well, there's your hit single", and the disc jockeys were saying that too, so we said, "DJs demand release of single" . . . and they were right.'

One slightly jarring note relating to 'Rock'n Me' was the track's opening passage, which to many sounded very similar to the beginning of Free's famous 'All Right Now' hit . . . 'I was talking to somebody about that, and mentioned it, and that turned out to be a real bad rap for me for a long time, like I was telling you about the characters. When I went through my press, there were two stories, the one about the characters and the other one about the Free riff on the front of "Rock'n Me". I do have a copy of Free's single, and I think their lick was a lot better, without a doubt, and I don't think what I did sounded very much like it at all. Their guy played much better guitar, I thought.'

Despite his absence from the public eye for the best part of three years, *Fly Like An Eagle* sold in huge quantities for Steve Miller, while all three singles taken from the LP made the top twenty in America. The British public even relaxed their apparent suspicion of Miller sufficiently to allow 'Rock'n Me' into the top twenty, and in 1977, *Book Of Dreams* was released, containing the balance of the tracks recorded at the same time as the contents of *Fly Like An Eagle*, but with some additional material also included. On what basis, we wondered, did Miller decide which tracks should be on *Eagle*, and which should be held over?

'I listened to the tracks over and over, while I was eating breakfast or riding around in my car, or reading a book, which is the way anybody listens to music. I wanted my records to flow like jazz records flow, and I didn't want to be interrupted by screaming lead guitar or something like that, and I didn't want something that was going to beat me up. I wanted something I could live with. So I looked for certain key ingredients an album should contain – it should have some singles on it, because singles sell albums and singles are played on the radio, so it's a requirement of making a good album. And it should have some long pieces included, so that you're not continually interrupted with twelve little stories all three minutes long – there should be a place where you can stretch out and relax, so I had to space it out, and find a way for the music to relax and evolve. Then I started getting into the sequencing and the segues, and once I knew what the tunes were going to be, it became a more interesting problem, until finally I was able to just work it out to where the timing was right, and the beat would happen where it was supposed to, and it pleased me – if it satisfied me, then I figured that was all I had to do at that point.

'In fact, the first album that I sequenced myself was *Sailor*, and it's really strange – we were there at that point, and then it was like I went off and did all those other things and finally got back to being there again, because for all practical purposes, the next album after *Sailor* was *Fly Like An Eagle*, as far as getting on the right track and staying there goes.'

Three tracks from *Book Of Dreams* were released in single form in America, 'Jungle Love', 'Swing-town' and 'Jet Airliner', all of which made the top thirty in the United States, but made no impression when released in Britain. '"Jungle Love" was a tune written by Lonnie Turner (Miller's original bass player, who had left in 1969, and returned during the tour which was undertaken to promote *The Joker*) and Greg Douglas (Steve's co-guitarist). Lonnie came into the studio and said he'd written this little tune which he and Greg had recorded in a garage, and gave me a tape of it. That was the first time I'd ever heard Greg Douglas play guitar, and I asked Lonnie who he was and whether he was in town. They came to the studio the next day and we recorded the song in forty-five minutes. I sang it, and that was it – all on the record, and then Greg joined the band for a couple of years. He's a really good guitar player.

'"Jet Airliner" is a tune written by Paul Pena, who's a blind guitarist and writer who I met through Ben Sidran. Paul had been involved with Albert Grossman, but things hadn't worked out very well, and it had left Paul feeling pretty bitter about the music business. I particularly liked "Jet Airliner", so I worked on it and reshaped it into what it became, and that turned out to be real good for Paul, because it got him off the street and into a better existence, and it was good for me because at that time, I was really on a streak of radio hits. We had six top singles one right after another, which is the way you should do it if you're going to do it, and if I saw a tune that would fit, then I would use it.'

'Jet Airliner' was released in America towards the end of 1977, after which came another lengthy hiatus for a full four years, only broken by the release of a *Greatest Hits 1974-78* album, which was extremely successful, containing as it did seven hit singles. It wasn't until the end of 1981 that an original Steve Miller LP was released, although this is not to say that he was idle over that long period. 'I finished three years of touring in the United States, and decided that I needed to take some time off for myself, so I bought a farm. I also decided to build a studio on my farm. Having done that, I started working on new material and recording it in the studio. The goal was to finish three albums, and then go on a really extensive world tour. I've obviously finished the first of the albums, *Circle Of Love,* and the other two should be finished by April 1982.

'I've actually been recording over the past two years, although that hasn't been every day by any means. At this point, I've finished it apart from putting it all together, but the ideas have all changed, because in October 1980, I discovered the video disc, and realised that it was a new challenge for me, and that I'd have to learn about some new ideas and new technology – I felt like I'd be making a mistake if I didn't incorporate video disc. Then I started looking at what everybody else was doing with video discs, and I realised that the way to really do it would be to write the music for the disc, and make the music for the disc, make a marriage between the two, so – "Change!" So it was back into the studio, but it's been a very interesting project – for all practical purposes, it was finished, because I'd written the lyrics, recorded the backings and sung on most of it, and I was at the part where I was doing solos and chang- ing the odd lyric here and there to clean it up, when I decided to back off and take another look at it. I've so far changed the target date for delivery of *Circle Of Love* about eight times.'

At the time of writing, *Circle Of Love* is the only Steve Miller album released during the 1980s, and as the better part of a year elapsed between the two interviews which have been combined to form this chapter, it becomes obvious that even after *Circle Of Love* was deemed complete in early 1981, things had changed by the time it was released at the end of the year. The track which is most obviously intriguing is 'Macho City', which takes up the whole of side two of the album. In many ways, it's interesting to first of all read Miller's description of it before anyone else had heard it, and then to hear his comments after the album's release. First, the description we were given some months before 'Macho City' was unveiled.

'There's a whole military section on the album, because I have a sort of nauseous military feeling, which I find sneaking into everything I do, so I've ended up writing a bunch of macho-military kind of sound effects tunes. There's one called "Choppers And Jets", there's "Macho City", "Macho Children", a whole macho section. In fact, I wrote a very long section, a thirty- to forty-minute group of tunes, and then I decided I didn't really want to come out with things like "Macho Slacks", "Macho Shoes" and all the rest, so I've backed off that. I figure there's enough of that kind of stuff in the world anyway, and one of the problems I've had in dealing with the record is that I want it to be a positive record.'

That was the preview. Nearly a year later, things had substantially altered. . . '"Macho City", which must be the longest single piece I've ever recorded, is the length it is because I became very annoyed with the concept of twelve little three-minute tunes, one after another, year after year, decade after decade – this is my third decade of recording – so I found that I started fiddling around with the music in that track on tape. I really liked the groove, but I didn't listen to it for about a year, and then I went back and started working on the section again. One day, I just copied it three or four times, edited it together and let it run for thirty-five minutes or some- thing – we had a huge roll of tape. The more I lis- tened to it at that length, the more I liked it, and then I started working on it as a long piece of music, and it became a mood piece that I really liked, and I found that, of all the music I was doing, it was the most mature, and the most relaxing to listen to. I found it far and away the most interesting piece, and I usually listen to my stuff for six months before I release it, to make sure that it'll hold up. It's music to live with, sort of like a good old pair of slippers or something.'

Having heard the lyrics to the song, the military aspects referred to by Steve in his preview are less noticeable than the political views expressed, which included a mention of the situation in El Salvador. Was that something to which he particularly took exception?

'I take exception to murder a lot; political murder annoys me, and I take exception to resorting to that kind of violence and force in this day and age to solve communication problems, and that's what "Macho City"'s all about, the callousness of the world when it comes to pure out-and-out murder, and the willingness to just report it on television like it's OK. It's not OK, and while I didn't want to belabour the point, I also didn't want to make this just a rock'n'roll album and act as if this wasn't going

On tour in Britain, 1982. Left to right: John Massaro, Kenny Lee Lewis, Gary Mallaber (drums), Steve Miller, Gerald Johnson, Norton Buffalo (not pictured: Byron Allred (keyboards)

on. I found it was something I couldn't ignore, yet I felt that I was inside an industry that's doing anything it can to ignore things – they just act like everything's hunky dory (because) there's no future.

'In America, we went through a period of the Vietnam war that was really significant, and unless you lived in America, and took part in the anti-war period, you can't really understand how much that war tore up our society and our government, and left huge wounds in it. The message is that you can't screw around with people like that and not get screwed around yourself. Generations of people were really destroyed by that war, and people got really tired when it was finally over, and then we got rid of Nixon, and then we had Carter and went through all the nonsense in Iran. It's like we've gone through a period of wanting to escape from all that – it gets to a point where you just can't absorb any more of it, and I think that's what's happened. That's the very point of "Macho City", the political point, that it's normal, isn't it? Of course, it's not normal, but it is normal, although it shouldn't be normal – economically, things are changing around the world too, so I think we'll probably be seeing a new period of conflict.'

Fortunately, 'Macho City' in musical terms has far more to it than a mere political diatribe, including some excellent examples of the Miller sound effects fixation. 'Yeah, I love to take electronics, sound effects and rhythm & blues and mix them together into this great electronic futurist rock'n'roll. The idea of the thunder at the end – which was an actual recording of thunder that I made – was that I wanted to bring in a little rain to wash things off, a symbolic cleansing of the situation. But even when I did that, I had to put a little helicopter in to indicate that the sharks are always hovering. . .'

The question of a video disc version of the album was very much to the fore when we met Steve again. 'We've been doing a lot of video work, and I'm not very satisfied with it, although I'm soon meeting a director who I think is brilliant. I've got an automated video clip that's nearly finished on "Heart Like A Wheel", and then we're going to go into production on the video disc for "Macho City". I've found working on video discs very time-consuming and it's been an unproductive period – I'm trying to develop a personal style, because I don't like most of what I see, and I've found it much more difficult to achieve perfection in video than in music, and more expensive, although I think it's going to become more and more important, and it's something I really want to do well in.'

Then there's the question of Steve Miller's choice of instrument. 'As far as acoustic guitars go, I've always used Guild guitars, which I love. I've got one of the prototypes, which is quite an interesting story – there was a man who was about ninety-years-old who designed the last series of big acoustic guitars made by Guild, and he built this prototype of what is now their fanciest 12-string, this huge wonderful instrument, but very simple and very plain, and it was given to me just through a coincidence. It was my favourite instrument, and I'd written half the tunes I've written on this guitar, and the thing got stolen a couple of years ago, and it just turned up again the other day, and it's coming in here tonight, so I'm really excited about that, because I haven't seen it for two years. As far as electric guitars go, I went through a lot of different ones. I played Gibsons for a long time, then I played (Fender) Stratocasters, and I'm now settled on a Japanese guitar called Ibanez. The Japanese have copied all the American guitars, and they now make better guitars than American ones. All their technology has been developed in this country by guys who play in bands, and I couldn't believe it when I met the people involved in it. They have built-in equalisation and electronically, they're excellent, so I've been using Ibanez guitars for something like five years, and I've been very happy with them. I also use a Stratocaster sometimes, and I still have a Les Paul, and I've got a large collection of guitars, because I've saved nearly every guitar I've ever had, rarely sold any of them. I think I've got twenty-six guitars, which is too many, so what I finally had to do was say, "These go to the Wax Museum, and these are the ones that I play". As for working guitars, I guess I must use about eight or nine electrics, a couple of basses, and some acoustics.'

In 1982, Steve Miller has almost effortlessly regained the ground he must have lost during his long layoff – at the time of writing, 'Heart Like A Wheel' had been another substantial hit single in America, while the *Circle Of Love* LP had been in the LP chart for several months, and was showing little sign of leaving. Unlike all too many rock stars of today, Miller is a thinker as well as a doer, and having learnt a number of valuable lessons during his comparatively lengthy career near the top of his profession, seems unlikely to throw away the vast experience he has accumulated on any kind of whim. While the vast majority of his early contemporaries have now been forgotten, Steve Miller, if anything, is growing in popularity – and deservedly so.

Steve Miller Discography

1968	Revolution (film soundtrack)	1976	Fly Like An Eagle
1968	Children Of The Future	1977	Book Of Dreams
1968	Sailor	1981	Circle Of Love
1969	Brave New World	1982	Abracadabra
1969	Your Saving Grace		
1970	Number 5		Compilations
1971	Rock Love	1972	Anthology
1972	Recall The Beginning – A Journey From Eden	1975	Best of Steve Miller 1968-1973
1973	The Joker	1978	Greatest Hits 1974-78

CARLOS SANTANA

Carlos Santana has continuously led the band which bears his name for nearly fifteen years, and maintained a substantial worldwide popularity, something which requires an exceptional talent, not simply in musical terms, but also with regard to finance, human relationships and the many other problems which confront the figurehead of a rock group. Carlos Santana appears to be almost the only guitar virtuoso who has enjoyed uninterrupted fame and success, and more to the point, is also a superb musician with particular reference to his chosen instrument.

Carlos Santana was born on 20 July 1947 in Mexico, to a musical family. 'My father was a street musician, and also played in local bars and terraces, as far as I can remember. It's funny, but even though it was 1947, and way down in Mexico, where they play mainly full tempo Mexican music, I can remember hearing Django Reinhardt and things like that. When I hear it now, for some reason I put it together with where I grew up – I only spent time there from '47 to '51 or '2, and the rest of the time I spent in Tijuana and San Francisco. The first musical things I did were to do with classical training – Minuet in C and things like that, learning how to read (music) and how to play the violin.'

Santana's early musical influences were generally in the blues/R&B field: 'When I got to Tijuana, Sugar Ray Robinson was probably at his peak, and music was just beginning to come out. I started to listen to the blues – Jimmy Reed was the first thing I listened to, then B. B. King, Bobby "Blue" Bland, early Ray Charles, stuff like that, but it was mainly B. B. King who knocked me right out. As soon as I heard a guitar player like that, I thought "Man, that's the stuff – this is the sort of music I want to do when I grow up". I got my first guitar in '57, '58 – my father came to work here in San Francisco while we were still living in Tijuana, and he brought me one of those big fat Gibson guitars.'

During the early 1960s, Carlos moved to San Francisco, which has remained his home base ever since. 'I was extremely frustrated when I came here because the main music that was happening was the Beach Boys, surfing music, and I hated it. To this day, I don't really like it, because it represents everything superficial about life that I don't relate to. I always related to black musicians, or rather black music but not necessarily by black musicians – for example, I like Bobby Darin – but I really didn't like that straight ahead south of San Francisco beach club kind of music.'

These sentiments were apparently expressed from the vantage point of semi-professionalism. 'I feel I started to play professionally even before I got here to San Francisco, because I was playing in Tijuana and earning money from being a guitar player in strip clubs. Black people would come from San José and Los Angeles to Tijuana, primarily for drugs and sex, but they'd wind up spending all their money really fast over the weekend, so they had to work in the club with us. They enjoyed our band, so they'd sing the blues and the strip joint would pay them money for gasoline to get back to the States. So we played for an hour, then the strippers would strip for an hour, then we'd play for an hour and so on, and that went on until six o'clock in the morning.'

Carlos' early work in San Francisco was less romantic – during the mid-1960s, he found gainful employment washing dishes. 'That was mainly because there were a lot of us in the family, and my father was the sole breadwinner, so I found a job as a dishwasher. I was doing that, going to school, and sneaking in to see concerts at the Fillmore West at the same time. I did that for four years, but it taught me something – dishwashing or whatever, it taught me a certain attitude about myself. I feel that whatever job I take on, I like to think that I can do two people's work – in other words, they could have fired two guys, and I could have taken their job, because I'm determined that whatever I do, whether it's cleaning garbage in the street or playing the guitar, I like to feel that I can take two people's work just because I'm so determined about what I decide to do.'

Becoming a full-time musician in San Francisco, however, was rather less to do with determination . . . 'I was sneaking into the Fillmore with a friend I went to stay with, and Bill (Graham, now manager of the Santana group) saw me jamming, strangely enough. They used to have Sunday matinées at the Fillmore West, and Paul Butterfield didn't show up for one of those, although his band did, and so they had a jam session. I think that was my biggest break – there was Jerry Garcia, people from the Jefferson Airplane, Michael Bloomfield and Elvin Bishop, and they were just jamming, and a friend of mine said "Hey, I've got a friend from Tijuana who plays the blues. Can he come up and jam?", and Michael (Bloomfield) was really kind, and said "Sure, come on up". He handed me his guitar, because he wasn't playing it, he was playing keyboards. They gave me a few bars to show what I could do, and this guy Sammy, who was in the audience, traced me. He said he'd been looking for me for two months, and he finally found me at this dishwashing, this restaurant place. He just walked in and said he'd been looking for me, and he wanted to start a band. I said OK, and he took me down to Palo Alto, and that's how I met Greg Rolie, and we started a band. We played mainly at that time things by the Bluesbreakers (John Mayall) and Paul Butterfield, and the Rascals and the Doors, but mainly the blues that was the happening thing – there was a tremendous blues revival, everything was the blues, and that's why the band was called the Santana Blues Band. By that time, my favourite players had changed a bit – it was still B.B. (King), although Jimi (Hendrix) hadn't jumped out yet, and Eric Clapton, Michael Bloomfield and the original Paul Butterfield Band, who were jumping like crazy, and the Spencer Davis Group, who were extremely significant.'

It was as a replacement for one of these idols, Mike Bloomfield, that Carlos Santana made his first released recording, on a double LP titled *The Live*

At San Francisco's Winterland Ballroom, 1970

Adventures Of Mike Bloomfield and Al Kooper in 1968. Prior to this, Bloomfield, Kooper and Stephen Stills had collaborated on a very successful LP with the title *Super Session*, the concept being to record off-the-cuff jam sessions in a recording studio. The idea was such a success that Kooper and Bloomfield decided to repeat the experiment, but this time before an audience in San Francisco. The first two nights of the scheduled three went according to plan, after which Al Kooper's sleeve note to the record provides the best explanation: 'After two nights of playing two sets a night, Michael's insomnia caught up with him, and just prior to going on stage the last night, I received a call that he was in the local hospital being sedated to sleep. I guess this is where the beauty of San Francisco lies, for in an amazingly short time Elvin Bishop, Carlos Santana, Steve Miller and Dave Brown had volunteered their services and had arrived at the Fillmore.'

Carlos' explanation is a little different: 'At that time, we were playing about three times a week at the Fillmore, or that's what it seemed like. Every time somebody would cancel, Bill Graham would call us, because he knew that we'd keep the audience totally interested. When he found out that Michael Bloomfield and Al Kooper were being recorded, he wanted me to play, but when I look back, it's like I would rather have not done it at all, because I really didn't get the chance to get into anything. But I'm still grateful for it.'

Carlos appears on a track on the album titled 'Sonny Boy Williamson', which according to the record was apparently written by Jack Bruce and Paul Jones, although it is difficult to ascertain whether such a credit is accurate. While he was nothing more than a guest on the one track of the album, it provided a certain amount of acclaim for Carlos, and introduced him to a wider audience than purely the local San Francisco crowd, although it was not the key factor which finally provided the Santana band with a recording contract, despite the fact that it was released on the Columbia (CBS) label to which Santana eventually signed. 'CBS came to see us because they had scouts out, and they heard that the band was outselling people who were already established recording artists, although we hadn't made a record. They came to see us in Santa Barbara one time when we were opening the show for the Grateful Dead, and this guy said that the thing he liked about the Santana band was that we could start with any song, or change the set around with any song, and it would still be happening. It came down to a big debate between Atlantic and CBS, and I never really liked Atlantic, even though they had all the black artists and I wanted to be with the black artists. I don't know – I didn't like Atlantic as much as CBS.'

Reasonable enough, except that the second record release by Santana appeared on an Atlantic subsidiary label, Cotillion Records, although it must be said that the label was incidental, as the record involved was the soundtrack to the film of *Woodstock*, a festival at which Santana played with immense success.

'We were very young, and it was a very wonderful time, before the concept of real hippies had been destroyed – a real hippy wasn't a harmful, dirty person, and it was a very constructive Bohemian type of thing between musicians and hipsters. You see, I would define a hippy as somebody who would go from Joan Baez to the Grateful Dead to Miles Davis to Cream to the Beatles and back – people who were creative as artists and all kinds of crafts and took pride in art, not in getting loaded and having free sex and all that dumb stuff. That's what Woodstock reminds me of – all that movement of people. It's still happening somewhere, you know. . . . When I went to see the film, it was scary – the dynamism that emanated from the band, and from the people themselves. We were very grateful for that opportunity, and Bill Graham, our co-manager then, was the one who really busted his chops to put us there.'

After a remarkable performance at Woodstock which was captured on film and on the first triple LP of the festival (with Santana contributing an eight-minute-plus version of 'Soul Sacrifice'), the stage was set for the release of the first Santana album, which was released in the wake of the Woodstock experience, and became a huge success. As well as a studio version of 'Soul Sacrifice', the LP contained a track which became something of a Santana trademark, 'Evil Ways', which was originally made famous by one Willie Bobo, a Latin-American musician whose work had strongly influenced Carlos.

'He was one of the first guys who tried to merge Latin music and blues together on record. He did it before us, because we were doing it on the street, and he was already doing it on records, but he was playing in a way that I call non-committed. I'll tell you what my definition of commitment is – Led Zeppelin is commitment to me. It's like shooting from the hip – a type of blues, a type of rock, whatever they do is shooting from the hip, and what he (Bobo) was doing was not really shooting from the hip, and it wasn't as powerful. So when we started to play his music, we would play the same songs, but there was a lot more striking intensity to them. I guess it's mainly because of the world that he grew up in and the world we grew up in – when we grew up, we went to see Procol Harum, Jimi Hendrix and Cream on the same bill, so we knew that you had to project. Even if it's a ballad and it's soft, you have to project – you can't be so introverted that you're the only one that's having a ball and the rest of the people are yelling at you. We learnt a lot about projecting at the Fillmore, and his music just needed more projection as far as I'm concerned.'

The following year, 1970, saw the release of the even more successful *Abraxas* album, which remained in the album charts for several years. '*Abraxas* was the peak of that band on that level, I would say. When I hear the word *Abraxas*, it brings to mind Miles Davis – he was hanging around a lot and calling us up, and he liked the direction of the band. And Jimi did too – a lot of people were becoming aware that this bunch of guys had something to say that musically was made in Chicago . . . and the Rolling Stones got congas and cowbells and all kinds of things. So that album is very significant, mainly because of the colours and the instruments that it brought to rock'n'roll. It injected a whole lot of stuff – Bo Diddley led to that beat, which comes from Latin music to the blues, and I feel we did it again to rock-'n'roll, to a certain extent. Not that we were the first, but we were just there in a way that nobody was doing it – Motown already had congas, but they didn't have them upfront, or timbales, and they didn't have a guitar upfront. That's what *Abraxas* reminds me of – a group of people who became significant, if you will.'

While it includes several classic tracks, the most interesting inclusion on the album is 'Black Magic Woman', written by British blues guitarist Peter Green, at the time the leader of Fleetwood Mac. Not the most obvious choice of material for a Mexican guitar player living in San Francisco. . . . 'By that time, we were jamming a lot with Peter – I used to go to see the original Fleetwood Mac, and they used to kill me, just knock me out. To me, they were the best blues band, because John Mayall seemed to disappear, Paul Butterfield's band broke up and he went into another kind of music, but Fleetwood Mac . . . it's always been extremely inviting to hear blues really executed by English people, because they take the best of the black and the best of the white, like Dionne Warwick or Johnny Mathis, so all of a sudden, blues becomes like water, and can take on any colour.'

By 1971, despite their success, the Santana band were still struggling for direction, two obvious pointers to this being that no less than twelve musicians played on the album (the first LP had featured a sextet), and that the record bore the scintillatingly imaginative title of *Santana – The Third Album*.

'We couldn't think of anything else to call it at the time. We just became a product of our environment, and the environment was too crazy – people were hanging around . . . Jimi and Miles and Eric (Clapton) and the Stones, but also just vultures and crazy people. I don't know why, but for some reason, the people who were hanging around with us weren't artists any more, they were just bozos and people who took too many drugs, and so at that time we became part of that, where music takes a back seat to all the other crazy stuff. But there is good music in the third album – I found that out in hotels where we stayed. If you went to Greg Rolie's room, you'd listen to the Stones and the Beatles, and if you went to Michael Shrieve, you'd listen to (John) Coltrane and Miles (Davis). If you went to (Mike) Carabello, you'd be listening to Sly Stone, and if you went to Neal Schon, you'd be listening to Jimi Hendrix. So it was very educational – I started to listen and began to realise that, as a musician, I wanted to do more than just crank up "Evil Ways" and "Black Magic Woman", and I started to have a yearning personally to understand what John Coltrane and Miles Davis were all about, and Joe Zawinul and all those people in Weather Report. So I wanted to see if we could fuse rock'n'roll and jazz, which is what I tried to do around that era, but I think it became frustrating to some of the musicians in the band because they wanted to retain the soul direction of Santana, but I don't think I wanted to as much as they did. The album took about a year to complete, and Eddie Kramer (a producer who worked with Jimi Hendrix) was involved with it, but we didn't like the direction he was taking us in. We recorded some stuff at Hammersmith (presumably live), we recorded all kinds of stuff, but we were travelling so much, and there were so many drugs, and secondary things took the primary role, that it took us a while to get our bearings together as far as where we were going.

'After that, unfortunately, the people in the band had very little empathy with each other. There was a lot of unnecessary resentment among the band, and the management fell apart and so did we.' Not long after the band collapsed, manager Bill Graham, a major influence on the Santana band, ceased to be their manager, although the choice, according to Carlos, was not Graham's. 'No, it was the contrary. We dismissed him, as I believe, because we took on accountants, although Bill advised us over and over that these accountants couldn't help. We didn't listen to him, and they did turn out to be no good. When we dismissed Bill, we told him that we wanted to do it on our own, and I believe he was hurt. We just wanted to prove that we could do it on our own, and we couldn't – we didn't have the knowledge or capacity.'

The next album featuring Carlos Santana was a collaboration with black drummer Buddy Miles, the two principals being backed mainly by musicians from the Santana group. Titled *Live*, the LP was recorded at Diamond Head Crater in Hawaii. In view of Miles' size and Carlos' later spiritual beliefs, the record was unkindly referred to as 'King Kong meets God', and in truth, it is not the best Santana album by any means.

'By that time, we weren't playing as much. It had almost been a year since I'd played in a band with those guys, and I just wanted to play with any Tom, Dick and Harry by that time – I was really getting ants in my pants. So they told me they were going to have this festival, and we practised for about a week

San Francisco superstars –
Jerry Garcia (left) and Carlos Santana

putting some songs together with Buddy Miles, just as a creative thing, so they told me they were going to tape it as well, and fine, you know . . . Buddy Miles at that time was still very much in pain, I think, because Jimi (Hendrix, with whom Miles had played) had passed on, so we found it a way to console ourselves in a soulful, creative way.'

In extreme contrast, the next Santana band album, *Caravanserai*, is widely regarded as the best ever by them, and was released during 1972. It seemed to mark a change of direction for the band which many thought was overdue. . . . 'Right – see, by that time, I have to say that I'd changed the records that were next to my record player. They became Weather Report, Mahavishnu (John McLaughlin), Miles Davis and John Coltrane. It became inevitable that that sort of music was what we gave birth to. I felt extremely stale on the direction Santana was taking, mainly because drugs were stale, and so was conversation – all people talked about was their conquests with girls and things like that, and eventually that becomes very uninspiring. So Mahavishnu and Weather Report and these kind of things were like valleys, extremely wonderful valleys, virgin land, if you will, that I wanted to get into.

'So for *Caravanserai*, when we first put the band together we went to England, and Mick Jagger and Stevie Winwood were there, and we didn't sing one single song like ''Oye Como Va'' or ''Black Magic Woman'' – none of those things. We just went straight ahead as if we were Sun Ra or Miles, or somebody like that, and people ate it up! And the

write-up in *Melody Maker* talked about ''the Gods from Olympus'' and all these things, which was very encouraging, and confirmed to me that it wasn't a bad thing to leave Greg Rolie and Michael Carabello – the bread and butter of the music, so to speak. And it worked. Miles was calling up, and Mahavishnu, and a lot of people wanted to become a part of that flow, and that's how we got to make an album with Mahavishnu. We started touring with Weather Report, and so I began to feel more confident about myself as a musician – I'm telling you, if you put Ted Nugent with John McLaughlin or Van Halen with Alan Holdsworth, there's paranoia and insecurity there, because there's two levels of playing. So playing with these bands gave me confidence as a musician that I could play with Chick Corea or Herbie Hancock, and now I can play with Paul McCartney or anybody, just about, and I don't need to have second thoughts about the ammunition that I have. I always say that Flipper and the Singing Chipmunks make platinum albums, so what? That's not necessarily success or progress, but when you combine musically music with rock'n'roll, or music with things like the creativity of the Beatles or Stravinsky, then you're talking my language, and that's what I like to do, and that's what *Caravanserai* was – the first approach to combining quality and quantity, if you will . . .'

During the same period (1972), something occurred which changed Carlos Santana's life – he met his guru, Sri Chinmoy, whose teachings were to influence both the music and the man substantially.

Serious business . . .

'Again, I have to say that it was John Coltrane. What he did was like a primary harbinger for most people like myself coming to terms with seeking our inner pilot, seeking a spiritual teacher, someone who has light and access towards the absolute, and who dwells in the heart with the supreme all the time. Once you go to drugs, once you go through physical pleasures and all these things, you realise that they stimulate the mind, but they do nothing to bring the soul forward. The most touching songs by any artist from Stravinsky to the Beatles are those that have nothing to do with their mind – it's when the soul comes forward, those are the most significant. So, through John Coltrane, I started to listen to Mahavishnu, and Mahavishnu introduced me to Sri Chinmoy, who I went to see at the United Nations. He changed my whole life and my concepts of God and Jesus – it's just like man's concept of the ocean, which is the Pacific Ocean, the Mediterranean Ocean (sic), the Indian Ocean, the Gulf Of Mexico, the Atlantic . . . There's only one ocean, that's what Sri Chinmoy told me – if you put your toe in the ocean, you've tapped all the oceans. So if you receive from that ocean, you become part of it – you please Krishna, Buddha, Christ – but most important, your music becomes more than music. Like there's music that bears can play and monkeys can play with accordions, and it's called entertainment, but there's also music to inspire the soul, to uplift the consciousness of humanity, and that's challenging. It's a whole other kind of stuff, and a lot of people back away from it because they know it's something insurmountable. First, you become an instrument for people to scorn and laugh at when you first embark on Jesus – you become "Oh, this guy's flipped out, he's going to wind up in some crazy ward", because he embraced God, but all it is, is that we're hungry for a whole other kind of nourishment. That's all it is – this experience of playing with name fame, power, occult powers, they're toys. That's exactly what they are. But embracing a spiritual path is embracing the mother, and the mother and father supply the toys. That's what that's about.'

Whether or not his new-found spirituality had anything to do with it, the next Santana album, *Welcome*, featured rather less of Carlos Santana, guitar player, than perhaps his devotees would have liked or expected, a rather odd occurrence considering the confidence Carlos had apparently gained first from impressing those he considered his musical heroes, and secondly from his new spiritual path.

'Right. At that time, I became Mr Humility, Mr Humble, and anybody who came in, I'd let them take solos, while I was just mainly digesting and absorbing from people. On stage, I was taking a lot more solos, but on records, I was mainly listening, for some reason. Again, I'm extremely grateful to Mahavishnu and Sri Chinmoy, because they made me aware of the importance of listening as well as talking, talking through your instrument, that is – it's really important to absorb also, and Miles Davis and Wayne Shorter are supreme proof of that. You learn how to say the right thing the right way at the right time, which is extremely important – Mr Subtlety, and that's what I was learning, I think, through these albums, by silence. That's how you learn, and of course, I'm very fortunate, because I get to learn and get paid as well.'

While *Caravanserai* is frequently cited as the best Santana album, claims are made that the best line-up of the band was the one which recorded *Welcome*, and perhaps more importantly, the remarkable *Lotus*, a triple live LP recorded in Japan, and wrapped in one of the most well-designed, opulent and intricate sleeves ever seen. This particular album was released in the Far East soon after it was recorded in 1972, but in Britain, it was not available other than as a very expensive import until 1975. Back to the line-up . . .

'I always think that that band was the best one of that era, but the band I'm playing with now wouldn't take back seat to that band, because the current band can go from walking to rock'n'roll to straight ahead heavy metal, or whatever you want to call it. That previous band was the best of one thing, which was mainly fusion music (jazz/rock) but I'm not sure how well we would have played Led Zeppelin type music, or blues, because they weren't that type of musician. So it was good for that era, but I don't think it was the best or the most versatile. I think the band I have right now is the most versatile, if I dare to say it, because we can play songs from *Caravanserai* and *Welcome* and from *Borboletta* (see below), where that other band couldn't play all those songs, not playing and making reality.'

Reverting to *Lotus*, was Carlos aware in advance of the remarkable packaging his album would receive? 'Well, I was aware of the artist, and aware that he had a tremendous sense of oneness and empathy with our music and with me personally. I consider him to be my brother through many incarnations – we are extremely in tune. I was with Bob Dylan at the Plaza Hotel in New York when they brought the packaging, and this Japanese representative of CBS threw it on the table, opened it up, and everybody's mouth just dropped – people in the band, Bob Dylan, just like "What's this?" There was so much depth and height, and the colour separation was just unreal. He says "There it is" and he bows, and he says "If you don't like it, we'll go back and try again". I thought he was joking, I couldn't believe it, and everybody started laughing. We couldn't believe how tremendous it was, and this is the thing about Japanese and Germans – as Americans, we have a lot to learn as far as integrity and quality goes, and that's all I'm going to say on that subject.'

Carlos Santana's next project in many ways mirrored the album he made with Buddy Miles, although on this occasion, it was musically of far more interest, with Carlos sharing the starring role with British born guitarist John McLaughlin, or 'Mahavishnu', as Carlos refers to him. This devotional name was given to McLaughlin by Sri Chinmoy, the 'guru' to whom he introduced Santana, who himself then became known as 'Devadip' Carlos Santana.

'The idea behind making *Love Devotion Surrender* with Mahavishnu was that I mainly wanted to get closer to Sri Chinmoy, and also, at the same time, make the masses aware of the Mahavishnu Orchestra.'

The style for which McLaughlin has become noted

is based on unbelievably fast, but very accurate guitar playing, a good example on *Love Devotion Surrender* being a song written by John Coltrane, 'A Love Supreme', which seemed a most ambitious piece of music to tackle. 'I think the only thing we added to that tune was that it became more accessible to the kids – if you listen to the original, it's like music for musicians, and we tried to make it more accessible and inspirational for the layman, so that you don't have to study music at university to understand it. So we added more simplicity – you always add something to anything, as long as it's coming from your heart, and as long as you're sincere.'

Carlos also explained the meaning of his devotional name. 'Devadip means to me what Muhammad Ali means to Cassius Clay – Devadip means "the eye, the lamp and the light of God", as the qualities that I embody within myself, so needless to say, I'm extremely grateful to Sri Chinmoy. He says he didn't necessarily give me the name – he just brought it forward because it was there to begin with, and he can see through it. It's like somebody who studies flowers – he says he'll give it a name because of the way it smells and its colours, because of the essence of what it is. But I'm very grateful to Sri Chinmoy, because only he could have the vision . . .'

Reverting to more widely understood matters, the Santana band of the time broke up around the end of 1973. Why was that? 'Because we did 312 concerts in one year, and we hated each other, couldn't stand each other. We were tired of each other, tired of our clothes, tired of the way we combed our hair, and we just wanted to jump on something new.'

The next project was also hardly a mainstream album – *Illuminations* was once again a collaboration, again with a fellow Sri Chinmoy disciple, 'Turiya' Alice Coltrane, widow of John Coltrane. 'She's a very good musician, who mainly plays concerts that she feels are according to her meditation significance. I'm grateful for my collaboration with her – it taught me more about freedom music, improvisation, the music of John Coltrane and learning how to work with strings. They call it "sheets of sound", which is what Elvin Jones and McCoy Tyner are into, and it's the same realm where Turiya Alice Coltrane abides. Somewhere in the Himalayas – they're soaring somewhere up there around Mount Everest.'

Illuminations had been released in 1974, as had a *Greatest Hits* album, but the barrage of either specialist or regurgitated Santana albums was ended with the release during the same year of an original album, *Borboletta*. 'We weren't into jazz, neither were we into being commercial, we were just into writing songs. If I may say it, I think we were like what Traffic were doing after their *John Barleycorn* album – not uninspiring, but not totally charging with vision. It was more like a breather after all those years of travelling and intensity with the *Lotus* band.'

It would be fair to say that then the Santana band was at a crossroads. 'The day that I went home after a rehearsal and realised that there was no more Santana and that I'd project all my energies into the "Lotus" band, I accepted at that very moment that I was kissing goodbye to a lot of my so-called audience. But I felt that I didn't want to be a monkey, where someone pulled the strings and I played what-

Carlos and Eric Clapton

Santana Band, 1980s

ever they wanted me to play – I have a soul, and it's a crime to ignore it, so I'll pay the price whatever it is, and whatever I have to do, I'll do it. So I wasn't too affected by the masses not coming, because I was having a ball – I still know that if I put a Safeway bag over my face and played in the streets, that somebody would listen, and that's my security. I'm a musician – I knew it then, and I know it now.'

Another kind of security which was missing for the next Santana LP, *Amigos*, was Carlos' long-time associate, drummer Michael Shrieve. 'Michael and I started to drift apart direction wise – I wanted a little more flexibility in a drummer, and I still wanted to play funk and jazz, and stuff like Bernard Purdie, but Michael wanted to go somewhere else, so we decided at that time that we'd part for a while. We learned a lot from Earth, Wind & Fire – I read a quotation from Maurice White (leader of EW&F) where he said his band was in between Miles Davis and Santana, and I thought that was funny – I hadn't listened to Santana in a long time, and I wondered what it was, and what Maurice seemed to be saying was that Santana was Latin/Afro/blue with guitars up-front energy. I thought to myself that that was very interesting, and I hadn't touched those things in a long time, so I decided to go back to see what was there, and that was how *Amigos* came about.'

While *Amigos* may have been inspired by Earth, Wind & Fire, many found that the album was dominated by percussionist Leon 'Ndugu' Chancler, whose influence appeared to be out of all proportion to his role in the Santana band, and who introduced a new singer and bass player to the group. 'It didn't take me

too long to work out what he was doing – I began to realise that there were cliques in people's cars and things. Unfortunately, some black people need to pamper themselves with slapping each other's hands and all that kind of stuff, for security, but others, of course, don't need to play that game. That first group of people have to play that role – hey, brother, and all that stuff – and it's just for security. I also realise that if you have five Japanese people in your band, you're going to sound Japanese, and the same with five Scotsmen, and that's not what I like – I like versatility, and I like to hit all the colours in the rainbow, so we had to dismiss people very soulfully, as much as possible, and start all over again.'

These 'dismissals' were in fact made somewhat easier for Carlos, since by this time, he and Bill Graham had buried the hatchet, and Graham had once again become the band's manager. 'It was easier than I thought it would be to get Bill to come back – we both swallowed a lot of the past, and neither of us wanted our pound of flesh from our relationship. I was very grateful, and I still am.'

The other Santana LP released in 1976, *Festival*, inevitably featured a different group of musicians, and was strongly influenced by salsa music, a Latin-American hybrid noted for its rhythmic qualities.

Nevertheless, *Festival* found little favour with critics, especially in Britain, and it seemed an appropriate moment to enquire whether or not Carlos was affected by other people's views of his music. 'Well, everyone's entitled to their opinion, but at the same time, I'm the one that I have to satisfy, and it's more important that I please myself than please the critics

Onstage in New York, 1981

Keeping cool amid the surrounding tension

– look at the critics: they all like so and so band, whose album goes platinum, but who, by my standards, sucked, so you'll always have differences of opinion. Santana will always be a band that finds it hard to please everybody, because people will want it to be like *Lotus* or *Abraxas* or *Borboletta*.'

One aspect of the Santana bands has been the great variety in the numbers of their personnel at different times. Did Carlos have a preference for either large or small groups? 'Some day, I'd like to try what Eric (Clapton) did, and just have a trio, because you have more room, but the only thing is that Eric knows more harmonically than I do, and that's how he gets away with it. I'm really a melodic person, and I need to learn more about harmonies so that I can cover more of a 360-degree area, but I'm also aware that as a trio, you're able to move around, where sometimes with a big band, you can't move around as much. But you also gain something – it's like cinemascope, where you gain variety.'

It's presumably easier for a guitar player in a big band ... 'It depends who the guitar player is. It's easier for me, because I don't consider myself a guitar player, and I listen to so many singers. You see, Eric to me isn't a guitar player, and nor is B. B. King – Joe Pass is a guitar player, and I don't like guitar players, although it's nothing personal. To me, Django Reinhardt isn't a guitar player – to me, people like that are instruments, artists, who create as a horn player, or as a singer, or as a baby crying. Like Francis Ford Coppola – they're artists, and they create on a whole other kind of spectrum, and that's why I like them. Eric and all those other people aren't guitar players, they're just something else.'

OK, but does singing, which Carlos has done from time to time, affect his guitar playing? 'Yes, because I don't sing all the time. Eric keeps getting mentioned, because for much of the time now, he sings, and I don't want to do that. I could have lessons, but all it is is having conviction about your voice, because at my age, my voice isn't going to change. When you're a kid, you're afraid you'll make a terrible noise in the middle of the song, and although my voice isn't going to change now, I'm still not knocked out by it. When I write songs, I sing a lot, but I'd rather sing through the guitar, so I don't like to spend too much time on the voice because I still need to perfect my craft as a guitar player. But let me say something else – I don't dislike Joe Pass or Kenny Burrell or any people that I could say were guitar players, like Segovia, because they're extremely significant. It's just that I grew up in a world where a guitar isn't played like that. So for all those people who want to send me to hell for saying those things, I'd like to say that I love Joe Pass and all those others, but it's just that I grew up in the Chuck Berry world where guitar players are infinitely more upfront.'

The only 1977 LP release was a double live album, *Moonflower*. 'Live albums are really good for me, because I haven't mastered the craft of recording live albums in the studio – I haven't had a producer or engineer who won't back away, because everybody's scared to death of a live album in the studio. They always want to pad and put make-up on it and all this kind of stuff, and that's why I like live albums a lot, because out there you don't have time to do anything else except just go, go for the heart. At this point, I appreciate to the fullest Led Zeppelin, because they did sound live, although at the same time they had make-up on the guitar. I don't like make-up on my guitar, but because of Jimmy Page, I'm learning to crave for make-up on my guitar, because of the way he uses certain things – he's one of the really significant producers and guitar players, I'd say, in making a band sound live and powerful, and I bow to him, because it takes a lot of know-ledge.'

The rather odd thing about the two major Santana live albums, *Lotus* and *Moonflower*, is that neither was recorded in America . . . 'That may be because in America, people scream – no, not really, but if you play in Japan or Europe, the audiences are infinitely more receptive, you ask any musician. For some reason, American audiences sometimes aren't con-ducive to just listening, and they want to put their own mark on everything, like "Hey, I'm here, make it happen for me, play one for me, can you play . . .", and they just won't shut up. They've begun to do that now in Japan and in parts of Europe, but when I first started touring, they listened.'

1978 saw just one album release, *Inner Secrets*, which was produced by the successful hit-making team of (Dennis) Lambert and (Brian) Potter, which seemed an odd choice for a band like Santana. 'At that point, Devadip was in one place, and Santana in another, in two different buildings. I have to do a Santana album, where CBS tell me how to play, and what and when to play, so that I can go in the studio as Devadip, or play with Miles or someone else. If Santana was to remain successful in CBS' eyes, and I was to maintain a certain integrity within myself, reaching all the people who come to see us in Europe and the few that come to see us in America, we had to get somebody like Lambert and Potter, someone who knows *Billboard*, because I don't really listen to AM or FM Radio or read *Billboard*. I just buy records, whoever knocks me out. But those people do (know about the radio), and so does Keith Olsen (who pro-duced the 1979 Santana LP, *Marathon*) and they gave us another perspective on putting Santana back into the auditoriums. So we did it consciously. And we're still doing certain things consciously – look at Stevie Wonder: the last two albums he did are magnificent works of art to me, but to laymen . . . people who go to Woolworths don't know the price of real jewellery at Tiffany. If they see it lying in the street, they won't know its worth, so they go to Wool-worths and buy this cheap jewellery. And that's my analogy for commercialism – it doesn't mean that Picasso isn't commercial, because there is a way to combine quality and quantity, and I'm still looking for it. It's really important to maintain integrity and dignity.'

Instances of the name of Santana appearing in the British singles charts are rare – prior to 1977, only 'Samba Pa Ti' had made the charts, while the biggest hit so far came in 1977 with a revival of 'She's Not There' (previously a hit for the Zombies) which was extracted from the *Moonflower* live double. 'Inner Secrets' provided the next (much smaller) hit with another revival, this time of the Buddy Holly song, 'Well All Right'. An odd choice of material? 'I always liked "Well All Right" since the first time I heard it, and when Blind Faith (Eric Clapton's shortlived 1969 band) did it, it sounded to me like James Brown, like Stevie Winwood, like B. B. King, like Buddy Holly, and it had all those things that Santana is – the cross-roads of all kinds of merging. It's what America is, a melting pot, and I persuaded the band to do it.'

One aspect of Carlos Santana's playing which has perhaps been ignored by all but his most avid fans is the remarkable consistency of his guitar work. Is maintaining that consistency easy for Carlos, in that he can naturally charge himself up, or is it sometimes a problem?

'People take coffee or cocaine, or they jog or medi-tate – it's by hook or by crook, outside stimuli, and you pay the price by becoming very cranky, very cal-lous, very weird, when you're coming down. Or you can take inspiration, which is the purest form of stimu-lus, and I'd rather take that, but I have to say that after two or three weeks on the road, four weeks at most, I lose my inspiration – I couldn't care less if the Queen of England or Mao Tse-tung is in the audi-ence, if I don't feel like playing, I don't feel like it, because my well has run dry. I need to come home at that point, and take a walk by the forest, or do certain things that inspire me. I have to see Sri Chinmoy, go back to old blues records, Little Walter, B. B. King . . . I have to do certain things that will inspire me to go back out there.'

1979 provided two Santana LPs, one by the band, *Marathon*, and a solo record by Carlos with the title *Oneness*. Presumably this must have resulted in a mild case of schizophrenia, especially since the solo project must have interested Carlos more than the

The sensitive artist

group LP? 'I told the band that if the Santana band was going to continue, that they'd have to keep me interested, and I told that to the management and everybody else as well. It's very natural for me to write for Devadip, but harder to write for Santana. Last year (1980) I was in Frankfurt and got together with Jimmy Page, and he charged me up by certain things he said to me about Santana – he liked the band, he came and saw us and liked us a lot. Now when we play live, there's Santana and Devadip happening together with this band, because they're that versatile, so there's no more schizophrenia.'

1980 saw a double solo album, *Swing Of Delight*, in which Carlos recorded with some of his idols, including Herbie Hancock and Wayne Shorter, which must have been most gratifying for Carlos. 'It was easier than I thought it would be to convince them to play with me, and I have to say that with anyone, musicians or other famous people, as soon as you hang around with them for more than half an hour, they lose all the greatness that you see in them, because you can see that they're just like you, equally fragile. But these people never lost that – I hold them in higher esteem now than when I first met them. As soon as they started playing, it was as if they'd grabbed me by the ankles and thrown me way up into space, yanked me right off the floor and thrown me up to wherever they're soaring. I discovered that I could keep up with them in a certain way, and I feel that this is the most significant album I've ever done – every second, I felt my inner self stretching, expanding, when we were playing and even when we were just talking. It would be like hanging around Jimmy and Eric all the time – these people are extremely significant, and I'm grateful to all of them.'

More recently came a new LP by the Santana band, *Zebop*, produced by Carlos with his manager, Bill Graham. 'I haven't been under this kind of pressure before – usually, I shake off pressure like a dog shaking off water, but I feel the pressure from CBS and from around the world, to get people listening to the band again. It's not so much finding an audience, but we want a new audience, because I know the Santana fans and the Devadip fans, and they're not enough. I want to reach more people, and to play with bands like Weather Report and the Police, and make sure that we don't sound like an antique when we play with those bands, to show that what we have to say is just as fresh and new and important as the Police – and we will prove it. Hopefully, this album will put us closer towards that aim, and if it does, that's fine. I play a Stratocaster, and I started to sound like Mark (Knopfler) from Dire Straits, and Eric, because I never played Stratocaster (before). When I started playing a Strat, it was so effortless to get that sound and that feeling that I thought I'd play the Stratocaster more often. I love the naked sound of the Stratocaster, but not cranked up and full, I like the way Eric and Mark play it, really juicy and nice. So I learned a lot from this album about playing other instruments.'

Which brought the conversation nicely round to Carlos' choice of guitars. 'I started with Gibsons, and I never really got into Fenders much, although I like Strats now. I'm also getting into the Telecaster now, because of the Police – I like the sound Andy Summers gets. And Yamaha made a beautiful guitar for me, and so did Paul Smith, who's a great master craftsman from Baltimore. And that's mainly what I'm playing now – a Yamaha, the Paul Smith, and an old Gibson Les Paul, which I've had since the early '70s. I used to play the Gibson SG for a while, but I don't like them anymore, because I find that they go out of tune too much, and God knows, it's hard enough for me to stay in tune – I need all the help I can get!'

While some may feel that certain of Carlos Santana's philosophies are too esoteric and/or antique, to meet him is to meet a survivor – after nearly fifteen years at, or close to, the top of his profession, Carlos is still a force to be reckoned with, both commercially and aesthetically, and such an accolade applies to only the very special.

Carlos Santana Discography

Santana Band
1969 *Santana*
1970 *Abraxas*
1971 *Third Album*
1972 *Caravanserai*
1973 *Welcome*
1974 *Greatest Hits*
1974 *Borboletta*
1975 *Lotus*
1976 *Amigos*
1976 *Festival*
1977 *Moonflower*
1978 *Inner Secrets*
1979 *Marathon*
1981 *Zebop*
1982 *Shango*
The Santana band also appear on *Woodstock* (1970), *Fillmore: The Last Days* (1972) and *California Jam 2* (1978)

Carlos Santana
1968 *Live Adventures of Mike Bloomfield & Al Kooper* (guest appearance)

1972 *Carlos Santana and Buddy Miles! Live!*
1973 *Love Devotion Surrender* (with Mahavishnu John McLaughlin)
1974 *Illuminations* (with Turiya Alice Coltrane)
1979 *Oneness – Silver Dreams Golden Reality*
1980 *The Swing Of Delight*

Sessions
Luis Gasca
1971 *Luis Gasca*

Papa John Creach
1971 *Papa John Creach*

Narada Michael Walden
1977 *Garden Of Lovelight*
1979 *Awakening*

Herbie Hancock
1980 *Monster*

Boz Scaggs
1980 *Middleman*

JOE WALSH

In 1969, The Who toured Britain, dragging around a support act who were, to say the least, an unknown quantity to all but a very few British rock fans. Pete Townshend, however, extolled to all who would listen (a considerable number) the virtues of The James Gang in general and their guitarist Joe Walsh in particular, and by the end of the tour, Joe Walsh was on his way to becoming a household name. A dozen years later, his status is unquestionably that of a celebrity, although Walsh's appeal has somewhat altered from those heady guitar days of yore.

Joe Walsh was born on 20 November 1947, in Wichita, Kansas, and not, as others have suggested, New York. The young Walsh was much travelled – 'I spent three- or four-year periods in Illinois and Ohio, and then I went to Junior high school in New York City, to high school in New Jersey, and then I went back to Ohio for college, so it's really difficult when I'm asked where I come from, because I don't know.'

The Walshes were a musical family, Joe's mother being a classical pianist. 'Yes, she still is – she's an accompanist for the New York Ballet, and I really owe her a lot, because she forced me to play various instruments and always made sure that I grew up hearing important classical works, and that influence surfaced later – for instance, *Pavane* was a piece I did on my *So What* LP, and that was something my mom

was always playing when I was growing up. She'd play a whole bunch of stuff, and I'd ask what it was, so I became kind of familiar with various forms of classical music, which really helped later on.'

Although he is obviously best known as a guitarist, Walsh is no beginner on several other musical instruments, having dabbled in his childhood with piano, clarinet and trombone before playing oboe in high school.

'Then I ended up playing guitar basically because I hated everything that I was forced to practise, and because guitar was my own little project, nobody forced me to practise, so that was really the instrument I enjoyed. It was kind of primitive guitar playing initially – I'm not even sure you could call it rhythm guitar, because it didn't really matter if I tuned it. Probably the reason I became interested in the guitar was because of watching a TV show in the United States called "Ozzie & Harriet", which was about the Nelson family, of which Rick Nelson was the youngest. It was like a serial, and every so often they would show Ricky Nelson playing at his high school dance, and of course his band involved James Burton, who played on most of his records.'

Walsh's first band was known as the G Clefs. 'Oh God! Where did you dig that up? That was a high school band. We had a piano player, a drummer and a trumpet player, and I played guitar, and that was the band. We did things like "Exodus", "Wonderland By Night" and "Walk Don't Run", if you can conceive of a Wurlitzer electric piano, a trumpet, one guitar and a drummer playing "Walk Don't Run" – it was a strange version. But that was the first band, and the most embarrassing thing about it was the name. We didn't know that there was another famous band called the G Clefs – it was just one of the two or three musical terms we knew, so that's what we called it. That had to be about 1962 or '63.'

The item which Walsh claimed changed his life was seeing the Beatles appearing on the 'Ed Sullivan Show' on television. 'I saw the Beatles, and I hadn't really listened to the album – they really surfaced over a period of four or five months in this country. I was a dumb kid going to high school in New Jersey in a band with a trumpet player, and I could play in one key, but I still have a really clear image of watching them, and my parents shaking their heads left and right and me shaking my head up and down, and that hit a spark inside me and I knew that was what I wanted to do. I thought, "Those guys are cool", and I'd like to do that, and that stayed dominant in my thinking, and because of that, I kind of negated college and fitting into the straight world.

'The next band I was in was called the Nomads – we had collarless jackets like the Beatles and tried to sound like them. Everybody did in those days. It didn't matter if you were good or not, if you could play some Beatle songs or songs from the English scene, you could play in front of people. If you had, for instance, a Gretsch guitar like George Harrison played, or a Vox amp, it didn't matter if you even turned it on, because if you had one, people would come. I was the bass player in the Nomads, although I didn't know anything about the bass – the only reason I wanted to play it was because I had two less strings to deal with. In retrospect, those were the

good old days where it was really important to do the top 30, and very few bands were doing original music. There were a lot of clubs and dances, a lot of opportunities to play. It's vastly different nowadays, and I think that one of the things I've always been thankful for, and a lot of people from the United States of my generation will always be thankful for, was that there was just such an influx of energy from England. It made things easier over here, and also gave a lot of musicians that are around today the ability to go out and play in front of people.

'We never played anything original – at that point, I didn't have an original thought in my head about anything. It was great training to be able to copy records for a period of two or three years and also have the feeling of being in front of people and playing just any music. Original thoughts came later . . . I was with the Nomads pretty much through high school, up until about 1965, at which point I graduated – I was going to try to say something funny about that, but it was a miracle that it even happened – and we all went our separate ways to various colleges. At that point in this country, Vietnam was dominant in the political outlook of things, and if you went to college, you got a deferment from military service, and if you weren't going to college, you went in the army. So I went to college – I was stupid, but I wasn't dumb! I went to college, and I didn't do well, but my creative energy was starting to focus at that point – I remember missing three and four days of classes and sitting in the dormitory practising guitar and listening to records, trying to steal every lick I could and writing a couple of very primitive songs, but at that point, I started to realise that I didn't have to play the top 20 note for note. Wait a minute, I can put this in here, improvise!'

Eventually, Joe did join a local band, the Measles. 'Oh boy! You're nailing me to the wall. Yes, that was the Measles, who were a local band who played downtown at weekends, and when the school year ended, I chose to stay in Kent, which is a suburb of Akron, Ohio, and play in the band in bars and clubs for the summer. I never really went home again after I left to go to college, and that was really the beginning of my career. I was starting to develop at that point, I think – I was writing more and more, starting to improvise, starting to get some licks that were my own that I hadn't stolen from other people. That was a good time – I was playing four sets a night, four nights a week, even if it was only fifteen or twenty dollars a night, and I was doing OK. Those were really good times, and even now when frustrated guitar players ask me what they can do to make it, I remember those times, when I really paid my dues. I played four and five hours a night, four and five nights a week for two or three years, and that's when you get good, that's when you get your licks, that's when you get comfortable, that's when you learn to fix your equipment when it blows up. So that would be my advice – "Hey, go play in front of people, don't be in a hurry to make it because nobody does overnight, and God help you if you do, because you go down just as quick".'

The next step for Joe Walsh was joining the band with whom he made his major recording debut, the James Gang, with whom he stayed for two and a half

Joe Walsh (left) in the James Gang

years, beginning in April 1969. 'The James Gang were good, a five-piece band who were one of the top acts in Cleveland, and by that time, I was one of the top guitar players in Kent or Akron. Their guitarist, Glenn Schwartz, was an amazing player, and to this day is kind of one of my gurus, and he left and I was invited to fill his shoes. So I joined the James Gang and we played about a year in various clubs around Michigan, Ohio, Indiana and Pennsylvania, but we didn't get along that well with five of us, so it ended up being a three-piece group, a bit like the Jimi Hendrix Experience or Cream, which was the really popular way to be in those days. Again, it was training for me, because I was the only melodic instrument – it was guitar, bass and drums – and I learned to enjoy playing rhythm and lead at the same time, and I also had to sing. I learned a lot about how to play guitar effectively. Right around then, I met Pete Townshend, who was and still is a great and special influence on my life, and he patted me on the back and said "You're doing pretty good, kid". We were the local support band when the Who came to Cleveland, and Pete arrived early and said he enjoyed our show. He kind of took me under his wing, advice-wise, and gave me confidence, and told me that I was intelligently going about being the only melodic instrument in the band very well, which was obviously very encouraging.'

The Who were in fact admired by Walsh but his previous influences and favourites were somewhat diverse. 'It's strange, because I really grew up listening to the singles of the '50s and early '60s – the Ronettes, Motown – and not really R&B, which was probably because of where I was geographically when I was open to that stimulus. Even so, my favourites were (Jeff) Beck and (Jimmy) Page in the Yardbirds – I thought they were incredible. And Clapton when he was in the Bluesbreakers (with John Mayall), Hendrix, of course, Mike Bloomfield, especially when he was with Paul Butterfield. At that stage, I was just beginning to get into B. B. King, Albert King, Freddie King, Albert Collins, those sort of people, but the only reason I was getting into them was because I had read everything I possibly could in terms of interviews with all these English guitar players who said that was where they got all their licks from. I feel silly that I wasn't into the American blues scene earlier than that, but I just wasn't.'

Things changed dramatically with the arrival on the scene of record producer Bill Szymczyk, whose name has continued to crop up in Joe Walsh's story to date. 'It's a strange story – he just showed up one night, when we were playing in Warren, Ohio, I think it was. He was a kind of in-house producer for ABC Records, and was looking for rock'n'roll groups, and while Cleveland, Detroit and Cincinatti was kind of a pocket of very good rock'n'roll, nobody really had got on to record at that time. He showed

Joe Walsh For President?

up one night and really liked the James Gang, and he and I became very good friends and related to each other, and that started about a fifteen-year friendship which has gotten nothing but stronger to date. He signed the James Gang to ABC Records, and we made *Yer Album*, our first album, which did very well in Cleveland, Detroit and Cincinatti!'

The precise history of the James Gang seems never to have been exhaustively documented – formed by drummer Jim Fox in 1967, the band also included Glenn Schwartz and bass player Tom Kriss, but had not recorded before Schwartz left and was replaced by Walsh. During the latter's time with the band, they recorded three studio LPs and a fourth live album. One aspect of that first LP, namely the title, has been disturbing these authors with its very Britishness. *Yer Album* – was the spelling of the personal pronoun intentional? 'Probably subconsciously – having just met the guys in the Who, having spent three or four years studying the chemistry of various English bands, and having spent a period of time trying to develop an English accent, which helped if you were singing English songs ... We couldn't think of a name for the album, and at some point we had to think of one – also "Yer" is a small reflection of the midwest kind of accent. It's yer, not your – it's a strange dialect.

'Just after that, we came to England for the first time, supporting the Who mostly, but headlining a couple of concerts ourselves as well. I really owe a lot to all the guys in the Who, because they believed in us and really took us under their wing – they gave us confidence and took us on tour with them, and that did us the world of good, just kind of showing us that we could do it. Europe was quite an experience in terms of gathering input which would help me write songs, and I really thought that I'd gain a lot musi-

cally from playing in Europe, but I didn't, although I did gain from playing in England and seeing the scene over there. I've always got a tremendous amount of positive input from visiting England, but Europe made me a little more mature, made me feel a bit more like a man of the world, instead of a dummy from Ohio.'

At this point in the interview, a rhetorical question was asked which presumed that *Yer Album* was actually Walsh's first released record – not so ... 'The Nomads made a record which sold four copies, because each guy in the band bought one, but that was very primitive and very silly. When it came to the James Gang records, each album did a little better than the one before. It was a means, really, a form of expression – during those times, I did a lot of experimenting and a lot of learning, about musical textures and how to put songs together. Of course, I studied Szymczyk a lot ... I can't say that we were really that successful, but the fact that each album did a little better than the one before gave us an amount of acceptance with the record company, and allowed us to continue playing in front of people.'

Arguably the best-known track by the James Gang is 'Funk 49', which in fact first appeared on the second album by the group, *James Gang Rides Again*, released in 1970. 'It's a good example of the James Gang. I came up with the basic guitar lick, and the words never really impressed me intellectually, but they seemed to fit somehow. It was a real good example of how we put things together, bearing in mind that it was a three piece group, and I don't think that there was any overdubbing. The only thing we really added was the percussion middle part, which the three of us actually played, putting some parts on top of the drums, but that's the three piece James Gang, and that's the energy and kind of the symmetry we were all about.'

While there may have been little in the way of overdubs on 'Funk 49', as time went on the group began to make more refinements in their recording, and that was one of the reasons for Joe leaving the band in November 1971. 'Yes, it's got too wonderful. There was a lot of overdubbing later on, and it was difficult to reproduce the records on stage, but there were two or three reasons for my leaving. Logically, I was trying to develop at that point, and I was starting to hear textures that showed up later in my career – I've always been obsessed with textures and the symmetry of things. It was very frustrating at that time to be the only melodic instrument in the band, because I wanted to have some harmony, I wanted to have piano and rhythm guitar live, and once again, when I stopped playing rhythm to play lead, there was no rhythm, so it was hard live, although it was fun, and I learned a lot. The second thing was that I felt I was starting to be stereotyped into being a heavy metal, loud, fast, American guitar player, and I felt there was more to me than that. I didn't want to turn into a Blue Cheer (a notorious American band, whose main distinction was their ability to be heard several miles from where they played) or a heavy metal thing, and I was scared I might have that label for life. I didn't want to be a heavy metal flash lead guitar player. I didn't want to be known for that, I wanted to be known to the public and to my peers as more of a songwriter, more of a musician, so at some point, I decided not to express myself in a three-piece very loud group anymore.'

During this period, Walsh assisted B. B. King, playing rhythm to B.B.'s lead on several tracks included on King's *Indianola Mississippi Seeds* album, almost inevitably produced by Bill Szymczyk. 'Yes, and I *loved* it! I was doing some session work at that time – not too much, most of it because of Szymczyk – but I did play for B.B. on a few things, and it really opened my eyes. I loved being able to play rhythm guitar without having to sing, and I loved being able to make records.'

At the same time as his departure from the James Gang, another guitarist, Peter Frampton, decided to leave Humble Pie, and Walsh was offered the chance to be Frampton's replacement, although he declined the position. 'I'm amazed that you were even aware of that – that was something I really wanted to do, but I think the problem was that I had definite commitments, if not to the James Gang, at least to my management and to my record company, which were kind of negative to me moving to England and joining Humble Pie. I very much wanted to – I've always had a high amount of respect for Steve Marriott and Frampton, and that was something that I really wanted to do, but I just couldn't.'

On leaving his band, the end of 1971 also saw Joe Walsh collecting together his belongings and relocating in Boulder, Colorado, a fairly intrepid move for a man whose prospects were, to say the least, uncertain. 'Without dwelling on it too much, I found when I decided to leave the James Gang that both my management and record company were disappointed, I guess is the word, because we were starting to realise material benefits, shall I say, and they were not real happy that I had chosen to leave.

And I didn't get much help from my management or record company at the start of pursuing a solo career. Moving to Colorado had a lot to do with my friendship with Bill Szymczyk, who at that point was an advisor who was helping me feel confident because I was scared to death.

'So I went to Colorado, took an amount of time off, and began forming Barnstorm, which was an arrangement of players conceived in a way to express what I was hearing and what I thought a band should be. They were strange times and it was hard, but it took me back to basic survival, which is always very positive in terms of creative energy – when you have to get yourself together and you're talking in terms of basic survival, you play differently from when you're rich.'

Somewhat curiously, in view of what Joe had said about his creative frustrations being at least partially the result of the James Gang being a three-piece band, Barnstorm was also a trio, at least in its first incarnation. 'That's a really good point, and that was the overall result of what I was trying to do – in other words, Joe Vitale and Kenny Passarelli were the two guys I could find who directly related to what I was trying to do. I would have had a ten-piece group, but I couldn't find the right people who would fit in, and believe me, I was in no hurry to form another group to cover myself. Towards the end of the first album, we found a keyboard player named Rocke Grace, who had played with Todd Rundgren, and really, that formed the foundation. Later on, there was

Hitting that note!

another guy, Tom Stephenson, who added second keyboards, and Rocke and Tom really gave me the melodic content I had been lacking with the James Gang. I know it's strange to quit a three-piece group because it's a three-piece group and then form a three-piece group – I can't really justify that, but there was a chemistry there, and to this day I'm proud of having put together Barnstorm, and everything we did. I would have had more people in the band, but I didn't want silly people in the band, and as I found people, they were interfaced in – it was a slow process and it wasn't easy, but that's all I could really do. At one time, the first Barnstorm album was my favourite of all the stuff I had done, although it's kind of primitive in that we were very new to each other, and it was recorded in a primitive manner, but I wanted it that way – the magic of the three of us, and with Rocke, the four of us, the magic of no overdubs, us being in a room and playing those songs, was there, and that's what I was going for. There are a couple of tracks from that album that I really like – I was always very happy with "Birdcall Morning", with the way that got from my brain to the tape, and "Mother Says". Both of those are very gratifying when I look back in terms of getting the songs on tape the way I conceived them, without losing anything.'

Although the first line-up of Barnstorm played no live dates during the first six months of its existence, soon after Rocke Grace joined the band they embarked on a punishing schedule of roadwork which took in 330 appearances in one year. 'The reason that we worked so hard came down to really basic survival. We were playing pretty much anything we could, just to be able to play and to be able to pay for the equipment – it wasn't particularly from choice, but it was good.'

During this hectic period, the band also found time to record a second album, which boasts the bizarre title of *The Smoker You Drink, The Player You Get*, the significance of which has eluded the vast majority of those who have ever considered its meaning (or lack thereof). 'Well – that's your problem! It's funny, I occasionally get asked "What do you mean by that?", and it just speaks for itself. It was something I thought of late at night, and it makes sense if you think about it. I'd rather not try to explain what it means, but there is meaning there – it's very true, but I'm not sure what it means myself.' So now we know . . .

The album includes a song which more than any other has become Walsh's virtual signature tune, 'Rocky Mountain Way', whose origins Walsh recalled. 'I always felt that was special, even before it was complete – we had recorded that before I knew what the words were going to be, but I was very proud of it. Again, it's a situation of performance – it was not a constructed record, like a lot of them are, that was pretty much one shot at it, all playing at the same time. The words came about – I got kind of fed up with feeling sorry for myself, and I wanted to justify and feel good about leaving the James Gang, relocating, going for it on a survival basis. I wanted to say "Hey, whatever this is, I'm positive and I'm proud", and the words just kind of came out of feeling that way, rather than writing a song out of

remorse. It was special then, and the words were special to me, because the words were like, "I'm goin' for it, the heck with feeling sorry for this and that", and it did turn out to be a special song for a lot of people. I think the attitude and the statement of that have a lot to do with it – it's a positive song, and it's basic rock'n'roll, which is what I really do.'

At the end of 1973, the group splintered, doubtless due to extreme fatigue following their on the road exertions. 'Fatigue, and also me being a little naïve, figuring that coming out of the James Gang I would immediately be recognised and all my problems would be over. Again, a band just really runs its course – nobody in the band has control of how long you stay together, and when you're done, you're done, and that's kind of up to fate. I'll go out on a limb and say that we were a very, very good band for a period of time, but unfortunately Barnstorm was only noticed and recognised as being a very good band after we had started to disband. The timing was just a little bit off.'

In view of Joe's feelings, it is particularly unfortunate that Barnstorm never released a live LP, although Walsh's next project, his 1974 LP *So What*, saw him making moves in a decidedly new direction and beginning to experiment with synthesisers.

'That's another story – I had one or two rare guitars that I had come across, and I sent one over to Pete Townshend, and he liked it a lot. I think he played it on *Who's Next*, or somewhere around that period . . . All of a sudden, I got a package at my house, and it was a synthesiser, a kind of "thank you" from Pete, so I plugged it in and stayed in the room for about three weeks straight! I got into synthesisers, and the texture again, and the sounds – the synthesiser is really an unlimited instrument, and the thing that really limits you on a synthesiser is you. So I kind of did homework and research on that, and I have subtly used synthesisers from around *So What* on. Not in the context of electronic music albums like *Switched On Bach* or Tomita or anything, but every once in a while, back in there underneath the guitars, you can hear synthesiser. And I like to tease with it, and there are textures you can get with synthesisers that are very teasing.'

One notable early example of the Walsh synthesiser technique is curiously enough the classical piece mentioned above and included on the *So What* LP, Ravel's *Pavane* – an unlikely choice for a rocker? 'Very strange, I know, but it's one of my favourite pieces of classical music. Maurice Ravel was an impressionist musician who wrote in the same time period as Debussy, and *Pavane Of The Sleeping Beauty* is part of *The Mother Goose Suite*, which is almost a ballet, almost a fairy tale, almost a children's story, and it's one of the movements. I think it's very haunting and something that I always wanted to do – I know that's really kind of way out there for a rock-'n'roller to do, but I loved it and just thought it was me, and I really wanted to share it with people. And it's all synthesiser.'

Equally significant as regards *So What* was the fact that Don Henley, Randy Meisner and Glenn Frey of the Eagles performed on the album, and within a year of its release, Walsh had joined that band. 'I met Irving Azoff during the Barnstorm period, and expressed to him my concern that I wasn't getting much help from my management or the record company, although at that point, he was in no position to do anything about it. He was also from the mid-west, and liked my music and my general attitude about things, and at some point, I told Irving that I wanted him to handle my affairs, and that in return I would try to maintain integrity and make him proud to represent me, so he became my manager. We spent an amount of time both starving, but he has always had a personal direct line with artists that he has represented. Around that time, I was just fed up with a solo career – I didn't have the energy to do it, and it didn't really look like it was going anywhere. Irving met the Eagles, who were kind of disillusioned with their management and the way they were being represented, and they also had some internal friction – it was kind of being in the right place at the right time, but what ended up was that the Eagles asked Irving to represent them and formed kind of a little family. I got to know the guys in the Eagles, they helped me a little bit with *So What*, and I went to some late night jams with them when they were working on *On The Border*, and just helped out as a guitar player while they were writing some of that. Later, Bernie Leadon, who was the guitar player that I replaced in the Eagles, decided that he didn't want to be in the group anymore, and they kind of had a stereotype of the "sons of the desert ballad" type – as the sun goes down over the banana trees and the cactus, you know – and they secretly wanted to rock-'n'roll a bit more. We got together and talked about it for quite a while, and the chemistry was really there, but they were scared to death to replace anybody in the band, and I was scared to death to join a band, but it worked out, and we had Irving, who was representing me and them in the middle, so it seemed like the best thing to do, because I wanted to be in a group and they needed to replace a member of the band, and they wanted a dominant-type guitar player. So it kind of worked out, and we made an agreement to abstractly try to get that together. We ran away for about six months, and an intense amount of energy went around between the guys in

Onstage with the Eagles – left to right: Don Felder, Don Henley, Joe Walsh

Joe wows Wembley Stadium, 1975

the Eagles, I was interfaced in, and out of that amount of energy came *Hotel California*.

Joe Walsh actually joined the Eagles at the end of 1975, and a year later, *Hotel California* was released and became a huge success. Joe also worked on many outside projects and this seems a suitable place to mention a number of them. 1974 had seen what appears to be the first Joe Walsh production for an outside artist, in this case a singer/songwriter named Dan Fogelberg. It's often true that a musician has more ideas in his head than he can easily use on his own records, but there must be a danger in sharing them with others in case they take the best ones ... 'At that point, I had been studying the art of recording for quite a while, under Bill Szymczyk, and I was running out of energy in terms of a solo career – it was very draining, and a lot of the benefits I thought I would get from leaving the James Gang I was finding out weren't necessarily true, and being in a solo career position and being the leader of the band, I was starting to feel kind of sterile, because I didn't really have anybody to write with and I was calling the shots. I think Danny Fogelberg is really a genius, really gifted, and I was in a position where I was pretty well drained as an artist, but I had a lot of energy in terms of getting someone else's brains down on tape – so I made a commitment to work with him on *Souvenirs*, although I'm not really sure, to this day, what a producer does. If I had to write it down, I would be at a loss, but basically, I think if you can get an artist's brains on tape without losing anything in the translation, you're an effective producer, and that's what I tried to do with Dan.'

Before his first LP with the Eagles was released, there came another 'solo' album, a live LP with another intriguing title, *You Can't Argue With A Sick Mind*, which was made by Walsh and a band of experienced session musicians, most of whom had backed Walsh for his appearance at a memorable concert held at Wembley Stadium or Midsummer's Day, 1975, the headline acts being Elton John, the Beach Boys and the Eagles.

'That was a good band. At that point, I knew I was going to be in the Eagles, although it wasn't yet on paper. There was Willie Weeks, Andy Newmark, David Mason the keyboard player, and at various times Rikki Fataar, Bryan Garofalo, Paul Harris, Joe Vitale, Jay Ferguson ... I had built up a bunch of songs through James Gang days, Barnstorm and post-Barnstorm, and I really had put together a pretty good group, although I was running out of energy to oversee it all. I was real proud of the band that played at Wembley, and that album was the live LP of that band, but it was also like my last statement, the end of a phase before I went back into a band situation.'

A notable track from the album is 'Walk Away'. 'That was a James Gang song that was done as a three piece, and I wasn't particularly proud of it, but with Andy Newmark, Willie Weeks and Rick Fataar, we worked it out and it changed, it really caught a groove and got real funky, and came out differently from the way the James Gang had performed it, and even differently from the way I had conceived it. It changed round, and I was real proud to have written it, couldn't believe that I had written it, but that's a good example of the energy and where I was at playing live at that point.'

An artist whose name has continually come up in the context of both this project and its forerunner, *The Record Producers,* is Rick Derringer, himself a guitarist, which makes it interesting that Walsh should have played on two tracks of Derringer's *All American Boy* LP. 'Rick was making a solo album and writing some songs, and possibly there were some parts that he couldn't quite figure out, or that he felt were weak, and wanted some external input.' Why does any guitar player, even Eric Clapton, need another guitar player? 'He doesn't, but there's a strength in that, an energy, that you could never think of. Another guitar player can come at you from angles that you could conceive in your train of thought, and although Rick can play circles around me, believe me, I think there were a few parts in his solo project where he couldn't quite figure out what he'd come up with and locked into, and weren't quite what he wanted to do there, so I was kind of involved on that as a specialist, kind of search and destroy.'

Another mid-'70s session project for Walsh was an album by Al Kooper, founder of both the Blues Project and Blood, Sweat & Tears, and also the keyboard player on Bob Dylan's highly influential 'Like a Rolling Stone'. 'Al is amazing – he's another guru of mine. He's an old timer and he knows so much, and when I get in a room with him, I just shut up and listen. He had used various guitar players, and hadn't quite found what he was looking for, so he gave me a shot at that, and I approached it very melodically, kind of flowing, and I think – I hope – I helped.'

A very different project was Keith Moon's solo album, on half of which Walsh played, which brings up the question of whether drummers (even the Who's drummer) should make solo LPs, since in many cases, they are heavily reliant on musicians who play melodic instruments to provide musical, as opposed to rhythmic, assistance, something which also applies to one of Walsh's erstwhile colleagues, Joe Vitale, to whose pair of solo LPs Walsh has also contributed. 'I don't like to pass judgement on that – if anybody wants to do a solo album, I think they should, and I think it makes them a stronger person. I think it's an outlet for people locked in various bands – if they can run away once in a while and make a solo album, they can blow off some steam, and that's good and healthy, rather than bad or anything, and I think it's very valid and positive.'

Another unusual undertaking was Joe assisting Ray Manzarek, keyboard player of the Doors, on one of the latter's solo LPs. 'The Doors were an amazing group, and the way I look at things, I appreciate musicians, and if I feel that they're pure and good and not full of baloney, and if their priorities are right, I'm happy to work with anybody.'

A few years before the Manzarek project, Walsh was involved in an album by Manassas, a neo-supergroup led by Stephen Stills, who, like Rick Derringer, is a fine guitarist but perhaps required some external input. 'They were an incredible band, and that was all part of the Colorado scene, where we had a little family – Chris Hillman, Stills, the Nitty Gritty Dirt Band, Kenny Passarelli, Rick Roberts, and I was there, of course . . . We kind of bumped into

each other through various concerts and hanging out, and I met Stephen – a couple of college friends of mine ended up being in the Manassas road crew, and I guess there were some late night road stories about me being crazy in college. Again, Stephen had always been one of my heroes, and it seemed logical that we got together, although we didn't actually go in and record a song for the album. These were late night jams in Colorado, and we got a chance to play, and I tried to play intelligent guitar and stay out of Stephen's way, which I think he appreciated, and I think he got energy from it, and one or two things we did really worked out to be good tracks.'

Another artist for whom Walsh played sessions was Michael Stanley, who has only very recently begun to achieve the success his cult following has for many years felt he deserved. Walsh played on Stanley's first two LPs which were recorded around ten years ago – 'Michael was a very early project of Bill Szymczyk's, and Michael was from Cleveland, and I always thought he wrote very good songs. Backaways, when I was frustrated being in a three-piece group and wanted to do sessions and play with other people, Mike was in a position to do a solo album, and asked me to relate to some of the guitar parts, which was really fun – there's a song called 'Rosewood Bitters', which was my very primitive early days, learning how to play slide guitar or bottleneck or whatever. I played on his second album too, but he never realised a big hit out of that.

'Another thing I did for Szymczyk was with a band called the Fabulous Rhinestones. Harvey Brooks, the leader of that group, was a real good old friend of Szymczyk's, and actually I got called into that as a synthesiser consultant. They wanted to use some synthesiser on their record, at the point where I was spending twenty hours a day playing my synthesiser, and I programmed the sounds, which can take hours. I came in, and based on what they said, programmed the synthesiser and played a little of it, although other guys in the band actually played the keyboard, but I got the sound together that they were looking for.'

Three more famous names with whom Walsh played on record are Rod Stewart, Jay Ferguson (ex of Spirit and Jo Jo Gunne) and Bill Wyman of the Rolling Stones. 'The Rod Stewart thing happened during the time we were recording *Hotel California,* or maybe between the time we finished it and the point it was in the shops. It was one of the sessions where I felt extremely humble, and almost got hung up – I could have played better if I hadn't felt so little playing for him, because of that incredible band with Rod and Ronnie Wood and Jeff Beck and Mickey Waller. Those first couple of Jeff Beck albums, when Rod was the singer in Jeff's band, really influenced me and my way of thinking about bands.'

Not only is Joe credited with playing on Jay Ferguson's *Thunder Island* album, produced by Bill Szymczyk, he also gets a 'special thanks' mention on Ferguson's *All Alone In The End Zone* album for 'saying stop'. 'Yeah, that's a good one! Jay and I are really good friends, and he's been involved with me a lot, and we really are close to being brothers. I wanted to help him with his record – of course, I loved Spirit and I loved Jo Jo Gunne, and Jay is a really good keyboard player. Again, he shares my frustration in being the leader of a band, or pursuing a solo career that's hard, but we think a lot alike, and we also conceive keyboards and guitars a lot alike. He had a list of things to be done when he was putting his album together, and I went in and listened to it – we were trying to figure out parts that I could play – and I felt that he was done. You lose perspective on a solo project, so I said, "Hey man, I think you're done – I think this list of eight things that could go on your record don't need to be there, and I think it's fine like it is", so that's my credit for saying "Stop". I've had some pretty interesting credits on various people's albums, besides even playing. The Bill Wyman record was another one that made me proud to play, because Bill's very wonderful and he's kind of a big brother. It's amazing to me that he's so normal and down to earth. His solo projects didn't really make it in terms of selling a lot of records and stuff, but I think it was really good music and I enjoyed doing it. I would much rather pull out an album like that, of really good playing, but not with a hit single in mind. After all, he can worry about the hit singles in his band – I don't think he particularly wanted to make an album with commercial potential in mind, he can do that in his day job, you know.'

Which finally brings us to the epic *Hotel California*, the extremely successful fifth album by the Eagles, and the first by the group with Joe Walsh as a member. No doubt it can be said that the end justified the means in this case, although the album took many months to complete, and presumably this was hardly what Walsh, whose previous LPs seemed to possess a certain spontaneity, would enjoy. Did he find making the album frustrating?

'It did take quite a while, but you have to realise that when I joined the Eagles and it was announced, I think probably 80 per cent of people said to themselves "That's stupid – how can that work? That's just downright silly and there's no way it's going to work." Before the album was released and I was in the band, there was no product out, and they had replaced a major creative force and we were all a little scared. Also, we were playing live concerts, so it wasn't like we took six months and went in to work on the album – we worked in the studio for a period of time, then we'd have to go out and play some concerts to make some money. So it did take a long time, but that to me was the essence of a band, and the magic. When *Hotel California* was done and we delivered it and it came out, I don't think anybody in the band had any idea that it would receive the recognition that it did. We were all so into it and we'd been working on it for such a long time that we weren't quite sure what was on tape, although we did know we were proud of it, and two years later, without a big head or without coming from a position of ego, it really was a kind of landmark project, but it was perfect chemistry, and that's the essence of a band situation.'

The two tracks on *Hotel California* which particularly featured Joe, and which he also co-wrote, are 'Life In The Fast Lane', a showcase for Joe's guitar, and 'Pretty Maids All In A Row', which he sings. The former song seems to in many ways reflect Walsh's penchant for comment on the often unreal lifestyle adopted by many residents of Los Angeles, and may even be the first of his songs to take this stance. 'I'm not really sure – I'd have to go through my record collection about statements on lifestyles – but "Life In The Fast Lane" kind of expressed the stereotyped LA "run around in your Porsche" 24 hour boogie mode that unfortunately is too true for a lot of people. It wasn't really a statement about the guys in the band, or about anybody in particular – just it's kind of disturbing to see the extremes that the bourgeois jet set will involve themselves in. For instance, disco almost turned into a lifestyle, and it's such a non-meaningful thing on which to base one's life.'

Several British rock critics would say that some of Walsh's colleagues may have been very symptomatic of the syndrome explored in the song.

'Yeah, that's probably true, and I think it was healthy, though, that we realised that running around and parties and fast cars are really not the answer – it's kind of a shallow way to approach why we're on this planet, and it probably came as a band consciousness.'

'Pretty Maids All In A Row,' by contrast, is gentler, and features Joe on piano and synthesiser rather than guitar, and seems not to be very typical of the Eagles, who were expected to perform songs reflecting the 'cosmic cowboy' influence. 'To make the Eagles really valid as a band, it was important that we co-write things and share things. "Pretty Maids" is kind of a melancholy reflection on my life so far, and I think we tried to represent it as a statement that would be valid for people from our generation on life so far. Heroes, they come and go . . . Henley and Frey really thought that it was a good song, and meaningful, and helped me a lot in putting it together. I think the best thing to say is that it's a kind of melancholy observation on life that we hoped would be a valid statement for people from our generation.'

Arguably the most impressive concerts which Joe Walsh has performed before a British audience were those which comprised the spring 1977 tour by the Eagles – no one present at Wembley could possibly forget the sound and spectacle of a vast string section being revealed from behind a curtain at the rear of the stage, and providing a sublime backing to 'Take It To The Limit.' *Hotel California* was certainly a successful album, but could it have been so profitable as to allow every city around the world to be similarly devastated?

'No, that was unfortunately too hard to do everywhere. We did it in Los Angeles, New York and London, and it was quite an experience – I got goosebumps just being on stage being a part of it. It was fairly overwhelming . . . I played 12-string guitar and sang background on it, but that was a special song, and that experience is really a fond memory, something I'll have for a long time. I would turn around and look at forty strings behind us and just forget what I was doing! It was really fun.'

Alone of the members of the Eagles, Walsh continued to pursue a solo recording career, albeit a fairly sporadic one. Was it a question of wishing to preserve an individual identity, or a kind of insurance, or was it a question of the other Eagles keeping quietly active between group projects but preferring not to rock the collective boat by releasing unilateral albums? 'Well, I can't say I had it in mind to pursue a solo career – I wasn't able to deliver what I was required to deliver in terms of solo recordings, which is an album every year, and a tour, then another album and another tour. I'm just not that fast – I suppose I could sell out and write a bunch of baloney and maintain that pace . . . I feel lucky that I have the option to go out with my own band or do a solo album, but that's really the way I am, and I don't think I need to apologise for it, and I think the guys in the Eagles knew that when I joined.'

In fact, Walsh's next solo LP, *But Seriously Folks*, released in 1978, was very successful, not least because it contained a substantial hit single in this autobiographical and wryly amusing 'Life's Been Good'. 'I wanted to make a statement involving satire and humour, kind of poking fun at the incredibly silly lifestyle that someone in my position is faced with – in other words, I do have a really nice house, but I'm on the road so much that when I come home from a tour, it's really hard to feel that I even live here. It's not necessarily me, I think it paraphrases anyone in my position, and I think that's why a lot of people related to it, but basically, that's the story of any rock star – I say that humbly – anyone in my position. I thought that was a valid statement,

because it is a strange lifestyle – I've been around the world in concerts, and people say ''What was Japan like?'', but I don't know. It's got a nice airport, you know . . . so it was kind of an overall statement.'

Another fascinating aspect of *But Seriously Folks* was its sleeve photograph, showing Joe eating a meal . . . under water. 'I had to do that a couple of times, but I did go down to the bottom of the pool, and almost drowned . . . but it was fun. Not at the time, but it was fun to do. We weighted everything down, but it was very involved and it took a long time, and I was real proud of it. As long as you have access to art, or visually presenting something with your record, I would like to use that, pursue it and try to make it an integral part of the music. It was hard to do, but when I look at it, I can't believe it either, I can't believe I was stupid enough to do that, but I was proud of it. I won't be repeating it, I can assure you!'

The next move for Walsh, and a very major one it became, was in his Eagles' guise, creating a follow-up LP to the monumentally successful *Hotel California*. *The Long Run* was released nearly three years after *Hotel California*, and was even more of a problem to complete. 'It's hard to explain. I think we felt a burden in that *Hotel California* had really gained

What's so weird about eating at the bottom of a swimming pool?

public acceptance beyond our wildest dreams, and we felt a burden in terms of how we could top it. That was a non-musical thing that kind of interfered for the first couple of months of working on *The Long Run* and I think we got a little hung up in that, and that slowed the process down a bit. At some point, we realised that we didn't particularly have to top it, or at least that that wasn't on the list of priorities, and if we could go in and make a good Eagles album, that was really all we needed to do. We were slow getting started, but I think that *The Long Run* is a really valid statement.'

One track included on the album, 'In The City', also appeared as part of the soundtrack to a New York street gang movie, *The Warriors*. The Eagles seemed one of the least appropriate choices to play music for a very urban film . . . 'That came out of having spent about three years of my life in New York City. *The Warriors* was made about gang-type city situations, and I related to that, having grown up in New York City, so again it was a positive statement to go against the desperation of miles and miles of concrete and growing up in a city – that really can affect you, and we thought it was a valid thing to put on *The Long Run,* and so we chose to do it.'

Another item from *The Long Run*, 'Those Shoes', features Joe playing the talkbox, the guitar attachment which allows an amplified guitar sound to be altered by diverting it into the player's mouth via a plastic tube, the effect being of an electronic voice. Jeff Beck, another of our subjects in this volume, also at one time used this device, although it has been mentioned by those who have used it frequently that too frequent use has a disturbing tendency to loosen the teeth of the player.

'Well, that depends. There's a country singer from Nashville named Dottie West who's a longtime friend of mine, and her husband is a pedal steel guitar player named Bill West, who actually came up with the concept of the talkbox, but never really got the credit for it. There was a record which I think was called "Forever" by Pete Drake in the late '50s, and they used it on that and various people used it. I met Bill and Dottie in Nashville, and Bill showed me this talkbox and gave me a prototype that he had, which I used for "Rocky Mountain Way", and Don Felder and I pursued that in the Eagles and worked out some double guitar parts, and it turned into a song, which was "Those Shoes", and that's actually both of us playing through talkboxes, which hadn't really been done. It's an old idea, but that was a new innovation.' Joe's teeth, by the way, show no sign of rattling out of context . . .

At the time of writing, the most recent Eagles LP has been a live double with the highly imaginative title of *Eagles Live,* which attracted a certain amount of critical flak, firstly because it seemed like a filler, released as a last resort since life might have been too short to await the completion of another album like *The Long Run,* a view to some extent reinforced by the fact that some of the tracks were four years old by the time the record was released, and secondly because the album was so musically perfect that it was widely assumed that a major part of the recordings were the result of subsequent studio overdubbing sessions.

'Well, it might have seemed like a filler, but the only real thing I can say is that I think it's very valid, because I think the Eagles are a very good band live. I know we're kind of into mega-production at this point, but that's not really our fault and – to my knowledge, no one's gone away from a live Eagles concert disappointed, so it's part of a phase, but I think it's valid to represent the way the band played live, as opposed to all the precision and attention to technical things in studio albums. There really weren't many overdubs, just a few patch ups, a few things that were re-done in the studio, honestly because there was feedback or one or two mikes hadn't been plugged in right, or there was a terrible hum. Really honestly, that is the essence of an Eagles' performance live, and any tinkering with it in the studio, which was really very minor, was based on things which were not representative because of technical problems. I think it's a good representation of the way we are live, and I feel good because I hope that we pointed out that we're not solely a studio band, and that we can represent our efforts live onstage.'

An intriguing potential future project in which Joe has expressed an interest was once described as 'a remake of *Fantasia*, the Walt Disney cartoon classic, although apparently Walsh himself sees it in slightly different terms. 'I would love to get involved with movies – there's a trend right now, I think, with the movie industry starting to realise that music is an important part of movies, where before, they didn't really care. One of my pet projects for the future is to be involved with a movie where the music is as important as what you see. *Fantasia* has been mentioned because nobody since then has combined what you see and what you hear so overwhelmingly. I don't know whether my project would be animated or not – I've been involved with a few movies in a minor role, but the frustration is that musically it's very hard at this point to have any quality control over the overall presentation. I would very much like to do a soundtrack and come up with the music during the process of filming the movie, instead of watching it and trying to think up 32.7 seconds of music to go between this scene and that scene.'

Another film idea which has been mooted was a cinematic version of the Eagles classic second LP, *Desperado.*' 'I don't feel that I can make a precise statement about that. It's been in the works for a long time – at this point, it's almost so old and so in the past in terms of the Eagles that it may be obsolete. Probably a good true Western where the good guy doesn't necessarily win, truthfully showing that period in America, might be justified in a film, but I don't think the Eagles want to pursue that unless it can be presented well and presented truthfully: and the good guy very seldom won. I don't know – that's really still up in the air, and really you should ask the other guys in the Eagles about that.'

When this interview took place, Joe had just completed work on a new solo LP, once again opting for an unlikely title, *There Goes The Neighborhood.* 'When you see the cover and hear the songs, it'll make sense.'

Presumably making a solo album involves a different process from writing a song for the Eagles to

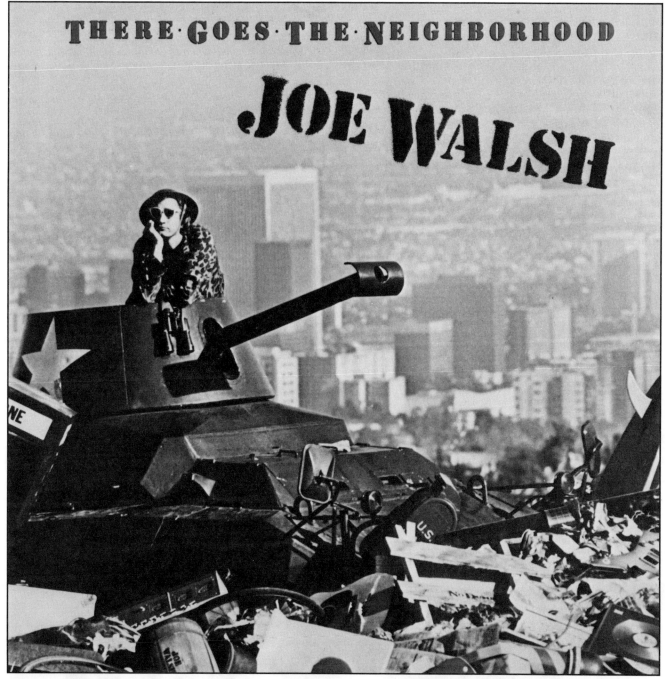

THERE·GOES·THE·NEIGHBORHOOD
JOE WALSH

Sleeve of the 1981 solo LP

record? 'A lot of my ideas are presented to the guys in the Eagles, and a lot of them are used, but a lot of them aren't. Basically, me releasing a solo album does not infer that I have chose to pursue my solo career – I just feel that I have a group of songs that are new and that are an organised statement of where I'm at right now, and it's a little outlet for me, and I think it's time to put out another solo record. That doesn't mean that I've left the Eagles or that we've broken up or anything. I've got Joe Vitale on the record, who was in Barnstorm, and was also involved with the bunch of Eagles' dates in the States, a bass player named Chocolate (Perry) from Miami, and Jay Ferguson and myself. That's the foundation for what I've been doing.'

It sounded like a very basic uncluttered sort of line up ... Did Joe feel he wanted to do that after the lush sound of the Eagles, and make a 'New Wave' record? 'That's a hard question, and I'm not really sure what category it is, although I'm sure that it's new songs, and it indicates that I'm progressing musically, and possibly maturing, although I'm not sure about that. It's a group of songs that really represent where I'm at right now, and I really think it's some of the best songs that I've written, and some of the best words, and I think it's presented well, and I think I'm singing better than I ever have, thanks to a couple of years of vocal coaching from Henley and Frey. I'm real proud of it. There's a track called "Things", and I heard the music before the words: I couldn't quite think what to write the song about, so I made a list of things that there were possibly to write a song about, and I ended up with a list about ten pages long, so I thought I should write this song about all the things there are – did you ever stop and think of how many things there are? So that turned into a song, and it's a little overwhelming to hear the first time, but if you listen to it three or four times, I think I covered most of the things there are. And there's another song on the album called ''You Never Know'' – I've spoken a lot about various non-musical things, and hype, and it's kind of funny how people will make something out of your songs, or your music, or you, that really isn't there, and ''You Never Know'' is about word of mouth, gossip, backroom whispering. Non-musical things which I don't particularly endorse.'

In fact, the name of Jay Ferguson is conspicuous by its absence on the album, and its fate in Britain and Europe can hardly have been helped by the fact that Joe was unable to tour on this side of the Atlantic due, apparently, to economic restrictions. He also predicted, most accurately, that the Eagles would be inactive for some time. 'We're going to take a period of time off and relax – we really worked hard in 1980, and I think we're going to try to reflect, meditate, and think about things that are important. We're five pretty dominant guys, and we don't want to keep going for anything more than purely musical reasons, and I think we've worked hard and earned and deserve a period of time off for each of us to get into side projects, and take a big look around, but at

some point, we'll get back together and there will definitely be more from the Eagles, but for the moment, I think it's going to be research, relax, think, search and destroy atmosphere, and I think that's very healthy at this point. Various people are going to try various things – we're going to get together in groups of twos and threes to write. I think Glenn would really like to do a solo album, and I think he should, and Don Henley is very interested in movies and screenplays – we'll just see. I don't think there'll be too much from the Eagles for a while, but we've definitely not broken up, and we'll be back – you'll know.'

A very positive way to end an interview, certainly ... regrettably, the ensuing months have carried rumours of apparently unbridgable rifts developing between the members of the group, although solo albums by various members are scheduled for summer 1982 release. It would be rather tragic if a group who have produced as much good music as the Eagles were to splinter acrimoniously, although disagreements are obviously inevitable. However, Joe Walsh will continue to make music for many years to come, whether in or out of the group, and his fans will be able to look forward to much more of his unique vision and masterly musicianship in years to come.

Joe Walsh Discography

With the James Gang
1969 *Yer Album*
1970 *James Gang Rides Again*
1971 *Thirds*
1971 *Live In Concert*
1973 *The Best Of The James Gang featuring Joe Walsh*

Solo Albums
1972 *Barnstorm*
1973 *The Smoker You Drink, The Player You Get*
1974 *So What*
1976 *You Can't Argue With A Sick Mind*
1978 *But Seriously Folks . . .*
1978 *So Far – So Good*
1981 *There Goes The Neighborhood*

With the Eagles
1976 *Hotel California*
1979 *The Long Run*
1980 *Eagles Live*
1982 *Greatest Hits Volume Two*

Sessions
1970 B.B. King
Indianola Mississippi Seeds

1971(?) Hedge & Donna
Evolution

1972 B.B. King
L.A. Midnight

1973 Rick Derringer
All American Boy

1973 Manassas
Down The Road

1973 Rick Roberts
She Is A Song

1973 Michael Stanley
Rosewood Bitters

1973 Michael Stanley
Friends & Legends

1973 Fabulous Rhinestones
Freewheelin'

1974 Ray Manzarek
The Whole Thing Started with Rock 'n' Roll . . .

1974 Joe Vitale
Roller Coaster Weekend

1974 Dan Fogelberg
Souvenirs

1974 Billy Preston
The Kids And Me

1975 Al Kooper
Act Like Nothing's Wrong

1975 Keith Moon
Two Sides Of The Moon

1976 J. D. Souther
Black Rose

1976 Rod Stewart
A Night On The Town

1976 Bill Wyman
A Stone Alone

1976 Fools Gold
Fools Gold

1977 Jay Ferguson
Thunder Island

1977 Emerson, Lake & Palmer
Works Vol. 1

1977 Dan Fogelberg
Netherlands

1977 Randy Newman
Little Criminals

1979 Graham Nash
Earth & Sky

1980 Andy Gibb
Greatest Hits

1980 Warren Zevon
Bad Luck Streak In Dancing School

1981 Joe Vitale
Plantation Harbor

1981 John Entwistle
Too Late The Hero

Joe Walsh also appears on the film soundtrack albums *The Warriors* (1979) and *Urban Cowboy* (1980)

BRIAN MAY

At the start of the 1980s, the rock band which was generally accepted, if not as the most popular group in the world, then as one of the top half dozen, was Queen. The conventional record markets were comprehensively conquered at the end of the previous decade, while the group had effectively opened the door for rock music in South America – at one point, Queen were not only top of the charts in Argentina, but allegedly occupied the top ten positions in the hit parade. To single out one member of the quartet as particularly responsible for this remarkable popularity would be invidious – vocalist Freddie Mercury is the obvious focal point, but the musical heart of the band is undoubtedly Brian May, certainly one of the most innovative British guitar players of the rock era, and equally important in view of the stance of many of his peers, a modest, unassuming and immensely likable person, from whom many could learn. .

Brian was born in Twickenham, Middlesex, on 19 July 1947. His father was an electronics engineer working on secret military projects for the Ministry of Defence, and this interest communicated itself to Brian, who nevertheless claims to lack his father's instinctive abilities relating to electronics, although he will admit to being well versed in the theory of the subject. More to the point, Brian's father was and is interested in music, and 'a pretty good pianist. He taught me to play ukelele-banjo in the style of George Formby – it's a pretty good instrument that's tuned the same way as a ukelele, but has the same sort of sound vellum as a banjo, and from the chords I learnt on that, I taught myself the guitar.'

Brian acquired his first guitar at around the age of seven. 'It was a very cheap acoustic Spanish type guitar with steel strings, and was much too big for me when I got it. I can remember being dwarfed by this thing, getting it in bed on my birthday morning, and I thought it was very shiny and new and exciting. The strings were a long way off the fingerboard, and I thought for a long time about whether I should try to modify it, to make it easier to play, because I thought I might ruin it, but eventually, I did carve down the bridge, and later, I put a pick-up on it, which my father and I made out of some button magnets with a coil wound round – it worked as well! We plugged it into a radio, into the auxiliary input, and it sounded pretty good, with a very sharp, penetrating clear sound, which I can't really get now.

'I found it quite easy to pick up playing the guitar –

Brian May, 1982

I was taking piano lessons at the time, which I never really enjoyed, because it was a chore to do the requisite half hour piano practice, and I always ended up banging the piano and swearing and walking away in disgust, whereas I always went to the guitar for pleasure, which is why, I suppose, my guitar playing progressed faster.' And his early influences? "Lonnie Donegan, Tommy Steele, and the guy who played on the Rick Nelson records, James Burton. Soon after that, the Shadows came along, and they were a big influence, although I was always a bit snobby, like all the people at my school – we thought that somehow the Shadows were beneath us, because we could play better or faster or something, which was definitely a mistaken opinion. I was very keen on the Ventures, probably partly because of the American mystique – the Ventures were cool, but the Shadows weren't – but now I think Hank Marvin had the edge, although some of those Ventures things were very good, and very hard to play.'

One of the legendary items for which Brian is famed is that during his teenage years, and with the help of his father, he built his own guitar. 'We didn't really have the money to buy a proper guitar, and my school friends had things like Hofner Futuramas or Coloramas, and later a couple had Gibsons, which we couldn't afford, so we decided to make one. I'd played other people's, so I knew roughly what I

The famous guitar

wanted, and I had some theories about what sort of properties it should have – I wanted a cambered fingerboard which was very close and fast, and I wanted three pick-ups, and to be able to vary the combinations of the pick-ups, which I felt was very limited on the guitars that I'd tried, where you either had them all on or all off, and that was about it. I think I'd just seen Jeff Beck at the time I was building it, so I wanted to be able to make it feed back like he did, because I was amazed at all this violin sound stuff, which I thought was obviously going to be the direction in which guitar playing was going – I thought if you could get a really good sustain which was foolproof, didn't just come out now and again, and was actually controllable, you'd almost have a new instrument, something really like a violin, where you can put some expression into the notes. So I had this idea of putting acoustic pockets into the guitar, because I realised it had to feed back through the body of the guitar and the strings, rather than through the pick-ups, which gives a microphone whistle effect – most of the guitars I'd played would just whistle if you held them near the amplifiers. I also wanted a good tremolo, which returned to its zero position, and didn't go flat once you'd pushed it down a couple of times, so we had to find a tremolo design which didn't have much friction in it – my dad and I did lots of tests with a sort of mock up, a piece of wood with some strings stretched over it, to see what sort of strains were involved. We were very scientific about it, and measured the stresses of the strings – and we designed one tremolo, a sort of cylinder device, which didn't work very well, because here was too much friction, so we ditched that, and went with the knife edge design, which I don't think had been done at that time, although there are some designs like that now. So we had an actual knife edge, which was a mild steel plate with a little "V" groove in it, and into the groove fits a plate which has a point, and the plate which holds the strings can rock backwards and forwards. We did the thing properly and case-hardened the ridge so that it would almost never wear out, which it actually never has, although I've used it constantly for the last ten years.

'It's very hard for most people to play, but as I grew up with it, I find it easy, and in fact, it's the only thing I can play properly, and I'm still using it. The neck was actually part of a fireplace which was just lying around in a friend's house, and the friend was a woodworking man – it was a lovely piece of mahogany with dead straight grain, which had probably been lying in his house for fifty years, and he said he got it from his father.'

Brian's early life was spent in the suburb of Feltham, not far from London Airport, and whether coincidentally or otherwise, the schools he attended had also educated several other notable musicians – Jimmy Page, Brian learnt, had attended the same infant's school in Feltham, while two of the Yardbirds, Jim McCarty and Paul Samwell-Smith, went to Brian's secondary school, Hampton Grammar School, which as a result became a fairly well-known nursery for rock musicians including Brian's own first group. Additionally, although neither of them knew it at the time, Freddie Mercury lived only a few hundred yards away . . . 'I didn't know – obviously, we went to different schools, and I didn't know who he was until we were at college and he was friendly with Tim Staffell, who went to the same art college as Freddie, in Ealing'. Staffell, in fact, was also a member of Brian's first group, 1984.

'1984 was purely an amateur band, formed at school, although perhaps at the end we once got fifteen quid or something. We never really played anything significant in the way of original material – it was a strange mixture of cover versions, some pop, Everly Brothers, Buddy Holly & the Crickets, some James Brown, "Knock On Wood" by Eddie Floyd, all the things which people wanted to hear at the time. This was about the time that the Stones were emerging, and later on we did Stones and Yardbirds things. . . I was in the band for a couple of years, although it wasn't very serious – we did a few dances and things, but I was never happy about it. I left because I wanted to do something where we wrote our own material. I just thought that was necessary to progress, and that was the time I met Roger (Taylor, drummer with Queen). I advertised on a notice board at college for a drummer, because by this time, Cream and Jimi Hendrix were around, and I wanted a drummer who could handle that sort of stuff, and Roger was easily capable of it. Tim Staffell, who had been in 1984, was our singer, and we formed this group called Smile, which was semi-pro – we travelled around the country a fair bit, as far as Cornwall, and Liverpool, and although we did well in some places, we never felt we were getting anywhere, because if you don't have a record out, people tend to forget who you are very quickly, even if they like you on the night. We tried for a long time, and wrote a lot of material, a little of which was carried over into Queen, and we also did a lot of improvising. We did get a record contract – we got very big time, thinking that was it, and we signed with Mercury Records of England, who were just setting up, headed by Lou Reisner, as an English branch of American Mercury, and we recorded about half-a-dozen tracks for them, but they didn't release any of them in Britain. They did put out a single in America, but it didn't do anything. It was a very bad experience, and we also had a bad management experience as well at that time, and it was all very disillusioning.'

It was also at this time that Brian first came across Freddie Mercury. 'He was a friend of Tim's and came along to a lot of our gigs, and offered suggestions in a way that couldn't be refused! Like "Why are you wasting your time doing this and that? You should do more original material, and be more demonstrative in the way you put your music across. It takes more than that, and you should put it across with more force – if I was your singer, that's what I'd be doing." At that time, he hadn't really done any singing, and we didn't know he could – we thought he was just a theoretical rock musician. He was a big Hendrix fan, and he played me all these little bits of Hendrix that weren't obviously audible – he was really a fanatic.'

At Imperial College in London Brian studied for an Honours Degree. 'It was about 50 per cent mathematics, with a little bit of electronics and a lot of pure physics. I intended to be an astronomer, and I attended the infra-red astronomy department of Imperial, although I didn't actually do infra-red astronomy – what I did was optical interferometry, looking at dust in the solar system. I did that for four years with the idea of getting a Ph.D., but I never finished writing it up – I was about two pages away from finishing, but I never got the final conclusions done, although we did publish two papers with the results and a brief interpretation of them, but there was going to be a third paper which unfortunately never got done. It all got beyond me, and I ran out of money in the fourth year, because the grant only lasted for three years, so I decided to teach in the daytime to make the money to support myself and be able to keep on processing the results. I did that for a while, and worked at night doing the calculations for the results, but that got way too much – anyone who's taught knows that teaching's a full time job. I taught at a comprehensive in Stockwell, and I found that I had to prepare for an hour or more each night to keep on top, and I just became tired, so something had to go, and also at that time was the beginnings of Queen. We were rehearsing, considering whether we'd go into it full time, and around the time we were offered the chance to sign a contract, I decided to forget the academic side at least for a while to see if Queen could become a proper group.'

After the inevitable finish of Smile, whose sole single coupled 'Earth' with 'Step On Me', came the eventual transition from that group into Queen. 'Smile completely broke up, and we gave up, and I think we all thought that we wouldn't try again after that, but Tim was the first to get back into music, and went off with a group run by a folk singer named Jonathan Kelly, who was trying to get into more rock-oriented material.'

With the departure of Staffell, Queen began to take shape, its initial members apart from Brian being drummer Roger Taylor and Freddie Mercury. 'Freddie was the driving force for getting us back together – he told us we could do it, and said he didn't want to play useless gigs where no one listened, and that we would have to rehearse and get a stage act together – he was very keen for it to be an actual act – and we started again, taking a couple of songs from Smile and a couple of songs from groups he'd been in, like a band called Wreckage from which we stole bits that went into "Liar" and a couple of other songs, and we set about it in a serious manner. We'd rehearse three or four nights a week in places like lecture theatres, and we managed to scrape together some equipment.'

Despite a level of musical expertise and originality which, in retrospect, was plainly evident, Queen did not enjoy the smoothest of rides in Britain at the genesis of their career, largely due to their choice of name – at a time when glitter rock was in vogue, the name 'Queen' seemed rather too obviously an attempt to cash in on someone else's fame. . .

'I think the name mainly came from Freddie, and I don't think I was too keen on it at the beginning – you toss around hundreds of names, and of all of them, that was the one that stuck, and in a way, the one which got the most argument. I'm not sure that Roger was that keen to begin with, either, but we felt it seemed to stick in the mind, and had a certain mystique and grandeur about it which we thought might catch people's imagination, so that was the one we kept.'

It will not have escaped the attention of those familiar with Queen's work that thus far, only three names have been mentioned as members of Queen. 'We did have a bass player, and we went through a few of them, but either the personality or the musical ability didn't fit, and it was a while before we found John, through some friends.' The first Queen LP refers to John Deacon as 'Deacon John' – what's that about? 'We used to call him that, and it appeared like that on the album, but after that, he objected to it, and said he wanted to be called John Deacon. I don't really know why we called him Deacon John in the first place – just one of those silly things.'

A discussion of Brian's guitar influences at the time of Queen's formation revealed some familiar names – Eric Clapton, Jeff Beck and Jimi Hendrix. 'When Hendrix came along, it just seemed to be such a great opening of the doors – he seemed to push it along so fast in such a short time. When I first heard ''Stone Free'', which was the B-side of ''Hey Joe'', there was this solo I couldn't believe, and as a guitarist, I've a reluctance to admit another guitarist's as good as he is but there's still nobody who can approach him for inventiveness, technique, pure sound and style and everything.'

One unique feature of Brian May's technique is the fact that he plays not with any kind of conventional

plectrum but with a coin, in fact a pre-decimalisation sixpence, of which he has a large supply. 'It's not crucial, because I can play with a new penny, or an American dime. I use coins because they're not flexible – I think you get more control if all the flexing is due to the movement in your fingers. You get better contact with the strings, and depending on how tightly you hold it, you have total control over how hard it's being played, and because of its round surface and the serration, by turning it different ways you can get different sounds, like a fairly soft sound, or a slightly grating sound on the beginning of the note which actually lends a bit of distinction to the notes, especially when you're using the guitar at high volume, as I generally do. Otherwise, the sounds tends to be very level and smoothed out.'

Queen's early days were, perhaps predictably, nondescript in terms of progress until they were invited to 'test' a new studio which had just been completed. 'I did have one real contact, a guy called Terry who was working at the time for Pye Studios, but was moving to the new DeLane Lea studios, and he said they needed people in there to make some noise, because they were testing the separation between the three studios, and the reverberation times, and they wanted a group to do it and Roy Thomas Baker came to DeLane Lea, completely by accident, as far as I know, and said that he liked what we were doing very much, and I think it was through him recommending us to Trident that they finally gave us a contract.'

The first Queen LP was made over a lengthy period at times when the recording studios owned by Trident were not booked by paying customers, which is not an ideal way for any band to make their first album – Brian confirmed that the group were less than happy about this arrangement, but added that since it was in the past, he felt it inappropriate to elaborate further on the subject.

At least a part of Queen had appeared on record shortly before any Queen product was released, in the shape of a single, 'I Can Hear Music'/'Goin' Back', credited to one Larry Lurex. 'As I said, the album took ages and ages – two years in total, in the preparation, making and then trying to get the thing released – and meanwhile, Robin Cable, who we also knew in Trident Studios, was doing this thing which was a re-creation of the Phil Spector sound, and he was very keen for Freddie to be the vocalist. Once Freddie was in there, he suggested that it should have some of my guitar work in this instrumental space they'd left blank, after they'd tried to do it with synthesisers, but it didn't seem to be working out too well, so I did a solo, although I didn't play the acoustic guitars which are crashing through it, and they also used Roger to do some percussion overdubs, like the maraccas and tambourines, which is a part of the Phil Spector sound. I like that quite a lot, and I thought it was a good piece of work, and it was done before we'd finished our own LP, so it was put out under the name of Larry Lurex, which was a joke, but which unfortunately backfired, because a lot of people took exception to the fact that we seemed to be taking the mickey out of Gary Glitter, so a lot of people refused to play it because of that.'

Just one dime, one thin dime . . .

Even when the first Queen LP was finally completed, it was not immediately released. 'After that, Trident had to go around all the record companies again to see what offers they could get for us, but unfortunately, they were selling us as part of a package of their production, which also included Eugene Wallace and Mark Ashton, and they wanted the package accepted as a whole. But suddenly, there was a move from EMI – Roy Featherstone sent us a telegram which asked us not to sign with anyone else until we'd talked to him, and he was very keen and he got us, and I think, in the end, he did sign the whole package of Mark Ashton and everything. But it had taken an awfully long time, partially because Trident had to do all the negotiations, as our hands were tied, and we actually put on the sleeve of the album that this was the result of three years work, because we were upset and felt that the record was old-fashioned by the time it came out. Lots of stuff had happened in the meantime particularly David Bowie and Roxy Music, who were our sort of generation, but who had already made it, and we felt that it would look like we were jumping on their bandwagon, whereas we'd actually had all that stuff in the can from a very long time before, and it was extremely frustrating.'

In America, the story was a little different, as neither Bowie nor Roxy Music were as immediately successful as they had been in Britain. 'We got a lot of FM radio play, and a lot of backing for that first album from people who played four or five tracks of it to death, and that gave us a really good grounding in America. We didn't tour in America, which was a shame, but we were just too busy doing other things at the time, and it's very much to the credit of Jack Nelson, who was brought in from America to manage us on Trident's behalf, and knew the American scene, that we toured America immediately after making our second album, supporting Mott the Hoople, and that was really one of the best things we ever did, and that was due to Jack.'

Another item of interest on Queen's debut LP was a note on the sleeve proclaiming 'No synthesisers', which was echoed on each new Queen album for several years. 'The guitars were making some sounds which people might have thought were synthesisers – I was using pedals and the long sustain stuff; and harmony guitars in the background – and we did some John Peel sessions for the BBC, and a lot of people thought we used synthesisers, so we wanted to make sure people knew it was all guitars and voices, and that stuck with us for a long time. I think that for the first nine albums we made, there was never a synthesiser and never an orchestra, never any other player except us on the records.'

Queen, mid-1970s – left to right: Brian May, John Deacon, Roger Taylor, Freddie Mercury

Relaxing royalty – left to right:
John Deacon, Freddie Mercury, Roger Taylor, Brian May

While 'Keep Yourself Alive' was the outstanding track for most on the first Queen LP, 'My Fairy King' seems to have been a foretaste of what would become one of the group's best known hits, 'Bohemian Rhapsody'. 'Yes, I think that was the first step in that direction, the first time we'd really seen Freddie working at his full capacity. He's virtually a self-taught pianist, and he was making vast strides at the time, although we didn't have a piano on stage at that point, because it would have been impossible to fix up, and we didn't want an organ sound. So in the studio was the first chance Freddie had to do his piano things, and we actually got that sound of the piano and guitar working for the first time, which was very exciting, and "My Fairy King" was the first of those sort of epics where there were lots of voice overdubs and harmonies, and a quite complicated structure, which Freddie got into, and that led to "The March Of The Black Queen" on the second album which is very much in that idiom, and then "Bohemian Rhapsody" later on.'

1974 saw the second Queen LP, *Queen II*, released, which saw the first British breakthrough for the group. The track from that album which seems to most bear Brian May's mark is 'Father To Son', which seems in retrospect to betray elements of both the Who and Led Zeppelin. 'They're probably in there somewhere, because they were among our favourite groups, but what we were trying to do differently from either of those groups was this sort of layered sound. The Who had the open chord guitar sound, and there's a bit of that in "Father To Son",

but our sound is more based around the overdriven guitar sound, which is used for the main bulk of the song, but I also wanted to do this business of building up textures behind the main melody lines. To me, *Queen II* was the sort of emotional music we'd always wanted to be able to play, although we couldn't play most of it onstage because it was too complicated, and so it was our first expedition into pure studio music. We were trying to push studio techniques to a new limit for rock groups, and we wore the tape literally to the point where you could see through it because we were doing so many overdubs. We were building up fifty piece choir type effects and loads of guitars to get this thick orchestra sound, and in a way, it was going over the top – it was fulfilling all our dreams, because we didn't have much opportunity for that on the first album, being stuck in at odd hours, and virtually reproducing what we could do on stage at that time, so the second album was an adventure into the world of what can be done and hasn't been done before, and in that sense it was over the top. We thought of it as almost baroque in some of the things we were doing, and in fact it went through our minds to call the album *Over The Top*.'

While he is best known as a guitarist, Brian is also a notable songwriter, and it seemed appropriate to enquire about the lyrical inspiration of 'Father To Son'. . . 'That was sort of a vision of things growing with the passage of time, not by overthrowing what's gone before, but by building on it – evolution as opposed to revolution, which is something I still believe in. So that was my little statement, although I don't know how much people actually get into lyrics.'

The track from *Queen II* which first attracted attention in Britain was 'Seven Seas Of Rhye', which had also been included, in a very short version, on the first album. Roy Thomas Baker, who produced both the first two Queen albums, had suggested that 'Seven Seas. . .' was no better than 'Keep Yourself Alive', but had become a hit because it was featured on *Top Of The Pops*, whereas the earlier single had been less fortunate.

'The first version was just a little trailer, because the song wasn't actually finished then – the shape of things which might come, although it was very plain on the first album, with no vocals or orchestration. As to the *Top Of The Pops* thing, there's probably a lot of truth in that. And on "Seven Seas Of Rhye" – the whole world happens in the first twenty seconds, and you've almost heard the whole song in that time. Great big swooping things, then the vocal launches straight in . . . maybe that had something to do with it, and it was a good, catchy record, but we were hot at the time, and that obviously helped.'

Shortly after embarking on the American tour on which Queen supported Mott the Hoople, Brian was struck down with a serious case of hepatitis. 'I really felt bad at having let the group down at such an important place, but there was nothing I could do about it. It was hepatitis, which I think you get sometimes when you're emotionally run down. And almost immediately after that, we were due to start recording the next album, *Sheer Heart Attack,* and I couldn't do much at the start. I seemed to recover, but then got ill again, and eventually, I couldn't eat anything and I was being sick all the time, which was sheer misery. They discovered that I'd had this ulcer business for fifteen years on and off, which had been aggravated by the hepatitis. So then I was stuck in hospital for a few weeks, and they did some stuff to me which was like a miracle, and it was like new life afterwards, because I thought I was dead. Being ill like that may even have been a good thing at the time, although it was pretty hellish going through it – I felt glad to be alive, and I became able to hold things in perspective more and not get so wound up and worried about them to make myself ill.

'With *Sheer Heart Attack*, it was very weird, because I was able to see the group from the outside, and was pretty excited by what I saw. We'd done a few things before I was ill, but when I came back, they'd done a load more, including a couple of backing tracks of songs by Freddie which I hadn't heard, like "Flick Of The Wrist", which excited me and gave me a lot of inspiration to get back in there and do what I wanted to do. I also managed to do some writing – "Now I'm Here" was done in that period, and came out quite easily, whereas I'd been wrestling with it before without getting anywhere. That song's sort of about experiences on the American tour, which really blew me away in more senses than one! I was bowled over, partly by the success we were having and partly by the amazing aura which surrounds rock music in America, which is hard to describe.'

Another notable song from *Sheer Heart Attack*

written by Brian is 'Brighton Rock'. 'I like to think that showed how my style was evolving, particularly with the solo bit in the middle, which I'd been doing on the Mott the Hoople tour and has gradually expanded ever since, although I keep trying to throw it out, but it keeps creeping back in. That involved using the repeat device in time with an original guitar phrase, which I don't think had been done before that time. It's a very nice device to work with, because you can build up harmonies or cross rhythms, but it's not a multiple repeat like Hendrix or even the Shadows used, which is fairly indiscriminate, although it makes a nice noise, but just a single repeat which comes back, or sometimes a second repeat as well, so you can plan or experiment to produce a fugue type effect.'

Roy Thomas Baker, who produced *Sheer Heart Attack,* has said that the album was designed to be more easily assimilable than its predecessor. 'Yes, that's probably true, although we weren't going for hits, because we always thought of ourselves as an album group, but we did think that perhaps we'd dished up a bit too much for people to swallow on *Queen II*.'

After the album was released, Queen embarked on their first trip to Japan which was a major occurrence. 'Oh yes, that was a big thing for us. Suddenly we were stars – we'd had some success in England and America, but we hadn't had adulation and been adored, and suddenly, in Japan, we were pop stars in the same way as the Beatles or the Bay City Rollers, with people screaming at us, which was a big novelty, and we loved it and had a great time. The only drawback was that we were a sort of teenybop attraction, but it was some years ago, and when we go back to Japan now, we're lucky enough to have made a smooth transition to having a pretty normal rock audience in Japan of older people of both sexes, rather than just the little girls screaming. But it was an inspirational experience, and I think it brought out the acting ability in us, and made us a bit more extrovert on stage.'

In the same period May received an offer from another group, Sparks, who were interested in his leaving Queen and joining them. 'They thought that because I was ill, Queen was breaking up, which wasn't really happening, although things were obviously a bit shaky at the time. I got on very well with Ron and Russell Mael, and I still see them occasionally, but despite the fact that I quite like their music, I didn't feel it would be quite right. I also felt a loyalty to Queen and thought that we'd get our strength back in the end.'

How does Brian feel his playing has developed during his years with the band? 'I don't think I've progressed that much technically in terms of pure playing, and I could play almost everything I can play now when I was about sixteen. I sometimes think that's a bad thing, but I see it in lots of other people as well, Jeff Beck and Eric Clapton. You fairly quickly reach a stage when you're practising very intensely and where you can express most of what you want to play, and after that, I think, you become better as an all-round musician and your taste improves, but I don't think your technical ability gets that much better and you reach a plateau.'

Queen, 1982

It must be, and has been, difficult for Queen to tour due to the enormous amount of amplification and lighting equipment they use on stage. 'Yes, even in the beginning when we couldn't afford a light show, we used projector lamps for lights, and we just got through somehow, getting someone to drive us, or borrowing a bigger van – it was scraping through all the way. It's still a big problem organising everything, but we're very lucky in having some great people working for us, notably Gerry Stickells, who was Hendrix's road manager throughout his career, and is an amazing person who I'd say was the best tour manager in the world, without any doubt. He's able to get it together in any circumstances and organise everything, even in South America, where you have no help because people don't understand what you're trying to do. We can go anywhere and know that when we walk on stage for the sound check, it'll all be working, which is a wonderful feeling of security. We also have other people working for us in different capacities, because we now manage ourselves and in the end everybody leaves the decision to us, but we have Jim Beach, who negotiates with record companies, agents, and merchandising people, and Paul Prenter, who runs our day to day operation. It's not a big operation – people tend to think of the vast Queen machine swinging into action, but we only have four or five people actually working for us, and we pick up the rest when we go on tour, although there are certain people who we rely on getting, like Trip Khalaf, who's our permanent sound mixer, and James Devenney, our permanent monitor mixer – that's so crucial, and I think one of the most difficult jobs in the world, because it's

equally important to have a good sound on stage as to get it good out front, and if either one's lacking, you do a bad show.'

Between *Sheer Heart Attack* and their next LP, *A Night At The Opera*, a basic change occurred in Queen's operations when they left Trident and started the organisation described above.

It was perhaps no coincidence that Queen's producer, Roy Thomas Baker, also left Trident during this period, and ironically followed Queen to their next manager, John Reid, who also manages Elton John. 'We went round and talked in person to a few managers, and it was quite an exciting time really, although depressing in some ways, because we felt very locked in. We thought if we could find someone who it was our idea to approach, then at least they'd be able to help us get out of our other situation, and we saw a lot of managers, all of whom had something useful to say, but John Reid seemed to be the only one we could all agree about – we liked his approach and the style of his operation, so we gave it to him, and told him to do the negotiating and get us out, and we'd go away to make the album. He did take the burden off our shoulders at that time, which was crucial, and allowed us to make that all important album.

'We later bought ourselves out of John Reid as well, but it was more out of a feeling that nothing was happening any more – it wasn't so much a conflict as a feeling that we weren't getting any further in the relationship, and the creative management thing wasn't there as much as it had been at the start. We obviously owe some of our success to both Trident and to John – Trident got us making records

Freddie Mercury (left) and Brian May on stage

and hits, for instance – but the whole John Reid time was a period when we made very big strides.'

A Night At The Opera was an extremely successful LP, perhaps largely due to the inclusion of the track which has become Queen's 'signature tune', the epic 'Bohemian Rhapsody'. 'That was really Freddie's baby from the beginning – he came in and knew exactly what he wanted. The backing track was done with just piano, bass and drums, with a few spaces for other things to go in, like the tic-tic-tic on the hi-hat to keep the time, and Freddie sang a guide vocal at the time, but he had all his harmonies written out, and it was really just a question of doing it. He even knew pretty much what he wanted in the way of guitar, although there's always a bit of freedom to do what I want on the guitar side, and I could do the solo as I wanted really, but it was very much Freddie's thing which was mapped out. It took a week just to do the vocals, and that was efficient working as well – we already had our methods well worked out, where the three of us would sing a line, then double or maybe treble track it. There were nine parts to some of those vocal pieces.'

Brian was responsible for writing no less than three standout tracks on the album, 'The Prophet's Song', 'Good Company' and ''39'. '''The Prophet's Song'' had been around for quite a long time, and I finished the lyrics off when we were making this album. I don't know exactly what inspired the words, because I don't pretend to have any supernatural vision of any kind – it was really just my feelings, and I had a dream about some of it, which I put into the song, but that's not my usual inspiration for song-writing. I'm not a very prolific writer, and I can never just sit down and write a song – there has to be something there, and usually, I get a couple of lines of lyrics and melody together, and then the rest of it's really working very hard, searching the soul, to see what should be in there, but then some of the stuff I've done without taking it too seriously, I've been more pleased with it in the end.

'With ''Good Company'', I indulged a little fetish of mine – all the things that sound like other instruments, like trumpets and clarinets, were done with guitar. To get the effect of the instruments, I was doing one note at a time with the pedal and building them up, so you can imagine how long it took. We experimented with mikes and various tiny amplifiers to get just the right sound, and I made a study of the kind of things those instruments could play to try to get that authentic flavour. It was a bit of fun, but a semi-serious piece of work because so much time went into it. '''39'' was different again, kind of a folky thing, close to skiffle, which probably comes from my Lonnie Donegan days. There was such a wide variety on those albums – Fred doing a really

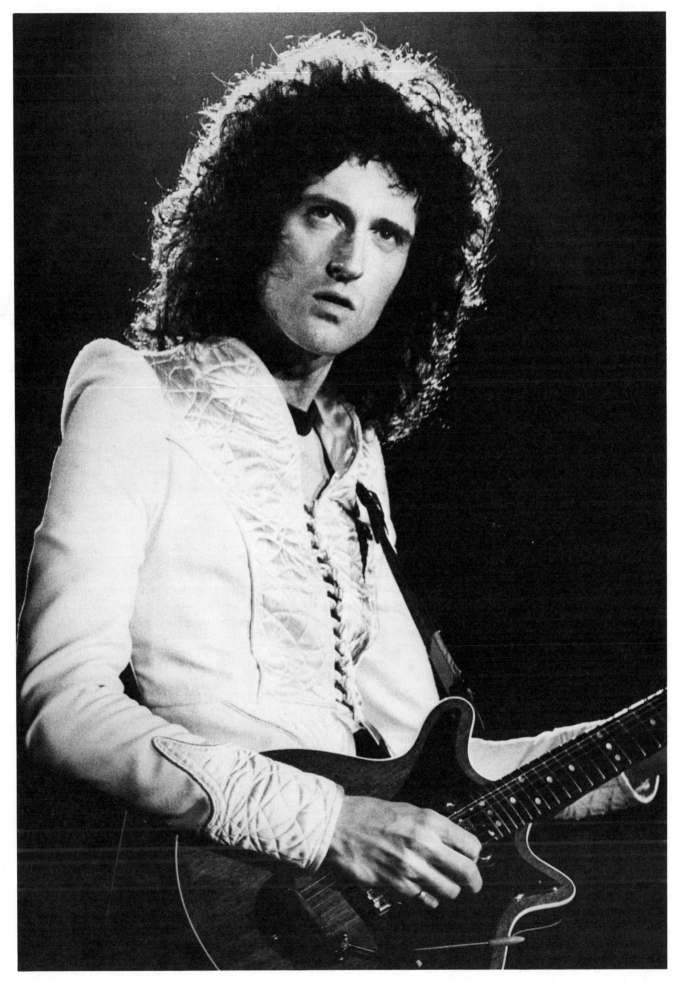

quite slushy ballad, then a heavy rock thing, then something else – and we were willing to try everything because we always wanted to expand our range.

Recently, we've become more selective, I think, and we try to make albums which don't go in so many directions at once – for example, *The Game* album was really pruned, and the others refused to include a couple of things I wanted on, because they said they were too far outside the theme of the album, and that we should be trying to make a slightly more coherent album. "'39" is a science fiction story I made up, it's a story about someone who goes away and leaves his family, and because of the time-dilation effect, where the people on earth have aged a lot more than he has when he returns, he's aged a year and they've aged a hundred years, so instead of coming back to his wife, he comes back to his daughter, in whom he can see his wife. I think I also had in mind a story by Herman Hesse, which is called "The River", I think, where a man leaves his hometown and travels a lot, then comes back and observes it from the other side of a river, and sees it in a completely different light because of his experiences. I felt a little like that about my home at the time, having been away and seen this vastly different world of rock music, which was totally different from the way I was brought up. People may not generally admit it, but I think when most people write songs, there's more than one level to them – they'll be about one thing on the surface, but underneath, they're probably trying, maybe even unconsciously, to say something about their own life, their own experience – and in nearly all my stuff, there's a personal feeling.'

The 1976 Queen album, *A Day At The Races*, continued the Marx Brothers title fetish, but in the opinions of many, was somewhat less impressive than *A Night At The Opera*. 'I wish in some ways that we had put the two albums out together, because the material for both of them was more or less written at the same time, and it corresponds to an almost exactly similar period in our development, so I regard the two albums as completely parallel, and the fact that one came out after the other is a shame, because it was looked on as a follow-up, whereas really it was sort of an extension of the first one.'

The period after the release of *A Day At The Races* saw Queen retreating into a kind of cloistered privacy from which they rarely departed, especially to speak to the media. 'This was imposed on us in a way – we had never really got on with the press and had a lot of enemies there, but by that time, just about everyone in the press was against us, and quite blatantly so. So our silence wasn't through choice, it was really having no one to talk to who was going to write anything which would be of any use to us, so we thought it best not to bother, although reluctantly, particularly in my case, because I like talking to people and I think there's always something to gain from it. I know it happens to everybody else as well, and it's a normal consequence of success in England – a lot of people resent your success, and a lot of people also resented Fred's demeanour on stage, interpreting it as a sort of arrogance in his private life, which he doesn't have. He's a performer first, and off stage, he's pretty shy on the whole.'

The mention of Mercury was appropriate at this point, as the 1977 Queen LP, *News Of The World*, saw Freddie less well-represented than usual as far as songwriting went, which led to some of the same press people to whom the group weren't talking to assume that a split of some kind in the group might be imminent. 'There was nothing like that really, except that possibly Fred was then getting interested in other things, and a bit bored with being in the studio, because we did studios to death with the previous two albums, when we'd be in there for months on end, just working away, although we weren't particularly inefficient, it was just that there was a lot to be done. We all felt we'd done enough of that for the time being, and wanted to get back to basics and do something simpler, but Fred got to the point where he could hardly stand being in a studio, and he'd want to do his bit and get out.'

Of the tracks on the record written by Brian, perhaps the most interesting is 'Sleeping On The Sidewalk', which evokes memories of the British R&B boom of the 1960s. 'That was the quickest song I've ever written – I just wrote it down, and I'm quite pleased with it as well, because it's not highly subtle, but it leaves me with a good feeling. It was the sort of thing any guitarist who had played a bit of blues would do, and I could very well have had Eric Clapton in the back of my mind. . . It was a one take thing as well, although I messed about with the take a lot, chopped it around and rearranged it, but we basically used that first take, so it has a kind of sloppy feel, but that works with the song.'

'It's Late', on the same LP, comes across as a typical Queen song. 'There's not much I can say to that – I suppose that's as close to typical Queen as you can get, and there's a kind of style in there, which I've often thought about, which is somewhere between my kind of thing on "It's Late", and one of Freddie's, something like "We Are The Champions". It's so easy for us to do, and we can slip into it almost without thinking, on stage and on record. Once Freddie starts playing E flat and A flat on the piano, which he very often does, it has a particular sound, and those are very strange keys for a guitarist to play in, so the songs being in those keys actually produces something different out of me, but as soon as that's happening, that formula's there, and we can do that sort of Queen sound all night and all day.'

The release of *News Of The World* more or less coincided with the rise of punk rock in general, and the Sex Pistols in particular, leading to Queen's fall from popularity being freely predicted in the media.

'We didn't really feel threatened, because we saw that it was still the same people attracting large crowds, like Genesis, Zeppelin and the Who, and even us, and we knew that the man in the street was still aware that music could have different forms, and that it didn't have to be one thing at a time, which is what I don't like about England, if you like. Going back to punk, that era took a lot of backward steps, like the idea that it was bad to put on a show because that wasn't musically valid, but the end result was good, as a sort of clearing out system, and it was a good time for people to reassess themselves, but I do wish it hadn't eventually destroyed the Sex Pistols – I would have loved to be able to talk to them, although

I'm sure they wouldn't have listened at the time, because we were something which punk was reacting against.'

1978 saw the release of *Jazz*, perhaps Queen's most controversial LP, and one whose title was inspired by a spray painting on a wall seen by Roger Taylor. It marked a reunion with producer Roy Thomas Baker, with whom the group hadn't worked since *A Night At The Opera,* having produced the two intervening albums by themselves. What did Queen hope to gain from the reunion? 'An easy life? No, I'm kidding – we thought it would be nice to try again with a producer on whom we could put some of the responsibility. We'd found a few of our own methods, and so had he, and on top of what we'd collectively learned before, we thought that coming back together would mean that there would be some new stuff going on, and it worked pretty well.'

The controversial aspect of the album concerned two tracks, 'Fat Bottomed Girls' and 'Bicycle Race' – it was decided to combine the ramifications of these titles to produce a live action video, which showed three hundred naked young ladies riding bicycles around Wimbledon Stadium, something which many might consider beneath Queen's dignity. . . 'It was just a bit of fun really – we thought the two songs went together, and the album was sort of European flavoured. We'd never recorded in Europe, and we absorbed some of the feeling, and talked about how to sell the album, eventually opting for something which was really crass and blatantly commercial. That's what we did, and I can't make any apology for it, but it was fun at the time. Now I'm pretty indifferent to it – I don't think it made much difference either way, to be honest. It alienated a few people, won over a few others, but on the whole, it was a pretty small thing.'

The 1979 Queen LP was a double live album, *Queen Live Killers.* 'Live albums are inescapable, really – everyone tells you you have to do them, and when you do, you find that they're very often not of mass appeal, and in the absence of a fluke condition, you sell your live album to the converted, the people who already know your stuff and come to the concerts. So if you add up the number of people who've seen you over the last few years, that's very roughly the number who'll buy your live album, unless you have a hit single on it, which we didn't – maybe we chose the wrong one, which was "Love Of My Life" in England and America.'

One interesting track which highlighted Brian's guitar was 'Get Down, Make Love', on which there appear some peculiar effects. 'That's a harmoniser thing which I've used really as a noise more than a musical thing. It's controllable because I had a special little pedal made for it, which means I can change the interval at which the harmoniser comes back, and it's fed back on itself so it makes all these swooping noises, and it's just an exercise in using that, together with noises from Freddie – a sort of erotic interlude.'

1979 also saw Queen active, appropriately enough, in live situations, which were however abnormal, first when they played smaller venues, and at the end of the year, when they assisted a number of other star names in a week of concerts whose proceeds were designed to provide relief to the people of Kampuchea.

1980 saw a departure as far as Queen's records are concerned in the shape of *The Game.* 'We approached that from a different angle, with the idea of ruthlessly pruning it down to a coherent album rather than letting our flights of fancy lead us off into different ideas. The impetus came very largely from Freddie, who said that he thought we'd been diversifying so much that people didn't know what we were about any more, so if there's a theme to the album, it's rhythm and sparseness – never two notes played if one would do, which is a hard discipline for us, because we tend to be quite over the top in the way we work. So the whole thing has a very economical feel to it, particularly "Another One Bites The Dust", "Crazy Little Thing Called Love", "Dragon Attack", "Suicide" – a very sparse feel to all of them, and for us, a very modern sounding album.'

One new element in the recipe was an engineer/ co-producer simply known as Mack. 'He had a great deal to do with the way the album sounds. His name's Reinholdt Mack, and he's the greatest of the unknown engineers, although he's now becoming known and quite rightly so. He's done a lot of work for ELO, and worked with all sorts of people like Deep Purple and Led Zeppelin, but he's been stuck there in Munich, and nobody seems to have given him a thought that much – the typeface used for his name was always rather small – so we thought that having found him, we should make a big thing of him because he's really quite a phenomenon.'

One important aspect of *The Game* to longtime Queen afficionados was that finally the group used synthesisers. 'Actually, they overflow from the *Flash Gordon* album, because we were working on that at the same time. Roger's really the guy who introduced us to synths, because he had this OBX which he was playing around with, which obviously produced some good sounds, and synths had advanced an awful long way since those early days. You can now get polyphonic synths with a device for bending the notes which is much closer to the feel of a guitar than ever before, so now we use the synth, but sparingly, I think, particularly on *The Game* – there's very little there, and what there is merely complements what we'd used already, so there's no danger of the synth taking over, which I would never allow to happen, although I'm much happier using them than I used to be. I get a good feeling from playing the guitar which you don't get with anything else – a feeling of power, and a type of expression.'

The Game was a remarkably successful LP, spawning no less than four top 20 singles in Britain, two of which Brian talked about in greater depth. '"Crazy Little Thing Called Love" was very untypical playing for me, and Mack actually persuaded me to use a Telecaster, which I'd never used on record before, and a Boogie amplifier, which I'd never have considered using. It's a very sparse record, and it was done with Elvis Presley in mind, obviously – I thought that Freddie sounded a bit like Elvis, but somebody's done a cover of it who sounds absolutely like Elvis, and the whole record sounds like a Jordanaires/Elvis recreation . . . A lot of people have used "Another One Bites The Dust" as a theme song – the

Contemporary Queen. Left to right: Roger Taylor, Freddie Mercury, Brian May, John Deacon

Detroit Lions used it for their games, and they soon began to lose, so they bit the dust soon afterwards, but it was a help to the record – and there's been a few cover versions of various kinds, notably "Another One Rides The Bus", which is an extremely funny record by a bloke called Mad Al or something, in the States, and you should hear it, because it's hilarious. We like people covering our songs in any way, no matter what spirit it's done in, because it's great to have anyone use your music as a base, a big compliment.'

Flash Gordon has already been mentioned, and was in fact an album of soundtrack music to the 1980 science fiction film of that name, with the music performed and written by Queen. 'It was in our minds that we would be up for writing a soundtrack if the right one came along. We'd been offered a few, but most of them were where the film is written around music, and that's been done to death – it's the cliché

of 'movie star appears in movie about movie stars' – but this one was different, in that it was a proper film and had a real story which wasn't based around music, and we would be writing a film score in the way anyone else writes a film score, which is basically background music, but can obviously help the film if it's strong enough. That was the attraction, because we thought that a rock group hadn't done that kind of thing before, and it was an opportunity to write real film music. So we were writing to a discipline for the first time ever, and the only criterion for success was whether or not it worked with and helped the film, and we weren't our own bosses for a change, which was quite interesting.'

The album contained a track which became a hit single, 'Flash', but rather more intriguing was 'The Wedding March', which seemed to be in the vein of Jimi Hendrix playing 'Star Spangled Banner' at Woodstock. 'Things like that go back a long way with us – we did "God Save The Queen", the beginning part of "Tie Your Mother Down", and there's "Procession" on the first album – those little guitar pieces. I'd heard Hendrix's thing, but his approach was very different, because he put down a line and then improvised another one around it, and the whole thing works on the basis of things going in and out of harmony more or less by accident – it's very much a free form multi-tracking thing, whereas my stuff is totally arranged and planned, and I treat it like you'd give a score to an orchestra. It lacks the improvisation part, but it's a complete orchestration, so it's a different kind of approach.'

The major new Queen-related item in 1981, a year which also saw a *Greatest Hits* LP, a Queen video and a book of photographs about the group, was a single titled 'Under Pressure', a collaboration between Queen and David Bowie, which not surprisingly, topped the UK singles chart. 'He lives near the studio we bought, in a little town close to Montreux, and when we were there, he'd often come over to see us, to chat and have a drink. Someone suggested that we should all go into the studio and play around one night, to see what came out, which we did, playing each other's old songs and just fiddling around. The next night, we listened to the tapes, because we'd left the tape recorder running, and picked out a couple of pieces which seemed to be promising, and then we just worked on one particular idea, which became "Under Pressure", for a whole night . . . an extremely long night.'

Otherwise, the album which eventually contained 'Under Pressure' – *Hot Space* – reflected a different method of creating songs from that which Queen had previously used, although there were some similarities in the evolution of *The Game*. 'We were thinking about rhythm before anything else, so in some cases, like "Dancer", the backing track was there a long time before the actual song was properly pieced together. We would experiment with the rhythm and the bass and drum track and get that sounding right, and then very cautiously piece the rest around it, which was an experimental way for us to do it. In one track called "Backchat", there wasn't going to be a guitar solo, because John Deacon, who wrote the song, has gone perhaps more violently black than the rest of us. We had lots of arguments about it, and what he was heading for in his tracks was a totally non-compromise situation, doing black stuff as R&B

artists would do it with no concessions to our methods at all, and I was trying to edge him back towards the central path and get a bit of heaviness into it, and a bit of the anger of rock music. So one night I said I wanted to see what I could add to it, because I was inspired by the backing track, which is very rhythmic and aggressive, but I felt that the song as it stood wasn't aggressive enough – it's "Backchat", and it's supposed to be about people arguing and it should have some kind of guts to it. He agreed, and I went in and tried a few things.'

Hot Space saw a further increase in the use of synthesisers. 'There's two there, really, an OBX, which fell into disuse a bit on this album, and a Jupiter 8, which we thought was more versatile in certain ways, and provided a lot of new stuff. But it's just a tool with which we're experimenting, and it hasn't really replaced anything except on a temporary basis.'

Brian May is one of the most genuinely rewarding people one could ever hope to meet. His contributions to the work of Queen may not have been more crucial than those of the other members of the group, but there can be little doubt that his temperament has been a vital factor in the quite remarkable consistency of both quality and success which has elevated Queen to the top of their industry and kept them there for longer than most, with little sign of deterioration. What does he consider the secret of Queen's success?

'I think change is part of it, but constancy of members is the biggest thing – it helps because we know how to work with each other, and also people identify with the four of us as a group, and know what we look like and who we are. It's also important not to have constancy of material – there should be some style to it, and maybe there should be some trademarks which crop up, but you should keep exploring new avenues, or else you die of boredom.' And how long can Queen continue?

'I don't know . . . it doesn't seem to be getting any harder, although it's always hard.' And can we expect a Brian May solo album? 'I don't really have the time, and I don't think the time's really right for me yet. I have a lot of ideas stored away in boxes, but I don't really want to do it at the moment, because there's enough to do with Queen and my private life.' So be it . . .

Brian May Discography

	With Queen
1973	*Queen*
1974	*Queen II*
1974	*Sheer Heart Attack*
1975	*A Night At The Opera*
1976	*A Day At The Races*
1977	*News Of The World*
1978	*Jazz*
1979	*Queen Live Killers*
1980	*The Game*

1980	*Flash Gordon* (Original Soundtrack)
1981	*Concerts For The People of Kampuchea*
1982	*Hot Space*
	Sessions
	Ian Hunter
1976	*All American Alien Boy*
	Lonnie Donegan
1978	*Putting On The Style*

INDEX